Field & Stream
International
Fishing Guide

BY A. J. McCLANE

SIP
SPECIAL INTEREST
PUBLICATIONS
HOLT, RINEHART AND WINSTON, INC.
383 MADISON AVENUE, NEW YORK, N.Y. 10017

Acknowledgements

We gratefully acknowledge the assistance of the following specialists in compiling the facts in this guide book:

Richard N. Barkle
Pan American World Airways, Inc.
Pan Am Building
New York, New York

Carlos M. Barrantes
Casa Mar Fishing Club
P.O. Box 2816
San Jose, Costa Rica

Peter Barrett
True Magazine
67 West 44 Street
New York, New York

Frederick H. Berry
U.S. Bureau of Commercial
Fisheries
Tropical Atlantic Biological
Laboratory
Miami, Florida

Sergio A. Betancourt
Cia. de Aviacion Pan American
Av. Roque Saenz Pena 832
Buenos Aires, Argentina

Jim Chapralis
Safari Outfitters Inc.
8 South Michigan Avenue
Chicago, Illinois

Guy de la Valdene
Palm Beach, Florida

Gilbert N. Drake
Deep Water Cay
Bahamas

Donald S. Erdman
Fish and Wildlife Division
Department of Agriculture
Commonwealth of Puerto Rico

Rex Forrester
Government Tourist Bureau
P.O. Box 527
Rotorua, New Zealand

Edward H. Gerhardt
Frontier Airlines
5900 East 39th Avenue
Denver, Colorado

Andrew Glaze
British Travel Association
680 Fifth Avenue
New York, New York

Douglas P. Bournique
Palm Beach, Florida

A. Cecil Harrison
Cape Piscatorial Society
73 St. George's Street
Cape Town, South Africa

Oddvar Kjelsrud
Mytravel Inc.
Norway House, 290 Madison Avenue
New York, New York

Bud Lewis
Lewis Co. Ltd.
8560 Sunset Blvd.
Los Angeles, California

Joe Malone
Irish Tourist Board
590 Fifth Avenue
New York, New York

Ed Meade
British Columbia Information Center
652 Burrard Street
Vancouver, British Columbia

Carl Nyberg
Finnair
10 East 40th Street,
New York, New York

T. Owen
South African Tourist Corp.
Rockefeller Center
610 Fifth Avenue
New York, New York

James B. Paterson
Eastern Jamaica Angler's
Association
Port Antonio, Jamaica

S. L. Perinchief
Bermuda Fishing
Information Bureau
Hamilton, Bermuda

Stojan Pudar
Tourist Association of Yugoslavia
Belgrade, Yugoslavia

John Squire
Rockresorts Inc.
1290 Avenue of the Americas
New York, New York

We also wish to thank the following organizations and individuals for their assistance in providing illustrations:

Cover photography by Arie DeZanger
Accessories by Abercrombie and Fitch
Fish illustrations by Richard Evans
Younger

Alaska Airlines
Ames Petroleum, Inc.
Stu Apte
Australian News and Information Bureau
Peter Barrett
Bermuda News Bureau
British Travel Association

Canadian Government Travel Bureau
G. L. Carlisle
Colombian Government Tourist Office
Robert Crandell Associates
Guy de la Valdene
A. Devaney, Inc.
Gilbert A. Drake
Farley Manning Associates
Field & Stream
Jim Hardie
Hawaii Visitors Bureau
Jamaica Tourist Board

Mexican National Tourist Council
Mytravel, Inc.
Oregon State Highway Department
Pacific Area Photo Service
Safari Outfitters, Inc.
Safari-Shikar Tours & Travel
Jack Samson
South African Tourist Corporation
John Tarlton
Hamilton Wright
U. S. Virgin Islands Government

Library of Congress Catalog Card Number: 71-150450

SBN (hardbound): 03-080131-1
SBN (paperback): 03-080129-X
HRW 25

Printed in the United States of America 600-017

Foreword

The June issue of *Field & Stream* in 1898 announced the opening of the Ozarks to anglers by the Frisco Line which also penetrated Indian territory. This latter qualification suggested that while the redskins were not actively pursuing the tourist trade, one could find primitive fishing by rail. The magazine further stated that although the mosquito dwells in the Ozarks, "he is retiring in disposition, not avid for blood." Many readers found this a reassuring detail. But as the diamond-stacker barreled through the night, American anglers were riding into the dawn of a new era.

Railroads are less important to the angler today than when our turn-of-the-century sportsman set out for the Ozarks. Modern jet transportation has brought a whole new galaxy of stars within the quick vacationist's reach, ranging from hibiscus *cum* chrome Acapulco to the barren lands of Alaska and the Promised Land of Argentina where no trout, much less roads, existed two generations ago. Where, when, and costs are still the key questions, and that is the purpose of this guide. Our 1971 annual covers 41 countries and more will be reviewed in subsequent editions.

The prices quoted for goods, services, and license fees are those prevailing at the time of publication. Although changes will occur, the rates given are useful in a comparative sense. There are also occasional changes in immigration requirements and other facts relating to travel abroad. We accept no responsibility for any inaccuracies or omissions pertaining to costs and documentation.

Al McClane

Fishing Editor
Field & Stream

PAGE 42

Franklin S. Forsberg
PUBLISHER

EDITORS
J. Robert Connor
Kenneth Anderson

Fred Tobey
DIRECTOR OF DESIGN

Ruth Fairbairn
MANAGING EDITOR

M. C. Gethman
SENIOR EDITOR

P. M. McClane
ASSISTANT EDITOR

ASSOCIATE EDITORS
Alice Nigh
L. J. Lowery
Arie deZanger
Richard E. Younger

Bert Westman
ADVERTISING DIRECTOR

Irving Herschbein
BUSINESS MANAGER

Stephen Grogin
PRODUCTION MANAGER

George Kiley
CIRCULATION DIRECTOR

PAGE 19

PAGE 113

PAGE 101

SPECIAL FEATURES

PAGE 87

PAGE 82

PAGE 223

PAGE 181

PAGE 31

PAGE 91

PAGE 110

PAGE 92

PAGE 253

PAGE 9

INTERNATIONAL FISHING GUIDE

Argentina

Patagonia is one of the great trout regions

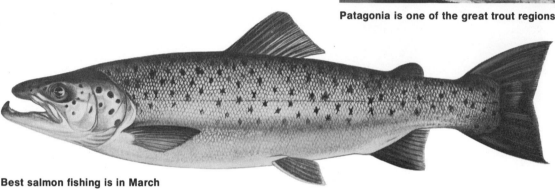

Best salmon fishing is in March

The 2,300-mile length of Argentina encompasses every climate from the purely tropical north to the frigid south. As a tourist you may visit Buenos Aires and find a city hardly different from London or Paris. It's more violently flavored in its isolation perhaps, but the night lights begin sixty miles out on the edge of the pampas, and instead of the Thames or the Seine you pass over the Rio de la Plata. At 6:30 every evening in the Hotel Plaza bar, politics, polo, and national strikes blend naturally in the soft Spanish of the Porteños. But these are sounds of the twentieth century. A thousand miles to the southwest across the pampas in the valley of San Martin de los Andes, vast herds of red stag roar at the rising sun, and the barred goose and the ashy-headed goose come in honking legions to the summer water holes of Patagonia.

This is a land of lonesome rivers and brooding peaks and great empty places that make a man look for the slow rising smoke of a campfire, or the moving streamer of dust made by a car on a distant road. During the day the sun lays a golden glow on the earth, then cools and falls in flame among the hills. Then abruptly the Cordillera challenges your passage in red and purple spires, and giant condors ride the thermals which form on the slopes. As the country narrows down to the Strait of Magellan, the eastern hills dwindle into desolate moors, but the Andes win out in the end.

Argentina is one of the great trout countries of the world. All of this fishing exists within Patagonia, which includes the provinces of Neuquén, Rio Negro, Chubut, Santa Cruz, and the federal territory of Tierra del Fuego. Although North American salmonids are not native to Argentina, a fish hatchery built in 1903 at San Carlos de Bariloche has been responsible for their widespread introduction throughout the country. The comparatively few freshwater fishes endemic to the Andes are of no angling importance; only the pejerrey (*Orestias* spp.) which generally resembles a large smelt and has considerable food value enters the sport fishery in any number. Rainbow, brown, brook trout, and landlocked salmon are the four principal species sought by angling. The initial success of their establishment is due to the thousands of miles of cold, unpolluted rivers and lakes which exist in Patagonia and the sparse human population (Patagonia represents 28 percent of the national territory occupied by 2½ percent of its people).

Until the early 1950's large trout of 10 pounds or more were common in Argentina. Brown trout exceeding 30 pounds and landlocked salmon of over 18 pounds were caught in Lake Nahuel Huapi, within sight of Bariloche. However, angling pressure increased rapidly and while trophy fish are still present today, and especially in the more remote streams and lakes, a 1½ pound average is to be expected on easily accessible waters. Nevertheless this is quality angling in beautiful country.

The angling in northeastern Argentina is entirely different from that found in Patagonia. The country itself, much like the hill country of Georgia with semi-tropical touches of Florida, is dominated by the Parana River. The 2,796-mile-long Parana River rises in Brazil and flows generally southwest forming the international boundary first between Brazil and Paraguay and Argentina before coursing south in Argentine territory to join the Rio de la Plata. In places the Upper Parana

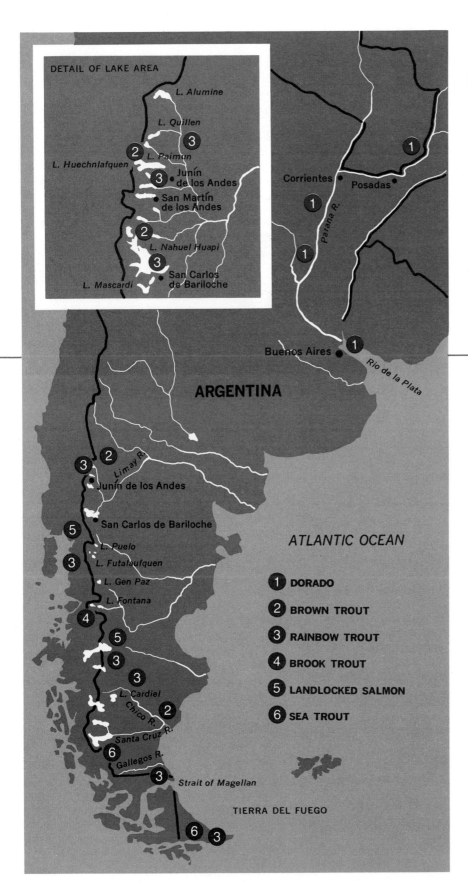

DETAIL OF LAKE AREA

L. Alumine
L. Quillen
③
② L. Paimun
L. Huechnlafquen
③ Junín
de los Andes
San Martín
de los Andes
②
L. Nahuel Huapi
③
L. Mascardi
San Carlos
de Bariloche

① Corrientes • Posadas •
①
Parana R.
①

ARGENTINA

① Buenos Aires •
Rio de la Plata

② Limay R.
③
Junín de los Andes

⑤ San Carlos de Bariloche
L. Puelo
③ L. Futalaufquen
L. Gen Paz
L. Fontana
④
⑤
③
③
L. Cardiel
L. Chico R.
②
Santa Cruz R.
⑥ Gallegos R.
③ Strait of Magellan
TIERRA DEL FUEGO
⑥ ③

ATLANTIC OCEAN

① DORADO
② BROWN TROUT
③ RAINBOW TROUT
④ BROOK TROUT
⑤ LANDLOCKED SALMON
⑥ SEA TROUT

A matching pair from the Cardiel

(Alto Parana) constricts to 1,500 feet in width, but below Corrientes the last 800 miles is from 2 to 4 miles wide even in low water, and during the flood season it can rise 60 or 70 feet and 10 to 20 miles beyond its banks. Unlike the clear waters of the Brazilian source streams, the sand-and-sandstone-bottomed Parana carries considerable silt in suspension; but the turbidity of the water has little if any effect on dorado angling.

South America's greatest native freshwater gamefish is an acrobat practically from birth; a 2-week-old, 2-inch-long dorado will eat a 1-inch dorado, and in fact, when grabbed by the tail (a favorite method of attack) the victim will turn around and grab the tail of the aggressor while they swim in circles until one fish exhausts the other. As a predator the dorado has few peers. This brilliantly colored fish (dorado means golden) is one of the most exciting fish to catch in freshwater. Dorado jump repetitively, often eight to ten times. As among all game species the largest ones jump less and run longer distances; but in weights up to 30 pounds a dorado stays airborne. The rod-caught record in Argentina is 68 pounds.

THE SEASON

The trout season in Argentina commences on November 15th each year and extends until April 15th of the following year. Weatherwise, this is the reverse of our Northern Hemisphere, where April corresponds to October in Argentina. Their spring season continues through December, with cold water bucketing off the Cordillera and hosing out of the clouds. The dying winds still worry the trees, and plover whimper under a brooding sky, but it's by far the best period for catching large trout and landlocked salmon in the lakes of Argentina. For the fly caster who prefers stream fishing, the latter part of summer, beginning in late February and running through March, is the ideal season. The air is calm then and the sun warm. What little rain may fall merely stimulates the trout into feeding. It spills with the high spirits of a rare Napoleon brandy and evaporates as quickly. If you are going to the end of the world at Tierra del Fuego (55° south latitude), February is the only real summer month, while March is likely to be a sudden jump into winter. The days run along mild and clear, then one morning the tent pegs pop and a 50-knot wind howls down from the peaks in vicious blasts of rain and snow.

The season for dorado fishing in Argentina is from the beginning of August until late in October. Although it is true that some fish may be caught during the summer months after November 1st, as a rule the Parana floods in the warm rainy season and it would be only by some unusual weather condition that you would find any angling. The tipoff to the best period is the many dorado "fiestas." Each year some thirty-odd fishing clubs along the Parana River in Argentina hold their annual Fiesta Nacional del Dorado—a dorado fishing contest that lasts for several days. The various Clubes de Pescadores are partisan bands representing townships on the river most

of which have a clubhouse, marina, restaurant, and other facilities. Their competition is fierce as from one to two hundred anglers divided into teams sally forth and give the golden one a fit. It's as much a social event as a contest ending in a great dorado *asado* with split fish sputtering over the coals and the *vino* flowing like Niagara. In fact, everybody likes the national tournament so well that six or seven of them are held in different weeks and locations just to make certain that nobody misses out.

August and September are winter months at this latitude. The weather is cool with temperatures ranging from 45°F to 65°F and one is well advised to bring along a heavy sweater and rain gear, as strong, chilling winds are common. By Christmas the air temperatures from Posadas north run over 100°F and insects make life impossible. Stock a repellent even for your winter trip, as this is not only mosquito country but the happy hunting ground of the blackflylike jejen (pronounced hay-hen).

SAN CARLOS DE BARILOCHE

The city of Bariloche, located 850 air miles southwest of Buenos Aires, is the principal angling center of Argentina. Although the fishing in the immediate vicinity of this popular winter and summer resort is limited, Bariloche is ideally located for visitors traveling north or south in Patagonia. Here guides and ground or air transportation may be obtained for the fishing in either direction.

NORTH OF BARILOCHE

The most popular fishing center in northern Patagonia is the village of Junin de los Andes. It is approximately 125 miles from Bariloche. The local angling headquarters is the **Hosteria Chimehuin** (Hosteria Chimehuin, Junin de los Andes, Provincia de Neuquén, Argentina), which overlooks the

Chimehuin River. Rates here run $8 single and $12 double per day. The Chimehuin gets considerable rod pressure but it is a good producer of 1½- to 3-pound brown and rainbow trout. There have been many large trout recorded for this stream in years past (a 24-pound brown was taken on the fly in 1961); however, these trophy fish are usually caught at night in the *boca* or first big pool formed below its source at Lake Huechulafquen. The Chimehuin flows for fifty miles in a southwest direction and joins the Collon-Curá; the latter is a broad, riffle-filled river where 2- to 2¼-pound rainbows are common. The experienced angler will have no difficulty in hooking one or two large trout on the Collon-Curá during a day's outing. The western end of Huechalafquen has two connected arms identified as Lakes Paimun and Epulafquén. These have to be reached by boat but both are good fishing grounds.

Continuing north from Junin de los Andes there are several more important trout waters: Lake Quillén and its outlet stream the Quillén River which flows into the Aluminé River and Lake Aluminé which is the source of the latter stream, and the northernmost point of the Argentinian Lake District. The Malleo River just a short distance north of Junin is also an Aluminé tributary, and where the two streams join, they form a large pool which is an excellent producer of heavy brown trout.

SOUTH OF BARILOCHE

South of Bariloche the chain of lakes continues to the tip of the continent. Most of these waters drain into Chile and ultimately the Pacific Ocean. Inevitably, those nearest Bariloche such as Lakes Mascardi, Hess, Fonk, and Roca in the Manso River drainage receive considerable fishing pressure although they provide good catches from time to time with the occasional large brown trout taken in the mouths of tributary or outlet streams. Lake Puelo and Lake Epuyen which are about a day's drive from Bariloche also offer modest trout fishing. The better angling begins at Futalaufquen which is approximately 130 air miles south of Bariloche. This river system encompasses Lakes Futalaufquen, Cholila, Rivadavia, Menendez, Verde, Krueger, and Situación. These are all large lakes connected by streams which offer primarily rainbow trout. Situación and the three lakes which drain into it also contain landlocked salmon.

Continuing south in Patagonia some of the outstanding waters are Lake General Paz, Lake Fontana, and Lake Cardiel. General Paz is noted for its big brook trout (3 to 8 pounds or more) while its outlet river called the Corcovado on the Argentinian side and the Palena River after it crosses the Chilean border offers equally large brook trout plus rainbows and browns. The Palena is a great wilderness stream and in its lower reaches attracts heavy sea-run trout from the Pacific. Lake Fontana produces large brook and rainbow trout as does its outlet the Alto Senguerr River. Lake Cardiel holds brook, brown, rainbow trout, and landlocked salmon.

The major trout rivers in southern Patagonia are the Santa Cruz, and Gallegos. This is about as far as is practical to drive over rough roads through Santa Cruz province, although it can be shortened somewhat by meeting your guide at an airport south of Bariloche, say in Esquel, or if you don't mind the world's worst roads, by making arrangements to drive north from Tierra del Fuego. Accommodations are scarce in this area although a small hotel can be found on the Chilean side near the Penitente River. (**Hotel Morro Chico**) and another adjacent to the Gallegos River in Argentina (the **Grand Hotel**). This is primitive country and while not easy of access, it is the reason the fishing remains above average. The hotels are functional with rates at about $6 per day single and $8 double.

Rainbow trout and landlocked salmon in the 10-pound class are fairly common in the remote region south of Bariloche

TIERRA DEL FUEGO
The only practical way to fish Tierra del Fuego is to fly direct from Buenos Aires on one of the regularly scheduled Aerolineas or Austral flights to Rio Grande. The cost is about $100 round trip. The most accessible, though by no means the only river in the eastern or Argentinian half of the island is the broad, wind-swept Rio Grande. Sea-run brown trout of 8 to 12 pounds are fairly common. The hotel here is **Hotel Yaganes** (Hotel Yaganes, Tierra del Fuego, Argentina) with rates at $10 per day American plan.

TROUT TACKLE
A fly rod or spinning rod is ideal for Argentinian fishing. Except on the broad wind-blown streams around Tierra del Fuego where stout 9-foot fly rods are essential, the caliber of the tackle depends entirely on the skill of the angler. Ideally, one can bring along a light 7½- or 8-foot fly rod for general stream fishing and the heavier rod for casting large flies or working the southern sea-trout streams. Spinning gear with 6- to 10-pound-test line is adequate throughout the country.

In the selection of trout flies for fishing in Argentina, it should be realized that mayfly hatches are the exception rather than the rule. Although there is an abundance of aquatic insects in some streams, the larger fish rarely seek their food at the surface. The major item of diet for rainbow and brown trout, as well as the landlocked salmon, is a brachyuran crab of the family Potamonidae (locally *cangrejo*).

Cangrejo is ordinarily 1- to 1½- inches in diameter. This crab accounts to a large extent for the excellent growth of Argentinian salmonids. The concept of fly fishing, therefore, must be modified to be effective. This change of tactics becomes even more apparent when one observes the surface of an Andean river rushing down the valley, presenting a succession of rapids and white water and only rarely developing into placid pools on its way to the ocean. Ideally, these are wet fly and streamer fly rivers. It is not implied that a dry fly, given the appropriate circumstances, cannot be used to good advantage, but it is always limited by prevailing wind and water conditions whereas a sunken fly will give results at all times, if properly handled. Although the importance of shape and size of the fly cannot be denied, its success or failure depends mainly on the way the fly is worked in the water to attract the fish. As a rule the darker flies are the more effective ones.

The range of size gives plenty of latitude to the preferences of the individual angler but is, to some extent, dictated by the characteristics of the water to be fished. Barring certain exceptions, the larger the body of water the bigger the fly required. Popular sizes range from No. 8 to No. 4 with a No. 6 hook probably the most universal selection. There are also many opportunities to use outsized (1/0 to 3/0) streamers, especially when fishing for big brown trout toward evening.

NORTH OF BUENOS AIRES

The important fishing north of Buenos Aires is for dorado on the Parana River. The best months for dorado fishing are the opposite to Argentina's trout season. Water level is of the utmost importance and these semi-tropical rivers reach their lowest volumes from July through mid-October. The most reliable angling occurs in August and September. However, if water levels remain normal in November and December, it is possible to combine early trout fishing with dorado fishing on the same trip.

Accessible facilities exist on the Parana River in the province of Corrientes. The jumpoff point is the town of Posadas (approximately 600 air miles north of Buenos Aires). A popular camp within three hours driving distance of Posadas is **Apipe Safaris** at Apipe, which consists of several thatched roof huts and the basic essentials such as a flush toilet and shower. Nothing fancy but the fishing can be excellent. From the city of Corrientes the only organized fishing camp is **Paso de la Patria**. However, excellent accommodations can be enjoyed by staying at **Gran Hotel Corrientes** in the city and arranging for a driver to make the short haul (20 miles) to Paso de la Patria each day, or to the fishing club at Empedrado where boats and guides are available. The entire reach from south of Empedrado north to Itá Ibaté is covered by Luis Oscar Schulz who presently operates 16 skiffs equipped with 40 hp. outboards; guides are assigned according to area. Two other popular locations are **Hotel de Turismo** in El Dorado and **Hotel de Turismo** in Mercedes; the latter is considered one of the best dorado locations on the Parana River. In the city of Posadas, check the fishing situation with the local *Club Pesca y Nautico*. This is not a "hot" location but good runs of dorado occur from time to time and a fine hotel is available at the **Gran Hotel Posadas.** If you are heading upriver from Posadas, there is only about 20 miles of paved road which turns into a red dust track, rutted by hundreds of trucks that make their daily haul of oranges and tung oil out of Misiones Province.

When it rains the road turns to red gumbo and every driver becomes a hotrodder speeding up and down hills at a breakneck pace just to keep forward momentum. The roads around Corrientes are all paved, but in either case there are no rental cars available. You can arrange for a taxi or query the local tourist office or hotel to hire a car and driver by the week. Everybody here is friendly and they go out of their way to see that a visiting *pescador* finds his dorado.

DORADO TACKLE

Unlike trout or most other familiar freshwater gamefish, the dorado are rarely seen (they seldom feed at the surface) and the angler must have confidence in his own ability to read the water and to present his lure properly.

The key to successful dorado fishing is the depth at which the lure operates. A plug or spoon that runs 5 to 15 feet under the surface, and capable of hitting bottom at times, is by far the most effective artificial. As a result, trolling is the most popular method of fishing among local anglers. The reason is twofold: it's the easiest way to swim a plug at the proper depth in fast heavy currents, and it's the only practical way to present a big plug on 40- to 60-pound-test monofilament lines. In more remote regions tourist sportsmen literally have to fight with the guide to be allowed to cast with light tackle. Fortunately, today, there is a contingent of European and South American regulars who are demonstrating that casting with spinning reels and multipliers is not only more fun, but often more effective.

The ideal tackle for dorado fishing is the kind of gear used in Florida for saltwater casting. A heavy-duty 5½- or 6-foot bait casting rod, or a 7- to 7½-foot spinning rod mounted with reels spooled in 12- to 20-pound-test monofilament are good choices. Although the line tests may sound a bit heavy, particularly for spinning, bear in mind that most dorado spoons and plugs are in the ⅝- to ⅞-ounce class and you may want to try 1- to 1½-ounce baits at times. Winter steelhead tackle and popping rods are popular among Argentinian sportsmen and a great many 8- to 8½-foot spinning rods are in evidence. For terminal tackle bring along either No. 5 piano wire if you wrap your own leaders, or the plastic coated ready-mades in a 3-foot length of about 40-pound test. Dorado will tear monofilament to shreds without the wire protection.

Despite the long-time popularity of spoons in dorado fishing, plugs are more effective over any period of time under variable water conditions. Spoons are often touted in the back country simply because they are cheap and readily available in South America. Jointed deep-divers in black, green, gold, or silver of 5 to 8 inches in length are most reliable. A plug with two joints is better than the standard one-joint model; the more violent the wiggle the more dorado it will attract. A slow, stop-and-draw retrieve is about one-tenth as effective as a medium-to-fast rod-jerking play-back. If the bait stops moving, a dorado quickly loses interest.

With respect to the hardware, avoid treble hooks. They are worthless on dorado lures. If a dorado crunches down on a bait (and it invariably does) just the movement of its powerful jaws will spring a treble out straight—even heavy-gauge saltwater hooks. such as we use for striped bass and tarpon. The local experts on the Parana mount their plugs with singles—one forward and one in the rear. These are 8/0 to 12/0 sizes.

A double-jointed plug with two single hooks is best dorado lure

Dorado can also be caught on a large streamer fly preferably with a thumbnail-size spinner flashing at its head. However, the conditions which make fly fishing practical are seldom experienced on big rivers like the Parana. For one thing, you are blind-casting 99 percent of the time, a mile or two from shore; and unless you *know* that a dorado is holding at a particular rockpile, it is arm-wrenching devotion to lay out a long line as the boat skims down at the target creating a serpentine belly of slack between rod and fly. As the skiff bounces safely away in the riffle, the fly, which never sank deep enough to begin with, is dragged over the surface. Some days you'll have to probe five, six, or seven rockpiles before a dorado shows. With over 100-foot casts the norm and perhaps a half-dozen drifts to cover the holding water completely, it's hard work even with a big plug. There are comparatively few fly fishing waters.

CONTACTS

A competent guide is a fundamental necessity in Argentina. Apart from his knowledge of geography, language, and customs, he will supply transportation. Car-rental services do not exist except in a few major cities, and these are invariably a thousand miles away from your jump-off point. Professional guides can save you a great deal of time and money. They can be contacted through your hotel or the sporting-goods stores of larger cities. Their rates vary, but the flat-fee system is by far the best. This should include all expenses incurred on the journey except for personal items such as liquor and cigarettes.

The most expedient way of making arrangements is to use a travel agency which packages Argentinian fishing tours such as *Safari Outfitters, Inc.,* 8 South Michigan Avenue, Chicago, Illinois 60603. For guided dorado fishing on the Parana River contact Luis Oscar Schulz (Paso de la Patria Corrientes Province, Argentina). For Patagonia contact Gerardo V. Gough, 9 de Julio 551, Esquel, Chubut Province Argentina. For all Argentina contact *Weckenheim Safaris Ltd.* (Box 484, Bariloche, Argentina)

ACCOMMODATIONS

BUENOS AIRES
There are first-class hotels in Buenos Aires including the **Plaza, Claridge, Presidente,** and the **Alvear Palace** with rates from about $13 single and $25 double European plan. Somewhat lower in price are the **Lancaster, Dora,** and **Crillon.** A room tax varying from 20 percent to 24 percent is added in all city hotels.

SAN CARLOS DE BARILOCHE
Top hotel here is the **Llao-Llao Hotel** with rates at $16 to $21 per person double and $17 to $22 single depending on the meal plan selected. Popular also are the **Hotel Tunquelen** and **Hotel Tres Rayes** with rates at $13 per person double and $16 single American plan. In the low price category but comfortable are the **Bellavista** and **Hotel Pilmaiquen** which run about $8 to $10 per person double and $9 to $12 single American plan. There is also an excellent hotel at the north or opposite end of Lake Nahuel Huapi, the **Hotel Correntoso,** which is located at the mouth of the Correntoso River.

ELSEWHERE
Beyond the Bariloche area and in trout country there are many lesser though by no means uncomfortable country "inns" such as the previously mentioned **Hosteria Chimehuin** in Junin de los Andes, and the **Hosteria Futalaufquen,** in Futalaufquen. In more remote places the accommodations may or may not offer a bath (and if so, it will be shared by other guests) but such hotels are a convenience in isolated regions; these would include **Hotel Las Horquetas,** near Lake Fontana, **Hotel Calafate,** near Lake Cardiel and **Hotel Tres Pasos** near the Pasos River. Most Argentinian fishing guides have the equipment for camping out and often trips are made where the clients spend several days under canvas then a night or two at an estancia or ranch; *Weckenheim Safaris Ltd.* specializes in trips on remote rivers.

CLOTHING
During the fishing season from November through March the weather parallels the spring to fall seasons of our Northern Temperate Zone. It can be cold until mid-December and beginning in March; it always gets cold at night particularly if you are camping out. So despite the warm sunny days which typify Andean trout fishing, bring along medium weight clothing and a warm jacket or wool sweater; colorful wool sweaters are a local specialty product in Argentina and may be bought inexpensively. Chest high waders are essential and rain gear is necessary particularly on the southern sea trout streams. Good sun glasses are a must. Biting insects are uncommon in mountain areas although one fly, similar to a deerfly, can be a nuisance.

LICENSES
A national Fishing License is required. This can be obtained for $2.00 in tackle shops.

TRAVEL NOTES
Argentina is serviced by Pan American Jet Clipper non-stop from New York and one-stop from Los Angeles to Buenos Aires. Local airlines service the major fishing centers within Argentina including Bariloche and Tierra del Fuego. Rental cars are available in Buenos Aires but are almost non-existent elsewhere. On location transportation to rivers is supplied by fishing guides or in a few instances by hotels.

LANGUAGE AND PEOPLE
The language of Argentina is Spanish, although different from Castilian in pronunciation. Large foreign settlements have maintained their native languages not only at home but in private schools. Thus, Italian strongly influences the Spanish of Buenos Aires, while German has flavored the tongue of Bariloche. English is spoken in most of the hotels and in trout fishing centers, as is German, Italian and French. However, very little English is spoken in northern Argentina, so a handy pocket dictionary or a book of useful phrases is essential. Pan American Airways issues one free of charge (Air Travellers' English-Spanish) which you can obtain at any district ticket office.

Australia

Giant grouper poses a real problem for
aborigines of Northern Territory

A record 1,064-pound black marlin taken by American Richard Obach

A rainbow brood fish typifies the active hatchery program of the Victorian Fisheries and Game Department

The most arid continent on earth, Australia nevertheless has claim to some of the world's best fishing in its surrounding oceans and its island state of Tasmania. While Australia appears to be small, a mere spot on the underbelly of the globe surrounded by the Pacific and Indian Oceans, the country is immense. In general shape and total land area (approximately 3 million square miles) Australia is comparable to the United States. Despite the kangaroo and Out-Back image, it is one of the most urbanized nations in the world with two-thirds of its population living in cities of over 100,000. But sports-minded Aussies are well aware of their outdoor heritage. In very recent years giant black marlin (record 1,064 pounds) have been caught around northern Australia in Queensland which fronts the Great Barrier Reef. The few boats working out of Cairns are making the area one of the most important fishing centers in the Pacific. Striped marlin, sailfish, swordfish, yellowfin and bluefin tuna, wahoo, and dolphin are also seasonally abundant. Shark fishing which has always been an Aussie preoccupation is popular among local anglers and some exceptional

white, mako, gray nurse, bronze whaler, and hammerhead sharks have been boated. The estuaries and tropical rivers of Australia also produce excellent angling to the light-tackle caster for barramundi, ox-eye, jungle perch, black grunter, riflefish, mangrove jack, flathead, Australian bass, and Murray cod.

At present the major drawback to Australian sports fishing is the lack of facilities in some key areas and the scarcity of boats for offshore work. Frequently, non-professional skippers will charter for visitors.

THE SEASON

South of the equator with summer beginning in November, autumn in April, winter in June, and spring in September. Climates vary greatly but in general you can expect mild weather with temperatures in the 60's and 70's. The trout season runs from January to the end of April with February a prime month.

NEW SOUTH WALES

Sydney, the major port-of-entry for most travelers is a big city with a kaleidoscopic population (2½ million) drawn from all over the world. Aside from the usual tourist offerings Sydney also provides some offshore fishing, particularly for striped marlin just outside North and South Heads, the massive rock bluffs guarding its harbor. However, the peripatetic angler might prefer to try the trout fishing, which, in New South Wales, is the best the mainland has to offer. One of the most popular locations is out from Cooma in the Great Snowy mountains south of Canberra. There are a number of fine rivers in the area including the Snowy, Murrumbidgee, Eucumbene, Thredbo, Geehi, and Tumut. Famous, but not as productive as it was during the initial years of impoundment, is Lake Eucumbene. Due to an abundance of forage the trout display a rapid rate of growth. When conditions are right, even the largest trout rise at times in the shallows near shore. Both browns and rainbows in excess of 10 pounds have been taken on large dry flies such as the Muddler.

Nearby Tantangara Reservoir, a

Lefroy Brook in the karri forests near Pemberton on west coast

This 60-pound Murray cod was caught on a spinner in the Murrumbidgee River

feeder lake of Eucumbene, also provides some wonderful flyfishing at times. Scientific investigation has shown that over 35 percent of the trout food in these waters consists of caddis larvae. Mayflies are less dominant food items, but other important insects are beetles, grasshoppers, and dragonfly nymphs (locally called mudeyes).

North of Sydney in the New England Range of mountains there are some good trout streams such as Jock's Water and the Styx River. Rainbows predominate, although they do not rise to a fly as readily as the brown trout, and wet flies, nymphs, and small streamers fished deep are very successful. The types of water range from rapid mountain streams to slowly meandering, meadow-type streams. Every year rainbows up to 8 or 10 pounds are taken. The center of the district is Armidale, and many streams are within forty miles. There is an active trout fishing club here.

SOUTH AUSTRALIA
There is very little fishing here for the trout angler. Streams such as Myponga Creek, Gawler, Finis Creek, and Onkaparinga provide some sport for anglers living in Adelaide. There is some saltwater fishing in South Australia notably at Victor Harbour, Kangaroo Island, Port Lincoln, and Streaky Bay. The latter is a popular port for big-game anglers, and several white sharks of over one ton have been caught here.

WESTERN AUSTRALIA
Western Australia is the largest state in the commonwealth with an area of nearly one million square miles. Its coastline is about four thousand miles in length, and although there are no important river systems, there is some fishing for trout from Ginhin north of Perth to Albany in the south. Two of the best-known streams are the Warren River and Big Brook.

Saltwater fishing is extremely productive all along the coast, but facilities for anglers are very scarce except at Onslow, Broome, Esperance, Albany, Fremantle, Geraldton, and Wyndham. Rottnest Island is good for surf and big-game fishing.

QUEENSLAND
The important fishing center here is Cairns (population 29,000). Cairns is serviced by daily propjet flights from Sydney via Brisbane. The town has ample motel accommodations; however, the number of boats in the local charter fleet is minimal at present and advance bookings are essential. Seven black marlin of over 1,000 pounds have been caught in recent seasons and it is likely that a new world's record will be taken here. The marlin season runs from September through December, with some blacks present the year round. Pacific sailfish, wahoo, dolphin, Spanish mackerel, and tunas are common. This area was pioneered by an American charter boat skipper, George Bransford, a former Floridian. A popular headquarters here is the **Trade Winds Motel** at $11.20-$12.35 per day single.

West of Cairns on the opposite side of the Cape York Peninsula is the Gulf of Carpentaria. This is largely unexplored from an angling point of view. The rivers emptying into the Gulf offer good to excellent barramundi and threadfin salmon fishing. This "threadfin" is the same species as the kawahi of New Zealand.

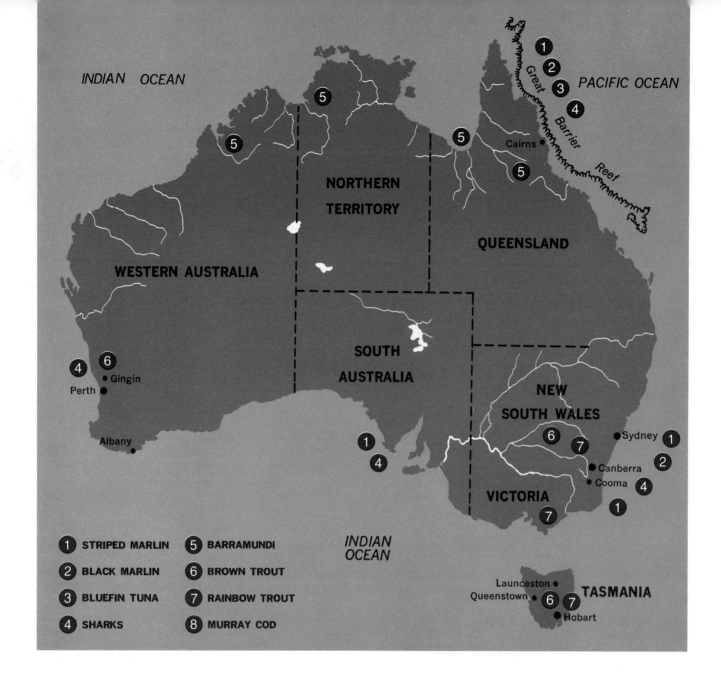

1 STRIPED MARLIN   5 BARRAMUNDI
2 BLACK MARLIN   6 BROWN TROUT
3 BLUEFIN TUNA   7 RAINBOW TROUT
4 SHARKS   8 MURRAY COD

TASMANIA

The island of Tasmania is a trout angler's paradise. Practically all its rivers provide suitable habitat for
browns and rainbows from their up-
permost reaches to where they enter
the sea. While caddis larvae are the
dominant food item of trout on the
mainland, in Tasmania the mayflies
are most important. Hatches are not
only prolific but much more predict-
able on the island, and consequently some wonderful dry-
flyfishing is possible. Good angling
can be found close to every town
and village. Some of the more famous trout waters are Great Lake,
Penstock Lagoon, Macquarie River,
Derwent River, Shannon River,
South Esk, and the Break O'Day.

However, there is superlative fishing
everywhere. Many rivers have fine
runs of sea trout. Generally, the best
season is from September to about
mid-December, and again in March
and April. Nymphs and wet flies can
be used, and streamer flies are often
productive in highwater.

Besides having the best trout fishing
in Australia, Tasmania has very
good saltwater fishing. Boats for
offshore work are available at Hobart; this capital city nestles in the
shadow of Mt. Wellington, the summit of which is about twelve miles
from the center of town. The **Wrest
Point Hotel** at Sandy Bay, Hobart,
is excellent. **Hadley's Hotel** and
Travelodge Motel are also recommended.

TRAVEL NOTES

By Pan American Jet Clipper. Flying
time has dwindled to a still impos-
ing 24 hours from New York to Sydney, or 17 hours from San Francisco
but the trophy collector has a variety
of stopovers to choose from including Hawaii, Tahiti, Pago Pago, Fiji,
Noumea, and Auckland. Trans Australia Airlines services via jet to
Cairns if you are bent on marlin, and
Hobart for Tasmanian trout.

Austria

Rainbow trout are uncommon to Austrian rivers but where found are usually large. Original stock was from Isonzo River

ACCOMMODATIONS

SYDNEY
Wentworth, from $17.40 single, $20.75 double; the smart **Chevron** and the **Menzies,** both designed for the international tourist, rates from $16.80 single, $22.40 double; the **Australia,** also in the center of the city, from $13.45 single, $19.05 double; the **Carlton-Rex,** opposite the Australia, from $13.45 single, $18.50 double. **Hotel Manly** is 7 miles from the city near a Pacific surf beach, single from $6.70, double from $13.45, including breakfast. **Astra Hotel,** overlooking Bondi surf beach, is 5 miles from the city, $8.40 single, $13 double; the **Coogee Bay,** handy to a surf beach, 6 miles from the city, from $6.45 single, including breakfast.

MELBOURNE
Hotels in Melbourne (with single rates given) include: the luxurious **Southern Cross,** an Inter-Continental Hotel that is completely air-conditioned and encompasses 9 restaurants and bars, and an open plaza with 70 specialty shops and a 300-car underground garage, $15.15-$19.80 single, $20.20-$25.80 double; the **Australia,** also conveniently located, $13.45 single, $19.96 double; **Ress Oriental,** handy to shops and theaters, $13.45; **Savoy Plaza,** $7.30; **Windsor,** $15.15; **Chevron** (10 minutes from city center), $11.10. In suburban Melbourne, the **Prince of Wales** is near shops and beach, $7.85 single, $12.90 double. Hotel reservations should be made well in advance, particularly during spring racing season from September to November, and during the March racing season. American-style motels are being built all over Australia. Rates for two average $11 per night.

Austria provides a limited mileage of quality trout and grayling fishing for the tourist. Angling in the "Salzkammergut" or Tyrol is a pastime that one enjoys while attending the Salzburg Music Festival — or as an exercise between bouts with *schlag und schnitzel.* To the man who has fished the best of South America and New Zealand, Austria is nine-tenths atmosphere and one-tenth results. Yet, it remains a most rewarding country in terms of casting to difficult fish in literally breathtaking Alpine scenery. Some rivers like the Aubach require a chamois' footing in abyssal gorges at 6,000 feet. All the streams rise amid bold, steep, fantastic masses of naked rock that tower from green valleys in amazing and endless contrast. In the beginning the currents are strong and the stream beds are broken by ledges. Below these the rivers run in long, smooth reaches, much beloved by the grayling, then drop into larger, green pools where the brown trout waits for the mayfly. Austria is one of few places in the world where the atmosphere dominates the sport. Your eyes constantly wander over carpets of buttercups threaded with deep violet gentians and red clover. You become hypnotized by the checker-board arrangement of pink and blue stones on the stream bottom, arranged as though somebody carefully laid each one in place.

Both the brown trout and the grayling are native to Austrian waters. Although some of the trout stocked each year are of hatchery origin, most derive from wild strains which are reared in protected streams and planted as two-year-olds. Brown trout are called *Bachforelle* in German. The *Lachforelle* here, as in Germany, is really a lake type brown trout with a minted silver body splashed with fine black crosses. They more nearly resemble a land-locked salmon than a brown trout. Lachforelle enter the rivers from time to time and usually weigh in excess of 5 pounds. Some large ones of 7 and 8 pounds are caught in the Traun on the dry fly, late in the evening and at night. The Traun is particularly well known for its big grayling. Exceptional fish may run up to 27 inches in length. In addition

The atmosphere may dominate the sport, but large brown trout inhabit the Aubach River

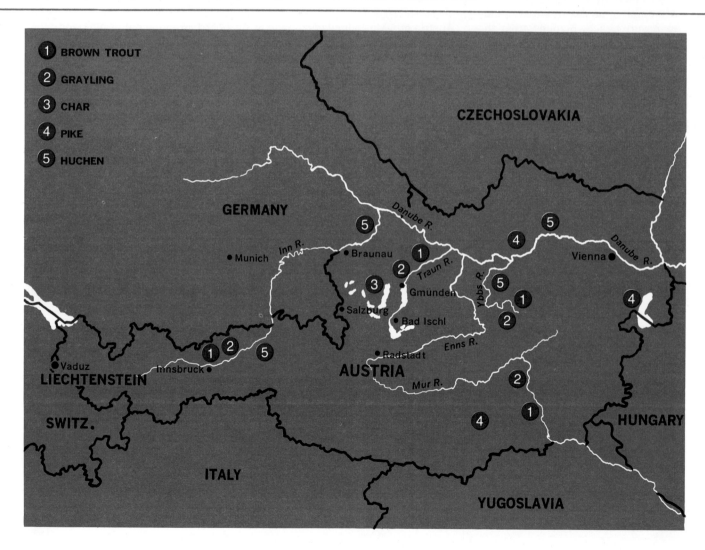

Light fly tackle is ideal in Austria

Traun River grayling average about 18 inches in length

to its size, the European grayling is often a difficult fish to catch in Alpine streams and displays none of the suicidal tendencies of the Arctic grayling found in North America.

Rainbow trout (locally *Regenbogenforelle*) were introduced to Austria by way of Italy during World War I. The original stock was brought from the Isonzo River by soldiers returning from the front. These Isonzo trout became established in a few rivers. Char (locally *Saibling*) are native to Alpine lakes and a purely Eurasian salmonid, the huchen is found in some of the larger rivers such as the Inn, Ybbs, and the Danube. Pike fishing is popular among Austrian anglers and one of the best locations is Offen See.

The Austrian fishing season opens cold with high water in May, and closes warm and low in September. For fly fishing the ideal period is from June on, with the best angling coming in July and August. The end of July and the first two weeks in August are the peak for dry fly work. Most of the rivers are big. Many of them are 200 feet wide in a normal flow but they can be negotiated with waders in the summer season.

WHERE TO GO
Austrian trout fishing is contained within a relatively small area, no more than a day's drive in any direction from Salzburg. Of the waters available to tourist fishing, the foremost river is the Traun which is a short distance east of Salzburg with its angling centers at Bad Ischl and Gmunden. The next choice would be the Mur above Lungau, the Koppen Traun near Aussee, the Lammer at Kuchl, the Gasteinache at Badgastein, and Enns at Radstadt, the Alm River, and the Aubach. Most of the west Austrian streams are too precipitous to support large trout, so the area beyond Innsbruck is better left to ski fans. A few other streams are found in the north along the Bavarian border of Germany and Czechoslovakia, or at least in the eastern half of the country. If you go up to the German border, there is a series of small streams near Brunau. Herr Bartzl at Altheim owns these waters and he welcomes guests.

TACKLE
Light fly rod tackle is ideal on Austrian waters. The trout are not usually large, nor are long casts required. Refinement is the keynote. Normally with the water running low and clear Austrian trout and grayling demand small flies on fine tippets. Any failure in presentation, a fly that drags, or one that is put down heavily will cause the fish to retreat. Fly sizes of No. 14 to No. 20 (American scale) on 4X to 6X points are the norm here. Light 7- to 8-foot fly rods matched with No. 4 or No. 5 lines and 9- to 12-foot leaders are ideal.

There are good tackle shops in Vienna and Salzburg. Buy some of the local fly patterns such as the Consul, Zulu, Pallareta, Traun Tricolor, Adjutant Quill, and Red Spinner.

CLOTHING
Summer weather in the mountains is warm by day but cool at night so include both cottons for stream apparel and warm clothing for rainy days and evenings. Chest-high waders are necessary despite the fact that some fishing will be done from the bank.

LICENSES

With very few exceptions, the state owns all the water in Austria. The rivers are rented by individuals or clubs from the government at a flat sum and usually on a 6-year lease.

The lessee of any stream can sell his trout on the public market at a fixed price. This in part reduces the cost of investing in a trout stream, and it's further supplemented by the fees collected from individual sportsmen. A tourist, for example, can get a day, a week, or a month of fishing for fees ranging from $10 to $20 a day. He must first buy what amounts to a county license (about 80 cents) then arrange for a stream through the Forest Service, a Fishing Club, or a private owner. To the serious angler, the cost is not prohibitive because he may get four or more miles of beautiful trout water at $70 to $140 for a week. Bear in mind, this is first-class river with plenty of fish available due not only to the fertility of the water but the basic stocking policy. From a tourist's standpoint it's an eminently fair arrangement.

TRAVEL NOTES

Salzburg is the jump-off point for Austrian trout fishing. It can be reached by Pan American Jet Clipper from New York to Munich, Germany (1½ hour drive Munich-Salzburg) or New York to Vienna (3½ hour drive Vienna-Salzburg). There is also local air, train, and bus service from Munich and Vienna to Salzburg. Car rentals are also available at each city.

ACCOMMODATIONS

For some reason many Austrian hotels seem to be built directly on highways and to get some sleep you might have to pay a few dollars more to reserve the back room or locate off the road. However, as a starter in fishing country on the Traun River try the delightful **Marienbrucke Hotel** near Gmunden. In same general area is the **Schloss Fuschl** located on Fuschlamsee which has several small nearby trout streams. These are reliable and cater to anglers.

Food is abundantly good throughout Austria, and you will find first-class restaurants everywhere. But sweet as the sound of the Traun's rapids are the meals you can find in old farm houses where big wheels of homemade cheese, hot bread, smoked wurst, and cold amber beer provide a lunch fit for the Emperor himself. The plain village taverns—where you can bring your trout and grayling to be cooked while a light white wine is frosting in the bucket—are the best of the lot.

Best period is July's end into August

CONTACTS

The major tackle shop in Vienna (Joh Springer's Erben, Graben 10, Wien I) can be most helpful in organizing a trip. English is spoken by one or more members of the firm. In Salzburg the major tackle shop, *H. Dschulnigg,* (Greisgasse 8) is a reliable source of local fishing information. Herr Helmut Dschulnigg (pronounced shool-nigg) takes great pains to see that visitors to his country are made welcome.

For a guide book you can't be without the government publication, *Fishing in Austria*. It contains an English and a French translation, and while not wholly complete with respect to licenses (one senses that the author just gave up trying to understand it himself), the basic facts from the stream's altitude to the kinds of fish caught are valuable. Besides the 237 waters listed there are excellent preserves controlled by the *Austrian Fishing Association* (Osterreichischen Fischereigesellschaft). The Association controls some fishing, including trout, in the vicinity of Vienna and in Lower Austria. Rights to fish these can be had on a daily permit basis that costs from 15 to 200 Austrian schillings (48c to $7.80 American). Information may be obtained from the offices of the OFG at Elisabethstrasse 22, Wien I, Austria, or *The International Sport Fisherman's Association*, Lenaugasse 14, Wien VIII, Austria.

LANGUAGE

The official language of Austria is German. There is considerable difference in dialects between one area and another. English is taught at high school level and is widely spoken in hotels and other tourist facilities. One phrase which the angler should remember is *Petri Heil!* or Hail St. Peter! (the patron saint of all fishermen), and the reply *Petri dank!* or Thanks St. Peter! These are centuries-old greetings among Austrian anglers.

Bahamas

The Bahama Islands are one of the great saltwater angling grounds of the world. The quality sport is reflected in the numerous IGFA records which have been tallied here but equally important the islands offer first-class resorts, widely available charter craft, and reliable point-to-point transportation. Composed of 700 low-lying islands and innumerable coral heads, the Bahamas lie off the east coast of Florida extending for 800 miles in a southeasterly direction from Walker's Cay on the north to Great Inagua off the east coast of Cuba. There are two other island complexes and banks — Caicos and Turks Islands and Mouchoir and Silver Banks — lying to the southeast that are geologically but not politically part of the Bahamian chain.

The Bahamas are flattened peaks of an ancient mountain range, but nowhere is there an elevation greater than 400 feet (Cat Island). The usual height above highwater is probably 5 to 10 feet. The channels and passages, Exuma Sound, the Tongue of the Ocean, and the Straits of Florida are the "valleys" of the range. In some places they drop away to great depths — 2,500 fathoms or more. Geologically the Bahamas are formed of loose coral sand beaches and weathered limestone rock of Pleistocene age. Although fresh water can be found under many of the islands, there are few active stream courses; the only permanent river is on Andros.

The rare black jack displayed by Mrs. Linda Drake

Tuna expert George Matthews, a regular Bimini visitor

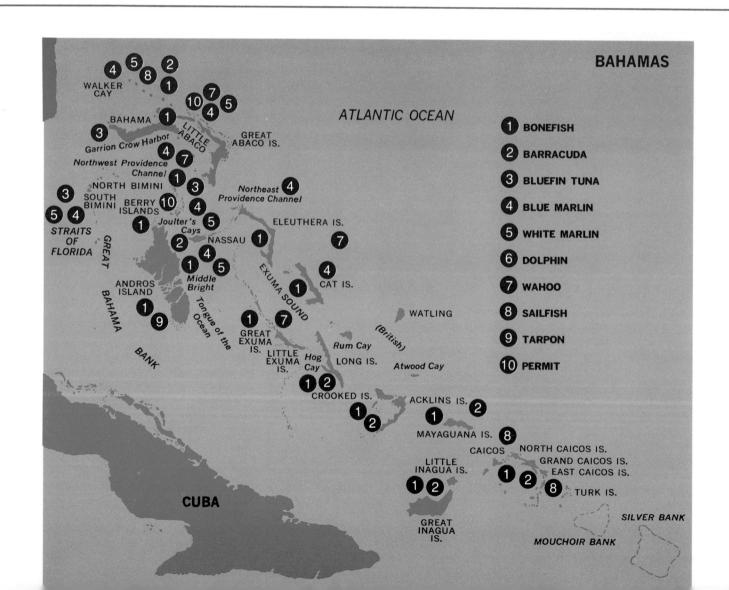

Fly reels should have a minimum of 125 yards of 18-pound-test backing

Bonefish usually travel in schools but large ones are often seen solo

THE SEASON

The Bahamas have an ideal climate. Despite occasional "northers" in the winter months, the average temperature is about 70°F. The summer months vary from 80°F to 90°F and the highest recorded was 94°F. The maximum rainfall is 50 to 60 inches per year. Fishing is possible the year round; however, seasonal peaks of abundance (marlin, sailfish, wahoo, dolphin, blackfin tuna) or occurrence during migration (bluefin tuna) make some game species scarce or absent at certain times. Fish which inhabit the flats such as bonefish, permit, and great barracuda are adversely affected by prolonged winds or chilly weather (below 60°F); northeasterly blows or sudden cold snaps will cause these shallow water gamesters to seek deep water temporarily.

Air boats are now being used by Andros Beach Hotel and Villas in the Joulter Cays. Craft can skim over one-quarter inch of water

FLATS FISHING

Poling or wading the tidal flats of the Bahamas can produce some of the best bonefishing in the world. Other countries may score heavier individual fish, or greater quantities of small bonefish, but large schools with high average weights are commonplace in the islands. Too, the conditions for fly fishing or spinning with artificial lures are ideal; although natural baits such as shrimp, crab, and strips of conch are used particularly by novices, the veteran flats angler favors artificials.

The Great and Little Bahama banks consist of wide expanses of shallow water. Over these banks the currents sweep back and forth with the tides, carrying enormous quantities of crustaceans and small fry to the deepwater along the dropoffs of the Straits of Florida, Northwest and Northeast Providence channels, Tongue of the Ocean, Exuma Sound, and Atlantic Ocean. Although bonefish are widely distributed throughout this area, only specific locations on certain islands contain the flats so necessary to this type of angling. Some of the most outstanding flats are found along

the southwest coast and Middle Bight of Andros Island, the Berry Islands, Cat Island, Great Exuma Island, Long Island, and the east end of Grand Bahama; here it becomes a series of creeks and small cays, stretching from Rummer Creek at the end of the Freeport road to Jacob's Cay some 15 miles away to the southeast. The tides ebb and flow from the deep ocean water of New Providence Channel, through a dozen or more of these creeks, to the large shallow-water sound known as the Bight of Abaco. Using Jacob's Cay as an eastern boundary, and the Cross Cays which connect Grand Bahama to Little Abaco as a western boundary, we have a vast area that offers what is probably the finest bonefishing in the Bahamas. The flats vary from pure white ocean sand, through the many sheltered creeks, to the thick turtle-grass and mangrove shoots of the bays and small sounds, making it possible to wade for tailing fish and to cast to the "muds" in the deeper channels. This entire area can be fished from Deep Water Cay located at the junction of Rummer Creek and Big Harbor Creek (known as Carrion Crow Harbor).

BAHAMIAN REAL ESTATE 1971

Anglers looking for a permanent winter retreat in the Bahamas are a significant factor in the real estate boom east of the Gulf Stream. Great Harbour Cay, located at the north end of the Berry Island Group, a prime location for bonefish and offshore fishing, has developed rapidly. The club house is now complete and the multimillion dollar marina is near enough to completion to dock a sizeable flotilla; however at the moment there is only one skiff for charter. The golf course is PGA caliber. Property is selling fast here with lots (¹/₃ acre) running from a low of $8,000 to one acre multi-family lots at $75,000. There is little waterfront property left.

On Treasure Cay located on the east shore of Great Abaco Island a new marina is being completed which should provide access to excellent offshore fishing, particularly for blue marlin and wahoo; there are also extensive bonefish flats along the east side south of Treasure Cay. Local charter boats and skiffs are limited in number. Treasure Cay Inn accommodates tourist anglers and prospective buyers. The general range on property here runs from a low of $5,600 for 11,200 square feet of interior scrub land to $40,000 for ¾ acre multi-family lots.

Although there are no prices available at press time for the fifty waterfront lots at Deep Water Cay, both the location and the property are ideal for the angler who doesn't want all the trappings of a formal resort development. Unique in every respect, all Deep Water Cay properties have 150 feet of ocean frontage and no back-to-back housing. The Deep Water Cay Club is open to transients and well equipped for light-tackle fishing.

The rarest trophy for the flats caster is the Atlantic permit. Although permit are distributed rather widely through the Bahamas, there are relatively few areas where the angler can anticipate seeing schools of these elusive fish. One such location is the vast white sand bank which extends from Red Shank Cay to Burrows Cay lying about 25 miles east-southeast of the East End of Grand Bahama. This can be fished from the **Deep Water Cay Club.** Permit are taken only rarely on artificial lures but the novice can expect a fair percentage of strikes using a whole live crab bait. The fish here run from 15 to 30 pounds or more.

Large barracuda are common to nearly all Bahamian flats and provide excellent fishing for the plug and fly caster. Sharks, particularly the blacktip and hammerhead, can be caught on artificial lures when foraging in shallow water. In the channels between the flats you can expect bar jack, yellow jack, horse-eye jack, mutton snapper, gray snapper, and small groupers.

Due to the scarcity of fresh water, tarpon are not abundant in the Bahamas. However, they do occur in fair numbers around Andros Island north to Joulters Cay and are often taken in the channels and blue holes using leadhead jigs, plugs, and flies. Elsewhere in the islands small schools appear from time to time but not in the quantity common to less saline Florida waters. The snook, another brackish water inhabitant, is totally absent from the Bahamas.

BIG-GAME FISHING
Bluefin tuna, yellowfin tuna, blue marlin, white marlin, sailfish, wahoo, dolphin and king mackerel are the principal big-game species of the Bahamas. Mako shark and swordfish occur less frequently. Other species incidental to the troll fishery are the blackfin tuna, bonito, greater amberjack, African pompano, and great barracuda.

Fisherman is angling for bonefish in a glass-bottomed boat

Bimini and the nearby island of Cat Cay were the pioneer big-game angling ports of the Bahamas. Today, however, boats troll over a wide sweep of blue water beginning with Walker's Cay in the north, Green Turtle Cay, Hope Town on Abaco, Deep Water Cay, West End and Freeport on Grand Bahama, Chub Cay in the Berry Islands, Nicolls Town at northern Andros, Grassy Cay near southern Andros, Powell, Bamboo, and Southeastern Points on Eleuthera, along the dropoff of the 10-Fathom Passage between Eleuthera and Little Cat Island, in eastern Exuma Sound off Hawks Nest, Cat Island, and west off Wide Opening in the Exuma Cays.

Generally speaking, the best period for the major gamefish is from January to August with the peak on white and blue marlin from March to May. Giant tuna fishing is limited to the northerly migration which usually appears over the Bahama banks from Bimini north to West End during the second week in May. The fishing reaches its peak here during the latter part of May and is finished by early June. Tuna fishing is spectacular in the islands because the schools can be sighted in the clear water and thus the trolling method rather than the more typical chumming method is used.

REEF FISHING
No trip to the islands is complete without a day or two spent trolling

or casting over the coral reefs. Although trolling with natural baits is a standard procedure, some of the most interesting angling is created by chumming the fish to the surface, then casting to these visible schools with flies, plugs, and leadhead bucktails. Yellowtail snapper, gray snapper (locally mangrove snapper), mutton snapper, Lane snapper, schoolmaster snapper, Nassau grouper, cero mackerel, bar jack, horse-eye jack, and many other species can be caught in this manner.

OUT-ISLAND CRUISES

Although there is no worthwhile fishing in the immediate vicinity of Nassau, many charter craft base here specialize in out-island cruises. These Bahamian skippers offer trips of a week or more through the remote cays where no resorts exist. The boats are standard sport-fishermen from 40 to 46 feet in length, equipped with ship-to-shore phones and accommodate from two to six anglers. Dinghy boats, or outboard powered skiffs are stowed or towed to be used on the shallow fishing grounds. This type of trip makes a marvelous vacation not only for visiting seldom fished waters but for skin and scuba diving. Although a list of charter craft is available from the Bahamas Fishing Bureau, it is advisable to meet the captain and check his equipment before making a prolonged voyage.

American charter boatmen based in Palm Beach, Fort Lauderdale, and Miami also make out-island cruises. Inquiries should be made at the City Docks.

TACKLE

There are no fully stocked tackle shops in the Bahamas. Some angling resorts inventory a small amount of equipment but generally speaking it's necessary to bring any light casting gear such as spinning, bait casting, and fly-fishing outfits. Tackle for big-game trolling is almost always aboard and is supplied by the captain. Charter boat tackle

which passes through many hands, is essentially on the heavy side, so the experienced angler usually brings his own gear.

For giant bluefins the standard outfit for deep-water fishing is a heavy-duty 39-thread or 130-pound-test-class rod, and 550 yards of 130-pound-test Dacron spooled on a 12/0 reel. In fishing the shallow water of the Bahamas it is possible to use a lighter 24-thread outfit; the rod should be an 80-pound-test-class fiberglass, with 550 yards of 80-pound-test Dacron or 24-thread linen spooled on a 9/0 reel. Although the heavy-duty outfit can be used with some degree of certainty, the 80-pound-test outfit requires expert teamwork between the angler and his crew. The tactics of a tuna in shallow water are more erratic and violent when hooked, and the captain must provide skilled assistance with the boat.

CLOTHING

The weather is ordinarily warm. However, a cool northeaster can occur any time from late November to April so it's a good idea to bring along a medium-weight sweater and a light-weight rain cap- to be worn over it; this will deflect the spray and wind aboard a running boat. Otherwise, light-weight summer clothing is the rule; sport shirts and slacks or shorts for men and blouses with slacks or shorts for women when fishing. Evenings are usually informal at out-island camps; few require jackets or ties. If you plan to visit Nassau, the latter are required.

Bring rubber-soled topsiders or similar foot gear for wading on

Some of the world's best big-game fishing boats are based in the Bahamas. Tuna tower for spotting fish from a boat was developed in these islands

FOR MILLIONAIRES ONLY

Big-game fishing everywhere has its moments of drama. But nowhere on the heavy-tackle circuit is the sport so spectacular as at Cat Cay in the Bahamas, when shoals of great bluefin tuna pass by in migration from Caribbean spawning grounds to their lush summer feeding pastures in the northern Atlantic. Tuna fishing at Cat Cay provides the ultimate in thrills. During their spring run the bluefins hug the eastern edge of the Straits of Florida, less than 50 miles from Miami. From early May until the second week in June the schools pour through. Some keep to the deep water of the Gulf Stream, but vast schools make their crossing in the shallows hard by the Stream dropoff, crowding together in incredible numbers. When light and sea conditions are right, anglers and tuna wage battles in the shallows that are unparalleled in heavy-tackle fishing. These fish are hard, lean 500-pound brutes, pushing along at a speed estimated at more than five knots on their way to a summer banquet on the herring of Nova Scotia, the whiting of Block Island, and the ling and butterfish of the Long Island and New Jersey coasts.

Cat Cay, a lush island on the western edge of the Grand Bahamas Bank, is a little more than two miles long and a half-mile wide, and 35 minutes by air from Miami via *Chalk's Flying Service* which operates daily flights to Cat Cay and Bimini with amphibious planes.

Cat Cay is presently owned by a group brought together by Willard F. Rockwell, Jr., board chairman of North American Rockwell.

Since 1931, this was perhaps the most exclusive and expensive angling club in the world frequented by captains of industry, titled Englishmen (although one name carved next to Wallis Simpson's among the thousands that decorate the walls of the bar simply reads "Edward"), actors, actresses, and just plain millionaires. In 1964 the club ceased to exist with the death of owner Lou Wassey. The demise of the island followed a year later in the winds of Hurricane Betsy.

Rockwell and his fellow investors bought the island in 1969 and a renaissance has begun in rebuilding the old club house, homes, and adding new reinforced concrete docks. Marshall Field, Jr., Roger S. Firestone, and August A. Busch are a few of the many new equity members who berth their yachts in the harbor. Several fishing tournaments are planned for 1971.

Cat Cay has no hotel and is definitely not for tourists. Those accepted as equity members of Cat Cay Limited, (Post Office Box 723, Buena Vista Station, Miami, Florida 33137) pay $12,500 and dues of $1,000 annually; yachting members pay $2,500 and annual dues of $500. Transient yachtsmen may put in at Cat Cay, purchase fuel and supplies, and use certain of the harborside facilities including the informal dining room.

bonefish flats. A good sun tan oil or cream is a must. Insect pests are seldom a problem although in brush-covered areas around fresh or brackish water (Andros Island) mosquitoes and sandflies can be a nuisance at times.

LICENSES
None required.

TRAVEL NOTES
The Bahamas can be reached via Pan American Jet Clipper from New York to the capital city of Nassau, or from London to Nassau via Bermuda. Service to the fishing camps consists of scheduled commercial flights from Nassau to the larger islands such as Andros, Abaco, Eleuthera, and Grand Bahama, or by reliable charter services to the smaller islands such as Great Harbour Cay, Green Turtle Cay, Walker's Cay, and Deep Water Cay. Anglers coming from the U.S. in regions other than New York may fly to Nassau via Palm Beach or Miami, Florida, or they may terminate in these Florida cities and use charter flights to the out-islands, which in some instances is closer and less expensive than the direct-to-Nassau route. There are no auto rentals available but they are not necessary; taxi services exist on the larger islands and elsewhere the resorts make arrangements to pick up guests by car or by boat.

No passports or visas are required, but you will need some proof of nationality. You may take in 200 cigarettes and 1 quart of liquor, unrestricted amounts of dollars, but not more than $70 in Bahamian, Bermudian, Jamaican or Bank of England notes.

ACCOMMODATIONS

NASSAU
There is an abundance of first-class hotels in Nassau. The winter season is the most fashionable time of the year, and hotel rates vary widely. Typical rates for Modified American

Plan (room, breakfast and dinner) are: **Balmoral Beach Hotel,** $26-$36 single, $42-$66 double. **Sheraton British Colonial Hotel,** $30-$47 single, $40-$55 double. **Carlton House,** $18-$20 single, $27-$30 double. **Coral Harbour Hotel,** $30-$50 single, $42-$65 double. **Montagu Beach Hotel,** $25-$45 single, $35-$55 double. **Emerald Beach Hotel,** $32-$55 single, $42-$65 double. **Nassau Beach Hotel,** $32-$55 single, $42-$65 double. **Nassau Harbour Club,** from $26 single, $38 double. **Pilot House Club,** $24-$36 single, $34-$46 double. **Dolphin Hotel,** $22-$26 single, $30-$40 double. **Cumberland House** $23 single, $38 double; **Prince George,** $24 single, $38 double. Representative of European Plan rates (no meals included) are the **New Olympia,** from $11 single, $16 double; **Royal Victoria Hotel,** $16-$30 single, $22-$40 double; **Towne Hotel,** $10-12 single, $16-$18 double. All these rates are reduced substantially from May 1 to December 15.

FREEPORT
Only 68 miles east of Palm Beach, Grand Bahama is developing at a rapid rate and is complete with shopping centers, traffic circles and all the other accoutrements of modern civilization while still maintaining an aura of existing solely for vacationers. Already the island has nearly as many hotel rooms as Nassau and more are on the way. Golf, beaches and water sports, gourmet dining and sophisticated entertainment are provided at the swank **Lucayan Beach Hotel** and **Marine Villas** (from $30 single, $35 double, European Plan) and there is a gambling casino too. The giant **Holiday Inn** is a beautiful place with lots to do; from $29.50 single, $37 double, Modified American Plan. The **Oceanus Hotel** has charming atmosphere, plenty of activity; from $34 single, $42 double. **King's Inn and Golf Club** has 800 rooms and 54 holes of golf; from $18 single, $20 double, European Plan. Just across from it is the *International Shopping*

Former King Edward VIII of England and Wallis Windsor were among the many famous visitors who enjoyed the facilities of the Cat Cay Club

Bazaar with exotic restaurants and merchandise from all over the world. Here, too, is *El Casino,* another fabulous new gambling establishment.

FISHING RESORTS
Out-island resorts which have the equipment and cater to anglers are the **Walker's Cay Club** on Walker Cay, the **Bluff House** on Green Turtle Cay, **Jack Tar's** at West End, Grand Bahama Island, the **Deep Water Cay Club** on Deep Water Cay, **Treasure Cay Inn** and **Hope Town Harbour Lodge** on Great Abaco Island, the **Great Harbour Club** on Great Harbour Cay in the Berry Islands, **Crown Colony Club** on Chub Cay also in the Berry Islands, **Andros Beach Hotel and Villas** at Nicolls Town on northern Andros Island, and **Club Peace and Plenty** at George Town on Great Exuma Island.

CONTACTS
Information on fishing resorts is obtainable through the Bahamas Fish-

ing Bureau. The Development Board, Box 818, Nassau, Bahamas. General travel information can be obtained from the Bahamas Ministry of Tourism, Churchill Building, Nassau. Pan American's office is on Mathew Avenue (Tel. 2-3394). Offices also in the British Colonial and Nassau Beach hotels. Information also from the Bahamas Ministry of Tourism at 30 Rockefeller Plaza, New York, N.Y., 10020; 1230 Palmolive Bldg., Chicago 60611; 1701 First National Bank Bldg., Miami 33131; 1406 Adolphus Hotel Arcade, Dallas 75202; 510 West 6th St., Los Angeles 90014; 707 Victory Bldg., 80 Richmond St. W., Toronto 1; and 5 Vigo St., Regent St., London, W.1, England.

LANGUAGE AND PEOPLE
English is the official language of the Bahamas. Native guides have a quaint dialect that may be difficult to understand at first (throw the crab becomes "Chow de crob" and reeling in is "making up") but you'll get the hang of it.

Bermuda

These most northerly coral islands lying about 750 miles southeast of New York have been by tradition a semi-tropical watering spot of royalty, honeymooners, and jet-setters; but no small part of Bermuda's attraction has been to anglers in the "high season," which is spring and summer here. There are approximately 150 "islands" in the Bermuda group ranging in size from large rocks to the 22-mile-long mainland which is no more than 1½ miles wide. The total land area of all the islands is a shade over 20 square miles. Natives proudly point out that these islands lie in the shape of a fish hook. Bermuda is entirely surrounded by shallow reefs which are the northernmost habitat of the bonefish. Bermuda is a plateau which, upon reaching the 35 fathom mark and within a matter of a very few yards, drops away sharply to depths measured in hundreds of fathoms. Fifteen miles to the southwest lies the 26-fathom-deep Challenger Bank; an additional 10 miles, in the same direction and approximately the same depth of water, brings one over Plantagenet Bank. This latter bank is more popularly known as Argus Bank, upon which is erected one of the famous "Texas Towers," which is named "Argus Island." As might be expected both banks are prime fishing locations, and the combined areas of the two banks form one hundred square miles of fishing grounds.

Fishing tournaments of interest to visiting anglers are the *Annual Bermuda Game Fish Tournament* (the 29th Annual puts to sea in 1971) which commences on May 1st and concludes on November 30th. This annual competition offers numerous trophies in all recognized tackle categories including spinning and fly casting. The other major tournament is by invitation only, the *Bermuda International Light Tackle Tournament* which is normally held in mid-July and lasts for three days. The I. L. T. T. draws expert anglers from all over the world. There are numerous other one-day and fish-of-the-month events.

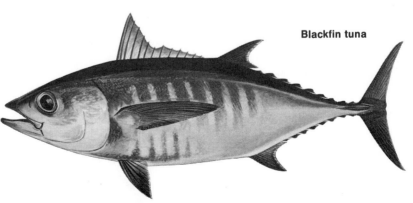

Blackfin tuna

Fishing in Bermuda is seasonal with the peak from spring to fall

Palometa are caught along beaches

World's record amberjack taken by Nelson Simons near North Rock weighed 142 pounds, 12 ounces

THE SEASON

Fishing during the winter months is uncertain at best and Bermuda does not promote itself as competitor to Florida, for example, which enjoys the peak of its sailfish run at that time. Good fishing in Bermuda begins to get under way in mid-April and is excellent by the end of May, and continues well into November.

Though situated far north of tropical latitudes, Bermuda nonetheless has a mild climate with an annual average temperature of 70°F. The lowest temperature ever officially recorded was a reading of 41°F. in 1955. Average annual rainfall is 57.6 inches and is evenly spread across the 12 months. There is a yearly average of 7.1 hours of sunshine a day. There has never been a year with less than 340 days on which sunshine has been recorded. The average is 351 days.

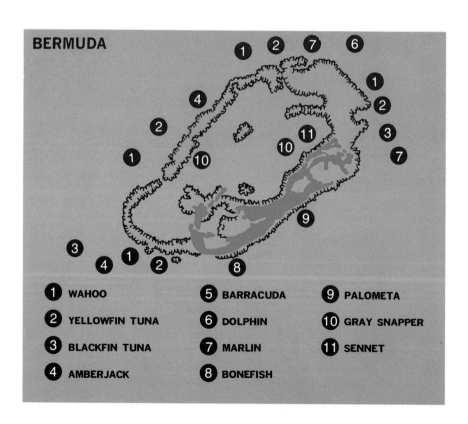

BERMUDA

1. WAHOO
2. YELLOWFIN TUNA
3. BLACKFIN TUNA
4. AMBERJACK
5. BARRACUDA
6. DOLPHIN
7. MARLIN
8. BONEFISH
9. PALOMETA
10. GRAY SNAPPER
11. SENNET

Bermuda's Whale Bay has produced many large bonefish. The productive months here are from July through October

Game and good eating, the blackfin tuna is a favorite among Bermuda anglers

OFFSHORE FISHING

WAHOO

Wahoo are taken year around, but the best angling is from May until the end of October. It is during May and into the first week or ten days of June that a minor run of wahoo takes place. The word "minor" is used because compared with the run in September and October, it is less significant. For the remainder of the summer and until the major run commences, wahoo are taken regularly. The trolling speed is important, and it has been established that 6½ to 7 mph will result in more wahoo strikes than any other speed. The favorite baits are balao (locally called garfish), flyingfish, and strip baits which are trolled from an outrigger or on a flatline. Feather jigs are extremely popular, but spoons are not generally used.

YELLOWFIN TUNA

Yellowfin-tuna fishing is popular on the Challenger and Argus banks. Although trolling accounts for a considerable number of fish each year, the best results are obtained by chumming. With the tide running from the banks toward the deep, two methods can be used. Anchor in 28 to 30 fathoms, and drift back until the boat is directly over the edge of the bank; then secure the anchor rope and commence chumming. Or run in over the bank until the boat is 400 or 500 yards from the edge, and drift back, letting out a steady stream of chum until the echo sounder indicates that the boat has passed over the edge. If no fish are hooked or brought in sight, return to starting point and repeat as often as necessary. It is seldom that fish fail to put in an appearance within the first hour. Anchovies or fry are most effective both for chumming and as bait. The yellowfin tuna is here throughout the year, but the best months are mid-April to the end of November.

BLACKFIN TUNA

Blackfin tuna have produced more world records than any other fish in

Bermuda waters. Skip baits and feather jigs work equally well. Like all members of the tuna family, the blackfin is a stubborn fighter, and a fish cannot be considered whipped until it is in the boat. Rainbow runners frequently flash into the chum line when fishing for tuna. There is little trouble in identifying this fish when it comes in sight—the tail is brilliant yellow and shows up clearly in the water. If a spinning rod with 12- or 15-pound-test line is aboard, tie a No. 3/0 or No. 4/0 hook to 3 feet of 20-pound-test monofilament leader. Secure a single anchovy or several fry to the hook, cast out, and get set for action. The rainbow runner is one of the marine world's most beautiful fish, and it always gives a rousing account of itself on light tackle. If no spinning tackle is available, try for the runners on 12- or 20-pound-test trolling rods.

AMBERJACK

Amberjack commonly reach a weight of 70 to 100 pounds in Bermuda waters and go to as much as 180 pounds. They are taken near the edge of the plateau and also the edge of the banks. Fishing from an anchored boat is usual, and the pre-continued on page 37

Islands In The Sun

From the Florida Keys east to the Bahamas and south through the Caribbean to northern South America is a saltwater fishing region without peer. The islands are an abstract wilderness even to anglers who have spent a lifetime on the Great Blue Stream. New areas are developed each year. Marlin fishing is now possible off Grenada, for example, and bonefishing has come to the remote Caicos Islands. But the idea is to get away from the rubbery smell of routine, and whether you choose the Bahamas, Virgin Islands, Jamaica, or any of the thousand coral atolls which are no more than an anchorage for passing ships, the water turns to the color of a key lime as you make landfall, and taut nerves relax in a world of long forgotten crusades.

Marlin, giant tuna, sailfish, wahoo, king mackerel, dolphin, yellowfin tuna, barracuda, bonefish—the list is impressive. And whether you wade the flats, pole a skiff, or ride a pair of 300 hp engines, there's fishing for everybody. It is possible to find fast action somewhere during the entire year although the hurricane months of August through October can be wet, hot, and blowy even if a tropical storm doesn't develop. The prime fishing months are from January into July. If light-tackle flats fishing is your choice, then all you need is calm weather without any northerly cold snaps (which reach down to the coast of British Honduras). If big-game fishing is your goal, then plan your trip on the peak periods, such as May for bluefin tuna in the Bahamas or July for marlin in the Virgins. These peaks are based on the migrations and feeding concentrations of each species and vary according to the locality.

Charter boats command from $100 to $200 per day with the average at about $125 on the present market. You can pick up the tab solo or make a split-charter with one to three other people, as most boats will fish four anglers. Some skippers feel that four is a crowd and we concur; splitting it two ways is ideal. Charter boats supply big-game tackle but this is usually on the heavy side to absorb the stresses of amateur handling.

Island resorts vary from posh high-rises to basic camps. Hotels in the 200-bed category can usually arrange for offshore fishing through the city docks and this is satisfactory in tourist centers like San Juan, Freeport, Montego Bay, and Willemstad. Family vacations are invariably planned around a variety of activities. Of course many small resorts offer almost as much at a less hectic pace, and these gems can be found from the Out Islands of the Bahamas through the Antilles. The serious angler will look for accommodations at well-known fishing grounds which cater primarily to sportsmen. With few exceptions, resorts in this category accommodate fifteen to twenty-five people but maintain their own fleet of boats and guides; this is essential to camps that specialize in light-tackle fishing for bonefish or tarpon. Beware of small operators who promise to "find a boat and guide locally," a fairly common, disappointing practice.

Guides' rates (including boat and motor) vary according to the equipment offered and locale. Average in the Florida Keys is $75 per day which includes a big skiff in the 20-foot class, fast motor, and the tackle. Elsewhere from the Mexican coast to the Bahamas prices run from $35 to $50 per day but skiffs are usually smaller and no tackle is provided. The angler is expected to purchase lunches and cold drinks when fishing independent of a camp. The guide's experience is of great importance to a successful trip; this is especially true in flats fishing for tarpon, permit, and bonefish where mutual techniques are complimented.

The real skills in bonefishing are the angler's ability to sight and stalk his quarry. Casting from a skiff is a team operation (top left) with the man at the push-pole maneuvering the angler into a favorable wind position

Where the bottom is firm, wading is an ideal method in stalking (top right). The angler is less visible and can get closer to the fish. Wear rubber-soled sneakers and long pants to protect feet and legs from sea urchins and coral

All good saltwater casters learn to do the double-haul (center left). The haul is valuable not only for distance, but to minimize rod motions. Bonefish often spook at first rod movement. No. 8 to 10 floating line is popular

Except for trophies, nearly all bonefish are released (center right). Bonefish's diet consists mainly of mollusks but they also feed on shrimp. Fly should sink to bottom and remain stationary for a moment before a slow retrieve

Polarized sunglasses are essential to the sport. Although live fish out of water displays dark markings on back (bottom left), this color is less intense in the water. Bonefish look like faint shadows against sand bottom

Conch, spiny lobster, and snapper are basic island foods (bottom right). Conch is made into chowder, fritters, and salad. The lobster is good steamed or broiled. Snapper is best poached in a bath of wine, herbs, and butter

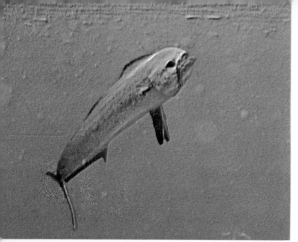

Underwater (*top and center*) a dolphin takes
a streamer fly and leaps in the air with
its dorsal fin erect. A top fly-rod fish,
the colorful dolphin runs from 10 to 40 pounds
or more. The gaping mouth posture of a big
barracuda (*right*) is typical. Barracuda are
crafty lure-takers and excellent gamefish
on light tackle in shallow water. World record
of 103 pounds was caught in the Bahamas

The Sunshine State

The 447-mile-long, mostly semitropical peninsula of Florida not only offers some of the finest saltwater angling in North America but a bonus in its largemouth bass fishing. Despite the fact that many of its once-famous rivers have been destroyed by pollution, dredging, and land development, a number of big lakes such as Jackson, Okeechobee, Kissimmee, and Tarpon (near Tampa) still produce an annual crop of 5- to 10-pounders, and trophy fish of 12 to 16 pounds are caught each season. A different type of water is the Everglades, a tremendous bass habitat at Conservation Area 3 with its access via Andytown.

The Florida bass season is open year-round, but spring is clearly the best period for big fish, and the peak months are from February through April. There are numerous public launching sites for the boat owner, and visitors can find guides with all equipment including canoes and airboats at the major bass waters.

continued from page 31

ferred baits are live bream, yellowtail snapper, mackerel scad (locally called ocean robin), and red hind. Another popular bait is a large squid, and it is practically impossible for an amberjack to pass up this hors d'oeuvre. The best angling for amberjack is September to April. The related Almaco jack (locally horse-eye bonito) is taken by the same methods as described for the amberjack except that the best months are April to October, with May producing the largest fish. The top weight is 50 to 65 pounds.

BARRACUDA
Frequently barracuda tear into trolled baits, feather jigs, and spoons when boats move over depths of less than 28 fathoms. Beyond 28 fathoms there is rarely any action from the species. A barracuda on light tackle is worthy of any serious fisherman's attention, and often during the fight it will put on an aerial display of no mean proportions.

DOLPHIN
The dolphin in Bermuda do not appear to have a definite season since they can be taken throughout the year. However, it has been established that they are most numerous from May to December. Also, when prevailing winds blow from the northeast or southeast, huge quantities of sargassum weed appear, and dolphin generally accompany it. Dolphin are just about the most obliging of all fish as far as anglers are concerned—just show them a fast-moving bait or lure, and let it be smaller than the fish. They will climb all over it, and if they miss on the first pass they will reverse and try again.

MARLIN
Blue marlin and white marlin are caught each year, but these are not species which can be deliberately sought. Their appearance behind a bait is sudden and unexpected, and it invariably happens when trolling for other species. The white marlin is one of the finest light-tackle fish that an angler can hope to catch, and the tackle used is apt to be entirely suitable for the task at hand. However, the picture is somewhat different when a big blue begins to stalk a skipping outrigger bait and the tackle is 30-pound test or lighter.

There are two options: go out ready for any emergency and use heavy gear, or adopt the philosophical attitude of the light-tackle angler and take your chances. In the former instance you may be lucky and raise a blue marlin. But it is far more likely that fish suitable to light gear will be caught, and these will provide little sport on heavy tackle.

July and August are the best months for blue marlin. The white marlin is taken in small numbers throughout the year. As is usual in the case of members of the billfish family, baits skipped from an outrigger are the top producers, and the following are used: balao, flyingfish, little tuna, and strip bait.

INSHORE FISHING

BONEFISH
Bonefish are found throughout the year with the best months being May through October. Bait, rather than artificial lures, will take more fish in May and June. No satisfactory explanation has been put forward as to why this should be, but the fish are extremely skittish when confronted with an artificial lure of any type during these two months. From July through October the bonefish are impartial and will take bait or lures, particularly small feather and bucktail jigs. The Bermuda record for bonefish is 14 pounds (1950) and the average size is about 6 pounds. Five of the top bonefish spots are Whitney's Bay (more often referred to locally as Whale Bay) in the Parish of Southampton; Long Bay in Somerset; Shelly Bay in Hamilton Parish; The Causeway, connecting

Hamilton Parish and St. George's; and Castle Point in St. George's. The latter location is accessible by boat only, since, in order to reach it from shore, one would have to cross private property. The first three named locations are ideal for the experienced bonefisherman, for he can wade, search, and cast to the fish. A falling tide does not bother local bonefish, and the best time for wading anglers is 2 to 2½ hours before low tide and the first 2 or 2½ hours of the rising tide; this gives waders a minimum of 4 hours' fishing.

PALOMETA

Palometa or "pompano" favor the south shore beaches from April through November, and are also found in harbors, bays, and around bridges. Lightest of spin tackle will give the greatest amount of sport. They are commonly taken at ¾ to 1 pound. Two and three pounders are trophies for the species. Anglers can give themselves an assist of real value by chumming with white bread broken in chunks about the size of a thumbnail and mixed with a generous portion of canned sardines and the oil in which they are packed.

GRAY SNAPPER

The gray snapper, better known as "mangrove snapper," appear inshore when the water temperature reaches 70°F. (about mid-April) and depart again about the end of October. These wary fish are one of the most difficult to take on artificial lures, but a persistent angler will achieve a measure of success by going after them at night. There is no substitute for bait (alive or dead) for those who really wish to catch the timid mangrove snapper. White grunt, bigeye scad, seaworms, mussels, anchovy, and fry are all good baits.

SENNET

The sennet, a small member of the barracuda family, is found along the shore, in bays and inlets, and, at night, around wharves and bridges,

particularly where a strong electric light or lantern casts its rays on the water. Small- and medium-size plugs, streamer flies, and jigs are made to order for these voracious little fighters. Bait is used at times but is seldom necessary if a supply of lures is at hand. A short wire leader is essential for sennet. November to April are the best months with peak angling from January to March. Fish of about a pound are average. A 3-pounder is exceptional.

Barracuda also frequent the shallow inshore waters during the summer months and are caught from skiffs and by wading fishermen. Fly-casting and spinning equipment give the ultimate in action. Bucktail and feather streamer flies, weighted jigs, and shallow diving plugs are best lures.

REEF-FISHING

Chumming with a bucketful of small minnow-like fish (called fry) mixed with fine sand is standard practice on all well-organized reef-fishing expeditions. This chum acts like a magnet and attracts such species as the yellowtail snapper, little tuna, mangrove snapper, amberjack, Almaco jack and the Bermuda chub. On or near bottom, various rock-dwelling species are numerous, and although delicious in the pan they can hardly be classified as game-fish.

For the angler who takes his sport seriously, artificial lures will attract all the reef species mentioned, even, on rare occasions, the mangrove snapper. However, due to the clarity of the water, it is not an easy task to fool these fish with any degree of consistency, and knowledgeable fishermen keep an open mind and switch to live bait when conditions demand.

Spinning equipment is the favored tackle for the reef-fisherman, with rods 6½ to 7½ feet in length. Line is 10- to 20-pound test with monofilament being the top choice of

material. Reels of sturdy construction, and capable of holding 200 to 300 yards of line, balance the outfit.

TACKLE

OFFSHORE

Light tackle is all that is required for offshore fishing. With the possible exception of that used by neophyte anglers, the tackle most used by fishermen is 12-, 20-, or 30-pound-test line matched to appropriate rods. Reels range from No. 3/0 to No. 6/0. Leader material is either light cable or straight (piano) wire 60- to 100-pound test, and its length varies from 15 feet (the maximum allowed for light tackle) to not less than 8 feet. The hooks used are No. 5/0 to No. 10/0. Serious anglers will bring their own gear but excellent equipment is available on all charter craft.

INSHORE

Spinning tackle suitable for bone-fish and other inshore and reef species should be in the 6- to 10-pound-test class. Standard salt-water fly fishing gear may be used for a variety of angling from bone-fish to yellowfin tuna (record on fly 53 pounds 6 ounces in 1969).

CONTACTS

A reliable source of information on Bermuda fishing is a department of the Bermuda Government—the *Bermuda Fishing Information Bureau* (Hamilton, Bermuda) directed by Mr. S. L. "Pete" Perinchief.

Although the Bermuda charter boat fleet is perfectly adequate to handle any number of visiting anglers, off-shore craft are not so numerous that you can afford to wait until the last minute to make a reservation. Hotels or guest houses will obtain bookings on behalf of guests on specified dates (a 25 percent deposit helps in getting confirmation) but dealing direct is advisable. The following are all captains who are members of the *Bermuda Charter Fishing Boat Association:*

CAPTAIN	BOAT	LENGTH	LOCATION	RATES	PHONE
Herbert Adderley	FAIR LADY	41'	Pembroke	$70 & $100	2-1191
Ronnie Boys	ARGOSY	36'	Pembroke	$70 & $100	1-4181
Walter Darrell	VALJOSHA	35'	St. George's	$70 & $100	2-4368
David De'Silva	TANGO	42'	Pembroke	$70 & $100	1-5876
Boyd Gibbons	CORAL SEA	37'	Somerset	$70 & $100	4-8515
Clyde Leseur	CHALLENGER	45'	Paget	$70 & $100	1-2109
David Martin	STAR DUST	39'	Southampton	$70 & $100	1-4882
Noel Parris	CONTESSA	32'	Pembroke	$70 & $100	2-2680
Edric Pearman	PARROT	38'	St. George's	$70 & $100	3-9433
Milton Pitman	MARLIN	40'	Somerset	$70 & $100	4-8302
					4-0700
Rudolph Richardson	ALRUJO	42'	Flatts	$70 & $100	3-1275
Reid Robinson	MARANDA	45'	Pembroke	$70 & $100	2-5535
Chris Smith	GINNY	33'	Southampton	$70 & $100	2-1045
Joe Stubbs	TROUBADOUR	41'	Somerset	$70 & $100	4-0685
	SEA MAID	38'	Somerset	$70 & $100	4-0685
Clarence Welch	HOPE	32'	St. George's	$70 & $100	3-9692
George Welch	BLANCHE II	41'	St. George's	$70 & $100	3-9507
Russell Young	SEA WOLFE	40'	Somerset	$70 & $115	4-8234
Frank Ray, Jr.	BONEFISH	23'	Flatts	$35 & $ 60	3-0104
					2-3099

TRAVEL NOTES

By Pan American Jet Clipper from New York on the new 747 or from Boston via 707 about two hours flying time. No passport or visa required but return ticket or onward transportation is essential and for U.S. Immigration authorities, proof of U.S. citizenship, such as an old passport, birth or baptismal certificate or voter's certificate.

Bus fare from Kindley Field Airport into Hamilton (12 miles) is $1.75; taxi fare is about $3.50, plus 15 percent tip. Airport porters are tipped 25c per bag. Departure tax by plane or ship is the equivalent of $2.40.

ACCOMMODATIONS

Bermuda's hotels are one of the chief attractions to tourists and the angler will have no difficulty in finding suitable quarters. Just remember that the place is apt to be jammed in the high season so make reservations well in advance. Most hotels here use the Modified American Plan (breakfast and dinner included) but an alternate in the Continental Plan (breakfast included) is often available. Rates are lower in winter and fall and the following are in-season prices double per day on Modified American: The

Castle Harbour at Tucker's Town, luxurious with swimming pools, golf course, dancing, and a private beach at $43 to $60: the Carlton Beach in Southampton, with every room overlooking the water, pool, $40 to $60; the glamorous Princess, with golf course, swimming pool, night club, $40 to $60. The Bermudiana Hotel overlooks the harbor on the outskirts of Hamilton, pool, $42 to $50. Elbow Beach Surf Club, on its own beautiful beach, is a gay social spot with dancing nightly, pool, $44 to $65. Inverurie on the harbor in Paget, swimming pool, nightly dancing and entertainment, $39 to $59. The Belmont Hotel and Golf Club in Warwick Parish overlooks the Great Sound, swimming pool, 18-hole golf course, $39 to $52.

Bermuda has numerous guest houses and cottage colonies, which offer the same service as hotels but provide a quieter, more private vacation. Rates are about the same as at hotels. All listed are Modified American Plan. The following are typical: Ariel Sands, South Shore, Devonshire, pool, from $46; Buena Vista, Harbour Road, Paget, $30 to $34; Horizons in Paget near Coral Beach, pool, $36 to $60; Palmetto Bay on

Harrington Sound, attractive cottages, $34 to $48; Waterloo House on harbor close to Hamilton has gracious service, good food, pool, $36 to $56; Pomander Gate in Paget is an old Bermuda mansion with picturesque cottages, magnificent flower garden, swimming pool, $38 to $60. Deepdene Manor, new pool, is $35 to $45. Cambridge Beaches in Somerset—small cottages, and rooms in main house, pool, rates $44 to $66. The Ledgelets in Somerset—small cottages, and rooms in main house, pool, $34 to $46; Lantana Cottage Colony also in Somerset, pool, $41 to $58; Bermuda Cottages in nearly all locales, $36 to $38 including breakfast, $42 to $48.

Most of the large hotels have nightly floor shows featuring either or both local and imported groups and personalities. Dancing is often out of doors during the summer months, and because of seasonal changes, entertainment is usually more informal during the winter months. There are also several night clubs in the City of Hamilton which present two floor shows nightly. There is nearly always a cover charge for dancing and entertainment throughout the colony.

British Honduras

British Honduras extends south of the Quintana Roo Territory of Mexico. It offers a variety of saltwater angling with the seasonal emphasis on tarpon and snook. The fishing may be divided between the mainland with its numerous rivers, lagoons, and mangrove bordered bays, and the Turneffe Islands which are located within a 190–mile-long barrier reef that parallels the mainland about 15 miles offshore.

The northern half of British Honduras is low (less than 200 feet above sea level) and the southern half consists in part of a plateau and the Maya Mountains. The climate is subtropical, with a dry season that lasts from February to April and a wet season from June to October. The mean annual temperature varies from 74°F in December to 83°F in July. The coolest weather is from October to December. Trade winds prevail through most of the year.

THE MAINLAND

The mainland of British Honduras offers snook and tarpon fishing in the many lagoons and rivers north and south of Belize City. Some of the better locations are the Northern River, Belize River and its tributaries, Sibun River, Manatee River, Stann Creek, Southern Stann Creek, Sapodilla Lagoon, Monkey River, Goldstream, Rio Grande River, and Moho River. The fishing is usually done in comfortable outboard powered skiffs but **Keller's Caribbean Lodge** also charters house-boats for extended trips to the more remote rivers. The house-boat, which has functional sleeping quarters and dining facilities, accommodates four anglers.

On the average, snook in these waters weigh from 5 to 20 pounds (the local record is 47 pounds), and the tarpon from 20 to 50 pounds with the occasional possibility of fish in the 100-pound class. Although some tarpon are present the year round with large individuals occurring far inland in the headwater sections, the major run extends from late April through June. The best snook fishing is in December. Bonefish, snappers, groupers, jacks, and some permit are found in suitable habitats along the 120-mile coast. An endemic species, unfamiliar to tourist anglers, is the so-called "bay snook" (*Petenia splendida*) which occurs in fresh and brackish water. Known also in Honduras as the blanco, this species averages from 1 to 4 pounds in weight and provides some sport on a light fly or spinning rod.

These are few all-weather roads in British Honduras so most of the coastal fishing areas are inaccessible except by boat.

TURNEFFE ISLANDS

These islands are a complex of low mangrove-covered cays lying within a barrier reef about 20 miles due east of Belize City. This reef extends 36 miles on a north to south axis. The fishing consists primarily of bonefish, great barracuda, mutton snapper, yellowtail snapper, mangrove snapper, dog snapper (locally reef snapper), yellow jack, horse-eye jack, cero mackerel, dolphin and king mackerel. There is also tarpon here beginning in April with fish running from 20 to 60 pounds which provide good sport on light tackle into July. Reef fishing for various groupers (the Nassau and black grouper are most common), snappers, cobia, jacks, ocean and queen triggerfish, and mackerels is excellent.

The Turneffe Island bonefish flats exist on the easterly shores inside the barrier reef. These have a hard bottom of coral, sand, and extensive turtle grass beds. They are easily waded. Due to the extreme tides on this type of flat much of the fishing is done in ankle to knee deep water. Fly fishermen should include buoyant patterns (light wire hooks and bushy hair wings) or weedless keel hook flies to avoid snagging in the bottom. During low tide periods bonefish gather in deep holes on or adjacent to the reef where they may be caught on artificial lures and natural baits in large number. Fish of all sizes may be present, and while the average is probably less than 3 pounds, fish of 6 to 9 pounds were caught in the 1969 season and a 14-pounder established the local record. Occasional permit may be sighted as singles or in schools. Both trunkfish and parrotfish forage on the reef flats and at a distance may be mistaken for bonefish by their tailing and grubbing behavior.

Lighthouse Reef (locally Half-Moon Reef) lying about 12 miles east of the Turneffe Islands is a vast shoal of over 25 miles in length with only a few widely scattered cays; of these, Long Cay on the southern perimeter provides fishing similar to that around Turneffe.

Isolated Lighthouse Reef produces excellent fishing for small tarpon as well as bonefish

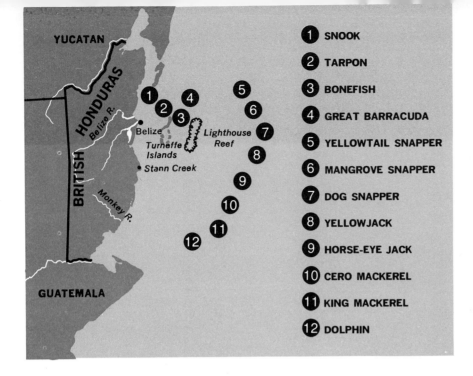

1. SNOOK
2. TARPON
3. BONEFISH
4. GREAT BARRACUDA
5. YELLOWTAIL SNAPPER
6. MANGROVE SNAPPER
7. DOG SNAPPER
8. YELLOWJACK
9. HORSE-EYE JACK
10. CERO MACKEREL
11. KING MACKEREL
12. DOLPHIN

TACKLE

A heavy-duty spinning or bait casting rod is standard in these waters. Much of the fishing is done close to mangrove shores in narrow rivers. A 12-pound-test line should be the minimum. Wire leaders are essential (No. 5 piano wire) as there are many sharp-toothed species and numerous snags in the form of coral heads and mangrove roots. Surface plugs are usually effective as are 1- to 3-ounce jigs for shore casting and deep fishing.

There are good possibilities for fly rodding both on the bonefish flats and in the rivers for tarpon and snook. A 9-foot saltwater fly-rod with a floating line is adequate for British Honduras waters.

There are no tackle shops in Belize City but some replacement items such as lines and lures may be obtained in the fishing camps.

CLOTHING

The climate throughout British Honduras is warm to hot so light-weight clothing is advisable. For wading on the bonefish flats an old pair of slacks and topsiders or similar foot gear affords the best protection from sunburn and coral cuts. Be sure to include an insect repellent, as sandflies and mosquitoes become active whenever the wind abates. Rain gear should be carried at all times.

LICENSES

None required.

TRAVEL NOTES

The only air service to British Honduras is on TACA Airlines via New Orleans and TAN airlines via Miami to Belize City. Rental cars are not available although taxis can be hired for both short and long trips within the country.

ACCOMMODATIONS

There is one major hotel in the capital city of Belize, the **St. George;** however, the fishing resorts are nearby and ordinarily guests go direct to camp from the airport. All reservations should be made in advance at one of the following: **Turneffe Island Lodge** (Room 6, 1329 St. Paul Avenue, St. Paul, Minnesota 55116). Operated by Bill and Dolly Haerr, veteran managers of Arctic sporting camps, this coconut palmed resort has pleasant accommodations in an idyllic beachside setting. The food is excellent with many native Caribbean specialties. Boats and guides are first-class. Turneffe Island is reached by the camp's launch from Belize City. Package price for an eight-day all-expense trip is $600 per person with a special "Couples Rate." The lodge is open from November 1 to July 31.

Keller's Caribbean Lodge (contact: Fred Keller, P. O. Box 459, Belize City, British Honduras). For those guests who want skiff fishing. The accommodations consist of private twin bedrooms each with private bath with shower. The cedar-and-mahogany-finished lodge contains the kitchen, dining room and lounge. Rates American plan are $25 per day single, and $35 per day per couple. The skiff including guide is $53 per day for one or two persons. The houseboat charter for extended cruising (3 day minimum) varies according to the number of anglers aboard: in a party of four $47 per person per day; in a party of three $54 per person per day; a party of two $70 per person per day. Each houseboat is equipped with two skiffs and an expert native crew consisting of captain, mate and cook. The crew attends to all services with excellently prepared meals.

Another popular angling resort is **Salt Creek Estate** (P.O. Box 187, Belize City, British Honduras). An old coconut and cattle plantation located 26 miles north of Belize City the resort offers all modern facilities.

Liquor is expensive in Belize but the tourist can obtain his favorite brand in the stateside Duty Free Shop of the Miami or New Orleans airports.

CONTACTS

None needed locally except for the resort operators.

LANGUAGE AND PEOPLE

The official language is English. Carib-speaking Negroes live in the southern coastal settlements and Maya Indians inhabit the inland region, speaking either Spanish or one of the Indian dialects. The English speaking tourist will have no language difficulty in the main fishing areas.

Canada

Few countries in the world today offer the abundance and variety of angling found in Canada. This independent nation of the British Commonwealth covering 3,851,809 square miles, bordered by three oceans, and deeply indented by Hudson Bay, is second only to the Soviet Union in size. With a population of about 20 million people, of which 90 percent is concentrated in the metropolitan cities of the southern provinces, most of Canada is only sparsely inhabited. The nation is outdoors oriented. There are literally thousands of lakes (over 10,000 on the Pre-Cambrian shield alone), as many rivers, vast forests, and extensive mountain ranges which provide recreation for residents and visitors alike. Sportsman's camps are a significant industry in Canada and foreign tourists will have no difficulty in finding exceptional angling at modest costs. Here, as in Alaska, the most remote areas can be reached by bush planes, while the motorist has access to quality waters at many points along the 5,000-mile span of Trans-Canada Highway.

TRAVEL NOTES
By Pan Am Jet Clipper from all parts of the world through New York, Boston, Chicago, Detroit, and Seattle to connecting Canadian airlines. Air Canada services the entire country. Native-born U.S. citizens need only some form of identification, such as a birth or voter's certificate. Naturalized citizens should carry naturalization certificates. Personal effects and sporting equipment may be brought in free of duty, as well as up to 50 cigars, 200 cigarettes, 2 pounds of tobacco, 40 ounces of alcoholic beverages per adult. Automobiles (proof of car insurance required in most provinces, with minimum limits of $35,000), motorcycles, bicycles, power toboggans, and private boats receive free registration cards at point of entry that are good for 12 months. Temporary pilot permits are also free to visitors with private planes. To re-enter the States, have all sales receipts and invoices handy for inspection. U.S. citizens returning from Canada may take back, once every 31 days, goods for personal or household use to the value of $100, duty-free.

Northwest Territories

Silvery sea-run char is top gamefish

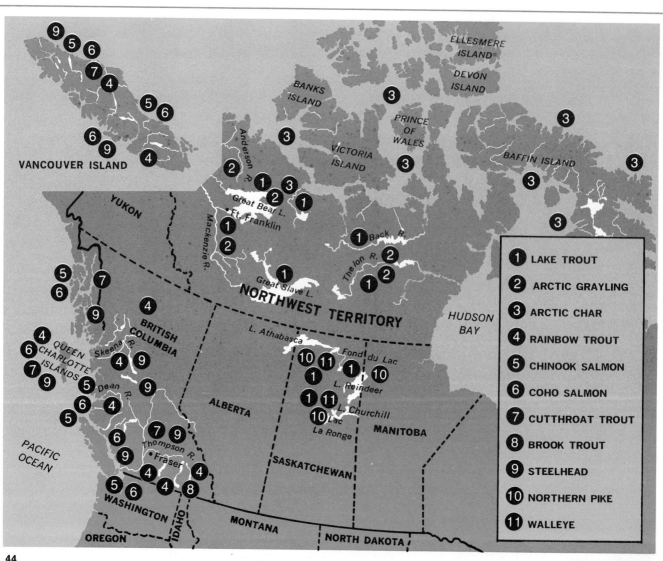

Fly fishing for lake trout is fast sport

Long as a canoe paddle. Great Bear produced record 65-pounder in 1970

The Northwest Territories encompasses an area of approximately 1,352,000 square miles, or about 38 percent of the total land mass of Canada. It sprawls 2,000 miles across the top of the North American continent from the Yukon on the west to Baffin Island on the east and another 1,700 miles from 60° N. latitude to within 500 miles of the North Pole. This vast land covers part of the Subarctic and virtually all of Canada's Arctic. It is populated by some 25,000 people, the majority of Indian and Eskimo descent. In the far northern and northeastern reaches day-to-day life has changed relatively little in the last hundred years, but in the more populated and heavily traveled areas, and more recently in even some of the isolated areas in the Arctic archipelago, new transportation routes, the search for oil and minerals, and nuclear age defense requirements have brought dramatic changes to the Territories and its people.

This is a land of infinite variety in topography, climate, and vegetation. At the western extremity lie the 9,000-foot Mackenzie Mountains, home of the snow-white dall sheep, grizzly bear, moose, and mountain goat. The mountains are cut by rivers such as the Nahanni, flowing through the now legendary "Headless Valley" to the mighty Mackenzie River. The miles-wide Mackenzie drains one-fifth of Canada and is one of the world's largest rivers. During the summer months, the Mackenzie is a 1,200-mile water highway from the outlet of Great Slave Lake to the Arctic Ocean. Its valley is relatively flat and well-forested, bounded on one side by the Mackenzie Mountains, and to the east by the Pre-Cambrian Shield.

The ancient granite of the Shield provides the basic character for most of the Territories. From the air, the land is a web of thousands of lakes and rivers, with treed valleys and bare-rock hills and ridges. To the north and east, the trees gradually become smaller and more scattered, until the tree line is past and the true Arctic begins—devoid of trees but blossoming in the summer with carpets of flowering shrubs and perennials. Farther north again, the land becomes more rugged, reaching a peak of magnificence in the 2,000-foot sheer cliffs of northeastern Baffin Island and the 10,000-foot mountains and permanent ice caps of Ellesmere.

One relatively small corner of the Northwest Territories is accessible by road. The Mackenzie Highway system, leading north from Grimshaw, Alberta (320 road miles northwest of Edmonton) serves communities in the Great Slave Lake area, including Hay River and Yellowknife. There is some good fishing for motorists who bring their own boats or who are prepared to rent boats in one of the communities. However, the best fishing locations are generally some distance from the settlements and some are accessible by only charter aircraft.

Lake trout of over 50 pounds occur in Great Bear

Char exceeding 20 pounds occur in Tree River

THE SEASON

The Arctic region is considered by many people as a land of eternal ice and snow, but this is true only of the few distant ice caps. Winters are long and summers are relatively short and warm. Throughout much of the Northwest Territories, there is little or no spring or autumn, at least not as it is known in southern areas. The arrival of spring is delayed by the large masses of lake and ocean ice. Break-up comes suddenly and then it is summer. Summers range in length from a scant 2 weeks in northern Ellesmere Island to 2 or 2½ months in the subarctic area around Great Slave Lake. Average summer temperatures range from around 45°F in southern Baffin Island to 55°F in the Great Slave Lake area, but temperatures as high as 100°F have been recorded. The crisp, clear summer climate of the Territories has many advantages for the visitors —up to twenty-four hours of sunshine per day, for this is truly the land of the midnight sun; very light rainfall; relief from the stifling heat of southern latitudes; and beautiful haze-free skies which range through literally the complete color spectrum in any twenty-four hour period.

CLOTHING

The type of clothing required depends to some extent on the location in the Territories. In the Great Slave Lake area during July and August, the mean daily maximum temperature is 70°F and the mean daily minimum 50°F. Temperatures occasionally go up to 85°F and down at night to 35°F. A warm windbreaker is essential and a set of long underwear is recommended. Farther north and east the temperatures gradually decline until at Cambridge Bay and Frobisher Bay on the Arctic Islands the mean daily maximum temperature during July and August is about 55°F and the mean daily minimum is 40°F. The equivalent of late fall hunting clothes is recommended for these areas.

Long sunny days (up to twenty-four hours) with very light rainfall are the general rule throughout the Territorial summer, but a rain coat or some type of waterproof clothing is recommended particularly in the coastal areas.

LAKE TROUT

The lake trout is the most widely distributed gamefish in the Territories and is found throughout the Mackenzie, Coppermine, Back, and Thelon drainage systems. The main angling locations, however, are Great Slave and Great Bear lakes, each more than 10,000 square miles in surface area. Modern fishing camps exist on both lakes. Fish in the 30- to 40-pound class are common and specimens of over 60 pounds have been recorded in these waters. Of the two, Great Bear Lake is the larger. Lying sixty miles east of the Mackenzie River and largely in the eroded crags of the Pre-Cambrian Shield, it presents a barren landscape with steep cliffs and hills along the east and low, timbered shores to the west. The Arctic Circle bisects the northern half of the lake. A number of things make Great Bear fishing unique. It's a remote lake and not fished commercially. The dominant gamefish are lake trout and grayling but there are also scattered populations of whitefish, northern pike, and walleye. Furthermore, the lake trout feed on the surface throughout the summer. Although the ice may break up any time from mid-June to early July, the surface temperatures remain at optimum for lake trout during July and August—with an average range of 40°F to 45°F. The water in a few shallow, isolated bays will reach 50°F. But these are in the minority. The average daily air temperature ranges within 44°F to 75°F, which is surprisingly comfortable. Because of the cold water and comparatively warm air Great Bear is largely covered by fog early in the morning and late in the evening. But the mysteries of Arctic weather are reducible to the dictum that for good or bad they generally favor the summer angler. It is not essential to use heavy tackle in Great Bear. The popular methods are casting and trolling at depths of 20 to 40 feet with all types of metal lures. Many anglers use spinning tackle with 8- to 10-pound-test lines and a spinner or wobbling spoon in nickel, copper, brass, or red-and-white finish. Although lake trout fly fishing is generally done with streamers and bucktails, catching them with dry flies is sometimes possible at Great Bear. Fly hatches are numerous in the gravel bays and whenever the water is calm it is possible to locate feeding trout.

ARCTIC GRAYLING

The Arctic grayling is particularly common in the Mackenzie, Coppermine, Anderson, Thelon, and Back drainage systems. During the summer months, grayling are found mainly in the cold, swiftly flowing rivers, but they also occur in bays of the larger lakes such as Great Bear. This species generally forages closer to the shoreline at depths to 5 feet, while Great Bear lake trout favor the 20-foot zone for their surface feeding. The grayling in the lake proper are somewhat larger and darker-colored fish than those found in nearby rivers. The lake form averages about 2 pounds and is a thickly built, brownish-purple fish wholly unlike the bright, brassy-blue tinted grayling in Great Bear River. A tributary to the Mackenzie, the river is an outlet near Fort Franklin on the west shore. In the clear swift currents these river fish often make spectacular jumps when hooked.

Due to the remoteness of Great Bear, the camps operate on a package basis for one week (or eight days) with rates varying from $700 to $900 per person which includes your round trip air fare from Edmonton or Winnipeg. The lodges in general are luxurious considering the location and inquiries should be made to the following: **Branson's Lodge** (R.R. 1, Box 710, Parker, Arizona 85344: Area Code 602-669-8543); **Trophy Lodge** (Box 9000, Panoka, Alberta, Canada: Area Code 403-783-4994); **Great Bear Lodge** (101 West 37th Street, Sioux Falls, South Dakota 57105: Area Code 605-336-2008); **Arctic Circle Lodge** (Box 3390, Saint Paul, Minnesota 55101: Area Code 612-459-4075).

The angling at Great Slave Lake is similar; however, it is fished commercially. The lake lies 550 miles north of Edmonton. Much of Great Slave is shallow, but in the vicinity of Christie Bay it drops to over 2,000 feet. The shoreline is irregular with many cliffs and with wooded sec-

tions. Lake trout are the most common gamefish and are distributed in all parts of Great Slave at depths of 15 feet or more. There are also abundant populations of grayling, northern pike, ciscos, and whitefish. Inconnu or sheefish are scattered throughout the lake and are most commonly caught during their spawning runs in tributary streams such as the Big Buffalo River and the Talston River. Walleyes are present but only in scattered locations.

For fishing in the Great Slave area try the **Arctic Lodge** (c/o International Inn, 1808 Wellington Avenue, Winnipeg 21, Manitoba, Canada: Area Code 204-786-5646) which offers an all expense one-week trip from Winnipeg and return at $750. Also at Great Slave is Jerry Bricker's **Frontier Fishing Lodge** (P.O. Box 5299, Station E, Edmonton, Alberta: Area Code 503-484-5571). Another popular spot is **Great Slave Lake Lodge** (Airliner Hotel, Winnipeg, Manitoba, Canada: Area Code 204-775-5131). Another package operator is Doug Finlayson's **Trophy Lodge** (Box 670, Yellowknife, Northwest Territories, Canada: Area Code 403-873-4555).

ARCTIC CHAR

Arctic char are found in clear waters from the rugged coasts of Baffin Island on the east to within a hundred miles of the Mackenzie River on the

west. There are two forms, the land-locked or freshwater char, and the anadromous or sea-run char. Even within these forms, there appears to be an appreciable variation in appearance and behavior between fish in various geographic locations. In general, the char is very streamlined in shape. Its back is dark green in color, shading to silvery sides and belly with pinkish spots on the sides. At spawning time, the males develop a protruding and hooked lower jaw, and the belly and sides may turn a vivid orange-red.

The Coppermine to Victoria Island area in the western Arctic is a popular region for char. While fish of 15 pounds are common in some rivers (they have been recorded to over 27 pounds in the Tree River), the usual run is 5 to 7 pounds. They can be taken with wet flies but gold, silver, or reddish-colored spinning lures are most commonly used. The char is not a spectacular jumper like the Atlantic salmon, but will frequently take off a hundred yards or more of line with one powerful drive and then jump or thrash on the surface in an effort to shake the lure. For Victoria Island fishing try **Arctic Outpost Camps Ltd.** (Box 1104, Edmonton 15, Alberta, Canada: Area Code 403-476-0946) which offers a one-week package trip including air transportation from Edmonton at $975.

Dog Rib Indian guide with the trophy lake trout he caught heads leisurely back to camp

British Columbia

Big steelhead enter the Babine in October

This westernmost province of Canada encompasses 366,266 square miles with a variety of geographical terrain which includes everything from heavily forested areas of fir and spruce and agricultural valleys to desert areas. Located in this vast region are innumerable lakes, rivers, and streams, many of them accessible only by pack train, where unfished waters still exist.

British Columbia has a coastline extending for some 16,900 miles from the state of Washington to the state of Alaska, with innumerable fjords and islands, and offers unlimited fishing for those who prefer their fishing in saltwater.

Climatic conditions are such that it can be safely said that in some part of this vast province fishing is available during all seasons of the year. A very active Provincial Fish and Game Department has in recent years engaged in a most successful replanting of gamefish in many of the lakes so abundant throughout the province. Waters that were stocked three years ago with fingerling rainbow trout are now producing fish weighing from 8 to 12 pounds. In most instances, these lakes are readily accessible to the motorist.

In the freshwater areas the steelhead is one of the great trophies available, followed closely by the resident rainbow or Kamloops trout, while in saltwater the chinook salmon, reaching weights as high as 80 pounds, is equalled by the very active coho salmon as a light tackle fish.

RAINBOW TROUT

The rainbow trout is native to British Columbia. Ideally suited to lakes and streams, this species is the most important freshwater sport fish in the province. The rainbow exists in a variety of fishing conditions. Waters such as the Lightning Lakes in Manning Park might be called family lakes; the fish are small (a 10-inch fish would be a big one) but so plentiful that no one leaves disappointed. However, in the larger lakes, such as Shuswap and Kootenay, trout may tip the scales at 25 pounds. In 1913 two huge rainbows, one weighing 56 pounds and the other 48 pounds, were taken from Jewel Lake in the Kootenay district. Giants like these (they were not caught by rod-and-reel) are extremely rare, and today the average size of a Kamloops or rainbow trout is about 1½ pounds.

Coho salmon provide excellent fly fishing in late summer and fall

Although there is no closed season for fishing in British Columbia lakes, fishing is largely carried out after the ice is gone. Generally, lakes are ice free in May. Lower altitude lakes, in the South Okanagan for example, may be open in early April whereas those at higher levels, regardless of latitude, may not be open until June.

CHINOOK SALMON

The coastal waters of British Columbia support five species of salmon—chinook, coho, pink, sockeye, and chum. All are important commercial species, but only the chinook and the coho are of interest to the saltwater angler. The pink salmon, although caught in fair numbers, is not highly rated as a sport fish when compared to either the coho or the chinook. There are size variations of chinook and coho entering the sport fishery; early maturing males in freshwater are known locally as jacks; 2-year-old coho are known as grilse; and blueback are young coho in their final year of sea growth.

A boat, powered if possible, is generally required for saltwater salmon fishing. Trolling and strip-casting are the two most popular angling methods. Coho, however, are good sport and in excellent condition for some time after they have entered freshwater, and here methods vary. Generally, fly fishing and bait-casting are preferable. The chinook is also called tyee, king, blackmouth, and spring salmon. Locally tyee applies only to chinook over 30 pounds. A world record was set in 1959 when a 92-pounder was rod-caught in the Skeena River near Terrace. The best chinook fishing is in July through September. Normally, the run reaches its peak in the first week of August.

COHO SALMON

Coho are not as large as chinook salmon. However, because they occur in greater numbers they provide more fishing. Coho will spawn in practically any running water where suitable gravel is available. They are found in almost all coastal streams of the British Columbia coast. In their last year of sea growth coho will weigh about 5 pounds in May and up to as much as 15 pounds in late September. Strong fish and highly prized by anglers, they put up a tremendous, leaping fight, particularly if hooked on light tackle. Unlike other salmon, coho provide good fishing after entering the spawning streams.

August and September are usually the best months for coho fishing in most coastal waters. Coho are still feeding extensively, and their movement toward the spawning streams has begun. However, June and July are also good months. Late in the season, in October, when coho congregate near stream estuaries waiting for fall freshets, they can still be taken on the fly. After they have entered the streams—and some will arrive as early as August—they are fishable until they begin to spawn.

CUTTHROAT TROUT

This trout occurs in virtually all lakes and streams along the entire coast of British Columbia. Like the rainbow, the cutthroat may be either anadromous or nonmigratory in freshwater. The sea-run cutthroat enters spawning streams in late November, and both it and the resident cutthroat spawn from February until May. The anadromous form is smaller than the steelhead but will run 1½ to 4 pounds. The resident cutthroat shows a greater weight range. Those in streams are usually small while those in lakes vary from a few ounces to as high as 17 pounds. The cutthroat is a popular fly fisherman's quarry.

BROOK TROUT

The brook trout was introduced into British Columbia in 1908, and is now found in waters of south and southeastern British Columbia and Vancouver Island. It is generally a small fish but runs occasionally to about 5 pounds. The brook trout does not compare with the rainbow as a sport fish. However, in some streams in the Kootenay area, it seems to be well suited to the habitat and provides angling of high quality. On Vancouver Island brook trout occur in tributaries of the upper reaches of the Cowichan River, Spectacle Lake in the Malahat District, and in Round and Semenos lakes near Duncan.

On the mainland, brook trout are found in many lakes and streams in the southeastern part of the province as well as in lakes and streams of the Princeton and lower Okanagan regions.

BLACK BASS

Smallmouth and largemouth bass have been introduced to British Columbia from the United States. In their native waters bass are highly valued as sport fish but in British Columbia they are of little interest to anglers. The smallmouth is the most important of the warmwater fishes and is better suited to local habitats than the largemouth. Introduced into a few lakes of Vancouver Island and the mainland in 1901, the smallmouth is now found in Christina and Boldue lakes and Kettle River below Cascade Falls, all in the Grand Forks area; it is reportedly found in Moyie Lake south of Cranbrook; several lakes on Southern Vancouver Island including Florence, Langford, Beaver, Durrance, and Spider lakes. The bronzeback also became established at St. Mary and Rosemergey lakes on Salt Spring Island in Georgia Strait.

The largemouth bass is believed to have entered British Columbia from Idaho some time before 1920. It is found only in lakes of the Columbia River drainage system; Vaseux, Osoyoos, Shannon, Christina lakes near Grand Forks; Duck and Kootenay lakes; Mirror Lake near Kaslo; and Wasa Lake near Cranbrook. Yellow perch inhabit a few lakes of the southern Okanagan Valley, including Osoyoos Lake, and occur in Duck Lake and Kootenay River sloughs.

VANCOUVER ISLAND

The island provides excellent steelheading on both coasts. On the west coast some of the better streams are the Ash River near Alberni, with summer and winter runs from June to October and from December to March, and the Stamp River near Alberni, with summer and winter runs from July to September and from December to March. Of the many steelhead streams on the east coast the following are outstanding: the Cowichan River near Duncan, with a good winter run; the Nanaimo, Little Qualicum, and Puntledge rivers with runs from December to April; Campbell River with a winter run from December to March; the Gold River with both summer and winter runs; and much farther up the island, Nimpkish River with a winter run from November to March.

Good coho fishing may be enjoyed in most of the sheltered bays and inlets on either coast. On the west coast, Barclay Sound is the main fishing area at present, and on the east coast two famous places are Cowichan Bay and, further up the coast, Duncan Bay near Campbell River. Several other places on the east coast of Vancouver Island also provide excellent coho fishing. A few of them are Comox, Nanaimo, and Oyster Bay.

For chinook salmon the popular centers on the island are Port Alberni, Bamfield, Campbell River, Cowichan, and Comox. However, as springs migrate from northern waters toward the rivers and larger streams, they are found in most inshore areas along both coasts of the island.

Sea-run cutthroat do not roam far from freshwater during their saltwater life. They move in and out of larger streams throughout the year, preying on salmon eggs in the fall, or salmon fry in the spring. Many such streams drain both coasts of the island. The larger lakes, particularly Nimpkish, Campbell, Buttle, Sproat, Great Centraland, and Cowichan also produce fine resident cutthroat.

The brown trout was introduced in the Cowichan and Little Qualicum rivers in 1932 and is now well established in these two river systems as well as Niagara Creek on the east coast of Vancouver Island. In the upper reaches of the Cowichan, brown trout to 12 pounds have been taken. As in the case of sea-run cutthroat the brown trout may migrate to saltwater but does not seem to stray far from its native stream. The brown trout is highly valued by fly fishermen because of its extreme wariness.

GULF ISLANDS

The Gulf Islands lie off the southeastern coast of Vancouver Island. Gabriola, Galiano, Salt Spring, and Pender (North and South) are the biggest islands, and all are accessible by air or boat from either Vancouver or Vancouver Island. The climate in this region is ideal. Temperatures are moderate throughout the entire year, rainfall is low (about 25 inches annually), and sunshine is the rule. The waters surrounding the Gulf Islands are well sheltered and, combined with the gentle climate, make fishing pleasant in any season. Both chinook and coho are found in abundance in this area.

LOWER MAINLAND

The Vedder, by far the best steelhead river in the lower mainland, has an excellent run from December to April. On the north side of the Fraser River, the Chehalis, Coquitlam, and the Alouette are good steelhead rivers with runs from December until March. Elsewhere in the lower mainland several streams provide fair steelheading. The Capilano and Seymour, both on the north side of Burrard Inlet, near Vancouver, have runs from December to April and in June and July. However, steelhead are in these two streams at other times of the year. The Nicomekl and the Campbell, both near the international border, produce light winter runs from December until March. The Coquihalla and Silver, near Hope, support summer runs that reach their peak in July.

Coho salmon provide good fishing here in the late summer and fall season. These salmon are found in practically all coastal inlets and bays. Some of the better known areas on the lower mainland are Howe Sound (reached by road), Sechelt Inlet (reached by road), Jervis Inlet (reached by boat), Powell River (reached by road or boat), and Toba Inlet (reached by boat). Don't overlook the Brem River at Toba Inlet for summer steelhead beginning in late

Vancouver Island's Cowichan River is one of few B.C. streams with brown trout

Coho salmon occur along entire British Columbia coast. Best fishing is late August to mid-October

June. The long fjords and remote bays of the mainland coast offer a world of fishing for the small boatman; a guided houseboat fleet (*B.C. Safari's Ltd.*, 408 Sixth Avenue, New Westminster, British Columbia, Canada) operates in this section of the province.

Cutthroat trout fishing is also popular on the lower mainland rivers. The Nicomekl River and the Serpentine River are heavily fished in January and February for the sea-run variety. The Nicomekl is the best. From Hope to the coast, bar-fishermen on the Fraser River enjoy good cutthroat fishing from August to late fall. Butzen Lake, on the north of Burrard Inlet, Alouette, Stave, and Harrison lakes on the north side of the Fraser all provide cutthroat as well as Dolly Varden. The Dolly Varden is widespread in the province. It occurs in lakes and streams throughout British Columbia with the exception of the Okanagan drainage. Like the coastal cutthroat and rainbow, the Dolly Varden may spend its entire life in a lake or stream or may migrate to sea. Dolly Varden are found in most of the lakes and streams which connect, or have connected, with the Fraser River. Sea-run Dolly Varden enter freshwater in July and August. In the southeast the Dolly Varden is present in most of the streams and larger lakes open to the Columbia drainage except the Okanagan River Drainage. Kootenay Lake is the most abundant source in this region, and Dolly Varden up to 22 pounds have been caught here. However, the usual weight of the species in the Columbia drainage is generally 3 to 4 pounds.

SOUTHERN INTERIOR

The Thompson River is the only important steelhead river in the southern interior and has become recognized as one of the finest in the province. Running through the dry country of the interior from the Rocky Mountains, it is a clean, swift-flowing river that joins the Fraser at Lytton. For 65 miles upstream, from Lytton to Savona, the fishing is excellent, and a road follows the river all the way. Though fish are taken from September until May, the better months are from October until March. The steelhead in this river are usually much larger than those in coastal streams and average 16 pounds.

KOOTENAY AND OKANAGAN

Fishing in these areas is best from May until September or October. In Okanagan and Kootenay lakes, which rarely freeze over, fishing may last from early spring until late fall. In the Kootenay district Kootenay, Upper and Lower Arrow, Christina, and Jewel are some of the better known lakes. A great many small lakes lie in the hills on either side of Okanagan Lake in the Oliver, Penticton, Kelowna, and Vernon areas. Okanagan and Kalamalka lakes have produced some large rainbow trout.

KAMLOOPS DISTRICT

The City of Kamloops is truly the heart of the rainbow-trout country and provides the regional name of the trout in that district. There are many camps in the area: **Echo Lodge** (P.O. Box 70, Kamloops, British Columbia, Canada) located on Paul Lake just twelve miles north of town offers cabins for American

Plan guests or modern housekeeping cottages. Southwest of Kamloops is **Le Jeune Lodge** (Box 780, Kamloops, British Columbia, Canada) with a main lodge, chalet units and rustic log cabins situated on Lac Le Jeune. Shuswap, the biggest lake in the area, produces some large rainbows; accommodations can be found here at **Little River Lodge** (Squilax, British Columbia, Canada) in modern housekeeping cottages located near the mouth of the Adams River. The Adams is an excellent spot in May and June. Numerous small lakes in the Merrit and Princeton areas south of Kamloops, and between Clinton and La Hache to the northwest also have fine trout.

CHILCOTIN AREA

The Chilcotin area is relatively unexploited. The western portions of this district toward Bella Coola, Anahim, and Nimpo contain many excellent trout waters. The Nimpo Lake and the Dean River are among the most productive in the province for rainbows. Nimpo is one of three lakes formed by the Dean (the others are Little and Big Anahim) which meanders across the Chilcotin Plateau before dropping precipitously toward the Pacific. Trout here run from 1½ to 4 pounds with larger ones a possibility. Steelhead occur in the lower reaches of the Dean below the falls; fish of over 20 pounds are taken here in July and August. **Duncan's Resort** (Cecil Duncan, Kleena Kleene, British Columbia, Canada) is well worth a visit. These waters can be reached by road from Williams Lake via Alexis Creek or also from Bella Coola on the west coast. In the Chilcotin district on the east slope of the coast range at Charlotte Lake is the **Rimarko Ranch** (C. H. Morse Jr., Box 250, Lake Forest, Illinois, 60045: Area Code 312-234-3458), a fly-in camp which specializes in rainbow, steelhead, and salmon fishing. The Chilcotin and Chilko Rivers are especially productive. The latter is best fished from **Chilko Lake Lodge** (Alexis Creek, British Columbia, Canada) a remote, but well-run camp that can be reached by plane or by one of the lodge's trucks from Alexis Creek. The Chilko is a fine fly fishing stream from July on.

BURNS LAKE AREA
About 140 miles west of Prince George, this area is relatively unexploited. Between Burns Lake and Tweedsmuir Park lie a number of excellent lakes, some large like Francois and Ootsa and many smaller such as Burns, Tchesinkut, Uncha, and Binta. Tweedsmuir Park,

liberally endowed with lakes and rivers, offers many opportunities for trout enthusiasts. North of Burns Lake several large lakes such as Babine, Stuart, Trembleur, and Takla offer not only rainbow trout but lake trout and Dolly Varden as well. A popular location for Babine Lake and River is **Norlakes Lodge** (Fort Babine, British Columbia, Canada). The peak of the steelhead fishing here is in October with 20-pound fish not uncommon (local record 32 pounds). The Babine is a big, fast stream that produces some of the best fly fishing in North America.

PRINCE RUPERT AREA
Several important steelhead rivers lie northeast of Prince Rupert in the Skeena River drainage, among them the Kispiox, Morice, Telkwa, Copper, and the Bulkley. The Kispiox is justly famous because it was from this river, in October 1954, that a

record steelhead of 36 pounds was taken. Easily fished, the Kispiox can be reached by road from Prince George via Hazelton or from Prince Rupert. The Morice, Copper, and Telkwa rivers are tributaries of the Bulkley, and all three offer excellent fishing.

QUEEN CHARLOTTE ISLANDS
West of Prince Rupert, these islands have for years had a reputation as being ideal fishing and hunting grounds. Although air and boat services from Vancouver are good, few tourists visit the Queen Charlottes. Copper River and Bay on Moresby Island is probably the best coho region in British Columbia. The Tlell and the Yakoun rivers also provide excellent coho fishing. Steelhead fishing is also available, particularly in the Copper, Tlell, and Yakoun rivers.

Saskatchewan

The borders of this Canadian province encompass 251,700 square miles, of which roughly one-eighth is composed of water ranging from tiny pothole lakes in the Great Sand Hills of the southwest to the vast lakes of the Pre-Cambrian Shield, and from tiny trout streams of the Missouri watershed to the mighty, clear, cold rivers of the north, such as the Churchill and Fond du Lac. These gigantic watersheds and the tens of thousands of lakes and ponds that drain into them comprise one of Canada's major inland fisheries. This resource played a vital role in the development of the province by providing a readily available supply of food for the explorers and the fur traders, and later for the settlers.

Sport-fishing enthusiasts, pursuing one of the main attractions of outdoor recreation, summer and winter, purchase approximately 100,000 an-

gling licenses annually. Thus, about one in every nine of the population is an angler, in addition to the thousands of Americans who visit Saskatchewan each year. During the fishing season, from the first Saturday in May to April 15 of the following year, anglers will harvest an estimated 6,000,000 pounds of gamefish—the second largest take of the total provincial fishery.

ACCOMMODATIONS
There are over 70 fly-in camps, 140 drive-in fishing camps, almost 200 motels, and over 500 hotels in Saskatchewan. These are classified by the Provincial Government according to the basic facilities offered as non-modern, semi-modern, and modern. To plan a trip obtain a copy of *Saskatchewan Tourist Accommodation* (Tourist Development Branch, Department of Industry and

Commerce, Power Building, Regina, Saskatchewan, Canada) which contains a complete listing of the fishing camps in the Province.

LAKE TROUT
The lake trout is a coldwater species, abundant in the deep lakes of the Pre-Cambrian Shield. Except for a few lakes in the central forest areas, its distribution in Saskatchewan is limited to the Shield. Its spawning season takes place in Saskatchewan during September and October as the water cools. The eggs are laid on the shallow, rocky, rubble bottoms of bays and inlets of the lakes. These lie dormant during the winter, hatching when the water warms again in the spring. During the spring and fall seasons, the adult laker is at its best as a sport fish, responding to spoons and plugs and putting up a good fight when hooked. In midsummer, as the

surface waters warm up, the trout go deep and can only be taken by trolling with heavy tackle.

Perhaps the most southerly of the outstanding lake trout waters in Saskatchewan is Lac la Ronge. This fabulous sport-fishing lake where anglers annually take approximately 200,000 pounds of lake trout, pike, and walleye is accessible by road, has an area of 450 square miles and has more than a thousand islands. The shoreline of the lake and its islands consists mainly of gray Pre-Cambrian granite, dropping off into water up to 140 feet deep. The water is cold enough to produce vigorous fish of the highest quality and is more fertile than the lakes farther north. Fishing usually commences between May 20 and June 1. In the first month, lake trout may be taken by casting before they migrate to the deeper waters where trolling equipment is then required to catch them. They again migrate to the shallower waters during the latter part of August, and angling usually lasts until the latter part of September.

For La Ronge fishing good accommodations can be found at **Van's Camp** (Van Bliss, 35—11th Street East, Prince Albert, Saskatchewan, Canada: Area Code 306-763-3597).

Fishermen may use Lac la Ronge as a jumpoff spot to fly into the other northern major lakes—Athabaska, Wollaston, Cree, and Reindeer. The same species of fish exist in these waters. Northward from Lac la Ronge, there are many smaller lakes which are rarely if ever fished. One of the largest lake trout ever recorded weighed 102 pounds, and was taken in a commercial fisherman's net in Lake Athabaska, in 1962.

Athabaska Lake covers 3,050 square miles of which approximately two-thirds is in Saskatchewan and the remainder in Alberta. The lake has an irregular shore, and is surrounded by granite ridges and stands of spruce or poplar except at

Northern Saskatchewan's fly-in camps produce many pike in 20- to 30-pound class

the south end where sand beaches and dunes predominate. The maximum depth of Athabaska is 405 feet near its geographic center, but there are considerable shallow areas as well as deep ones. The dominant gamefish is the lake trout which attains very large size. There are also grayling which can be taken by fly fishing along the rocky cliffs of the north and east shores; most of the grayling run 12 to 16 inches (1½ pounds). Goldeyes are numerous in the river channels at the west end of Athabaska, and are frequently caught on dry flies in weights up to 2 pounds. Walleyes and northern

pike are taken by casting or trolling. Whitefish and ciscos are present.

NORTHERN PIKE

The northern pike is one of Saskatchewan's most widely distributed fish species, occurring in almost every stream and lake in the province which is capable of supporting fish life. Due to their availability, more pike are taken by anglers than all other species combined. The big ones of the northern lakes, which can put up a good fight, are prized by fishermen who fly into the Pre-Cambrian country. Some of the better known pike waters of northern Saskatchewan are Athabaska Lake, Beaverlodge Lake, Black Lake, Careen Lake, Deception Lake, Fond du Lac River, Foster lakes, Frobisher Lake, Grease River, Hatchet Lake, Hickson Lake, Jewett Lake, Reindeer Lake, Riou Lake, Tazin Lake, Unknown Lake, Wapata Lake, Waterbury Lake, and Wollaston Lake. Camps exist throughout the area, and are usually reached by floatplane service from Lac la Ronge, Meadow Lake, Buffalo Narrows, Carrot River, and Flin Flon.

In the more southerly and accessible portion of the province the following lakes are popular for pike fishing: Besnard Lake, Bear Island Lake, Churchill River, Drinking Lake, Emmerline Lake, Lac la Ronge, Little Deer Lake, MacKay Lake, McIntosh Lake, Nemeiben Lake, Nipew Lake, Histowiak Lake, Otter Lake, and Wapawekka Lake. Heading east into the provincial park area, anglers catch pike in Buffalo Pound Lake, Crooked Lake, Crystal Lake, Echo Lake, Fishing Lake, Good Spirit Lake, Greenwater Lake, Katepwa Lake, Kenosee Lake, Last Mountain Lake, Madge Lake, McBride Lake, Mission Lake, Moosomin Reservoir, Pasqua Lake Qu'Appelle River, Round Lake, Souris River, and York Lake.

WALLEYE
Of the sixty-one species in Saskatchewan the local favorite is the walleye. The walleye is not a spectacular antagonist, but as a table fish it is considered unsurpassed by any other species, particularly when cooked by the waterside on a wilderness lake. Although one may seek larger or more active gamefish, veteran anglers consider it almost essential to catch a few walleyes for a shore lunch.

The walleye ranges throughout a lake in its search for food and is far more destructive of young whitefish, ciscos, and suckers than the pike. It has been estimated that a mature walleye accounts for 2,000 to 3,000 small fish annually, in addition to a substantial number of crayfish, smaller crustaceans, and insect larvae. In spite of its tremendous appetite, this active predator grows very slowly, adding only 6 or 8 ounces to its weight each year, and does not begin spawning until the age of 6. A spring spawner, the walleye moves upstream in April, in some areas traveling up to 35 miles or more to find ooze bottoms suitable for spawning. The eggs are extremely small, and a large female of 6 pounds will deposit about 200,000 eggs in a season. The average size of walleye caught in Saskatchewan is about 3 pounds, although 13-pounders have been taken.

Among the better known walleye lakes of southern Saskatchewan are Buffalo Pound Lake, Cannington Lake, Crooked Lake, Crystal Lake, Echo Lake, Fishing Lake, Good Spirit Lake, Greenwater Lake, Katepwa Lake, Kenosee Lake, Last Mountain Lake, Lenore Lake, Little Quill Lake, Madge Lake, Mission Lake, Moosomin Reservoir, Pasqua Lake, Qu'Appelle River, Round Lake, and Souris River.

In the northwest portion of the province, walleyes are caught at Beaver River, Brightsand Lake, Canoe Lake, Chitek Lake, Clarke Lake, Cold Lake, Delaronde Lake, Dore Lake Flotten Lake, Green Lake, Greig Lake, Jackfish Lake, Keeley Lake, Lac des Iles, Lac Ile a la Crosse, Makwa (Loon) Lake, Meeting Lake, Murray Lake, North Saskatchewan River, Perch Lake, Pierce Lake, Smoothstone Lake, Turtle Lake, and Waterhen Lake.

Elsewhere in the north walleyes occur in nearly all of the major lake trout and pike waters.

ARCTIC GRAYLING
The Arctic grayling is one of the most beautiful freshwater fish on the North American continent. It has been often called the sailfish of the north. It is easily distinguished by its magnificent dorsal fin which is a deep blue color, with white spots and a gold and purple band along the outer edge. As an angler's fish, the Arctic grayling has few equals in North America. It is found in the purest, clearest water in Saskatchewan's far north. Weighing up to 4 pounds (occasionally more), the grayling is found in large schools in the rapid portions of the rivers and streams. In August or September, or on most summer evenings or cloudy days, it responds to almost any lure, including dry and wet flies. Taken on light tackle, this fish provides a fight that tests the angler's skill. As a table fish, the Arctic grayling is perhaps equal to the brook trout and is superior to most others. The grayling is mainly insectivorous, and in the evening may be seen rising from the fastwater to feed on low-flying caddisflies, mayflies, and midges. Insect larvae probably make up a large proportion of its diet, but in the winter months smaller fish may be important as food.

Generally speaking, grayling anglers seek their fishing in the same waters where lake trout are abundant. The fish occur both in the lakes and tributary rivers. Among the better known spots are the aforementioned Athabaska Lake, Black Lake, Careen Lake, Cree Lake, Cree River, Fond du Lac River, Geikie River, Hatchet Lake, Reindeer Lake, Tazin Lake, Wapata Lake, Waterbury Lake, and Wollaston Lake. For the Cree Lake area try **Cree Lake Lodge** (Box 1074, Saskatoon, Saskatchewan, Canada); this is a fly-in camp with weekly rates at $385. At Waterbury Lake good accommodations can be found at **Jackson's Lodge** (c/o Transair Ltd., Lynn Lake, Manitoba). **Camp Grayling** (Box 2, Moose Jaw, Saskatchewan, Canada) offers all facilities on Black Lake and has special rates for charter aircraft groups. At Wollaston Lake the popular location is **Wollaston Lake Lodge** (Miss Evelyn Miller, 325—9th Street East, Prince Albert, Saskatchewan, Canada).

Quebec Wilderness Angling

The Mingan Reserve, a 20,000 square mile wilderness region located in Quebec on the north shore of the Gulf of St. Lawrence and extending to the border of Labrador can now be fished out of the **St. Lawrence Fishing & Hunting Club** (245 Welsh Road, Huntingdon Valley, Pennsylvania 19006: Area Code 215-947-2583). Brook trout of over 7 pounds have been caught in the club waters but there are other species available in the many lakes and streams including ouananiche (landlocked salmon), lake trout, whitefish, northern pike, and Atlantic salmon. Ouananiche fishing is especially good. The club has exclusive rights to the numerous waters it leases from the Quebec Government. One can reach the club's base headquarters at Longue Pointe de Mingan, Quebec, by commercial airline, or if flying in a private plane, there are two 5,200-foot hard-surfaced runways at Mingan, and a float plane dock is at Patterson Lake a mile away. Guests may also travel by car to Sept-Iles (Seven Islands), Province of Quebec, which is ap-proximately 500 miles east of Montreal. Then by commercial airline from Sept-Iles to Mingan (about 100 miles), where the main lodge is located. There are no roads between Sept-Iles and Mingan.

Excellent commercial air services are maintained daily between Montreal or Quebec City and Mingan. This is a heavily traveled route during the summer, particularly between Sept-Iles and Mingan (which is operated by Nordair, a subsidiary of Quebecair), and reservations should be made long in advance of travel dates.

From the main lodge in Mingan, which serves as a staging area, guests are transported by Norseman aircraft on floats to one of a number of widely separated bush camps, which are located 55 to 140 miles from Mingan, and can only be reached by float planes. Accommodations at each bush camp are restricted, at any one time, to a maximum of 4 to 6 guests, in addition to the guides and a cook.

Big water means big fish in remote Quebec

COSTS

Bush camps have a minimum rate of $300 per person for 5 days (or less) with additional days at $60 per person, American Plan. Overnight in main lodge at modest price. The charge for air transportation between the main lodge and the various bush camps is figured on a mileage basis: bush camp 55 to 75 miles at $50 round trip and 128 to 140 miles at $100 round trip.

LICENSE

A Quebec fishing license is required ($5.50) and may be obtained at the main lodge.

Quananiche is heavily spotted form of landlocked salmon

Labrador Brook Trout

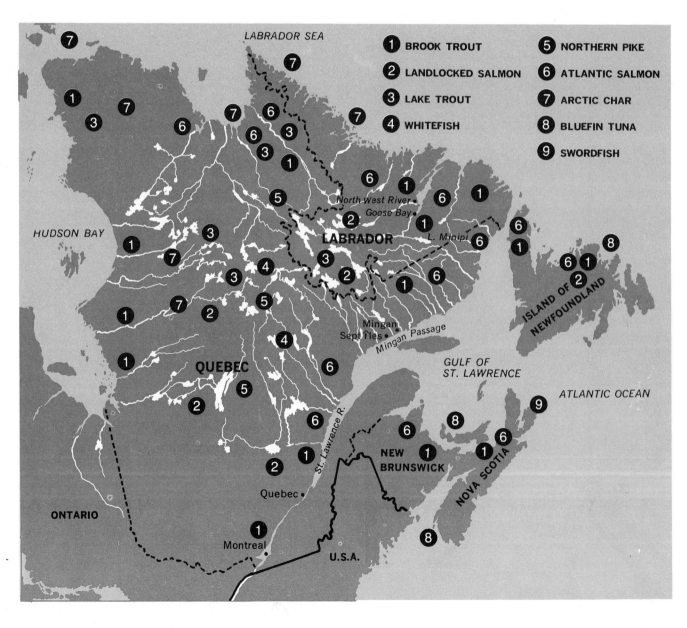

LABRADOR SEA

1	BROOK TROUT	5	NORTHERN PIKE
2	LANDLOCKED SALMON	6	ATLANTIC SALMON
3	LAKE TROUT	7	ARCTIC CHAR
4	WHITEFISH	8	BLUEFIN TUNA
		9	SWORDFISH

North West River
Goose Bay
LABRADOR
L. Minipi

HUDSON BAY

ISLAND OF NEWFOUNDLAND

Mingan
Sept Îles
Mingan Passage

GULF OF ST. LAWRENCE

QUEBEC

ATLANTIC OCEAN

St. Lawrence R.

NEW BRUNSWICK

NOVA SCOTIA

Quebec

ONTARIO

Montreal

U.S.A.

Sherman L. Lowell of Springfield, Massachusetts, proudly displays prize-winning ouananiche caught in the Kaniapiskau River, Labrador. The salmon weighed in at a hefty 10 pounds 8 ounces, was 31 inches long and had a 15½-inch girth

Exceptional fly fishing for big squaretails can be found at Ray Cooper's **Northern Labrador Camps** (P.O. Box 8, Northwest River, Labrador, Canada). These wilderness camps (two lodges plus tent-camps) can be reached via Montreal to Goose Bay on Air Canada and from there on a short hop to Anne Marie Lake about 50 miles southwest on Wheeler's Northland Airways. Brook trout in 4-pound class are common in Anne Marie Lake, Minonipi Lake, and the

Minipi River. Because of the exceptional quality of the fishing, it is restricted to fly only.

The fishing season opens as soon as the lakes are clear of ice which is around June 10 and the camps remain open until the close of the season on September 15. The fishing remains good throughout the whole season. Almost all the fishing is done in the river sections except during the main mayfly hatch which lasts for several weeks during the

period mid-June to late July depending on the water temperatures, and at which time many of the large trout move out into the lakes. Dry fly fishing is excellent during this main hatch but with smaller hatches occurring almost every evening right through into September, dry fly fishing has proven successful throughout the whole season.

In 1968 during 345 rod-days 1,644 brook trout were caught with an average weight of over 4 pounds and

The vast watershed area at Northern Labrador Camps provides abundant brook trout

Fish are large and the rule is fly only

of these, 1,288 were released. 218 trout weighed between 5 and 6 pounds; 68 weighed between 6 and 7 pounds, and 24 weighed over 7 pounds.

In 1969 during 908 rod-days 3,969 brook trout were caught with an average weight of over 4 pounds and of these, 3,272 were released. 377 trout weighed between 5 and 6 pounds; 163 trout weighed between 6 and 7 pounds, and 52 weighed over 7 pounds.

Transportation between Goose Bay

and the camps is in four-passenger DeHaviland Beaver aircraft or six-passenger, twin-engined Beech-craft. The cost of the charter of these aircraft, which is not included in the rates for accommodation at the camps, is based on mileage flown. A one way charter between Goose Bay and **Minonipi Lodge** costs $90.00 with the Beaver, and $100.00 with the Beechcraft. A one-way charter between Goose Bay and **Matimek Lodge** costs $99.00 with the Beaver, and $110.00 with the Beechcraft.

These costs are for the planes and not a per person rate.

The rates for fishing and accommodation at both **Matimek Lodge** and **Minonipi Lodge** is all-inclusive and is $70.00 per person per day, based on parties of two, four or six persons. Non-resident fishing license, which may be purchased at the camps, costs an additional $5.00. An advance deposit of 25 percent is required to confirm reservations; this is refundable with thirty days written notice in the event of cancellation.

Cayman Islands

The Cayman Islands are located 480 miles south of Miami. Consisting of three islands, Grand Cayman the largest, Cayman Brac 86 miles to the east, and Little Cayman 74 miles to the east-northeast, this Caribbean paradise is rapidly developing as an angling resort. The islands are projecting peaks of the Cayman Ridge, a range of submarine mountains extending from the Maestra range of Cuba and running to the west to the Misteriosa Bank toward British Honduras. Geologically, Grand Cayman is a flat topped mountain of about 22 miles in length (east to west) and from one to eight miles in width. Cayman Brac, which is 12 miles long and a mile wide, rises 140 feet above sea level at one point. Little Cayman is 10 miles long and one mile wide but surrounded by reefs and extensive flats. Known among amateur beachcombers as a place to vegetate among the sea grapes and cocoanut palms, the Caymans remain unspoiled. Nevertheless inter-island transportation is a reality and the essential facilities for fishing such as boats and accommodations are now more readily available.

THE FISHING

Fishing in the Caymans is typical of the Caribbean area with an abundance of offshore, reef, and flats species with the emphasis on bonefish around Little Cayman and Cayman Brac and the winter run of wahoo, which is spectacular at times. A half mile offshore the water is 3,600 feet deep. Ten miles west of Grand Cayman are the Cayman Banks, a shoal area fifteen miles long and about a half mile wide. The depth varies from about 60 to 110 feet with sharp dropoffs where wahoo, blue marlin and dolphin concentrate. Wahoo are ordinarily caught by anglers who are seeking other species such as sailfish, marlin, or tuna. In Grand Cayman, however, where the wahoo school (December is the peak month) fantastic fishing is often had just off the beach from 16-foot outboards as well as larger sportfishermen.

The most common trolling bait is the balao (ballyhoo), but mullet and other small fishes are also successful. The majority of wahoo are caught on flatlines rather than on the outriggers, and at a fairly close distance to the boat; their strike is swift, and the automatic dropback of

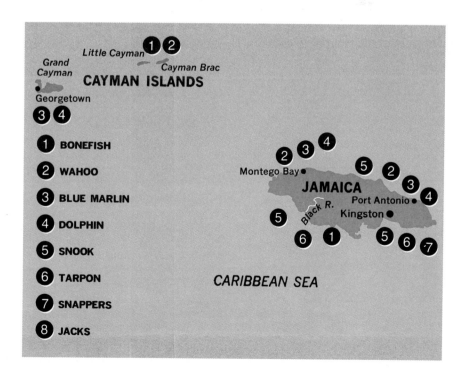

①	BONEFISH
②	WAHOO
③	BLUE MARLIN
④	DOLPHIN
⑤	SNOOK
⑥	TARPON
⑦	SNAPPERS
⑧	JACKS

an outrigger bait does not help in setting the hook. Wahoo also hit artificials, particularly feathers in the 1/0 to 5/0 sizes. They are also taken by drift-fishing with live bait on hook sizes from 5/0 to 8/0. In common with the king mackerel, wahoo often strike a swivel or a light-reflecting leader wire, and breakoffs occur often when the fish are abundant. Although wahoo do occasionally leap from the water when hooked, swift runs with sudden changes in direction are more typical of their play. The most popular tackle for wahoo fishing is the 20- or 30-pound-test class.

One resort specializing in wahoo fishing is Eric Bergstrom's **Tortuga Club** on the north shore of Grand Cayman. The Tortuga gets $30 single and $50 per day double American Plan.

Bonefishing in the Caymans is excellent with fish averaging 2 to 4 pounds but 6 pounds is not uncommon. The island record (Little Cayman) is currently 12 pounds, 4 ounces. All standard methods are used with spinning and fly tackle by wading or casting from a skiff. At present there are only two accommodations on the bonefish grounds, the **Southern Cross Club** on Little Cayman, and Anton Foster's **Buccaneer's Inn** on Cayman Brac. Rates at the Southern Cross run $17.50 double in season, and $32 to $45 double (American Plan) at the Buccaneer's.

TRAVEL NOTES
No passports are required for U.S. or Canadian citizens. However, proof of identity, such as voter registration, is required as well as your return ticket. A smallpox certificate is also required.

Grand Cayman is served by two airlines and is the home base of operations for Cayman Airways. Both LACSA (an affiliate of PAA) and BWIA serve Grand Cayman. Air fare from Miami round trip is $59.00.

ACCOMMODATIONS
Hotel accommodations on Grand Cayman are excellent. Quarters are roomy and comfortable. Many of the hotels have swimming pools, large dining rooms and landscaped courtyards. Other lodges offer choice one and two bedroom apartments, charming unpretentious cottages and a few luxuriously furnished villas. Most of the hotels are oriented to provide guests the ultimate in casual beach living. Hotels with Modified American Plan rates (with two meals) are the fully air-conditioned **La Fontaine,** $46 double; the deluxe **Beach Club Colony**, $50 double; **Coral Caymanian** and **Galleon Beach**, $40 double; **Anchorage**, $33 double. American Plan rates (with three meals) are $50 double at the **Tortuga Club** and **Rum Point Club**; $35-$38 at the **Pageant Beach**. The **West Indian Club** has luxurious apartments with maid service; daily rates are about $40 for 1-bedroom, $60 for 2-bedroom. **Cayman Kai Sea Lodges** are $30-$45 daily for 1-bedroom, $60-$75 for 2-bedroom, 3-bath lodges. **Bay View**, a commercial hotel, has a swimming pool; $36 double, MAP. The homelike **Glen** and **Sandy Cottages** are $25 double, EP. **Sunset House** is $24 double, with meals. All rates appreciably lower from April 15 or 30 to December 1 or 14.

LANGUAGE
Dialect and vocal intonations used by Caymanians have puzzled linguists. It's a mixture of American southern drawl and the English slur, with a Scandinavian lilt to end a statement, all combined to fall charmingly on the ears. V's are pronounced as W's: "Prewailing" or "Warying Wind" are classic examples used by these seafaring people, and nautical terms are used unconsciously. You'll enjoy the twist, a fascinating sing-song of Cornish, Irish, Scottish and Welsh, and have no difficulty communicating with the Caymanians.

INDIA

Pulk Straight

CEYLON

Colombo · Nuwara Eliya · Badulla · Pottuvil

Adam's Peak

1 **SAILFISH**

2 **BLUE MARLIN**

3 **YELLOWFIN TUNA**

4 **STRIPED MARLIN**

5 **BLACK MARLIN**

6 **WAHOO**

7 **DOLPHIN**

8 **BARRACUDA**

9 **JACKS**

10 **MAHSEER**

11 **PERMIT**

12 **POMPANO**

13 **RAINBOW TROUT**

Ceylon is in the Indian Ocean, separated from the southeastern tip of India by the 20-mile-wide Palk Strait. Occupied by the Portuguese and Dutch for almost three centuries and ruled by the British until 1948, this independent Asian nation has many tourist attractions derived from its polyglot culture. Ceylon is 270 miles long and 140 miles wide and encompasses a variety of landscapes. It also has extreme climatic differences. Around the palm-fringed coast and in the wide alluvial plains of the south and west it is hot and humid with temperatures in the 90's; in the jungle plains of the southeast and the central-north (the unique Tank Country) it is hot and generally dry. In the mountains at the island's center where elevations reach a peak of 8,298 feet, temperatures vary from cool (average 55°F) to cold, and the weather

Ceylon

from wet to dry. Rivers cascade down the wooded hills, creating a number of waterfalls including Diyaluma Falls, the sixth highest in the world. Distinct from the southern portion of the island is the hot and dry northern peninsula, which ranges from sandy desert to thick forest in a few watered areas. Rainfall throughout Ceylon is equally extreme with 25 to 250 inches annually according to altitude.

THE FISHING

There are several types of fishing available in Ceylon. Foremost of these is big-game fishing, which as a sport is not yet fully developed. There is a good run of sailfish off the west coast of Ceylon near Colombo from August through October. Blue marlin and yellowfin tuna also occur during this period. Striped marlin and some blacks appear from October to March with the peak beginning in January on the north, south, and west coasts. On the east coast off Trincomalee and Batticaloa the peak fishing period is probably from February through May. May produced good marlin and tuna fishing in 1969. Wahoo, dolphin, barracuda, jacks, and smaller oceanic species are in evidence most of the year. Charter craft and on-location accommodations can be obtained through the *Ceylon Sea Angler's Club* at Clappenburg, Trincomalee.

Surf fishing offers unusual possibilities in Ceylon. The lagoons along the southeast coast open up during the flood season (from November to January) which triggers mullet runs into the sea; these baitfish are attacked by many species of gamefish including huge jacks (*Caranax ignobolis*) up to 100 pounds in weight. This type of fishing is most productive at Arugam Bay, Panama, Pottuvil, Yala, Kirinda, and Bundala. Two species of Pacific permit (*Trachinotus blochii* and *T. mookalee*) which also attain large size are com-

mon along the coastal beaches. In addition, there are two unusual species of spotted pompano (*Trachinotus russellii* and *T. Bailloni*). For information and rental of small craft for surf and inshore fishing, contact the *Ceylon Angler's Club* at Galle Buck, Fort Colombo.

Freshwater fishing in Ceylon consists principally of rainbow trout in the higher altitude streams between Nuwara Elyia and Adam's Peak. The streams are stocked by the *Ceylon Fishing Club* at Nuwara Elyia and their quality is modest; the average catch is less than a pound and 5-pound fish are exceptional. At lower elevations the rivers contain small mahseer (*Barbus tor*) which average about 5 pounds but occasionally range up to 20 pounds in weight.

TRAVEL NOTES

By Pan American Jet Clipper from New York to Karachi with connections to Colombo. Connections also from Calcutta, New Delhi, Singapore.

Valid passport, but no visa needed for a visit of a month or less. Cholera and smallpox vaccination certificates required; yellow fever certificate needed if coming from an infected area. No restrictions on U.S. currency, but no rupees of Pakistan, India, or Ceylon may be taken into or out of the country.

Free bus service from Katunayake Airport to Colombo hotels. Porters are tipped Rs. 1 per bag. Departure tax Rs. 2.50 (53c).

ACCOMMODATIONS

COLOMBO

Best hotels in Colombo are the **Taprobane** in the city, from $10.50 single, $18.50-$20 double American Plan (with meals), **Galle Face,** on the sea, apartments $9.45 single, $14 double European Plan, and the **Mount Lavinia**, a complete resort hotel 7 miles from the city on a

lovely beach, from $11.50 single, $20 double American Plan, plus 10 percent for service. Air conditioning extra. Throughout the island in rural spots of special interest there are Government-owned rest houses of considerable charm; American Plan rates here are about $7.50 per person a day; 20 percent less May to October.

KANDY

Only 72 miles northeast of Colombo, Kandy is 1600 feet above sea level. **Queen's Hotel** overlooks Kandy Lake, and across the lake is **Chalet Guest House. Peak View Hotel** is 2 miles from town. Most famous landmark is the ornate Temple of the Sacred Tooth. Buddha's Tooth is carried during the Kandy Perahera, 10-day festivities in July/August, a stupendous pageant and procession of unforgettable costumes and extraordinary dancing accompanied by the throbbing of Kandyan drums. Peradeniya Botanical Gardens, among the finest in the world, and the University of Ceylon are near Kandy.

NUWARA ELIYA

A cool climate resort at 6,250 feet elevation and center for trout fishing. The **Grosvenor** and **Grand Hotel** with rates at about $3 per day single.

CONTACTS

Ceylon Government Tourist Bureau, Chaitya Road, Colombo 1. Ceylon Embassy, 2148 Wyoming Avenue., N.W., Washington, D.C. 20008. Pan Am's agents are Shaw Wallace & Hedges Ltd., 363 Kollupitiya Road, Colombo 3 (Tel. 78271-5: 3977).

LANGUAGE

There are two principal language groups among the Ceylonese—Sinhalese and Ceylon Tamil. However, due to the long British rule much English is spoken and little difficulty is encountered in hotels or restaurants.

Chile

Spectacular trout fishing, majestic scenery, and world famous big-game angling make Chile a prime vacation spot. The crest of the Andes dividing the country from Argentina is jagged and in places too steep even for snow to cling to it. Through each valley between the peaks a clear river roars and tumbles, gliding seaward. Most have their origin in the perpetual glaciers of the Cordillera and gain stature from countless gushing springs and tributary brooks. Here, as in Argentina, trout are not true natives of the lakes and rivers but were first introduced from Germany in 1905. Habitat and food conditions were so ideal that the fish quickly became established in all the major watersheds south of Santiago. Although there has been a noticeable decline in angling in some watersheds due to natural catastrophes such as volcanic eruption and earthquakes, mismanagement of forest lands, and inadequate law enforcement, Chilean waters continue to produce some very large trout each season. Trout of over 20 pounds have been recorded, and fish of 8 to 15 pounds are taken in considerable number each season. A trout of 2 to 3 pounds is common in Chile. Nevertheless, including all the small fish caught, the angler's average is often lower. Much depends on where the fishing is done and at what time of the season. The rainbow and brown trout are the two principal species. There are some brook trout in the Laguna del Inca at Portillo, a famous ski resort 9,000 feet up in the Andes mountains. Brookies are also found in the Manso and Puelo rivers, which flow from Argentina where the species is widespread.

THE SEASON

Chile is a country of great climactic extremes. The north is an arid desert but precipitation increases south of Santiago and from Puerto Montt to Tierra del Fuego rainfall prevails. A cyclonic belt which moves north in the winter and south in the summer causes violent winds to sweep the Andean passes. Moving low pressure areas in southernmost Chile produce very strong winds and create a constant succession of storms for which the passage around Cape Horn has been famous. The cold Peru Current flows northward along the entire coast of Chile, and keeps temperatures low and uniform. Nevertheless, the climate is pleasant, comparable to northern California, with January the warmest month and July the coldest month of the year. The spring fishing season in late October to December may be accompanied by high water levels from snow runoff but the summer months of January into March normally find the streams running clear.

FLOAT TRIPS

Due to the large size and turbulent nature of the trout waters which attract most tourist anglers, float trips are more or less standard procedure in Chile. As a rule the *botero* (boatman) will cover about ten miles in a day, as access roads are widely separated. The boats are comfortable, and the fisherman is seated and facing downstream. He can troll or cast, or, when the river is low in summer, he can wade. Float-fishing is a delightful form of angling if you want to see a lot of country and enjoy a wonderful *asado*. The guides double in brass as rowers and camp

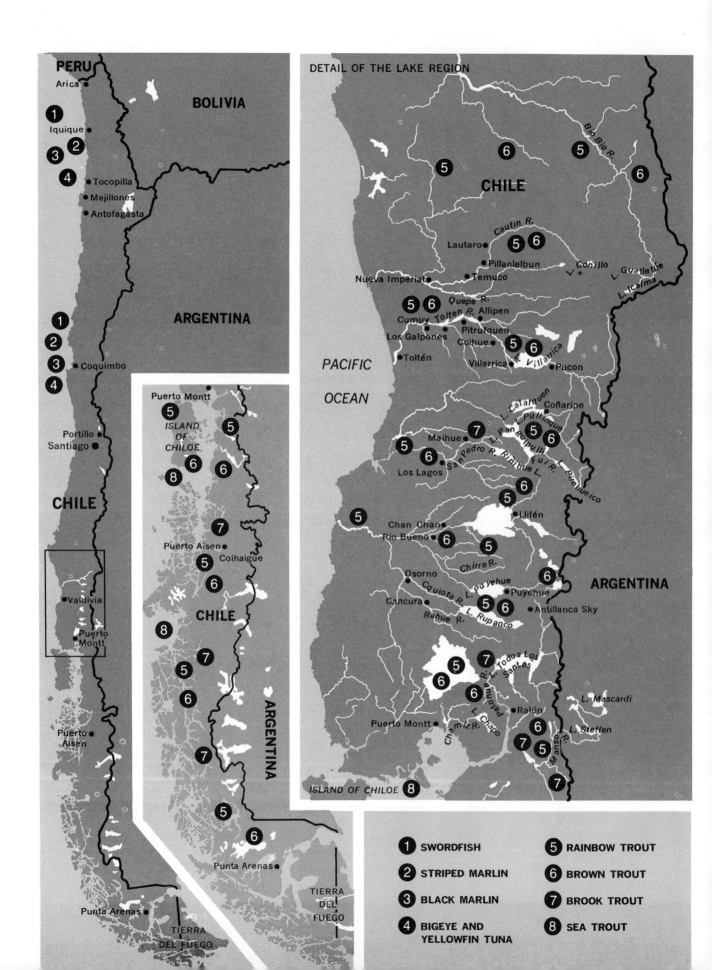

PERU

BOLIVIA

Arica

Iquique

Tocopilla
Mejillones
Antofagasta

ARGENTINA

Coquimbo

Portillo
Santiago

CHILE

Valdivia

Puerto
Montt

Puerto
Aisen

Puerto
Aisen

TIERRA
DEL
FUEGO

Punta Arenas

TIERRA
DEL
FUEGO

DETAIL OF THE LAKE REGION

CHILE

Bío Bío R.

Cautin R.

Lautaro

Pillanlelbun
Temuco

Conillo
L. +

L. Gualletue
L. Icalma

Nueva Imperial

Quepe R.

Cumuy   Tolten R. Allipen

Los Galpones

Toltén

Pitrufquen
Coihue
Villarrica

L. Villarrica
Pucon

PACIFIC

OCEAN

L. Calafquen   Coñaripe
L. Pullinque
L. Panguipulli

Maihue

Los Lagos

San Pedro R. Rinihue L.
Fui R.
L. Pirehueico

Llifén

Chan Chan
Rio Bueno

Chirre R.

Osorno

Cquiota R. L. Puyehue
Cancura
Rahue R.

L. Rupanco

Puyehue

Antillanca Sky

ARGENTINA

L. Todos Los
Santos

Puerto Montt

L. Chapo

Ralún

L. Mascardi

L. Steffen

ISLAND OF CHILOE

Puerto Montt

ISLAND
OF
CHILOE

CHILE

Coihaigue

Puerto Aisen

ARGENTINA

Punta Arenas

① **SWORDFISH**	⑤ **RAINBOW TROUT**	
② **STRIPED MARLIN**	⑥ **BROWN TROUT**	
③ **BLACK MARLIN**	⑦ **BROOK TROUT**	
④ **BIGEYE AND YELLOWFIN TUNA**	⑧ **SEA TROUT**	

cooks. The noonday break is initiated by kindling a fire. Lunch is a simple affair of trout right out of the stream pan fried in butter and a barbecue of either steaks or a rack of lamb. All this is washed down with local wines, white and red, or a very excellent Chilean beer.

If the weather is really warm, everyone—guides and anglers alike— siestas for a half-hour after eating. That noontime catnap has merit. It's really amazing how a fellow can cork off for a brief spell on a bed of volcanic sand and gravel and wake up a new man.

CAUTIN RIVER

Temuco is the gateway to the lake district and lies about 400 miles south of Santiago. Here is the great Cautin River flowing right through the town. Some fifteen miles north is the main hatchery at the town of Lautaro, which is a good place to start a float trip down the Cautin. Or you can start at the village of Pillanlelbun. The float can be extended below Temuco to the town of Nueva Imperial where the Quepe joins the Cautin. The Quepe was once a fine river with good-size trout, but intensive fishing ruined it, and the yield now is mostly small fish.

LOWER TOLTÉN RIVER

The lower part of the Toltén River, from Pitrufquen flowing toward the Pacific, is fished from Temuco. Here the Toltén is a very big river, but it divides in many arms and is ideal for fly fishing. A good two-day float trip can be made as far as Cumuy, leaving the boats at Los Galpones, returning for the night to Temuco, and proceeding next day to Cumuy. Trout of 3 to 7 pounds can be expected. This trip has one disadvantage. At times the river is not clear due to volcanic ash which comes from a feeder stream on the Llaima Volcano. The best time is before January 15 and again at the end of March. Temuco is also the starting point to fish Lake Gualletue and Lake Icalma, near the Argentine border. By road it's about an 80-mile trip. There is an airstrip near Icalma, at 3,500 feet. Most lakes in the district are between 700 to 1,000 feet.

BÍO BÍO RIVER

Out of Gualletue flows the Bío Bío River, and for miles and miles there is fine trout fishing amid beautiful scenery. In the central valley, a long distance away, the Bío Bío is most likely the largest river in Chile. A lake worthy of mention is Concillo, behind the Llaima Volcano. Not too long ago the lake was full of 3- to 8-pound trout, but the fishing today is modest.

UPPER TOLTÉN RIVER

The most concentrated fishing is about five hundred miles south of Santiago, at Villarrica, a small town at the west end of Lake Villarrica, or Pucón which lies at the east end. The Toltén River, which empties from the lake, is the most beautiful of all the float streams, winding at the beginning between high banks heavily overgrown with thick vegetation and wild flowers. The water is crystal clear, flows rapidly between large pools and many rapids. The Toltén is fished as far as Allipen, where a river of the same name enters the Toltén. Access roads are located at Prado Verde, Catrico, and Coipue. The float from Coipue to Allipen is quite different as the river divides in many smaller arms, forming islands. In the last mile or so, the river again flows in one bed, and large fish are caught here. The Toltén holds rainbows and brown trout. Heavy fishing, especially during the summer months, made it less productive than in former years, and many small fish of a pound or so are among a daily catch of larger-size trout. The best is at the beginning of the season and at the end.

LIUCURA RIVER

Pucón is the best-known trout center in Chile, and its fame dates many years back when fish were plentiful and of large size. But the eruption of Villarrica Volcano in 1948 and again in 1964 has done some damage to the fishing. In spite of this, the lake is still productive. The Liucura, which joins the Trancura, is a major tributary. A float trip on the Liucura is the prettiest fishing trip in Chile. At the starting point, the bridge, the river is small for several miles and

then gets bigger after the Carvello joins it. The river has a constant speed as far below as Mata Quila. From then on it is all shooting rapids between great pools. Just below the point where the Liucura enters the Trancura is Martínez Pool which usually holds good-size trout. There are still a few more tricky rapids, but the *boteros* are real experts. The Liucura is always clear, whereas the Trancura runs very muddy after the end of January due to volcanic ash brought down by the Turbio River. In such cases the Trancura can be fished further up, from Curarrehue downstream. Lots of small trout, all rainbows, but plenty of action all day which makes fun-fishing.

HUANEHUE RIVER

The next lake south is Calafquen, and in years past it was *the* place in Chile. Trophy fish of 20 pounds and more were caught in the Huanehue River, the outlet of Calafquen, and in Lake Pullingue. Farmers came on horseback to Villarrica with trout hanging on their saddles, the tails dragging in the dusty road. This is ancient history. A hydroelectric dam was built at Pullingue which contributed to its decline. There are still trout in the lake, and at Conaripe, at the mouth of the river of same name, good fishing can be had. This small village was partly destroyed by the eruption of Villarrica Volcano in 1964.

ENCO RIVER

Chan-Chan at the west end of Lake Panguipulli is where the Enco leaves the lake to join Lake Riñihue. It is a short link of only about 4 to 5 miles, and mile for mile it was the best fishing water in all Chile before the earthquake in 1961. The stream gradient was over 90 feet, but after the quake it literally disappeared. Nearby at Kankahuasi is the club house of the **Rainbow Fly Fishing Club of Chile** formed by a group of American sportsmen, but now owned by the duPont interests. In the good old days there wasn't an angler coming to Chile who didn't pay a visit to Kankahuasi. The Enco is still a fine river, and it may come back again, as it is the main link of an enormous lake system.

FUI RIVER

The Fui River is another water to fish at the Rainbow Club. It is a lovely, fast, and broken river coming out of Pireihueico Lake and entering Panguipulli Lake a few miles away from the club house. The river is floated in part, but some stretches can be waded. The largest fish, of 4 to 8 pounds, are caught mostly at the *barra* or in the pools directly above it.

SAN PEDRO RIVER

The river flowing out of Riñihue Lake is the San Pedro, one of the great rivers in Chile. This river suffered most in the 1961 earthquake. However, it recovered rather quickly, as a trout of 27 pounds was taken here in 1964. A very fine piece of water is the stretch from the Malihue bridge down to the small town of Los Lagos; this should produce good-size rainbows and browns.

CALCURRUPE RIVER

Continuing south comes Lake Ranco, the second largest lake in Chile. At the east end is Llifén, at the west end Puerto Nuevo, and to the south Riñinahue. All three have a good reputation in Chilean fishing. The principal river at Llifén is the Calcurrupe, coming out of Lake Maihue, about fifteen miles to the east. This river produces very large trout of 10 to 15 pounds. The float trip is usually made in two days. Start at Maihue, leave the boats at *medio rio*, and return next morning to continue down to the lake. Down to *medio rio* the water is perfect, and most trophy fish are caught in this part of the river. There is an award for the largest trout caught each season, and generally it is a brown of about 16 pounds or more. It is worth while to be on the water at daybreak near the *barra*, as this hour is most productive. A good place to stay is the **Hosteria Chollinco** which is right on the river. At Llifén is the **Hosteria Hadida.**

CAUENAHUE RIVER

North of Llifén a small river enters the lake, called the Cauenahue. The *barra* still yields good-size trout, but unfortunately the former lava pools about a mile above have filled with sand and gravel and hold only small trout. The Cauenahue can be waded about ten miles or more following a road to a sawmill. It's ideal water for the angler who is content to work a dry fly over 1- to 3-pound fish. There are several smaller rivers emptying into Maihue Lake, and one worth visiting is the Blanco River. It can be reached by road or with an outboard from the outlet of the lake. Where the Blanco River enters the lake many trout of 4 to 8 pounds or more are caught. There is good wading water above this point.

RIÑINAHUE RIVER

The Riñinahue River has been in the past twenty years the most astonishing river for its continuous and constant fishing of large-size trout. There was nothing comparable in Chile or Argentina. The river is rather a small one, and its water extremely cold. This is noticeable in summer when the temperature of the lake is considerably higher. Most large fish are caught at the mouth or immediately above it. Fishable water extends only for about a mile to where a high waterfall forms a barrier to upstream migration. The Riñinahue has been under heavy pressure in recent years, but the fishing is as good as before. The average trout is 4 to 5 pounds. From the Trahuilcho Farm one can fish a beautiful mountain lake called Encanto or Pichi (*pichi* in Indian language is small). This lake is full of rainbow trout of 2 to 3 pounds. A daily catch of 20 to 30 trout is ordinary. This is a horseback trip of under two hours. The fishing is done from boats.

BUENO RIVER

At the west end of Lake Ranco the Bueno River leaves the lake. The Bueno plunges out of the lake with a roar into white water through a canyon for a half a mile. This is perhaps the most beautiful outlet in Chile. The view looking over the lake towards the Cordillera and the many islands is very scenic. Most of the fishing is done at this outlet, and trout of over 20 pounds have been caught here. A boat is necessary, but there is on both sides a short stretch of water for wading. The best fishing occurs very early and again in the evening with preference to the morning. A recommended excursion is from Puerto Nuevo to Huapi Island, inhabited by Indians. A steamer can be chartered which brings the anglers and their boats to the island. The fishing is done by trolling around the island which produces very good results; trout of 4 to 10 pounds are not unusual. It is also productive to cast with spinning equipment toward shore from the boat. A half-day float trip can be arranged from Puerto Nuevo to Puerto Lápiz. From here the Bueno River can be floated in two days to the town of Río Bueno, and boatmen can be hired there at the **Hotel Plaza**. This float trip is delightful; the river is fast and has two difficult rapids which the *boteros* go through alone. The river is flanked by high banks of the type of the Toltén but still more spectacular. This water is lightly fished by local anglers, and therefore it produces more trout and of larger size. Rainbows and brown trout of 4 to 8 pounds are common. It is advisable to leave the boats first day at the Ramírez Farm and stay overnight at Río Bueno if you are not camping.

PILMAIQUEN RIVER

Fine float trips are on Pilmaiquen River which is a short distance from Río Bueno. The Pilmaiquen comes out of Lake Puyehue. One day float is from the Lumaco Farm to the bridge of Trafun, where the Chirre joins the Pilmaiquen. The Pilmaiquen is a much smaller river than the Bueno River, and it produces good fishing for 1- to 5-pound trout.

The Toltén, one of the more accessible and popular rivers, still holds good trout. Large wet flies are ideal here

RAHUE RIVER

At the town of Osorno is another large river, the Rahue. The boats are owned by local fishermen, and it's advisable to make reservations through the **Gran Hotel Osorno**. There are several floats to be made on the Rahue, but the best is from the outlet at Lago Rupanco down to the village of Cancura. The Rupanco is a big, long lake and well known for large trout. There are two small rivers entering the lake, the Pulelfu coming from north, and the Gaviota, larger, at the very end of the lake.

GOLGOL RIVER

The village of Puyehue is a hot spring settled over a hundred years ago by Indians. The principal river nearby is the Golgol. It can be floated starting at the sawmill and down to the lake. The largest fish are generally caught at the inlet. During the earthquake of 1961 the formerly inactive Puyehue Volcano came to life for about twenty-four hours and did considerable damage, especially to the river bed of the Golgol. The inlet is not as good as it was before. A few large trout are still caught there. From here, on the road to Antillanca, a ski resort, are several lovely mountain lakes to fish such as the Espejo, Encanto, Torito, and Toro. Toro Lake is the best, and rainbows of 2 to 6 pounds are common. Virgin forests surround all these small lakes, and the fishing must be done from a boat.

PETROHUÉ RIVER

Petrohué is best known as an access point for tourists crossing the lakes from Chile through the lakes to Bariloche, Argentina. The Petrohué River flows out of Todos los Santos Lake. It is a large river, and it runs very calmly for about ½ mile to where a cable crosses the river to measure the outflow of water. Below the cable the river gains momentum and behaves like a wild horse—a turbulent river with occasional pools at intervals. The largest trout are caught just above and below the cable, and a fish of 15 pounds is not at all rare—mostly rainbows and browns and an occasional smaller brook trout. Downstream the trout are much smaller (1 to 5 pounds) but nevertheless hard-fighting fish. An interesting place to visit is at the big waterfalls several miles below the lake. At the sightseeing bridge, leading to the falls, a small arm of the Petrohué is formed which is fed by a big, cold spring. This section looks like an English chalk stream and at times, generally early season, offers fine fishing. Where the arm again enters the main river, the pool is called Ultima Esperanza (Last Hope), and it is seldom disappointing. All this fishing below the cable is by wading, above it from a boat. A boat is used again further down where the river calms down, at the ferry, and from there to Ralún. Some large fish are caught in this part of the river as this stretch is not often fished.

CHAMIZA RIVER

Puerto Montt is an important seaport and at the same time the end station of the Chilean Railroad and of the road system. The vast continent to the south can only be reached by sea or by air. For the fisherman, a good river near town is the Chamiza. For best results the tide has to be taken in consideration. The river comes out of Chapo Lake, and from there down to the sea there are many fine places to fish. There are no organized facilities, and it is advisable to get in touch with the Club de Pesca through one of the hotels for information. The best hotels in Puerto Montt are the **Hotel Perez Rosales** and the **Hotel Molina.**

ISLAND OF CHILOÉ

Off the continent but still part of Chile, a short distance south of Puerto Montt, is the island of Chiloé. Chiloé has some lakes and rivers, and all hold trout, mostly browns. Its important streams are the Puntra and Putalcura. The color of their waters is like strong tea, created by decaying vegetation. After they join, the river is called Chepú, and empties into the Pacific. There is an airfield for small planes located here, and the river offers interesting fishing. Some accommodations can be found in the village of Chepú—not fancy but adequate.

continued on page 74

That Other Season

When snows are chilling the Northern Hemisphere it's a simple matter to hop a southbound jet and find some of the greatest freshwater fishing in the world. A winter vacation in the land of summer has become a regular habit for many trout anglers. And more and more tourists are discovering that South America's winter, which roughly corresponds to June through November depending on latitude, has a big bonus to offer in its tropical rivers, notably for the mighty dorado. But the choice is academic, as no year is complete without sampling both.

South America's trout fishing centers in Argentina and Chile. Although many of the great rivers of a decade ago are only modest producers today, the quality of the sport is still above average; and for the angler who is willing to travel off the beaten path and arranges to camp out or make a float-trip, the fishing can be exceptional. Fish of large average size (over 5 pounds) are still common to the wilderness regions of southern Chile and southern Patagonia in Argentina. A reliable outfitter is essential in both regions. Check the appropriate sections for travel agencies or guides who offer back-country trips. Do not rely on finding a professional locally, as there are not that many good ones without bookings. Equally important is to get all-inclusive rates for camping trips (excluding any personal items) to cover transportation as well as food and essential equipment. Domestic airlines in Argentina offer a special $90 excursion fare to non-residents. This entitles you to travel anywhere in the country within a one-month period.

Some top spots for 1971 are the Yelcho, Palena, and Senguerr Rivers.

Brook trout of over 5 pounds are common, and browns and rainbows exceeding 8 pounds are daily fare. With fast jet transportation today a two-week vacation would allow ten days of fishing in many areas but camp-outs require a minimum three-week vacation for a visitor coming from San Francisco, New York, or London. Bear in mind that foreign round-trip excursion fares, usually 23 to 30 days, favor the longer stay.

Although five or six species of dorado are distributed throughout tropical South America, the big one is limited to Argentina, Paraguay, and a portion of Brazil. The best and most accessible river system for this kind of angling is the Parana and its tributaries. The difference between a trout trip and a dorado trip is simply a matter of direction; instead of heading southwest of Buenos Aires for the former you will fly north for the latter. Actually dorado occur right in downtown Buenos Aires, but the muddy Rio de la Plata is not the water that made this fishing world famous. The hotspots are mostly in the Province of Corrientes, which borders Paraguay, and the Province of Misiones on Brazil's border. This northeastern corner of Argentina is also convenient to tourists coming from Sao Paulo, which is no more than two hours flying time north of Iguassu Falls on the upper Parana.

Dorado fishing is done from a base camp or even a city hotel with the help of a taxi. New resorts are under construction in this region due to the increase in the number of visitors to the Falls—an awesome 2½ mile wide cataract that is well worth a detour. Bargain rates are the rule rather than the exception in this part of South America.

A golden dorado (*top left*) greets visitors at the Paso de la Patria fishing camp on Argentina's Parana River. Top outfitter here is Luis Oscar Schulz, many times winner of local tournaments. Fishing is from July through October but may run into November in dry years

A sleek 30-inch-long rainbow (*top right*) taken from Chile's Rininahue River. Float fishing is popular method on this country's big streams. Streamer flies and salmon wet flies in dark colors imitate the brachyuran crab which is favorite food of these fast-growing trout

The enchanted land of Patagonia offers exceptional fishing to anglers who camp out. Trout in the 5-pound class are common but visitors should allow a minimum of three weeks to get into the remote streams such as the Palena, Futaleufu, and Yelcho

Larger lakes of Argentina, Chile can yield 20-pound rainbow trout

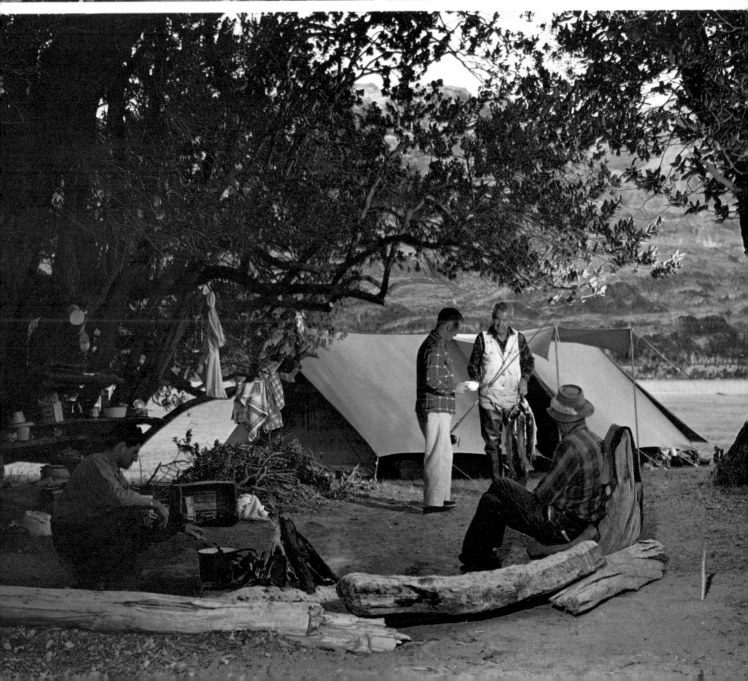

**Angler Jacques d'Hunval (*top left*) holds a 12-pound rainbow taken in Lago Verde, Argentina.
Typically, large trout and landlocked salmon are found around inlet and outlet streams of Patagonian lakes
Perched on a hill overlooking Argentina's Lake Nahuel Huapi, the first-class Llao-Llao Hotel
(*bottom left*) is headquarters for anglers traveling north or south. Record for lake is 38½- pound brown trout**

**The Martinez Pool of the Trancura River in Chile is
one of the classic stretches of fly water. Due to size of most
Andean rivers here anglers bring along hip-boots and
make occasional stops in a float-trip to try likely spots**

One of the most powerful freshwater gamefish in the world, the dorado fights aerially. Fish frequent rocky shoals

This is a common sight in the annual Fiesta Nacional del Dorado each August. Hundreds of anglers compete

A pair of 35-pounders taken at Paso de la Patria. Fish of this size are common. Record is 68 pounds

Rio Grande River in Patagonia region of Argentina is well-known for its rainbow and brown trout

Secret Of The Blue Trout

Blue trout recipes invite a turgid flow of metaphor from European cooks, but they always fail to explain where the color originates and this, obviously, is important. There are no plums in plum pudding, no duck in Bombay duck, and no blue coloring in a trout's skin. The color comes from the same lubricant that makes a fish slippery—the film that keeps our trout waterproof. Without it he would drown and without it there can be no blue. Consequently, the idea has existed that the trout must be cooked alive. Something is always lost in translation, but this calculated sadism grew out of the phrase "in a live condition," meaning that the trout should not be washed or scaled before going into the vinegar bath. Actually, your fish should be quite dead, but killed and gutted within an hour or two before bluing. Part of the dogma handed from kitchen to kitchen also reveals that more than one restaurant has made a practice of using trout that are not exactly fresh. Numerous

recipes suggest running a cord through the trout from mouth to tail, or piercing the fish's head with a toothpick and trussing him tail to head. The idea, one would gather, is to serve curved trout, and in a manner of speaking the curve is essential but the methods are contradictory. The final gesture of a freshly killed trout is to curl, and he will do this with no help from the chef. String and toothpicks are necessary only when the fish has been dead for many hours and the muscle tissue will no longer contract.

TRUITE AU BLEU

The first step in making *truite au bleu* is to brew a good court bouillon. In a large kettle add two quarts of water, a cup of dry white wine, and a tablespoon of lemon juice. While this is warming, drop in two stalks of celery including the leaves which you have cut in small pieces, one cut carrot, one cut onion, two springs of parsley, one sprig of thyme, a tablespoon of crushed bay leaf, six peppercorns, and one mashed clove of garlic. Now let this cook until the vegetables have added their juices to the pot. It should bubble merrily for half an hour, but

in the meantime dilute some tarragon vinegar in another kettle at the ratio of two-thirds vinegar to one-third water and bring to a boil. When the bouillon is ready, strain off the vegetables and you are ready to blue your trout. Nine- to 12-inch-long fish are ideal for this dish.

With large kitchen tongs, grasp each trout firmly by the lower jaw and lower them in the hot vinegar and, when properly blue, place them in the fast boiling court bouillon. The bouillon will cease bubbling for a few minutes, but when it comes to a boil again, remove the pot from the fire and cover. Let this stand for about fifteen minutes and your trout are cooked. The fish should be removed carefully and drained.

Classically, blue trout are served with marble-size new potatoes bathed in butter and garnished with parsley. There should also be a side dish of garden fresh asparagus smothered in mousseline sauce (simply a hollandaise mixed with an equal part of stiffly whipped cream). After the cream has been added to the hollandaise, heat it very carefully and stir until the sauce is hot. A dry and lively champagne would be the proper mate to such rich fare.

Due to the turbulent nature of many Chilean rivers, float-fishing is the only practical method of angling

continued from page 67
PUELO RIVER
Some of the best trout rivers in Chile today lie south of Puerto Montt. The first of these is the Puelo River. There is a steamer service several times a week to the village of Puelo where the river empties into the Estuario de Reloncaví, a long, narrow branch of the sea. Rainbow, brown, and brook trout can be caught in the brackish water. The Puelo comes a long way from Argentina and enters Tagua Tagua Lake about 7 to 8 miles above the village. The outlet is called "El Baraco" where large fish are caught. On the way down are great fishing pools like El Salto, Quita Calzones, Pangal, Urupa, La Carrera, Vacilio, and others. Fish of 4 to 8 pounds can be expected. Probably the easiest place to fish the Puelo is at the Argentine border. The Chilean air force maintains an airfield at Segundo Corral in the Distrito Llano Grande. A small plane can be chartered at Puerto Montt to reach the river. The most experienced and reliable charter pilot locally is Manolo Gil (Casilla 429, Puerto Montt, Chile).

MANSO RIVER
The Manso River holds large rainbows, browns and brook trout. A 5- to 6-pound average is not unusual. A good location here is about 6 miles upriver from its confluence with the Puelo River. There is a small airfield nearby suitable for light aircraft at the Gallardo Farm. The Manso rises on Mt. Tronador on the Argentine side and enters Lago Mascardi, then passes through Lago Hess and Lago Steffen before coursing into Chile. Some good fishing can be found in Argentina also where the Manso leaves Mascardi.

SIMPSON RIVER
In the Province of Aysen, the Simpson was a fine brown trout stream until several years ago when a flood destroyed many of its pools and channels. However, the river is still worth while particularly in the stretch below its juncture with the Coyhaique River. There is good air service from Santiago to Coyhaique via LADECO Airlines or to Balmaceda via LAN Airlines (Balmaceda is 40 miles from Coyhaique). Accommodation locally would be the **Hosteria Coyhaique** (Coyhaique, Aysen, Chile).

SERRANO RIVER
Near Punta Arenas the most important river is the Serrano which produces trout of 10 to 15 pounds with an average of about 4. Punta Arenas, a free port and navy town (90,000 population) is also one of the largest sheep farming areas in the world. Clinging to the edge of the Strait of Magellan the city has good accommodations in the **Hotel Cabo de Hornos**. The Chilean airline LAN services Punta Arenas out of Santiago.

SALTWATER FISHING
Chilean saltwater fishing is exceptionally productive because of the upwelling of nutrient-rich waters as the Humboldt or Peru Current flows northward along Chile fairly close to shore. The multitudes of plankton offer a rich food supply for bait species such as anchovies, sardines, sauries, and squid, which abound off the coast and which in turn attract and hold the large game fishes along Chile's 2,600-mile coastline.

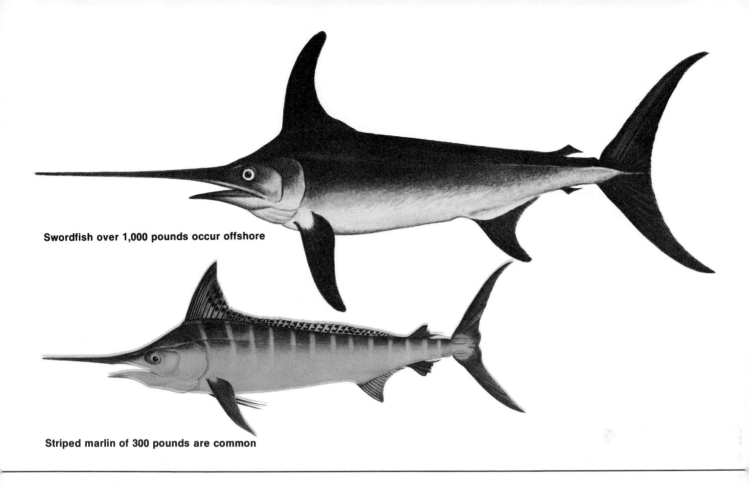

Swordfish over 1,000 pounds occur offshore

Striped marlin of 300 pounds are common

Tops in Chile's saltwater gamesters is the swordfish, known locally as *albacora* or *pezespada*, and a record 1,182-pound fish has been taken at Iquique, the prime angling port. The usual catch is from 300 to 900 pounds, but commercial fishermen have harpooned broadbill swordfish in these waters weighing over 1,500 pounds, and reliable persons have sighted fish that would probably exceed 2,000 pounds.

Swordfish prefer warmer waters, and are thus concentrated in the northern waters of Chile, although they occur at least as far south as Valdivia. The chief commercial fishing ports are Iquique, Tocopilla, Coquimbo, and Antofagasta, so good sport fishing should be expected there. The best months are March, April, and May. Swordfish are not fished blind, but are seen finning-out and then the bait (usually a bonito or small tuna) is presented.

Striped marlin (*marlin*) run large off Chile, with 300-pound fish fairly common and specimens of over 400 pounds being caught each season. The fishing is from January through October with a peak in March and April.

Black marlin (*pezzuncho*) are occasionally taken in the north parts from Arica to Mejillones, but only when a thin surface layer of warmer water from the north flows southward, as occasionally happens in April. Similarly, occasional sailfish (*pezvela*) are taken in the north.

Among the tunas, the bigeye tuna (*atún*) is perhaps the largest of the Chilean tuna, but is not always distinguished from the yellowfin tuna (*atún de aleta amarilla*). The bigeye approaches 400 pounds, but fish of 100 to 150 pounds are the rule. They are usually caught in the deeper strata by commercial fishermen.

CHILEAN SWORDFISH TECHNIQUE

Swordfish only rarely strike blind on a trolled bait. Generally, the fish is first seen on the surface. Then the trolled bait is presented carefully and as quietly as possible, for swordfish seem to be easily frightened by the approach of a boat.

They seem also to be very finicky about taking a bait, and presentations may be made time after time before the fish either takes the bait or becomes alarmed and disappears.

The method of baiting the broadbill is the same in all oceans. The squid, oceanic bonito, and small tuna are good baits. A double hookup is used. The forward hook is inserted below the gill, the second hook close to the tail. Large hooks, 14/0 or 16/0, are preferred. Off the west coast of South America 16/0 is better, since the fish run very heavy in these waters. The broadbill has a very soft mouth, and a big hook is needed so that it can hold better. Naturally, the big hook also gets a better bite in case of foul hooking whether it be in fin, body, or tail. The leader must be strong. The bill of this fish is a formidable weapon; therefore stainless-steel cable is essential. For general broadbill fishing the cable should have a breaking strength of 450 pounds, but if there are really big bruisers in the water, such as one finds in the Peru Current, a 900-pound-test is better. Thirty feet of cable is the preferred length, due to the tendency of the fish to wrap itself around the leader.

When stalking the broadbill, one or two men stand in the crow's nest as lookouts. The boat cruises faster than at trolling speed since the bait is seldom tossed into the water until a fish is spotted. Most anglers prefer this method of stalking fish to blind trolling since it permits a rapid coverage of the area. The broadbill is fairly easy to spot because the fin and tail stand high out of the water and can be seen at a considerable distance. If it is definitely known that broadbill are in the area then it is wise to troll, often as deep as 400 feet, at which time the boat should proceed at a snail's pace while everybody aboard searches the area for a fin. The general procedure, however, is watchful cruising with the rod kept ready in the rod holder, bait and leader attached for immediate use. At the electric moment when a broadbill is spotted the angler picks up the rod and jumps into the chair, quickly attaching his harness. He now tosses the bait into the sea and proceeds to peel off about 200 feet of line. The bait should troll a good distance behind the boat.

The mate stands in the stern and holds the line at approximately the 200-foot mark, between his thumb and first finger. The angler peels off another 75 feet of line which drags in the water forming a loop between the tip of the rod and the angler's finger. At the strike this loop permits a slow and uninterrupted dropback.

The boat should move at a very slow speed. The bait is kept approximately 2 feet under the surface and at no time is permitted to make a disturbance or a wake. The boat is maneuvered so that the bait is presented to the fish within 20 to 25 feet of its bill. Since the swordfish has a tendency to run in circles, it often turns away from the bait.

When this happens the boat must maneuver repeatedly, until the fish dives for the bait. Any disturbance, such as the wake or motor vibrations, has a tendency to cause the fish to sound. The captain must use great precaution at this point; for instance, if the boat moves too fast or closes in precipitously the fish will sound. This does not necessarily mean it is gone forever. It may remain in the vicinity. The boat usually idles or slowly cruises the area, while everyone aboard is on the alert. This happened when the 1,182-pound record broadbill off Chile was spotted. The fish sounded; the area had to be stalked at least a half hour before it reappeared. Drifting was necessary, and care was taken to cause no disturbance. After what seemed an eternity Eddie Wall, the guide, spotted the fish a little over a mile away.

ACCOMMODATIONS
The capital city of Santiago is usually included in the tourist's itinerary. Hotels here offer good food and service. The **Carrera Hilton,** a 17-story hotel with rooftop swimming pool and garden, is one of the best in the city. Single rates from $10, double from $12, European Plan. Other first-class hotels in Santiago are the **Crillón, Emperador, Panamericano, Grand Palace, Carlos V** and **Santa Lucia,** with rates considerably less than at the **Carrera.** The **Kent, Lido, Ritz, Savoy** and **City** hotels are comfortable and inexpensive. Hotels add up to 21 percent to your bill to cover service and taxes.

Restaurants are inexpensive. The hotels **Carrera** and **Crillón** have superb continental food. English is spoken at **El Parrón,** famous for meat and mixed grills, Chilean dishes. It also has an outdoor patio. The **Waldorf** has American and French cuisine, a good orchestra. **El Escorial, Nuria** and **Chiaranda** for continental food. The **Due Torri** specializes in Italian dishes; **El Danubio Azul** in Chinese food. Also try **La Portada Colonial, Shorton Grill** and **Mervilles** for Chilean specialties. **El Pollo Dorado** is excellent for chicken and beef served in a typically Chilean atmosphere. Try **Parrilla de Venancio** for barbecues.

The native wines are the thing to buy and drink. Tops are *Santa Carolina,* a white wine; *Tarapacá ex-Zavala* and *Tocornal* in the burgundy class. Some Chilean Rieslings are well known in the States and there are many more brands available.

CLOTHING
It's necessary to bring along rain gear, warm clothing, and lightweight clothing. During warm midday hours in the mountains khaki pants and light flannel shirt are adequate; however, when the sun goes down a sweater or down jacket is ideal. The daytime temperatures may range around 75°F and drop to 45°F or less at night depending on altitude. Just keep extremes in mind and pack accordingly.

TRAVEL NOTES
For U.S. citizens, passport, vaccination and health certificates are required. No visa is required for U.S. and countries with which Chile has diplomatic relations. Tourist cards, valid for 90 days, are issued gratis to U.S. citizens. No duty on articles for personal use, including fishing tackle and cameras. Five hundred cigarettes and two tins of tobacco allowed duty free.

There are no mosquitoes in Chile but one insect similar to a horsefly in appearance with an orange head and tail called the *coli-huache* can be a nuisance at times; a small pale-colored deerfly called the *tobane* also bites as does a small blackfly or *polce.* None of these insects are normally abundant; however, they are reason enough to bring along a repellent. River water is not safe to drink in Chile unless you see it running out of a snow bank, or unless it's boiled.

LANGUAGE
To the visitor, Chile seems to be less Latin than other countries of South America, perhaps because many Chileans have English, Irish, or German ancestry, and so many speak English.

Colombia

It has become a cliché to say that South America is a land of contrasts, yet the absolute division between civilization and wilderness is the very factor which provides some of the world's most diverse angling.

Colombia is bordered by the Pacific Ocean and the Atlantic Ocean (Caribbean Sea). It is the northern terminus of the Andean Ridge which branches into three principal mountain ranges with peaks reaching over 18,000 feet. From the arid land of the Guajira Peninsula to the swamps of the Magdalena and from the Llanos or eastern plains to the volcanic western cordilleras and south to the luminous green rain forest of the Amazon is an area of 440,000 square miles. Between these extremes of oceans and altitudes exist an amazing variety of saltwater and freshwater fish. Colombia has thousands of streams which form three major watersheds; those that drain into the Pacific, those that flow into the Caribbean, and those that enter the Atlantic through the Amazon and Orinoco Rivers. Because of this diverse habitat, anglers in Colombia can run the gamut from rainbow trout to dorado and blue marlin to peacock pavón.

Much of the country is still undeveloped from a tourist angler's point of view, but facilities in remote areas are growing, and for the adventuresome the Colombian jungles are uniquely rewarding.

THE SEASON

Colombia lies almost entirely within the north tropical zone. High temperatures prevail in the lowlands including the coastal plains and the larger river valleys. Cooler climates prevail at higher altitudes with subtropical weather found at elevations up to 6,000 feet and temperate zone weather from 6,000 to 10,000 feet. Above 10,000 feet the weather is *cold*. Most of Colombia's major cities are at 3,000 to 9,000 feet above sea level so the temperature in Bogotá, for example, will average about 58°F the year round.

Colombia has a wet season (*invierno*) and a dry season (*verano*). The area of highest rainfall is in the Department of Chocó where the annual average exceeds 400 inches and there is no dry season here. Generally speaking, the January through March period is the dry season in lowland jungle rivers and is the best time for freshwater fishing. For the high-altitude trout waters, the best period is June through September. Along the Atlantic coast April-May and October-November are generally rainy periods.

SALTWATER FISHING

The inshore Atlantic Coast region of Colombia has a great variety of marine species dominated by snook and tarpon because of the many brackish estuaries and bays. These fish also occur in the lower reaches of the coastal rivers and penetrate quite far inland for at least 250 miles in the swamp regions of the Atrato and Magdalena River systems. The waters of the lower Magdalena are dissipated over a wide area of marsh, lakes, and lagoons; concentrations of tarpon are found around Ayapel and El Banco. The more accessible fishing of this type is at the port cities such as Barranquilla at the Magdalena River mouth in the Cienaga Grande area. A major fishing resort was scheduled to open in June of 1970 at Santa Marta, east of Barranquilla. The **Carib Inn** (Santa Marta, Colombia; information and reservations *Adventure Associates,* 301 Outdoors Building, Columbia, Missouri 65201 U.S.A.) The **Carib Inn** is a beachside resort located near the Buritaca River mouth and has access to a variety of angling as well as charter boats for offshore fishing. The blue water species seasonally common to Colombia's north coast are blue and white marlin, sailfish, wahoo, king mackerel, dolphin, barracuda, yellowfin and blackfin tuna. Presently, the Del Rosario Island group is a popular location for boats working out of Cartagena. Charters can be made here through the local *Club de Pesca.*

The Pacific Coast region of Colombia is largely undeveloped. There are many short, precipitous rivers coming off the Western Cordillera which is heavily forested and humid. The coastal lowlands are sparsely populated in the Departments of Chocó, Valle, Cauca, and Nariño. Rainfall exceeds 200 inches per year. Exploratory vessels have reported good fishing along the coast from Cabo Marzo to Isla Gorgona for black marlin, sailfish, amberjack, roosterfish, dolphin, yellowfin and big-eye tuna but there are no on-location facilities for visiting anglers. Occasionally boats run down from the Panama Canal Zone to fish the Cabo Marzo area but this is a two-day trip and requires a long-range craft suitable for living aboard.

TROPICAL FRESHWATER FISHING

The largest family of freshwater fishes found in South America is the Characidae. There are 1,350 known species which includes the dorados, piranhas, pacus, payaras, the trahira and many pikelike species without common names. The great majority of characins are carnivores and nearly all of the larger species are excellent gamefish.

The local names of fishes in South America are extremely confusing, as they are derived from Spanish and Portuguese and a great many dissimilar Indian dialects. The Spanish word *picuda*, for example, which means "beaked," is applied to at least thirty different species ranging from the saltwater barracuda to the freshwater dorado. The serious angler can profit greatly by learning at least a few of the Latin as well as the common names of important native gamefish. With the exception of the well-publicized piranha (Portuguese)—known elsewhere in South America as the caribe (Spanish)—Spanish common names are preferable as they are more widely used.

There are two dorado (locally picuda, picua, dorada, or rubio) found in Colombia; *Salminus affinis* is confined to the upper Magdalena River and its tributaries (the Cauca system) which flows north into the

Atlantic; the second is *Salminus hilarii* which is distributed in the Orinoco watershed (notably in the Meta and Guaviare Rivers) and the upper Amazon. Neither species attains the large size of the Argentine dorado (*Salminus maxillosus*) which is known to exceed 65 pounds. Colombian dorado in general range from 2 to 8 pounds and 12-pounders are uncommon. Both Colombian species are more slender than *S. maxillosus* and very silvery rather than gold in color. They are found in fast flowing, gravel-bottom streams and will take a variety of lures. Spinning and fly tackle provide excellent sport.

Another characin of major importance as a gamefish in tropical South America is the payara. There are two genera (*Cynodon* and *Hydrolicus*). The payara is a formidable predator, related to the African tigerfish. It is distinguished by a pair of long canine teeth in the lower jaw which project through the snout. There are four species distributed in Brazil, the Guianas, Venezuela, and Colombia. Payara are large (to 30 pounds or more) powerful fish. They make strong runs and frequent leaps. Their sharp mouths also make them difficult to hook solidly. Almost any artificial lure and especially topwater plugs will attract payara.

Tropical South America has a vast and unknown number of species in the Cichlidae family. Among these in the genus *Cichla* and *Cichlasoma* are some of Colombia's most important gamefish. The *Cichla* are represented by the pavóns. These fish are generally basslike in appearance with a hump developing on the posterior region of the head in males which becomes most prominent as the April spawning season approaches. The adult body coloration is a gray-green or purplish-green on the dorsal surface, shading to golden yellow or bronze on the sides. The belly coloration varies from snow white to dusky yellow and is often bordered by bright

orange. Most species have three black to dusky bars on their sides; one has a prominent black stripe with 7 or 8 indistinct dusky bars; another species has 3 or 4 horizontal rows of white spots in addition to the three dusky vertical bars. All species possess a prominent ocellated black spot on the base of their caudal fins, which suggest the vivid eye of a peacock tail plume, hence the popular American name—peacock bass. The pelvic, anal, and lower half of the caudal fins are yellowish-green to brick red in color.

The dorsal fin and the upper half of the caudal fin are a translucent blue-green, sometimes with white spots. Some of the *Cichla* species are characterized by an interrupted lateral-line canal, while others have a continuous lateral line. The caudal fin is slightly rounded and completely scaled; the anal and pelvic fins are partially scaled. The peacock pavón attains weights up to 28 pounds or more, with the average in some Colombian streams running 5 to 6 pounds.

There are two common species of pavón in Colombia and possibly more in isolated streams along the Venezuelan border. The peacock pavón (locally pavón rayado, pavón cinchado, or tucunaré pintado) is indigenous to the Orinoco and upper Amazon watersheds in Colombia but since 1950 has been widely transplanted by the Ministry of Agriculture to lowland streams and farm ponds. Inland from the Pacific coast on the plateaus and higher river valleys is a well populated agricultural region extending northward from Popayán. The Popayán to Cali region probably represents the westernmost distribution of the peacock pavón although this species was stocked rather than native to the area. The second species common to Colombia is the butterfly pavón (locally pavón amarillo, pavón mariposa, or tucunaré común).

Pavón are caught with essentially the same lures and techniques used

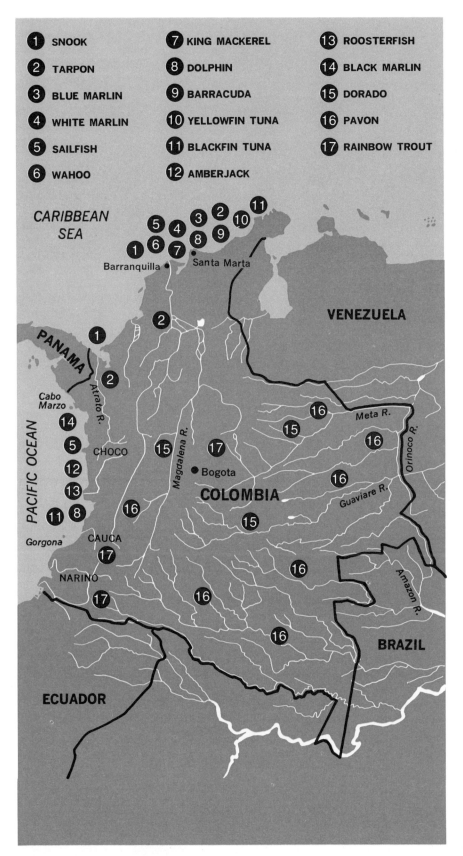

1 SNOOK
2 TARPON
3 BLUE MARLIN
4 WHITE MARLIN
5 SAILFISH
6 WAHOO
7 KING MACKEREL
8 DOLPHIN
9 BARRACUDA
10 YELLOWFIN TUNA
11 BLACKFIN TUNA
12 AMBERJACK
13 ROOSTERFISH
14 BLACK MARLIN
15 DORADO
16 PAVON
17 RAINBOW TROUT

CARIBBEAN SEA

Barranquilla
Santa Marta

VENEZUELA

PANAMA

Cabo Marzo

PACIFIC OCEAN

Atrato R.

CHOCO

Magdalena R.

Bogota

COLOMBIA

Meta R.

Orinoco R.

Guaviare R.

Gorgona

CAUCA

NARINO

Amazon R.

BRAZIL

ECUADOR

for North American black bass. During the dry, low water season when both forage and gamefish are concentrated in small areas, the sport can be phenomenal at times. In general, pavón feed sporadically and in the course of a day there will be bursts of action followed by lulls although large numbers of fish can be caught during the active periods. Pavón are strong fighters and leap repeatedly from the water when hooked. Pavón are a superior table fish and gourmet travelers rate them among the world's best.

Organized facilities in the primitive fishing regions of Colombia are extremely limited. There is a new fishing camp at Miraflores, less than three hours by air from Villavicencio and an additional hour by boat, the **El Dorado Lodge** (Adventure Associates, 301 Outdoors Building, Columbia, Missouri 65201) which offers excellent pavón fishing. This is a modern, fully equipped wilderness camp.

For a varied program, outfitter Kjell von Sneidern offers the choice of three different safaris, each of two weeks duration. Von Sneidern, a Swedish adventurer who came to Colombia in 1930, is an experienced angler and an authority on the country's wildlife. His trips are custom-tailored for one to five persons at $68.00 to $98.00 per day depending on the size of the group. The *South Colombia Safari* includes both tropical fishing and rainbow trout fishing; the *East Colombia Safari* is strictly tropical river fishing; his *North Colombia Safari* emphasizes tarpon and dorado fishing in the Magdalena watershed. For details contact *Safari De Colombia* (P.O. Box 557, Popayán, Colombia).

TROUT FISHING

There is some good trout fishing in Colombia. It is not comparable to the angling found in Chile and Argentina but the quality is above average—and can be uniquely combined with fishing for tropical species on the same trip. The most

The remote Meta River which flows through Colombia into neighboring Venezuela produces some excellent fishing in its headwaters

popular spot for trout is Lake Tota near Bogotá. Anglers headquarter at the **Hotel Rocas Lindas** (Allen Lowrie Travel Service, Apartado Aéreo 7262, Bogotá, Colombia). Tota produces fish in the over 10-pound class each season. Big rainbows are also taken in Lake Cocha near Pasto in the Department of Nariño, and in the streams near Popayán in the Department of Cauca.

TACKLE

There is little tackle available in Colombia and whether you plan an offshore trip or a safari into the jungle, it is necessary to bring appropriate gear. The usual equipment popular in U.S. saltwaters is suitable here. Freshwater anglers, however, are well advised to select somewhat heavier tackle than ordinarily used in river and lake fishing. Bait casting and spinning equipment in the 15-pound class should be the minimum. Many tropical species average quite large in size and are caught along densely wooded banks where snags are common. In addition, wire leaders (18-inch stainless steel coated with vinyl in 30-pound-test) provide needed protection from the various sharp-toothed gamefish. Bring plenty of lures; floating and sinking plugs, jigs, spoons, spinners, and bucktails, large streamers, and popping bugs for the fly rod.

TRAVEL NOTES

By Pan Am Jet 4½ hours from New York to Caracas, which is 1½ hours from Bogotá. Miami-Barranquilla 3¼ hours, Panamá to Bogotá nonstop 1¼ hours; Quito-Bogotá 1¼ hours; Panamá-Barranquilla 1 hour; Panamá-Medellín 45 minutes; New York-Cali 8¾ hours; Quito-Cali 50 minutes.

Need proof of citizenship, 2 photos and tourist card issued by Pan Am, and smallpox vaccination certificate. Commercial travelers may obtain business visas or transit cards. Ticket to a point outside Colombia also required.

Bus fare from El Dorado Airport into Bogotá (8 miles) is 2.50 pesos (14c); about U.S. $1.75 by taxi to the Tequendama Hotel. Luggage porters are tipped the equivalent of 25c to 30c for an average load, 10c to 15c for just one bag. International air departure tax is 75 pesos.

ACCOMMODATIONS

BOGOTÁ

Best in Bogotá is the **Hotel Tequendama,** which, like other Inter-Continental hotels, is beautifully equipped and operated by American standards. It has studio-type rooms with a view of mountains and city. Singles about $12-$16; doubles, $16-$20. The **Hotel Continental** is also new and good; from $8 single, $12 double. Small, but new and modern, are the **Cordillera, Bacata, Alexia, Comendador, Del Duc,** and **Presidente.** Also good: **Residencias Santa Fe** and **Santa Fe de Bogotá.** Hotel rates are subject to 5 percent tax, but no service charges are added.

BARRANQUILLA

El Prado Inter-Continental (About $9-$12 single, $12-$15 double), has a swimming pool and gorgeous gardens. Its *Patio Andaluz* night club is known for good food. The **Central, Riviera,** and **Caribana** are good, less expensive hotels. **Brande's** restaurant, **El Pez que Fuma, La Colonia,** and **Alfredo's** have European cuisines; **Chi Kong** is good for Chinese food. The **Yacht Club** has charter boats for the offshore fishing. The **Country Club** has an 18-hole golf course, swimming, tennis, and dining facilities.

SANTA MARTA

Only 15 minutes by air or 2½ hours by car from Barranquilla, Santa Marta is a year-round resort with a vast sandy beach lapped by the warm Caribbean Sea; an ideal spot for skin diving and fishing. Founded

A 12-pound dorado is large in Colombia

Santa Marta, located just 22 miles from the 19,000-foot snow-capped "Bolivar," has modern hotels and sun-bleached beaches

in 1525, Santa Marta is the site (3 miles from town) of a national shrine and museum containing the room where Simón Bolívar died in 1830. The new **Carib Inn,** a major resort, is expected to open in 1971. The **Hotel Tamaca** and **El Rodadero Motel** on Rodadero Beach, from $8 single, $12 double. The **Tayrona,** facing Santa Marta Bay, is from $5 single, $8 double. The **Irotama** and **Marlindo** hotels are also good. A gambling casino, near the beach, is set at the base of the spectacular Sierra Nevada mountains.

CARTAGENA

Only 20 minutes by air from Barranquilla is an old walled city which lies on a sandy peninsula. There are many interesting old buildings and fortifications dating from the 16th century, especially San Felipe fortress, the clock tower, and Fort Boca Chica. There is good swimming at Boca Grande Beach. The **Hotel del Caribe,** on this beach, is fine and so is the new **Hotel Americano,** which is on top of a gambling casino. The **Flamingo** and the small **Bahia** are also good. Rates are about $5.50 single, $8 to $10 double.

CALI

Cali is located in the rich Cauca Valley with altitude of 3,000 feet and pleasant year-round climate. The **Alférez Real** is on the Cali River; another first class hotel is the **Aristi;** both about $8 single, $12 double. Good restaurants are the **Martin Fierro** and **Don Carlos; Cali Viejo** for regional specialties. **Club Campestre de Cali** is the most important social center of Cali and among the best in Latin America. Among its attractions, an 18-hole golf course, nine tennis courts, a riding school, private lake for boating and fishing, and an Olympic-size swimming pool.

MEDELLÍN

This is the "second" city of Colombia situated about 150 miles northwest of Bogotá and has the climate of late spring. It is an industrial

The harbor of the oceanfront town of Santa Marta on the Caribbean is spacious and protected from the elements

center. The **Nutibara** is the leading hotel and compares with the best; from $7 single, $11 double. The **Medellín Country Club** has excellent food, golf courses, tennis courts, and swimming pool. (Invitation by a member required.)

MANIZALES

Built on a ridge of the Cordillera Central at an altitude of 7,062 feet, Manizales is a comfortably cool city, an important coffee center. The people are extremely hospitable. Every tourist is welcomed with a free bottle of *Ron Caldas.* The city goes in big for fiestas and corridas de toros.

LANGUAGE

Spanish, with native Indian dialects in isolated areas. However, English is spoken in city hotels and the tourist will have no difficulty in making himself understood.

Costa Rica

Giant palms are backdrop as anglers cast for tarpon on Parismina River

Guy de la Valdene bills fly rod trophy

Big snook enter the rivers in September

Costa Rica is a new frontier, and though comparatively few facilities exist for the sportsman, it can provide exceptional Pacific sailfish and tarpon angling. The country is made extremely diverse by its geography; broadly speaking, the Atlantic or Caribbean side of Costa Rica consists of rain forests and mangrove swamps but inland it varies from deciduous woodlands and savannas to alpine and semiarid (xeroptic) terrain. It can be pleasantly cold on a Costa Rican trout stream yet tropically hot on a coastal tarpon river just a hundred miles away. This second smallest country in Central America probably has the greatest variety of fishing contained within a land area of 19,652 square miles.

Here you can find the jungle rivers of the Caribbean coastal plain plus an offshore fishery for Atlantic big-game species, high mountain streams cold enough to support trout, and the tidal rivers of the Pacific coast at lower elevation and its offshore fishery.

Although there is no winter or summer season in the Temperate Zone sense, it is important to plan a Costa Rican visit between December and the middle of May. The mountains (one volcanic peak reaches 11,322 feet) in part determine the rainfall, which can make fishing impossible in either Atlantic or Pacific shore rivers. During the wet season they become extremely muddy. However, in offshore fishing where turbidity is not a factor, the prevailing winds must be taken into account and the better period for moderate seas is from April through September. The mean annual temperature in Costa Rica varies from 80°F. in the low areas to 59°F. at 5,000-foot altitude.

ATLANTIC SIDE

The principal gamefish on the Caribbean shore of Costa Rica is the tarpon. All the fishing is done within rivers or their estuaries which flow clear from January through April. Large runs of tarpon enter freshwater during that period, notably in the Parismina River and its tributaries (the Cabo Blanco, Cabo Negro, the California River and Tarpon Creek). The tarpon range from 20 to over 100 pounds with progressively larger fish entering the rivers until the peak period in April and May. The average weights are uniformly high with 50- to 70-pound tarpon

A sailfish leaps against mountain backdrop on the Gulf of Papagayo. Peak fishing occurs in July

common. The fish are taken primarily by trolling and plug casting, or casting leadhead bucktails; due to the depth of these coastal rivers fly fishing has only a sporadic success. Snook also occur in weights exceeding 20 pounds although not in great number except at the river mouths and in the surf which is generally muddy. However, there is an excellent run of large (25- to 35-pound) snook in the Colorado River in late September.

Other good tarpon rivers are the Colorado River and its tributaries near the border of Nicaragua, and the Frío River and its tributaries which drain into Lake Nicaragua. Like the Parismina, these are sparsely settled jungle streams. There are accommodations on the Colorado River at Barra del

Colorado but no facilities on the Frío. The San Juan River, which in part forms the northern border of Costa Rica, offers good tarpon fishing at the rapids near El Castillo in Nicaragua. Although the rapids are 70-odd water miles inland, sharks follow the migrating tarpon right up the San Juan and can "apple-core" a hooked fish if you don't work them fast—or get lucky.

There are several small freshwater gamefish endemic to these same river systems such as the guapote, mojarra, and machaca. Of these, the machaca is probably the most interesting from the angler's point of view; it feeds to a large extent on seed pods that fall from jungle trees. The pods can be simulated with a small (No. 4) plastic or cork-bodied bass bug by slapping the

lure on the surface. School oriented and therefore greedy at the strike, a machaca moves swiftly and hits the lure hard. Machaca seldom weigh more than 4 pounds but provide wonderful action on a light fly rod or spinning rod. They are usually found in quiet places under overhanging trees along the river banks.

PACIFIC SIDE
The Pacific coast of Costa Rica offers excellent sailfish, wahoo, and roosterfish, and an abundance of dolphin. Occasional black and striped marlin also occur. Sailfish are numerous, particularly in the Gulf of Papagayo on the northern end of the Pacific coast; here thirty-five strikes per day (in July) is a recorded average. Rustic accommodations exist at Bahía del Coco,

west of Liberia, which can be reached by rental car from San José. Check San José tackle shop on availability of charter boats in this area. The only established Pacific coast camp is located near Palmar Sur in the southern portion of the coast. Here, a twin-diesel craft is available.

The west coast rivers (which only run clear during March and April) such as the Tarcoles and Terraba are fished for black snook, corvina, various snappers, jacks, and jewfish. Black snook up to 64½ pounds have been caught. Trolling with deep-running plugs is the commonly used method.

TROUT FISHING

Unknown to most tourists is the trout fishing which exists in Costa Rica. Both rainbows and browns have been introduced to many rivers flowing at high altitude and only a very limited angling pressure exists. Fish of 2 to 4 pounds are fairly common. There is good fishing in the Savegre, Macho, Poas, and Coto Brus Rivers. The latter has produced rainbows up to 9 pounds in weight. The closed season for trout is from November through February with the best period for fly fishing and spinning from April into June.

TACKLE

A heavy-duty spinning or bait casting rod is preferred for the tarpon rivers on the Caribbean side. Trolling with large (1- to 2-ounce) plugs is the most effective method and most anglers use 20- to 30-pound-test monofilament lines and 30- to 40-pound-test wire leaders. Naturally, more experienced fishermen will go lighter. Leadhead bucktails of 1 to 2 ounces in white and yellow are frequently effective; best lure for snook is the Creek Chub Darter in yellow. Although these waters, like most inland rivers, are not ideal for fly fishing, you may want to try it, in which case a 9-foot fly rod calibered for No. 11 floating and sinking lines is recommended.

Illinois angler Don Dobbins admires 132 pound tarpon caught in Colorado River

The same spinning or bait casting outfit can be used on the Pacific shore for casting and trolling, but suitable big-game tackle is necessary for offshore work (4/0 to 6/0 reel, 20- to 30-pound-test line, and a 9- to 12-ounce rod.)

There is a well stocked tackle shop in San José where all replacement items can be obtained. Tackle and lures purchased in Costa Rica are approximately 20 to 30 percent higher than in the United States due to high import duties.

LICENSES

No license is required for saltwater fishing. A license is required for freshwater (trout) fishing obtainable at the Ministerio de Agricultura, Calle 1, Avenidas Central and First, Marshall Building. Must present a valid passport or tourist card and two passport-size photos. Fee $10 U.S.

CLOTHING

The climate in San José (altitude 3,000 feet) is pleasant and medium-weight clothing is comfortable. In the coastal fishing areas the weather is usually hot, and here light-weight clothing is more suitable. In the mountains at trout stream elevations it can be cool and a warm sweater or jacket is advisable. Be sure to bring rain gear as heavy but brief rains are common to the subtropics.

TRAVEL NOTES

Costa Rica is serviced by Pan American Jet Clipper from San Francisco, Los Angeles, Houston, New Orleans, and Miami. Rental cars are available in San José. Light aircraft can be chartered for remote points such as the Parismina River or Colorado River. A domestic airline, buses, and a railroad connect a few major cities outside of San José.

ACCOMMODATIONS

There are several good hotels in the capital city of San Jose such as the **Gran Hotel Costa Rica,** the **Gran Hotel Europa,** and the **Royal Dutch.** Generally speaking, the rates are low to moderate ($8 to $12 single and $11 to $12 double).

Accommodations for fishing are relatively scarce:

PARISMINA

The **Parismina Tarpon Rancho,** not fancy but a perfectly adequate camp which accommodates twelve guests in six clean, twin-bedded rooms; each has running water, showers, and electricity. Good food with bottled or purified water. Located at mouth of Parismina River and accessible by small aircraft from San José ($45 round trip). Rates at camp are $50 per day per person when two persons share same boat; $65 per day when one person fishes one boat. For reservations: Sr. Carlos Barrantes, Parismina Tarpon Rancho, P.O. Box 2816, San José, Costa Rica (telephone 22-14-70).

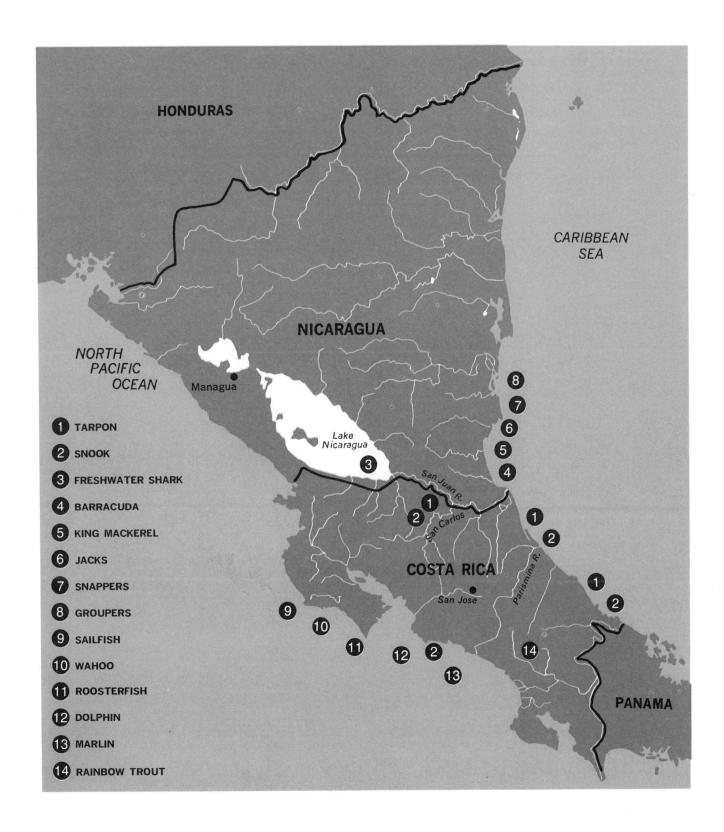

HONDURAS

CARIBBEAN
SEA

NICARAGUA

NORTH
PACIFIC
OCEAN

Managua

Lake
Nicaragua

③

⑧

⑦

⑥

⑤

④

San Juan R.

① TARPON

② SNOOK

③ FRESHWATER SHARK

④ BARRACUDA

⑤ KING MACKEREL

⑥ JACKS

⑦ SNAPPERS

⑧ GROUPERS

⑨ SAILFISH

⑩ WAHOO

⑪ ROOSTERFISH

⑫ DOLPHIN

⑬ MARLIN

⑭ RAINBOW TROUT

①

②

San Carlos

①

②

COSTA RICA

San Jose

Parismina R.

①

②

⑨

⑩

⑪

⑫

②

⑬

⑭

PANAMA

BARRA DEL COLORADO

The **Casa Mar Fishing Club** consists of large comfortable cabins set apart from the main lodge, each with two twin-bedded rooms and private baths. Overlooks the Laguna Agua Dulce. Accessible from San José by small aircraft ($100 round trip). Rates at club are $50 per day per person when two persons share same boat; $65 per day when one person fishes one boat. For reservations: Sr. Carlos Barrantes, Casa Mar Fishing Club, P.O. Box 2816, San José, Costa Rica (telephone 22-14-70)

PALMAR SUR

The **Rancho Estero Azul** (Blue River Lodge) operated by American Jerry Thornhill is located on the Pacific side of Costa Rica. Special 7-day all-expense trip as low as $195 per person including room, meals, boat, and guides. The fishing here is for snook, corvina, roosterfish, sailfish and marlin. For reservations: Jerry Thornhill, c/o LACSA Airlines, Palmar Sur, Costa Rica, or Drawer 1780, Lexington, Kentucky 40500; telephone Area Code 606 252-0391.

LANGUAGE AND PEOPLE

The official language is Spanish. Some English, French, Italian, German, Portuguese, and Dutch is spoken on the commercial and cultural levels but the tourist is well advised to bring along a Spanish dictionary, particularly when traveling in the back country.

The population of Costa Rica is mainly of Spanish descent, and 95 percent is of the white race. Of the aborigines that were inhabitants of the territory during the Pre-Columbian Era, there remain only, 2,000 Indians distributed in small tribes to the south in the Cordillera de Talamanca, the Valley of the Dui close to the Panama frontier, on the marginal regions of the Frío River in the north of the country and the headwaters of the Terraba and Coto in the south.

Jungle cabin at Casa Mar Fishing Club

Ecuador

A great fishing country which until recently had no first-class facilities for sportsmen. Located on the northwest coast of South America, Ecuador is tropical along the sea coast but cool in its snow-capped mountains. Quito, the City of Eternal Spring, at 9,248 feet elevation is also the second highest capital in the world (next to La Paz, Bolivia) and its temperatures average in the mid-50's. The great banana port of Guayaquil, a key city in Ecuador travel, is about 60 miles inland from the ocean on the Guayas River and is usually hot and humid. The coastal area does not have the distinct wet and dry seasons that one normally expects in the tropics, but there are variations. During December through April the Humboldt Current swings further out from the coast and the days are usually bright and cloudless. This is summer here. During the remainder of the year this cool current flows closer to shore and frequently produces a cloud cover, but no rain.

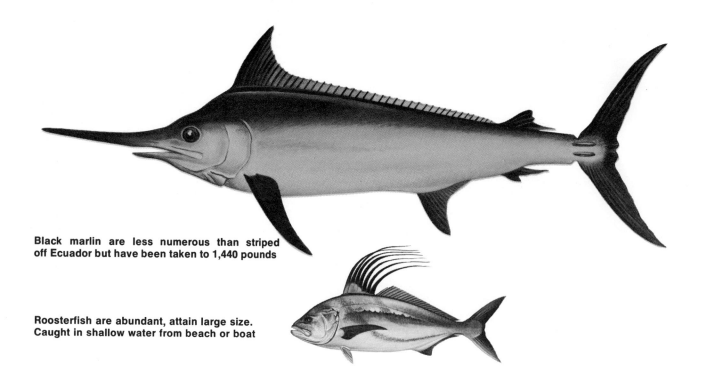

Black marlin are less numerous than striped off Ecuador but have been taken to 1,440 pounds

Roosterfish are abundant, attain large size. Caught in shallow water from beach or boat

SALTWATER FISHING

The principal species taken off Ecuador are the black marlin, striped marlin, swordfish, Pacific blue marlin, wahoo, big-eye tuna, sailfish, roosterfish, yellowfin tuna, dolphin, mako shark, sierra mackerel, amberjack, albacore, white sea bass, and corvina. All standard methods of big-game angling are used here. Trolling is fundamental and the billfish are usually sighted rather than fished blind. The Humboldt Current, which has followed a rather erratic path to the south off Peru in recent years, shows more stability off Ecuador and the fishing grounds are reached in less than an hour's run. There is a good fleet of 28- to 34-foot boats at Punta Carnero.

Current and weather conditions being compatible, it's commonplace to see twenty to thirty striped marlin in the 120- to 160-pound class in a day. The larger black marlin (local record 1,440 pounds) are less abundant but in hot periods a half dozen blacks will be seen finning-out just beyond the next set of seas. Swordfish are numerous about 30 miles south of Punta Carnero. Predicting the whims and feeding variations of these billfish becomes an obsession; one local theory is that there is a current reversal approximately every ten days and when the water is flowing north the fishing peaks.

Inshore light-tackle fishing here is typical of the western coast of South America. It is accomplished primarily with skiffs and outboard powered dugouts casting to the rocks and along sandy beaches. Roosterfish, groupers, snappers, jacks, corvina, and snook are the chief targets and tend to run to larger sizes. Casting with bottom-bouncing feathers and jigs usually produces action.

Despite the glamour of billfishing, one of the stellar attractions in Ecuador is the roosterfish. Roosterfish (locally *papagallo* or *pez de gallo*) range from Cabo Blanco, Peru, north into the Gulf of California and up the western coast of Baja California to Turtle Bay. However, they appear in greatest numbers off the coast of Ecuador. The maximum size recorded is a specimen 5 feet, 2 inches in length, weighing 111 pounds. Roosterfish are exciting gamefish, being strong runners and occasionally jumping when hooked. When swimming at the surface they often "flash the comb" by erecting the long spines of the first dorsal fin out of the water. This species is found along sandy beaches in the surf and offshore to moderate depths. It is a fine light-tackle fish usually taken by trolling with spoons, feathers and plugs (large red-and-white Mirrolure is an effective artificial).

THE SEASON

Black marlin appear to be most plentiful from May through October, but blue and striped marlin are more numerous from November through April with the peak on stripes from February through April. Wahoo are taken most frequently in the fall, tuna appear in the winter, and sailfish, swordfish, and dolphin are plentiful at all seasons. If there is an "edge," the December through April period is prime. At this season the sea is very calm, the sun is bright, and marlin are easier to spot. Fishing is always good in these waters, however.

TACKLE

All tackle for offshore trolling is supplied by the charter craft. For inshore casting from outboard powered skiffs bring a standard saltwater spinning or bait casting rod; if you plan to fish from the beach, a 9- to 12-foot surf rod with either a spinning reel or multiplier is advisable.

FRESHWATER FISHING

There is quality trout fishing in the high lakes of the Andes around Quito. The introduced fish are rainbow and cutthroat hybrids which have been planted in waters at 9,000 to 13,000 feet altitude. Trout 4 to 6 pounds are not uncommon. Colonel Sam Hogan (retired U.S.A.) operates a tour from Quito via Land Rover

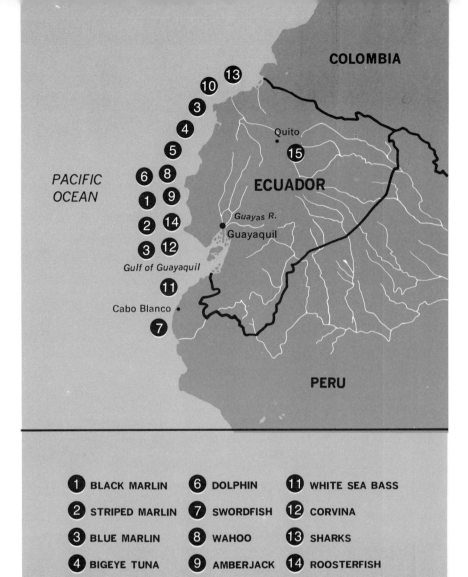

①	BLACK MARLIN	⑥	DOLPHIN	⑪	WHITE SEA BASS
②	STRIPED MARLIN	⑦	SWORDFISH	⑫	CORVINA
③	BLUE MARLIN	⑧	WAHOO	⑬	SHARKS
④	BIGEYE TUNA	⑨	AMBERJACK	⑭	ROOSTERFISH
⑤	SAILFISH	⑩	ALBACORE	⑮	RAINBOW TROUT

and horseback into the *altoplano* using tent camps as a base. Boats, motors, and guides are available where necessary. The cost varies according to the size of the party (about $400 per week for one person or $300 per week for one person in a party of four). For reservations contact: *Safaris Ecuatorianos C. A.,* (P.O. Box 122, Quito, Ecuador, South America) or its U.S. representative *Adventure Associates,* (301 Outdoors Building, Columbia, Missouri 65201; Area Code 314 449-0038).

ACCOMMODATIONS

QUITO

Luxurious **Hotel Quito,** with spectacular view of the Andes, has swim-

ming pool, night club, gambling casino, coffee shop and elegant dining room. Single from $8, double from $12. **Hotel Humboldt,** centrally located, has singles from $5.75, doubles from $10. **Hotel Savoy,** also central, has rates from $4 single, $7 double. The **Colon,** 10 minutes from the center of town, has a friendly atmosphere and very good food. Rates from $6 single, $11 double, including American-type breakfast. American Plan rates available, too. The **Embajador,** 12 minutes from the center of town, has comfortable rooms and good service. Rates from $5 single, $14 double, European Plan. The **Majestic** and **Crillon** are commercial hotels in the center of Quito. All hotel bills are subject to 10 percent service charges and 10 percent tax.

GUAYAQUIL

The **Humboldt International Hotel** on the riverfront offers rooms with private balconies, and there's a swimming pool. Rates from $5 single, $9 double, European Plan. The new **Palace Hotel** is in the center of the city, is air conditioned and has good dining facilities. The **Hotel Continental** near the heart of the city is modern and comfortable, good food. Other hotels are the **Majestic** and **Crillon.** There are several good restaurants, including **Salon Rex** and **La Maison Doree.**

PLAYAS

Beach resort 60 miles from Guayaquil. The **Hotel Humboldt** here has rates from $7.25 single, and from $10 double, European Plan. You may swim in the sea or in a pool. There is deep-sea fishing in the Humboldt Current. Guests have Shangri-la Golf and Country Club privileges, and use of all sports equipment.

SALINAS

About 90 miles from Guayaquil, this beach resort has the air conditioned **Hotel Miramar.** There are the *Yacht Club* and *Club de Pesca* with boats for deep-sea fishing. Horse racing every Sunday at the Hipodromo from February to April, which is also the rainy season.

PUNTA CARNERO

A mecca for anglers the one million dollar glass-and-marble **Carnero Inn** (80 miles from Guayaquil) is hosted by Ramon Fernandez. An olympic-sized beauty is carved out of the Carnero cliff overlooking the frothy swells dashing into the rocks below. This facility offers an opportunity for swimming, sunning, and sightseeing all in one place. Rooms are spacious, beautiful. Each features a private balcony with an ocean view, a carpeted floor, telephone, all of the conveniences you would expect to find in a new U.S. hotel. Several suites are available at increased cost above regular package prices.

Food is delightful at **Carnero Inn.** Lobsters, stone crabs, oysters, fillet mignon, crepes suzette, and other palate ticklers. Sensibly, breakfast is served early enough to allow fishermen to get to their boats before 8:00 a.m. and the dining room remains open until 10:00 p.m. Special package rates are in effect and special rates are available for children. Carnero Inn, (Box 5013, Guayaquil, Ecuador. U.S. Reservations Office— Box 16512, Oklahoma City, Okla. 73116. Tel (405) 843-7235)
Special packages include the following:

7-DAY BIG-GAME SPECIAL $368
For the serious big game angler who desires to devote his time exclusively to the pursuit of big billfish. Package includes Customs assistance, round-trip transfers from the Guayaquil airport, six nights accommodations, all meals, and five full days fishing with cruiser, crew, bait and tackle furnished. (Price is based on two anglers sharing one boat.)

An 8-pound bonito is just right for black marlin bait in Ecuador

7 DAYS INSHORE FISHING $206
Light tackle action with roosterfish, snook, corvina, mackerel, and a variety of other saltwater gamesters. The package includes assistance through Customs, round-trip transfers, six nights accommodations, all meals, and five days fishing inshore waters with boat, motor, and guide furnished. (Tackle is not furnished. Price is based upon two anglers sharing same boat.)

7 DAYS COMBINATION $272
The most popular fishing package. Offers a chance to battle big billfish and sample the fast-paced light-tackle fishing that Carnero waters offer. Includes Customs assistance, round-trip transfers, six nights accommodations, all meals, two days offshore fishing with cruiser, crew, bait and tackle furnished, and three days inshore fishing with boat and guide furnished. (Tackle not included for inshore portion. Price based upon two men sharing the same boat.)

5-DAY PACKAGES
(4) Big Game $264
(5) Inshore $156
(includes everything in 1, 2, and 3 except only four nights' accommodations and three days' fishing.)

NON-FISHING RATES
(6) 7 Days $140
(7) 5 Days $100
(wife rate for two-couple party with men sharing cost of fishing boats.)

LANGUAGE
Spanish with a little English spoken in resort centers. Between 10 and 15 percent of the people are white of Spanish blood, with some Central European refugees; the remaining 2,000,000 are Indian Mestizo, Negro or mulatto. There are also a few Asiatics.

England

The Pheasant Inn at Bassenthwaite caters to anglers fishing the Derwent River

Trout in the fluvarium at the Mill

Dermot Wilson with a typical day's catch on the dry fly from the Itchen

This is where it all began. In the 17th century, Izaac Walton, the Father of fishermen, sat by the River Dove finding solace not in some imaginary world, but in the real world of the waterside. His words, penned over 300 years ago, are relevant to our times, for his England knew a Civil War, one of the Great Plagues, the Great Fire of London, the Execution of Charles the First—yet this simple and gentle man advised the world "to study to be quiet and go a-fishing." Fishing, of course, is the framework for Walton's philosophy. While he wrote of silver streams that "glide merrily by"—a sight that "possessed my soul with content," his book, *The Compleat Angler,* not only reveals the mystique of fishing but its philosophy.

England's wealth of angling lore is universally recognized. The birthplace of Izaac Walton is symbolized by centuries of literature pertaining to salmon and trout, and, technically, England still produces some of the finest tackle in the world. The art of fly fishing was developed here, and ever since the publication of Dame Juliana Berners' *The Book of St. Albans* in 1496, British authors have figured prominently in the establishment of now common

practices—dry-fly-fishing, nymph-fishing and the fixed-spool reel, to mention a few historic innovations.

Angling in England, or at least quality angling, is not easy to obtain. Yet, the visitor can enjoy excellent sport at times particularly for brown trout and sea trout through many of the country hotels, associations, and private individuals who have rights on the better streams.

ATLANTIC SALMON

Atlantic salmon occur in most of the faster flowing streams. Starting at the northeast border with Scotland, salmon appear in a number of rivers south to the Whitby Esk. However, from this point down to Southampton the rivers are either too slow-flowing and lack the gravel necessary for reproduction, or they are too polluted. From Southampton westward through the West Country (Somerset, Devon, and Cornwall), through Wales and the northwest coast up to the Scottish border, most of the rivers have a salmon run. The most famous in the south are the Avon, Itchen, Test, and Frome. Although these chalk streams are better known as trout rivers, in some places they are

dammed to prevent the salmon from ascending too high and therefore maintain separate fisheries. In the west, the Exe, Dart, Teign, Tamar, Tavy, Taw, Torridge, Severn, and Wye are best known; in the northwest, the Ribble, Lune, Edem, Derwent, and Border Esk are popular. In the northeast, the Tweed, Coquet, and Whitby Esk are major salmon rivers. Boats can be rented on some streams, and the country hotel which offers fishing to its guests is very much a British institution. Most of the hotels are well run and provide good accommodations. Some clubs and associations issue tickets for days and longer periods.

Salmon vary greatly in size in England. On the Wye and Avon, for example, one or two 40-pound fish are

One of the world's most historical trout rivers, the Itchen flows near the city where Izaac Walton is buried

caught each season. In the West Country the fish run much smaller, and a 15-pound salmon is considered a good fish. The season differs slightly from river to river, opening as early as January and ending as late as November. Normally, it extends from mid-February to the end of October. Fly-fishing is, of course, the traditional method of taking salmon. A big wet fly is fished early in the year and a smaller wet fly at season's end. The greased-line method is popular during the warm weeks of summer. The dry fly is little used and is generally conceded to be ineffective. Experiments have shown that salmon can be caught on dry flies in Great Britain but not with consistent results.

Unlike Canada, where salmon fishing is restricted to the fly only, any sporting method can be employed in the British Isles with local and seasonal exceptions. Spinning (a collective term in Great Britain which encompasses bait-casting) is permitted, and the spoon, plug, and devon minnow are commonly used in high cold water and particularly when the rivers are roily after a rain. The worm, shrimp, and prawn are also legal in some streams.

SEA TROUT
The sea trout is one of the world's great gamefish, and fortunately it's not difficult to obtain good angling for these migratory browns in England. Many hotels and clubs own water where the visiting angler can purchase day or week tickets. Furthermore, the angler is not as dependent on the right water conditions for sea trout as he is for salmon.

Sea trout forage on Britian's coastal waters, and grow to a substantial size. They enter most rivers to spawn beginning as early as March. However, the main run commences in June or July and extends to October. Although some sea trout are caught in the slow rivers of the south and east, the best fishing is in the West Country on rivers like the Tavy and the Torridge and the streams of the northwest. Many fish run 3 to 10 pounds although the majority are in the 1- to 2-pound class.

Sea trout are caught by all methods but fly fishing is the more interesting game. These are shy fish, and they feed primarily at night. Consequently, fishing after dark is most effective. A warm night provides the best sport. Sea trout are difficult to catch during daylight hours except in discolored water. They take dry flies and wet flies, as well as spinners and live bait. Favorite sea-trout fly patterns are the Black Pennel, Peter Ross, Mallard and Claret, and Silver March Brown. On some rivers the Demons and Terrors (two- and three-hooked feather lures) are very effective. During the day, spinning with a 6 to 7 foot rod and 4-pound-test line using a small spoon or devon is considered a sporting way of taking these fish.

BROWN TROUT
The native trout of the British Isles is the brown trout. This species is found all over England, and like the salmon and sea trout it prefers fast-water and is most plentiful in the hilly regions. Rainbow trout have been introduced, but apart from a few rivers like the Wye in Derbyshire and the Chess near London this species has only thrived in lakes and reservoirs. Perhaps the most famous brown-trout fishing in England is in the southern chalk streams, particularly in the counties of Hampshire, Wiltshire, Dorset, Berkshire, and parts of East Anglia and Yorkshire. These are extremely clear, spring-

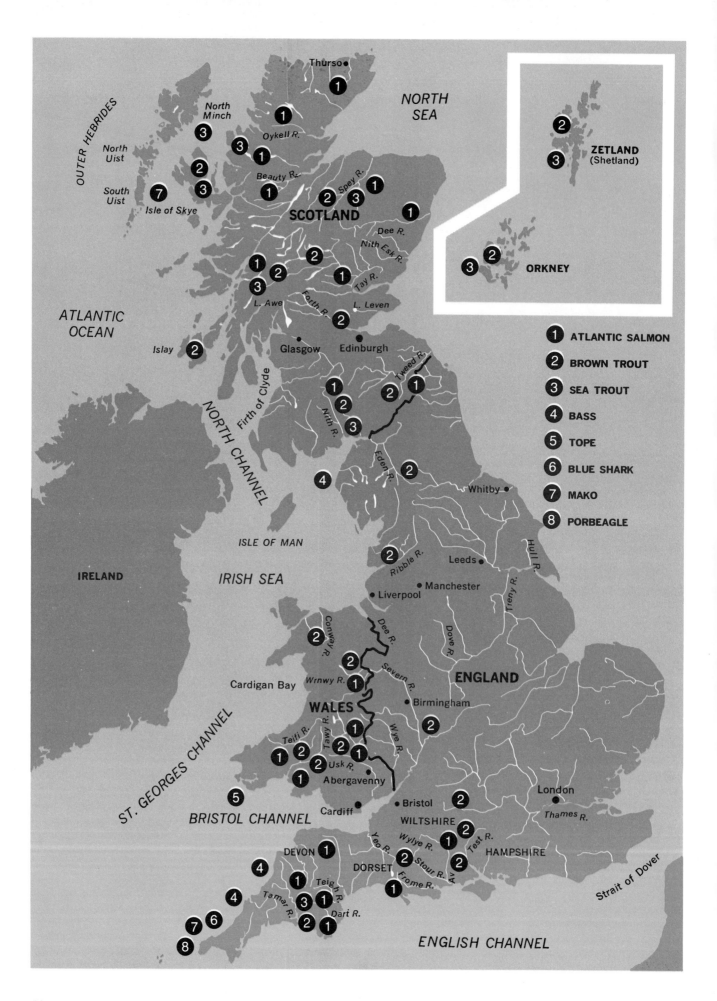

ATLANTIC SALMON
BROWN TROUT
SEA TROUT
BASS
TOPE
BLUE SHARK
MAKO
PORBEAGLE

fed rivers which originate in chalk hills and are therefore highly alkaline. Their water-plant growth is both fast and dense, and such rivers are very fertile. Under these ideal conditions trout grow rapidly and are free rising. A 2-pound average is not unusual on some streams, and trout of 4 pounds or more remain surface feeders. On a carefully managed river such as the Test, big trout come freely to the dry fly. Although the Test fishing of world fame is wholly private (the Houghton Club), it is a classic example of a controlled fishery. The annual catch on the club's 14 miles of stream exceeds 15,000 fish averaging 2½ pounds. The Test is stocked with both brown and rainbow trout which have been selectively bred for fast growth. As on all productive chalk streams, systematic weed cutting is essential to maintaining a flow through the stream channels which are the important lies of the trout. The vegetation holds vast quantities of insect life as well as freshwater shrimp and snails. Among the best trout streams in England are the Test, Itchen, Ribble, Avon, Kennet, Dove, Wye, Derwent, Wharfe, Lune, and Eden.

Reservoir fishing is also very popular in England. Many of the public-utility reservoirs are stocked with browns and rainbows. In such habitats their rate of growth is often rapid, and the condition of the fish is uniformly excellent. At Chew Reservoir, for example, near Bristol, 3-pound trout are common, and some 5- to 6-pound trout are caught each year. This fishing is available in many parts of England on a day ticket basis.

Hotel fishing is the principal means available to the tourist for angling in the British Isles. The tradition and business of offering fishing rights to guests, or in some cases making day tickets available, is highly satisfactory, and good sport can be obtained. Hotel fishing is mainly for brown trout, sea trout, and Atlantic salmon. The cream of English trout

Wallop Brook, a tributary of the Test, produces large trout in late summer

fishing in the chalk-stream counties of Hampshire and Wiltshire is virtually all in private hands; however, the **Bull Hotel** on the Avon at Downton, near Salisbury, yields some good trout fishing during the mayfly season, and any student of fly fishing will certainly enjoy **The Mill** at Nether Wallop.

A CHALK STREAM SAMPLER

Author Dermot Wilson who lives at the village with that unlikely name Nether Wallop (and there *is* an Over Wallop), provides one of the most unique fishing vacations in the British Isles. In the heart of the Hampshire chalk stream country, Mr. Wilson makes his headquarters at an old mill which is recorded in the Domesday Book and sits on a tributary of the River Test, only a mile or two from the water Halford used to fish. On the Itchen Mr. Wilson has two stretches of water near Winchester, the cathedral city where Izaac Walton is buried; one section is just above the water Skues fished and just below Lord Grey's fishing cottage. The other stretch is one of the three little streams that form the headwaters of the Itchen. This is all dry fly water with wild trout. The choice of fishing is considerable:

1. *Itchen.* A short stretch of the main Itchen, and also a small side stream branching off it and some adjoining river. This is famous water, and

holds a large number of wild trout. They are not huge—ranging between 1 pound and 2 pounds—but they are the best-shaped fish, the tastiest on the table, and probably the most difficult to catch.

2. *Itchen-source stream.* About a mile of this. It is a tiny stream, completely wild and unspoiled. The trout are very free-rising and some are extremely large. Wilson's best fish here, a record for the Itchen, was 7 pounds 1 ounce, caught in July. The stream produces trophy fish nearly every season and has the advantage of fishing well in hot weather, since it is fed by many cool springs.

3. *Test tributary.* This is the stream where the mill is located. The trout are perhaps the readiest of all to rise. Large fish are in the minority during the spring, but there are plenty of trout of 1 pound or so. The bigger fish appear from mid-summer onwards, and the mill race is a sure spot for them.

4. *Other Test beats.* Wilson can take you to fish on other good Test beats. They are all in private hands but the necessary arrangements will be made for you. There are a number of beats, including stretches adjoining the renowned Houghton Club water at Stockbridge. They are stocked with both brown and rainbow trout, usually running rather larger than the wild fish up to 4 pounds and over.

5. *Upper Wallop Mill Lake.* This is a

lake on the Wilson property. It is full of the wild brown trout, and is also stocked with rainbows and a 7-pounder was caught here in 1969.

At the mill you can see and study a full-scale stream "fluvarium" which reveals all the life of the river. Here in glass tanks, everything that goes on under the water is brought into full view and magnified. You will see the aquatic plants and all the tiny water creatures that go to make a chalk stream trout so pink and portly and fast-to-grow. You can study the aquatic insects in their natural habitat and see plenty of trout. The Freshwater Biological Association of Britain helped build this, and it is said to be the only installation of its kind.

The cost varies from $70 to $100 per day per person; the charge is made according to the time of year and the type of accommodation selected. The price covers fishing, the ghillie, room, breakfast, lunch, and local transportation and all other fishing needs. It includes the loan of any tackle you need. You are, of course, welcome to bring your own, but Wilson can supply anything you lack. He can also supply rubber boots and rainwear (though no other clothing). Most people use 8- to 9-foot rods on the chalk streams, but he can fit you out with lighter tackle if you prefer it, down to midge rods. If by any chance you feel you would like instruction in either casting or fishing, there's no extra charge.

Out of the charge you will become a member for one year of the Test and Itchen Fly Fishing Association. This association does very good work for the preservation of fishing on Britain's most famous chalk streams. Your membership will entitle you to be sent all its publications and news.

Wilson feels he cannot do justice to his guests if he tries to entertain too many. You are very welcome by yourself, or with a maximum of two friends. Accommodations can be had three miles away in Stockbridge

at a pleasant little hotel called **The Sheriff House Hotel.** The drawing room was once the cell of the local jail. A side stream of the Test (with trout on view but fishing is not allowed) flows through the garden. The rooms are simple but all have showers. Another hotel in Stockbridge is a typical British pub called **The Greyhound.** It has a good cuisine and cheerful atmosphere. Also in Stockbridge is **The Grosvenor Arms.** This hotel is headquarters for the Houghton Club, and is pleasantly quiet. The Houghton Club have first priority on bookings.

For real comfort, in a luxury hotel, Wilson can arrange for rooms with bath, or for a suite, at the **Wessex Hotel** in Winchester. It is eleven miles from The Mill but it's the most modern hotel in the district.

For reservations (from April 1st to September 30th) write: Dermot Wilson, The Mill, Nether Wallop, Hampshire, England.

OTTER RIVER
The River Otter is midway in character between the rough rivers of western England and the limpid chalk streams of the counties to the east. Both banks are fairly open, and

the water is relatively clear. There is some weed growth, and fairly good hatches of mayflies occur, especially in spring and in September. Spent spinners and dusk-hatching caddisflies may also give rise to good sport in the evenings. Knee boots are usually adequate for the Otter.

Headquarters here is the **Deer Park Hotel** (Deer Park Hotel, Honiton, South Devon). This hotel, standing in its own spacious grounds, controls both banks of three miles of the River Otter. The beats are all easily accessible, the nearest being only 150 yards from the hotel itself, and car parking is available downstream, just off the busy main road from London to the west. This water has been closely preserved for sixty years as a brown trout fishery. Dry fly only is the rule, and the number of rods is strictly limited. The river is restocked annually. Detailed records of catches are available for inspection in the fishing register, which shows that baskets average ¾-pound and that a number of 2- to 3-pound trout are taken each season. This weight is much above the usual average for west-country waters.

In the lush weed growth of a chalk stream such as the Kennet an abundance of aquatic food makes trout selective

Part of Wilson's Chalk Stream Sampler is the Itchen source stream which holds many large wild brown trout

TAMAR RIVER

The Tamar River rises in Cornwall and empties into Plymouth Sound. Although the fishing is primarily for brown trout, it also yields some sea trout and the occasional salmon. A popular location for the Tamar is **Arundell Arms Hotel** (Lifton, West Devon) which has 18 miles of fishing rights with 20 individual beats. Chest-high waders are desirable for salmon fishing on the Tamar.

For trout the rule is fly only, both dry and wet fly being employed. The hotel issues a handy booklet describing each beat in detail, together with fishing methods recommended for each. The water is not over-fished, and on most stretches there are plenty of trout of varying size. The hotel also owns a lake which is stocked with rainbow trout. A resident fishing instructor gives lessons in fly tying. Fishing begins in mid-March and is usually good right from the start of the season.

Cornwall River Board licenses are available at the hotel. Day tickets may occasionally be available.

TORRIDGE RIVER

The Torridge rises near the Cornish border of Devonshire and joins the Taw estuary. It is an excellent salmon, sea trout, and brown trout stream. The upper Torridge valley is rich in bird life, and in spring wild flowers bloom profusely along the river banks. Fishing begins in mid-March and continues to the end of September; March to mid-May are the best salmon months with sea trout running from July to September. For brown trout fishing try the **Woodford Bridge Hotel** (Woodford Bridge Hotel, Milton Damerel, North Devon). This delightful, thatched hotel, standing in its own beautiful gardens, has 4 miles of brown-trout fishing on the upper reaches of the River Torridge. Though small, trout are plentiful and fight hard in relation to their size. Fly only is the rule, and the dry fly is generally rewarding. Upstream nymph-fishing pays good dividends during the daytime in summer. There are plenty of 9- to 10-inch fish above and below the bridge. Daily catches are recorded in the fishing register, and it is the cus-

tom for good baskets to be displayed in the hotel in the evening.

For salmon and sea trout fishing the **Half Moon Inn** (Half Moon Inn, Sheepwash, Devon) offers 5½ miles of good fly water. The salmon average from 8 to 12 pounds but fish of over 20 pounds have been taken here. Record sea trout is 14 pounds. Rates at Half Moon Inn run $51 to $63 per week.

Reservoir fishing is available in the district, and fishing for sea bass can be enjoyed in the Torridge estuary at Brideford about twelve miles away.

Another quality hotel for salmon and sea trout on the Torridge is **Weare Giffard Hall** (Bideford, Devon or 29A Kensington Church Street, London W. 8). Built in 1462 the hotel is a beautiful and historic setting. The Hall offers 10½ miles in cooperation with the Lower Torridge Fishery. Excellent meals with rates from about $52 to $72 per week.

DART RIVER

The Dart rises in Dartmoor and divides into two branch streams, the

East Dart and West Dart, then re-joins at Dartmeet. Salmon, sea trout, and small brown trout provide fishing on this stream. The **East Dart Hotel** (East Dart Hotel, Postbridge, Yelverton, Devon) has rights on a considerable stretch of the river. There is good sea trout fishing in the West Dart, and brown trout in both branches as well as tributary streams such as Cherrybrook and Blackabrook.

TAW RIVER

The Taw rises on Dartmoor and joins the Torridge Estuary at Instow. Salmon fishing is prime here from March to May and again in September with sea trout on the move from July into September. Brown trout fishing is good. The **Rising Sun Hotel** (Rising Sun Hotel, Umberleigh, Devon) has 3½ miles of water on the Taw. Rates for accommodations run $46 to $51 per week. Rod charges run about $45 per week during the peak season (March to mid-April). The **Fox-and-Hounds Hotel** (Fox-and-Hounds Hotel, Eggesford, Chulmleigh, Devon) offers 7 miles on the Taw and Little Dart. The latter hotel has been a mecca for anglers since Victorian times and its resident owner Alan R. Chappell provides a bountiful table and good wine cellar at about $50 per week. Rod charges run from $26.40 per week during the peak season for salmon (March through May) or $5 per day if fishing for less than a week. The salmon and trout season closes on September 30th.

DERWENT RIVER

The Derwent River is located in the Lake District and rises north of Scawfell flowing to the Solway Firth. Fishing is for salmon, sea trout, and brown trout. A beautiful river, the Derwent winds through a pastoral valley with many large pools and long riffles. The Derwent is a late river. The peak period for salmon and sea trout is from July to October; trout fishing is good through the season but best in April to June. A popular location here is at Bas-

The River Dove immortalized as the meeting place of Cotton and Walton

senthwaite where the **Hotel Swan, Armathwaite Hall,** the **Red House,** and **Pheasant Inn** cater to anglers. Most of the better water is syndicated but stretches are periodically available through *Castle Fisheries* (address inquiries to the Secretary, Estate Office, Cockermouth Castle, Cumberland, England). Rod fee runs about $80 per week without ghillie. Hotel rates average from $40 to $50 per week.

SALTWATER FISHING

Saltwater fishing in England is similar in its methods and tackle to the Northeastern United States coast. Surf-casting, spinning, and bottom-fishing from rocks, piers, and boats are all popular. While fish are plentiful, they do not run large, and real game species are scarce. The most sporting is probably the bass (*Morone labrax*) a relative of the striped bass (*Morone saxatilis*) of the western Atlantic. Known as *loupe de mer* in France, and sometimes called gray bass, or European sea bass, it is a much sought gamefish along the southern and western coasts of England and Ireland. Under favorable conditions bass may attain a weight of 20 pounds; however, the average size is very much less. Bass are an inshore species during the warm months of the year and the fishing usually begins about May and lasts until October. Favorite places to seek bass are beyond the

pounding breakers on storm beaches, over low weedy rocks covered by the incoming tide, in tide races off rocky headlands, and in creeks and estuaries, where they penetrate into brackish water. The bass has a varied diet and feeds on crabs, squids, small fish such as sand eels, clams, prawns and many types of marine worms, all of which make excellent baits for fishing.

For wariness and cunning the bass has few equals, and tackle must be as light as conditions allow: for surf casting, a long light fiberglass rod, capable of casting a 3-ounce sinker, used in conjunction with a fixed-spool or multiplying reel loaded with 200 yards of 15-pound-test line, would be appropriate. In more sheltered conditions, when fishing in estuaries or from rocks, a spinning outfit is ideal. Spoons should be of the narrow wobbling type and should be retrieved fast. Fly fishing with bucktails or streamers is also practical in estuaries. Bass perform many antics when hooked; they run swiftly, altering course abruptly to head for any snag around which to break the line. They rarely, if ever, leap, but have a habit of running swiftly towards the angler to gain slack line.

Particularly good bass fishing is found all around the coastlines of Devon and Cornwall, or on the western beaches of Wales.

Another popular saltwater gamefish is the tope *Galeus vulgaris,* which is a small European shark. This active shark is much sought after by British sea anglers, and although it rarely attains a weight exceeding 70 pounds (British record 74 pounds), it makes up for lack of size by its fine qualities. The fight of a hooked tope consists of long fast runs alternating with powerful dives, and in shallow water it often leaps spectacularly.

The tope in search of food visits old wrecks, where it preys on the whiting and sea-bream which congregate there; sometimes it rises to the surface to attack dense shoals of mackerel. But the main diet consists of small flatfish and sand eels, which are captured by foraging over sand in medium depths.

For the most enjoyment tackle should be as light as conditions of tide allow, but a flexible 7-foot hollow glass boat rod used in conjunction with a multiplying reel loaded with 300 yards of 25-pound-test monofilament line makes a practical outfit. The leader must be of strong but flexible wire to counteract the tope's sharp teeth and abrasive skin. Bottom fishing from an anchored boat using an oily bait such as a fresh slice of mackerel mounted on a 7/0 hook is the favored method. When tope feed near the surface they can also be caught from a drifting boat, using float tackle or feather jigs. A chum pot filled with fresh minced mackerel makes a useful attractor when ground fishing, as tope, like other sharks, possess a keen sense of smell.

Noted tope fishing areas around the British coast are the Wash in Norfolk, the Thames estuary, the Goodwin Sands off the coast of Kent, and the west coast of Wales.

In recent years fishing for blue, mako, and porbeagle sharks has become a popular sport off Cornwall. The blues run to 200 pounds while the mako and porbeagle reach 400 pounds. The common Atlantic mackerel and the gray mullet *Mugil chelo* provide good sport on light tackle. Other angling species of seasonal importance are the whiting, sole, skate, conger eel, cod, and pollack. Bluefin tuna were caught in years past off the Yorkshire coast, but this fishery has declined.

LICENSES

No permit is required for saltwater fishing, but separate licenses are necessary to fish for salmon and migratory trout, and trout and coarse fish. These licenses are issued by each River Board, which is the authority responsible for the administration of a particular river or group of rivers. The cost depends on the quality of the angling, but broadly speaking, a season's license is nominal. The funds so provided are used by the River Board for restocking, river improvement, wages of bailiffs (game protectors), and other management expenses. Licenses for shorter periods are available on many rivers. No distinction is made between residents and non-residents.

TRAVEL NOTES

To London by Pan Am's new 747 Jet Clipper services, 6¾ hours to London from New York. Also direct service from Chicago, Boston, Philadelphia, Baltimore/Washington, Atlanta, Detroit, New Orleans, Dallas and Houston. Jet Clippers fly from U. S. West Coast via the polar route in 9½ hours. Bus fare from Heathrow Airport into London (14 miles) is 84 cents. Taxi fares vary, depending upon destination in this vast city, but the minimum to Kensington and West End hotels is about $6, plus 25 percent tip. Airport luggage porters are tipped 1 shilling each for one or two bags, sixpence for several small pieces.

Your American passport is all you'll need for identification. If you plan to hire a car to drive yourself, bring your driver's license, which is also valid in Great Britain.

ACCOMMODATIONS

LONDON

Visitors arriving in London have a wide choice of excellent hotels. Perhaps the most elegant is **Claridge's.** Also in the luxury class is the **Dorchester, Berkeley, Grosvenor House,** and the London **Ritz.** The London **Hilton** and **Londonderry House** overlook Hyde Park. The **Connaught** near the U.S. Embassy and the **Savoy** on the Strand are smart. Room rates in London's deluxe hostelries average about $23 per day single, and $31 per day double. In the Mayfair area, and somewhat less expensive are the popular **Park Lane,** the modern **Europa** and small but charming **Meurice, Stafford** and the new **Cavendish.** Rates in these hotels average about $18 single, $27 double. In the Baywater area between Paddington Station and Hyde Park are the **Royal Lancaster** ($14.40-$16.80 single $24-$25.30 double); the **Hertford,** with studio-type rooms ($11.50-$13 single, $16-$18 double) **Leinster Towers,** with kitchenette rooms ($10.50 single, $19 double); the **Cumberland** and **Mount Royal** at Marble Arch (both about $13 single, $20 double). In Knightsbridge, south of Hyde Park are the very deluxe **Carlton Tower** (from $22 single, $24 double) and the less expensive **Hyde Park** and **Normandie.** A little farther west below Kensington Gardens adjoining Hyde Park, are the **De Vere, Kensington Palace,** and **Royal Garden,** averaging $16 single, $27 double. In Bloomsbury, near the University of London and the British Museum are the modern, moderately priced **Bedford, Cora, Grand, President, Russell** and **Tavistock;** rates average $9.45 single, $15 double. Hotels within the general area of Oxford Street include the ultramodern **St. George's,** the **Stratford Court, Londoner** and **Mandeville,** all reasonably priced. Soundproofed hotels at the airport are the **Ariel, Excelsior, Skyway** and new **Centre Airport Hotel.**

Fiji Islands

Fiji's offshore fishing is limited only by the number of boats available

The Fijis are a group of 250 islands lying 3,000 miles south of Hawaii. Nandi airport, long considered a way-stop for travelers headed to New Zealand or Australia, is now a terminus for big-game anglers seeking the South Pacific's big three— black marlin, sailfish, and wahoo. New hotels and charter craft have created an angling resort complex which didn't exist a few years ago. The larger islands are volcanic in origin, mountainous (highest peak 4,341 feet) and surrounded by coral reefs; the smallest islands are coral atols close to sea level. Dense forests of breadfruit, acacia, Tahitian chestnut, and mulberry trees occur on high ground with screw pine and ferns on the slopes. Mangroves and cocoanut palms are common to the shores. Suva, the capital of this British colony, is on the southeast coast of Viti Levu (4,114 square miles). The second largest island, Vanua Levu (2,393 square miles) is about 40 miles to the northeast. The other islands in the Fiji group are considerably smaller.

At present the offshore fishing in the Fijis is limited only by the number of charter craft available. There are good accommodations and potentially excellent fishing grounds but relatively few boats and these are in great demand. Although the larger Fiji Islands have some beautiful freshwater rivers flowing through remote gorges, the only native gamefish is a sunfishlike species (*Kulia rupestris*). This genus is widespread in the tropical central Pacific as well as parts of South Africa.

THE SEASON

Though Fiji is in the tropics the climate is temperate with a range between 60°F and 90°F. The average annual rainfall on the windward coasts is 120 inches distributed throughout the year and 70 to 90 inches on the leeward coasts; most of the latter occurs in the hot season between December and March when there are northerly winds. Fiji is in the South Pacific hurricane belt. Although hurricanes may occur from November to April, these storms are more common in January and February.

THE FISHING

Some offshore fishing is available the year round but the best period for black marlin and sailfish is from October to April. Yellowfin tuna appear between February and June. Mako and bronze whaler sharks, dolphin, dogtooth tuna, wahoo, barracuda, and various jacks, groupers and snappers are caught throughout the season. Wahoo are particularly numerous and run to large sizes with fish of 70 pounds not uncommon (local record 118½ pounds).

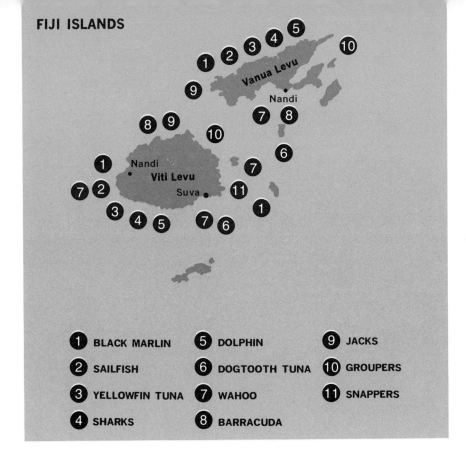

FIJI ISLANDS

1 BLACK MARLIN **5** DOLPHIN **9** JACKS

2 SAILFISH **6** DOGTOOTH TUNA **10** GROUPERS

3 YELLOWFIN TUNA **7** WAHOO **11** SNAPPERS

4 SHARKS **8** BARRACUDA

The Korolevu Beach Hotel on Viti Levu

ACCOMMODATIONS

VITI LEVU

In Suva is the **Grand Pacific Hotel,** set in tropical gardens on the edge of the harbor; air-conditioned rooms from $9.50 single, $17.50 double. The **Club Hotel** is completely air-conditioned; single from $5.90, double from $9.15. **Hotel Suva,** from $5.90 single, $10.20 double. The **Outrigger Motel,** 5 minutes from downtown Suva, is air-conditioned and fronts on the sea; from $8.90 single, $12.60 double. Charter boats operate out of Suva and also out of the **Trade Winds Hotel** on the nearby Bay of Islands.

On Viti Levu's northern highway twenty miles north of Lautoka is the **Ba Hotel,** and beyond it the **Tavua Hotel.** Situated on a tiny reef-protected island offshore and reached from Lautoka by schooner (three hours) is the **Castaway Resort Hotel** with bungalows from $18 to $22 double per day American plan.

Along the south shore of the island at Korolevu is the **Korolevu Beach Hotel** (about 75 miles from Nandi Airport). Taxi fare from the airport is $15. Accommodations are in airy native *bures,* each with private bath. A Polynesian trio plays nightly; war dances and native ceremonial entertainment on Saturdays; skin diving, deep-sea fishing, boating, tennis, horseback riding; sightseeing trips arranged. Rates, depending upon room, suite, or *bure,* $11.75 to $20.85 double, European plan. East of Korolevu on the southern (Queen's) road is the deluxe **Reef Lodge** with superb beach, fishing, skin diving amid coral reefs; single $15, double $10 per person.

YANUCA

Yanuca Island is reached by taxi from Nandi Airport by causeway. The **Fijian Hotel** with singles at $14 to $23 and doubles at $16 to $28 per day European plan. Three twin diesel charter boats are available here at $65 to $75 for a half-day and $125 for a full day charter.

VANUA LEVU

The second largest of the Fiji Islands, reached by Fiji Airways. Sugar, copra, and cocoa plantations dominate the landscape. On the ocean in the town of Savusavu is the **Hot Springs Hotel,** single with bath $6.75, including breakfast; spear and deep-sea fishing facilities.

Finland

Beaching Teno River Salmon is not an easy task with light tackle. The Teno River is 250 miles north of the Arctic Circle and fishermen require warm clothing

Situated northwest of Russia and east of Norway and Sweden, Finland's 130,085 square miles contain over 60,000 lakes and uncounted streams. Rising as a low plain from the Baltic Sea, it is a country of eroded granites and forested in pine, spruce, alder, and maple. Beyond the Circle dwarf Arctic birch and pygmy willow screen the reindeer herds grazing on the hillsides. The average altitudes in Finland are only 200 to 400 feet above sea level but the northwest mountains rise to

over 4,000 feet. Due to the topography of Finland its fishing regions are sharply defined. In the vast southern lakes district the pike is the most common gamefish. Although 4 to 6 pounds is average, fish exceeding 30 pounds are occasionally caught, especially in the Baltic Sea west of Helsinki to Turku and south to the resort area of Aland Island. The northern third of Finland which lies within the Arctic Circle is dominated by grayling and Arctic char; both species tend to run small (½ to 1

pound average) and only the occasional 2- to 4-pound fish is taken.

Many streams throughout the country contain introduced populations of rainbow and brook trout as well as the native brown trout. While numerous in some waters the brookies tend to be small also, seldom exceeding a pound. Sea trout (anadromous brown trout), appear more as an error in translation from *Sports Fishing In Finland* published by the State Board of Forestry (1969) which lists the fish in some 40 rivers; they occur only in the Tornio River. Trout streams in general are heavy flowing, deep "thoroughfares" between lakes which are mostly fished by boat and the better waters produce browns and rainbows in the 1- to 1½-pound class with the chance of a 5- or 6-pounder. Rich in insect life, with tremendous mayfly and caddis hatches, these rivers contain fat, red-fleshed trout. Due to the violent nature of the waters, streamers, nymphs, and wet flies are more effective than dry flies.

ATLANTIC SALMON FISHING

Atlantic salmon occur in three Finnish rivers—the Tenojoki, the Näätamojöki, and the Tornio. The word "joki" means river and while attached to most names on local maps, it is usually dropped in conversation. Known to neighboring Norwegians as the Tana River, the Teno produces the largest salmon with yearly records exceeding 45 pounds (the world record of 79 pounds was caught on the Norwegian side and is therefore listed as a Tana River catch). However, including large numbers of small grilse in the 2-pound class which are abundant, a total would be closer to 10 pounds for the average. You can reasonably expect 20- to 30-pound salmon in the Teno. The Näätamö on the other hand is a quantity stream with plenty of small fish to 12 or 15 pounds and only the rare large salmon. The Tornio, more or less lost to hydroelectric development—which is the history of Finnish rivers—produces few salmon but a modest run of sea trout. Although the border streams are commercially netted, by international agreement the nets have to be lifted three days a week which provides a fair number of salmon for the angler. With few exceptions Finnish streams are not wadable. The torrential flows in both trout and salmon waters barely provide a foothold along the stream edges and a visiting angler can get along with a

pair of lightweight hip boots. The Teno River has a number of lies that can be fished by wading in knee deep water. The Lap guides who are commercial fishermen and take their job seriously work the channels and midstream riffles. Fish are sometimes hooked by local fishermen on long casts from shore, using spoons and plugs, but the river is ½ to 1 mile wide, and it would require a perfect knowledge of the stream to know that you are covering a hold. Although casting lures are legally used by the local people, tourists are restricted to fly only. It's customary for the guide to troll two lines while his client fishes with one or two fly rods. The same "harling" method used on big Norwegian rivers is applied here with the guide rowing back and forth across current in a series of drops while the lures and flies are left swimming 50 to 60 feet downstream. If you stand up to cast, you will (1) fall out of the boat which is tippy and no more than a yard wide, or (2) be rebuffed by the rowman who already *knows* where the fish are and hates to see a fly in the air when it should be working in the water exactly where his oars have maneuvered it.

THE SEASON

The peak period for salmon fishing is from late June through July with a good run of fish sometimes appearing in mid August. Waters become ice-free about the beginning of May in southern Finland and usually a month later in the north. Air temperatures are ideal in the lakes district ranging between 60°F and 80°F, sometimes going as high as 90°F. In Lapland, however, the mercury can drop from 80°F to freezing in a 24-hour period and the fishing hours are normally cold. There are almost fifteen hours of sunshine daily during the summer months and no real night in the far north. From about 10 p.m. to 3 a.m. which is considered the most productive time for salmon (guides try to be on the water by 8 p.m. and return at 6 a.m.), the light is best described as a heavy over-

cast. Long hours of sitting in a boat in 30°F and 40°F temperatures requires warm clothing—thermal underwear, mittens, and a lightweight waterproof parka with hood to deflect spray and neck chilling breezes. The Teno River is 250 miles north of the Arctic Circle.

TACKLE

There are well stocked tackle shops in Finland's major cities. Items are mainly Swedish and American origin but local plugs are world famous. The Rapala balsa plugs and the Nils Master plugs are made here both of which are exported to the U.S.

Any standard 9-foot fly rod calibered for No. 8 to No. 10 lines is adequate for Finnish salmon fishing. Though broad, the rivers are shallow and a floating line, or in early season at high water, a sinking tip line, is recommended. Tackle need not be as heavy as that used in Norway. Leader tippets should test 15 to 20 pounds. Fly sizes range from No. 2 to 6/0 with the emphasis on 2/0 and 3/0 dressings. Despite their own preference for plugs, Laps are extremely critical about the flies used. The fly must be sparsely tied, which eliminates many traditional Norwegian and British dressings. You can buy locally tied Teno flies which are not only unique patterns, but perfect swimmers. There are two classic fly tyers in Finland: Erkki Vaalama at Imatra, and Jouko Lukkari in Utsjoki on the Teno River. Their originals like the Peuran yö, Jussin yö, Jarim, Tivri, Tenon Valkea, Lohi suvanto, Teno No. 1, Teno No 7, Schröderin Special, Eversti, and Kuparinen are not only works of art but designed with slender wings and sparse hackles for perfect balance. How the fly is knotted to the leader is vitally important, and there are several popular jams which place the bulk of the knot in back of the hook eye so that the dressing is always upright in the water at all current speeds. There is a ritual testing before each trip; a Lapp will flap your fly in the current

continued on page 110

Lands In The Midnight Sun

Among the group of five countries known as Scandinavia, Norway and Iceland hold most of the world's salmon fishing by virtue of a combined total of 181 rivers where the fish spawn in significant numbers. If poured end to end, this represents about 10,000 miles of the most valuable water on the globe. And where the salmon is king, the sea trout is his crown prince. The anadromous brown trout is a spectacular quarry which enters nearly all coastal streams including many that are bypassed by the salmon. Sweden and Finland each have a few rivers where angling for both species can be enjoyed, but Denmark's fjords are limited to the sea trout only. Arctic char, grayling, and brown trout are the other important native gamefish throughout Scandinavia, while northern pike are distributed primarily in the Baltic and the lake region of Finland.

In the latitudes where salmon fishing is done, you can be on the river twenty-four hours a day during most of June and July. If you are in the sub-Arctic or Arctic zones, the local preference is for "night" rather than day fishing. The sun pales and perhaps disappears for an hour, depending on how far south you happen to be, but more fish are caught in the late p.m. and early a.m. hours than in bright sunlight. It is disconcerting at first to have dinner and go to bed at 6 a.m. and arise at 4 p.m. for breakfast, only to have lunch at 1 a.m. on the streamside; yet after a few days it all seems perfectly normal. Whether you have a koldtbordt, smorgasbord, or smorrebord, the table will be of Viking proportions—an essential in the cold, often damp weather that characterizes the Arctic salmon season.

Fishing in Scandinavia is a summer sport. It takes place at a time when tourism is at a peak and hotel accommodations are not easy to find. If you do not use a travel agency or a fishing-tour operator, make certain you hold confirmed reservations at your port of entry in a city hotel. As a rule of thumb, figure on $15 single or $20 double per day in a first-class hotel. Luxury hotels run over $30 double; however, there are comparatively few of these, and the lesser option is adequate. In the best restaurants, dinner averages about $10 per person. Except for aquavit and vodka, drinks are expensive, and smart travelers buy their favorite labels in duty-free airport shops. Scandinavian beers are among the world's best.

Once you make the scene at the fishing camp, prices can be very much less—or positively awesome, depending on the location. Finland's Teno River, for example, can be explored from a $10 per day double with bath, and counting every necessity including guide, boat, and tips, you shoot the works at $300 per week. Norway's Alta, on the other hand, may run from $1,800 to $3,000 per week. That differences exist is obvious, but more important is the fact that there are alternatives.

Again, as a rule of thumb, expect to pay $550 to $750 per week for most Norwegian fishing, which includes room, meals, guide (known here as a klepper), and boat.

The typical Norwegian guide is a Norse descendant and a farmer during most of the year. Frequently, he is a co-owner of the fishing rights made available to visitors. This is often true in Iceland also. In the extreme north and particularly in Finland, most guides are Lapps.

Lapland is a band across Norway, Sweden, and Finland. Probably the earliest settlers in Arctic Europe, the Lapps were once nomadic; but these hardy people have settled down with their reindeer herds, as the meat and hides find a ready market elsewhere in Scandinavia. During the summer months when the reindeer are grazing on the high ground, the Lapps supplement their incomes by guiding. Although few Norwegian guides speak English, and the Lapps have a language uniquely their own, little technical difficulty will be encountered, as the profession is over a century old (since 1862).

While the Scandinavian fishing season is from mid-June through August, the peak period is usually from about June 20 to July 20 for salmon and from July 15 to August 30 for sea trout. Large sea trout arrive toward the end of the major salmon runs. This varies by days according to latitude; at the southern limits of the trout's range in Scandinavia these anadromous browns make two distinct runs: May and September in Sweden and September through October in Denmark. The largest sea trout in the world are taken from Sweden's Morrum River (over 30 pounds); however, the number of fish caught each season is a modest 700 to 800 total for both salmon and trout.

Despite the fairly mild marine climate of Scandinavia and the occasional 80°F. day, by all means bring along thermal underwear and rain gear with a parka hood. The thermometer makes frequent drops, so go prepared for drizzly 50°F weather, which feels colder after long hours of inactivity sitting in a boat. Include a topcoat and a light woolen suit for city wear.

A husky 9-foot fly rod is adequate in most Scandinavian rivers, but local preference on big boat streams such as the Alta is a 12- or 13-footer matched to a No. 11 sinking line. Favorite flies here are 5/0 and 6/0 sizes on double hooks. This is not simply an accommodation to the fish but a means of getting the fly down in deep, swift water. In the north, warm weather continues to melt the snows in the mountains as summer advances, so that instead of having a spring runoff and then a gradual shrinking of the river, July may see the water level at flood stage. It's likely to be August before most of the snow water has run off and you can employ light tackle and small flies on most streams. It's best to bring along both a light and heavy outfit; a No. 8 is suitable for the former and No. 11 for the latter.

American visitor Carl Tillmans holds 20-pound salmon from the Teno River. Tri-corner hat of Lapp guide signifies salmon run

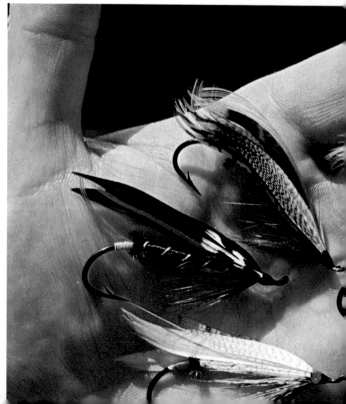

Hardy Lapp guide *(top lefthand page)* has his midnight pipe on the Naatamo River in Finland. Anglers set out in 8 p.m. sun on the Teno River *(bottom lefthand page)*. Boats are hand carved from solid log. Slimly tied Teno salmon flies *(center)* are local favorites. Finnish boy and his dog *(top left)* explore a woodland brook for trout. New York visitor Ralph Straus *(top right)* has reason to be proud of this 45-pound Alta River salmon. Oslo businessman Hans Gustav Myhre *(below)* displays a night's catch of seven salmon from the Alta

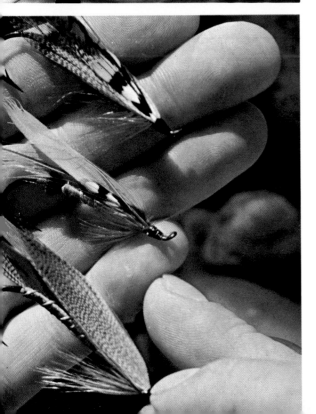

Linstroms Hotel in Norway (*above*) is an angling
landmark in the lovely little village of Laerdal

Vossa River is a wide and deep one and usually
is fished from a boat rather than by wading

Salmon (*below*) of over 60 pounds are taken
from Namsen River. This is also boat stream

Author Al McClane holds up the hefty 38-pound
salmon that he fished from waters of Stryn River

Opposite page
Platform fishing (*left*) on the Laerdal is typical of
the many rivers that cannot be waded

Aurland River (*bottom left*), one of Norway's most
beautiful, boasts sea trout from 12 to 18 pounds

American angler Tom Lenk (*center*) with Flaam
River salmon, which averages about 14 pounds

Annual Norwegian visitor seeking the 40-pound-
plus Alta salmon is Charles Ritz (*left*) of Paris

The Teno River (Tana in Norwegian) produced the record 49-pound salmon

A real trophy at bargain prices

continued from page 103
for a half hour or until he is convinced that it's riding true. He will trim, reknot, and go through fifty patterns if necessary. They know what they're doing so be patient.

Many streams in Finland are bordered by marshlands and swamps where the delectable cloudberries abound but standing waters also produce literally clouds of mosquitoes.

LICENSES
The licensing system in Finland is fairly simple. Except for the border rivers between Norway and Finland, you need a State Fishing Card which only costs $1.25 and can be bought at any police station. In some waters local fishing permits are also required and these cost between 50c and $20 per week depending on the quality of the water. Permits can be obtained from the Forestry Board offices, tourist hotels, and local fishing associations. Taking one typical trout stream as an example, the Hannulan Koski, a permit costs $17.50 per week in addition to the State Fishing Card. Norway and Finland have a mutual

agreement on fishing the border—no card is required and a permit costs about $3.50 per day.

TRAVEL NOTES
The Teno River is a thousand miles north of your port-of-entry at Helsinki. By any standard the additional air fare would be considerable. Happily, Finnair, the national airline of Finland, offers a Holiday Ticket which is only available to residents of countries outside of Scandinavia. It provides unlimited flights within Finland during a 15-day period for $80, which means you can fly beyond the Arctic Circle and back for what amounts to $40 each way. Finnair flies both jets and turbo props, so you can leave your hotel in Helsinki in the morning and arrive at Utsjoki Tourist Hotel in time for the evening fishing.

If you rent a car ($4 to $10 per day plus 6c to 15c per mile) to make a grand tour, the road signs are international pictograms, so you won't have any difficulty. Finland has over 43,000 miles of road and you can drive everywhere—right to the Arctic Ocean.

ACCOMMODATIONS
Comfortable hotels and inns can be found throughout Finland. A reliable chain with establishments everywhere is the **MR Hotel** which includes the **Utsjoki Tourist Hotel** located on the Teno River. Rates are low. At Utsjoki $6 single without bath (sauna available) or $10 for a double with bath, both with free continental breakfast. Rooms in nearly all hotels including the major ones in Helsinki tend to be miniature so if you are heavy on luggage and rod cases pay extra for the double. Meals at the Utsjoki run from $1 to $4 with a large menu and nicely prepared food.

In transit you will stay in Helsinki. It's a swinging city situated on the Gulf of Finland and its hotels are modern, comfortable, and impeccably serviced. Among the best and centrally located are the **Vaakuna, Torppa Marski, Palace,** and the **Helsinki.** Rates run from $8 to $15 for a single room and $12 to $22 for a double. Space is usually tight, so advance reservations are essential. There are all kinds of restaurants,

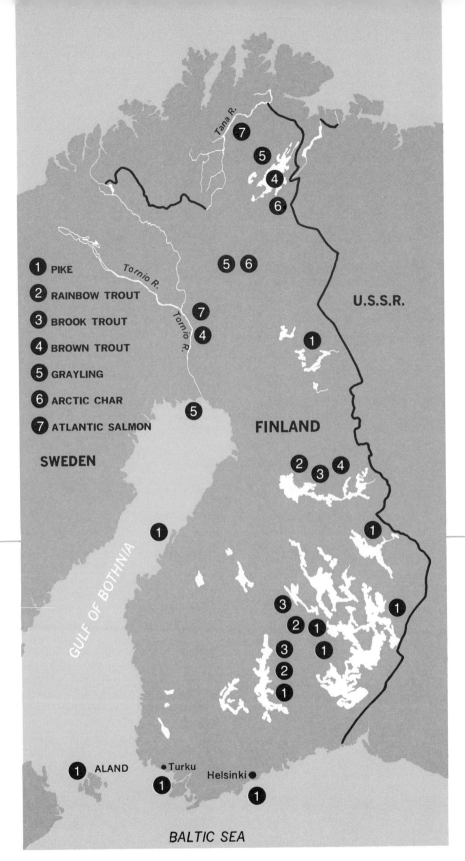

1 PIKE
2 RAINBOW TROUT
3 BROOK TROUT
4 BROWN TROUT
5 GRAYLING
6 ARCTIC CHAR
7 ATLANTIC SALMON

SWEDEN

Tornio R.

Tornio R.

U.S.S.R.

FINLAND

GULF OF BOTHNIA

ALAND ● Turku

Helsinki ●

BALTIC SEA

Tana R.

Smaller salmon run the Naatamo

CONTACTS
To organize a salmon trip on the Teno River, write direct to the Manager, Utsjoki Tourist Hotel, Utsjoki, Finland. The hotel honors all reservations and will make arrangements for guide and boat (standard rate $15 per fishing day). For general information contact the Finnish National Travel Office, Scandinavia House, 505 Fifth Avenue, New York, N.Y. 10017.

LANGUAGE AND PEOPLE
Finland is a bilingual country where approximately 90 percent of the population speaks Finnish and the rest Swedish. The tourist can get oriented in Helsinki and other big towns since hotel and airline personnel usually speak English too. In the back country practically nobody speaks English, and Finnish being a language that doesn't lend itself to a quick course in useful phrases, you'll have to rely on hand signals. However, Finns are also among the most friendly people in the world, and in this outdoors-minded nation, somebody carrying a rod case will receive any assistance he requires.

but after a careful survey we recommend the following: For lunch try the **Savoy, Monte Carlo, Royal, Motti,** the **Marski,** or the bar and grill on the second floor of the **Palace.** For late dining try the room on the tenth floor of the **Palace,** which overlooks Helsinki harbor. Our favorite is the **Kalastajatorppa** (or Fisherman's Cottage) located on the waterfront. Another showplace is the **Walhalla,** an old fortress carved out of rock, located on an island ten minutes from town. For sophisticates the **Brando Casino** with its wide screen view of the Gulf of Finland is worth the tab. Finnish beer is world famous.

Grenada

This beautiful Isle of Spice, the most southerly of the Windward Islands, lies about 90 miles north of Trinidad in the eastern Caribbean. The 120 square mile island is volcanic in origin and a mountain range runs from north to south which reaches its highest point at Mt. Saint Catherine (2,756 feet). A lake, Grand Etang, occupies the crater of an extinct volcano and another crater lake lies on the northeast shore. There are also several large freshwater streams and many springs which create brackish-water habitat, particularly along the eastern coast where tarpon and snook occur.

Grenada (pronounced *Gre-nay-da*) is primarily an agricultural island with the emphasis on nutmegs, cocoa, and bananas. Fishing as a tourist attraction is little developed at present. However, it has excellent potential both offshore and inshore, especially for sailfish, blue and white marlin, dolphin, yellowfin tuna, wahoo, and dolphin. Charter craft suitable for big-game fishing are scarce.

THE SEASON
Grenada has a tropical marine climate. An average annual range is 76°F to 79°F at the capital city of St. George's. Temperatures vary with altitude, but the rainy season lasts from May to December and the peak fishing season is from December through March.

THE FISHING
Due to the proximity of the 100-fathom curve to Grenada, gamefish migrate through these waters in large numbers within a mile of the coast. Captain Martin Mathias (Grenada Yacht Services, St. George's Grenada, West Indies) who has been pioneering the area for several years again found good concentrations of sailfish and blue marlin in December of 1969 and through January 1970. Large yellowfin tuna were also numerous early this year although the peak tuna runs are expected from April through June. Little else is known at present.

TRAVEL NOTES
By Pan American Jet—New York to Trinidad or to Barbados, then short connecting flight to Grenada. Taxi fare from Pearls Airport into St. George's (16 miles) is $6.00 or $2.00 per seat in a shared car. Departure tax $2.00. Need only proof of citizenship and a return ticket.

LANGUAGE
English with a French patois common among the native people.

ACCOMMODATIONS
There are good accommodations available on Grenada and the rates given are for a double per day Modified American Plan (two meals) except where noted: The **Silver Sands** on Grande Anse Beach, $40. The **Grenada Beach** with air-conditioned rooms, from $34 to $54. **Spice Island Inn,** air-conditioned, separate cottage suites along Grande Anse Beach, $32. The **Calabash** features Indian and French cuisines, $60 double American Plan in winter. The **Islander** overlooks harbor of St. George's, $28 American Plan. **Ross Point Inn** on the sea with private beach specializes in West Indian cuisine, $19.50 to $40. The **Crescent Inn** with home-like atmosphere, overlooks the Yacht Basin, $19 to $27. At the **St. James** in St. George's rates are $19 to 22. **St. Ann's Guest House** has year round double rates at $12.50 American Plan.

For further information and the pamphlet *Where to Stay in Grenada,* write the Grenada Tourist Board, St. George's, Grenada, West Indies, or contact the *Caribbean Tourist Association,* 20 East 46th Street, New York, N.Y. 10017.

GRENADA

St. George's

Grand Etang

1 SAILFISH

2 BLUE MARLIN

3 WHITE MARLIN

4 DOLPHIN

5 YELLOWFIN TUNA

6 WAHOO

An Icelandic farmer rides his pony between pools while fishing the Haffjardara River

Iceland

A Viking's endurance is an asset here; if you fish in southern Iceland during the summer months, you run into only two hours of darkness every day. In the north, the midnight sun penetrates the gloom and you can fish for twenty-four hours, or forty-eight, or as long as you can stay awake. Iceland has sixty major salmon rivers, hundreds of trout streams and no trees. You can't hang a backcast unless you get so tired that you drop one in the grass.

Iceland, the second largest island in Europe (approximately 40,000 square miles) lies crouched just south of the Arctic Circle. It's an independent republic, grubbed out of lava rock, a living saga, a tough ice-berged, hard-drinking, I-don't-give-a-damn country with a sensitive core. Its language is rooted in Old Norse or German of the year 1000 that came over with the Vikings, and you won't learn more than a few words of it. But the language of running water is universal, and so is the soft towel-snapping of duck wings, the lonely honk of geese, the finger-

rubbed-balloon sound of startled ptarmigan, the flop of an up-again down-again salmon, the plaintive cry of golden plover and the bleat of satanic black sheep.

In the old days, fishing in Iceland was slow to get at because you had to travel by ponies—gentle little head-to-the-wind Mongols in the south and Arabian stock in the north. Now they have roads—paved in Reykjavik for the Mercedes and Pontiacs but made of clay or volcanic ash in the back country.

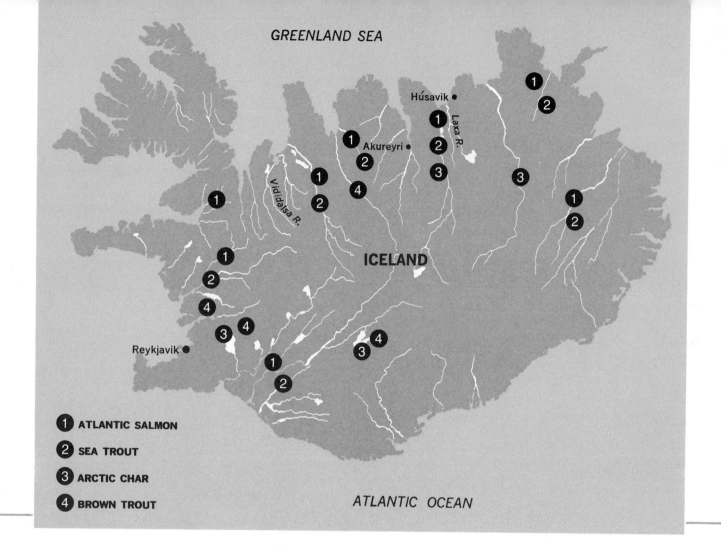

GREENLAND SEA

Húsavik •

ATLANTIC SALMON
SEA TROUT
ARCTIC CHAR
BROWN TROUT

Akureyri •

Laxa R.

Vididalsa R.

ICELAND

Reykjavik •

ATLANTIC OCEAN

Where the roads won't take you a charter plane will, and there are plenty available. Iceland is an air-minded nation. For big hops from the south coast to the north or from east to west, Icelandic Airways provides inter-city service. But everywhere you will see ponies and people with tents and fishing tackle going into the mountains.

There are two ways to get on Icelandic salmon water. One is to rent a river, which is expensive and the price is going up every season. The other is to work through an organization that can obtain fishing rights for you. The latter is the easier way for people who don't speak Icelandic or don't have the time and money to chase landlords. A reliable outfitter for fishing in this country is *Mytravel* (Norway Travel House, 290 Madison Avenue, New York, N.Y. 10017; Area Code 212-532-6055). Mytravel has many subleases on first-class rivers. An American broker with excellent leases available each season on the best Icelan-

dic rivers is Elisha F. Lee (W.E. Hutton & Co., 75 Federal Street, Boston, Massachusetts; (Area Code 617-482-8230).

THE SEASON
The Icelandic salmon season is open from June 15th to September 15th, but the fish are seldom in the rivers in any appreciable numbers much before the first of July. Regulars agree that July 15th is the optimum date for both salmon and sea trout. Unlike the British Isles, there are no early and late rivers in Iceland, so that in a year when the fish are late in arriving, the angler's disappointment is apt to be as great in the west coast rivers as it is in those of the northern section. We favor the last week in July and any time in the month of August. For good fishing, the weather should be bad before you get there and alternately wet and sunny during your stay. Daily summer temperatures will range from 40° to 65°F with a mean of 52°F in the three months of the salmon season, from mid-June

to mid-September, the noonday temperature is apt to rise close to 70°F and there is midnight sun, at least over the northern half of the island, for almost all of the season's first month. Even in late August and early September, when the season's end is approaching, there are only a few hours of real darkness, from around eleven at night until around three in the morning. Conversely, in the depth of winter in Reykjavik, the country's one major city, there are only about four hours of actual daylight, from late morning to early afternoon.

ATLANTIC SALMON
Icelandic salmon average about 8 pounds in weight although fish of over 20 pounds are not uncommon on the better rivers and the national record stands at 38½ pounds. The Laxá near Husavik has consistently produced some of the largest salmon in Iceland. It's important to remember that there are a number of "Laxá" rivers in this country; the suffix á (pronounced *ow*) simply

Angler Bing Crosby with a nice
salmon from the Laxa River

Sea trout *(below)* typical of Iceland

Dry-fly expert Arnold Gingrich plies his art on the beautiful Haffjardara River

means river, and Lax means salmon and when combined they mean salmon river. Thus, the Laxá near Husavik is separated from the others geographically. Three other very productive north coast rivers are the Hŕutafjardara, Siká, and the Vídidálsa (in the 1969 season two anglers caught 49 salmon ranging from 8 to 21 pounds in one week on the latter stream).

The Snaefellsnes section, on the west coast has three outstanding rivers, the Straumfjardará (pronounced Strum-fidar-ow), the Haffjardara, and the Stadara, the last being exceptionally good as a seatrout stream. Nearer to Reykjavik are the Grimsa, the Sogid, and the Bruara. The best rivers are on the north, northeast, and west coasts.

They are rugged streams, flowing fast and deep. There are a few good rivers in the south, and these are shallow and easily waded. Many other rivers provide excellent salmon fishing, and it is a general rule that in large streams the fish range 12 to 18 pounds; in the smaller ones, 6 to 8 pounds.

Except from the standpoint of his own creature comfort, Icelandic weather need not concern the angler, as the fishing there is as nearly weatherproof as it can ever be anywhere. Since the surroundings of the rivers are volcanic rock, overgrown with tundra, and there are no trees whatsoever, there is also an almost total absence of mud. Hence the clear streams never really muddy up in even the foulest weather. They may "pearl" a bit for a few hours, but they never turn that chocolate color that is so frequently the fly fisherman's despair.

SEA TROUT

Apart from salmon, the great sport in Iceland is sea-trouting. The sea trout here is a migratory brown trout that spends some part of its life in

the ocean. When it comes back from salt water, it is deep-bodied and its brownish coloration is covered by a silvery coat heavily marked with charcoal-black spots. The fish are of good size in Iceland at an average of about 4 pounds with individuals sometimes exceeding 15 pounds. A 24-pound sea trout was caught in the Stadara River. Sea trout come readily to both wet and dry flies.

TACKLE

The angler going to Iceland will be well advised to take his own rods and leaders, and the rod should not be more than 6 ounces at the very most, since nine out of ten of the salmon hooked will run under 10 pounds. And, since most Icelandic rivers offer a simultaneous chance at two of the five kinds of fish prevalent (that is salmon and sea trout and anadromous char, as well as the nonmigratory strains of both trout and char) almost any salmon pool is equally likely to yield a trout or a char of 2 to 4 pounds. The latter, of course, are a picnic on rods of from 2 to 4 ounces, but somewhat anticlimatic if played on heavier tackle. Because of the comparative lack of stream obstructions and the relative ease of finding a bank favorable to beaching the fish, the angler need not feel underequipped with a trout rod and terminal tackle no heavier than IX. The reel is important. It should have at least a 100-yard backing capacity and 150 yards is advisable. There are no boats to follow your salmon, and the rough-cut volcanic-rock streambeds are not easy to walk on, let alone run over.

The basic-size salmon fly is on a No. 4 hook, but go prepared with dressings from 3/0 down to No. 8. The larger ones work best on the big streams and during high water. Icelanders prefer patterns with some blue in them, like the Blue Doctor, Hairy Mary, Blue Charm and Silver Wilkinson. The Green Highlander is very good also. Dry flies will take salmon in Iceland but generally floaters are less effective than sunk patterns.

There are tackle shops in Reykjavik and Akureyri. Most of the gear is British-made, although some American equipment can be had at rather high prices. The rods and reels available are uniformly heavy because Icelanders prefer 15-foot, two-handed outfits that will sling anything from flies to spoons. Favorite bait is a clutch of night crawlers which grow to serpent size in the south Arctic.

CLOTHING

Clothes are important in arctic climates, and even though temperatures may soar to 65 degrees at midday, the polar winds bite through several layers of wool. A 50-mile-per-hour wind is not unusual in August. You may be unlucky and have nothing but sunshine without wind. If you planned the trip right, however, there will be plenty of salmon-moving rain. It takes rain and rising water to bring them up the rivers, and the rain will generate fog the like of which you never saw in your life. Alaska has fog and williwaw winds, but they lift or you can get out or get behind a tree.

You should have a parka equipped with a hood. You need long johns and wool shirts. Two lightweight wool shirts are better than one heavy one because they hold body heat, and if you have to walk a lot you can always peel off a layer. Wool pants and knee-length wool socks are essential. As for sweaters, it is economical to buy them in Iceland. The island is crawling with sheep, and the Icelanders make a lamb's-wool sweater that is not only handsome but inexpensive. A government-sponsored shop just a few blocks from the Hotel Borg in Reykjavik sells them for as little as $15.

Bootfoot waders are preferable to the stockingfoot type, since the abrasive action of the omnipresent volcanic rock dust (even the roads are of volcanic rock) will quickly wear through waders at the ankle, where brogues and wading socks make a too convenient catch basin for the diamond-hard particles. The lava river beds, too, are extremely slippery, so hobnailed wading sandals, or at least a set of chains or a pair of wading grips, are a must. As for the rest in the way of stream clothes, it is important that it be both rain-resistant and windproof. A rain jacket, preferably with a hood, should be in the back pocket of whatever tackle pack, vest, or coat the angler normally wears on the stream. It is almost certain to be needed for protection from wind if not from rain.

ACCOMMODATIONS

Adequate accommodations are provided on each of the rivers. These are best described as farmhouse without bath; the food is plain but wholesome. You'll be uncertain about when you'll get to eat, because Icelanders are not concerned about time. Dinner at midnight is not unusual, and if you wander off the beaten track you may run into a ritualistic smorgasbord served three times a day, every day. All breads are homemade and good. Everything American bakers take out is left in Icelandic bread.

Smoked char and ptarmigan called *riupa*, (pronounced rue-pa) are excellent but the dried cod and shark (called *Hakarl*) are tough to get down. The shark is buried for five or six months, then excavated. The chocolate bars, which you will devour for body heat in cold weather, are comparable to the best offered in Holland and Norway, and these are superlative. Boiled salmon and trout are constant companions and become montonous unless you complain to the cook.

For a bath you will have to go to the hotel at Akureyri or wait until you get back to Reykjavik.

Aside from a soul-warming nip on the stream, drinking is done in Iceland before and after dinner. Available are Scotch, cognac, and (from the local alembics) an explosive Brennivin, known to Icelanders as

COSTS FOR 1971

Icelandic leases are expensive ranging up to $1,000 or more per week per rod. *Mytravel* offers the following for the 1971 season on the Laxá River at Adaldal. This is one of the top producing rivers with an average weight of 12 pounds on its salmon; best fish in 1969 was 27 pounds.

June 20 through July 10	$750 per rod per week
July 11 through August 14	$950 per rod per week
August 15 through August 28	$750 per rod per week
August 29 through September 11	$650 per rod per week

Black Death. This is a triple-distilled extract of old Vikings. Icelanders drink everything straight, and when you pass the bottle they throw the cork away. Skoal is pronounced "scowl" in Iceland, and it is a formality not to be ignored. No matter what the occasion, everybody present must be toasted, and neglecting the before and after salutes is worse than putting your foot in the mashed potatoes. The potatoes, incidentally, are inclined to be black but tasty.

REYKJAVIK
Newest hotels in Reykjavik are the **Holt** and the **Loftleider**. The **Saga** and **Borg** are also good. Rates about $13 double, plus 15 percent service charge and 7½ percent tax, but there is no tipping. Local food specialites include *hangikjot* (smoked lamb), and various forms of dried fish. The *Naust, Glaumbaer, The Club* and *Saga* restaurants have fine seafood and smorgasbord. Magnificent view from the Saga Hotel *Grillroom.*

TRAVEL NOTES
To visit Iceland you need only a passport. Duty-free customs allowances include 1 bottle of liquor and 200 cigarettes. The krona is the monetary unit; 42.95 kronur equal $1, each krona being worth about 2.3c. Good buys are sheepskins, Icelandic handmade silver, ceramics and other handicrafts. Duty-free shop at Keflavik Airport.

LANGUAGE
Icelandic, Danish, German, Norwegian, and some Swedish and English are spoken. You can almost always find somebody to get you out of a scramble—except at breakfast when the maid brings you ham and eggs and you ask for toast. Then you get another order of eggs.

TRADE BOOK

Ireland

Bank fishing at famous Butler's Pool

Ashford Castle is a trout and salmon anglers hotel

This 18-pounder from the Laune River

Trout average 2 pounds at Lough Ennell

There is a line in the song *Galway Bay*, "just to hear again the ripple of a trout stream." In a country so saturated in angling lore that its major rivers have appeared on paper currency, leaping salmon on its coins, where pubs bear names like Angler's Rest and Last Cast—not to mention the world famous Limerick and O'Shaughnessy hook patterns and where signs along the road read "Salmon and Sea Trout Fishing, Inquiries Invited," no writer of songs could neglect what is so obvious on the Irish landscape. The Emerald Isle has perhaps the only victualler-tackle salesman in the world, one Paddy Tiernan of Foxford in County Mayo who combines a tackle shop with his butcher shop. Although the sign over the storefront claims "Best Quality Beef, Mutton, and Spring Lamb" the showcases are laden with fishing lures which compete with the well marbled cuts for customer approval. That Mr. Tiernan sells more tackle than meat comes as no surprise. If every other Irishman is a politician—every *other* Celt is a fisherman.

Ireland provides one of the principal salmon and trout fisheries in the world due to a normally well dispersed rainfall and a minimum of industrial pollution. The great beauty of the countryside and the low cost of the angling are unique. The best rivers are held by riparian owners, and these are rented out to local fishing clubs or groups of anglers who exercise their options from year to year; or as is customary in many waters, fishing rights are issued by the day, week, or month. Some hotels have fishing rights which they reserve for their guests on payment of a weekly or daily charge, which varies with the status of the fishery and the period of the season. The greatest demand for hotel fishing exists during July and August, and charges are highest during these months.

Ireland's rugged west coast rivers contrast with the gentle limestone streams of the Central Plain region

THE SEASON

The salmon season opens on a few rivers on January 1st (Liffey, Garavogue). The opening date on most rivers is February 1st, but others open later, on dates varying from February 26th (Slaney) to 1st May (parts of Bangor district, Mayo). The season ends on September 30th on a majority of waters, but ends in the Slaney on August 31st and on the Boyne on September 15th; while some western waters remain open until October 12th. Unlike the rivers of Canada, Newfoundland and Norway, none of the rivers in Ireland becomes ice-bound during the fishing season, even in January or February. Generally, the best spring fishing in Ireland is over before salmon season in Canada or Norway has begun. For the tourist who wants to combine salmon and the best of the trout fishing, May and June are the peak months.

Rainfall over four-fifths of Ireland averages 30 to 50 inches per year with higher totals on mountains and exposed shores on the coast. The rain is normally distributed through the year and the number of inclement days reaches 155 in the east and 200 in parts of the west. The number of sunny days is relatively low with June being the best month, averaging 6 hours of sunshine per day. Despite this norm, Ireland has had below average rainfall during the past few years and water levels were extremely low on rivers and lakes at the end of the 1969 season.

ATLANTIC SALMON

There are two major runs of salmon in Ireland—the "spring salmon" which ascend the rivers from January until June, and the grilse (locally *peal*) that appear with the first rains of June and continue until October. Summer run salmon are less common but large fish do come into west coast waters such as the Ballynahinch River and provide fishing until the last day of the season. Spring salmon weigh from 10 to 30 pounds with an average of about 12 pounds on the better rivers; grilse range from 4 to 8 pounds with an average of about 5. Prime spring rivers include the Boyne, Suir, Nore, Slaney, and Munster Blackwater. Some of the best summer salmon fishing is found in the large lakes which are physically part of the river systems in Kerry, Connemara, and Donegal. These lake fish are often caught by anglers casting small wet flies for trout but they are more commonly taken by trolling with a spoon.

BROWN TROUT

Ireland offers exceptionally good brown trout fishing in both rivers and lakes. Generally speaking the browns found in the coastal regions of Cork, Kerry, Connemara, and Donegal are small with an average of less than one pound. These are acid waters with a low pH value in the hill regions or peat bog drainages. The largest trout are found in the clear limestone region of the Central Plain, notably Loughs Sheelin, Derravaragh, Owel, Ennell, Carra, and Arrow. The average weight in these waters is close to 2 pounds and may be as high as 4. Fish of 8 pounds and over are caught on the fly each year. The somewhat less highly alkaline lakes such as Corrib, Mask, Conn and Derg hold fish averaging 1 to 2 pounds, but these lakes also produce fast-growing, piscivorous brown trout, taken chiefly by trolling and spinning, and growing to over 20 pounds.

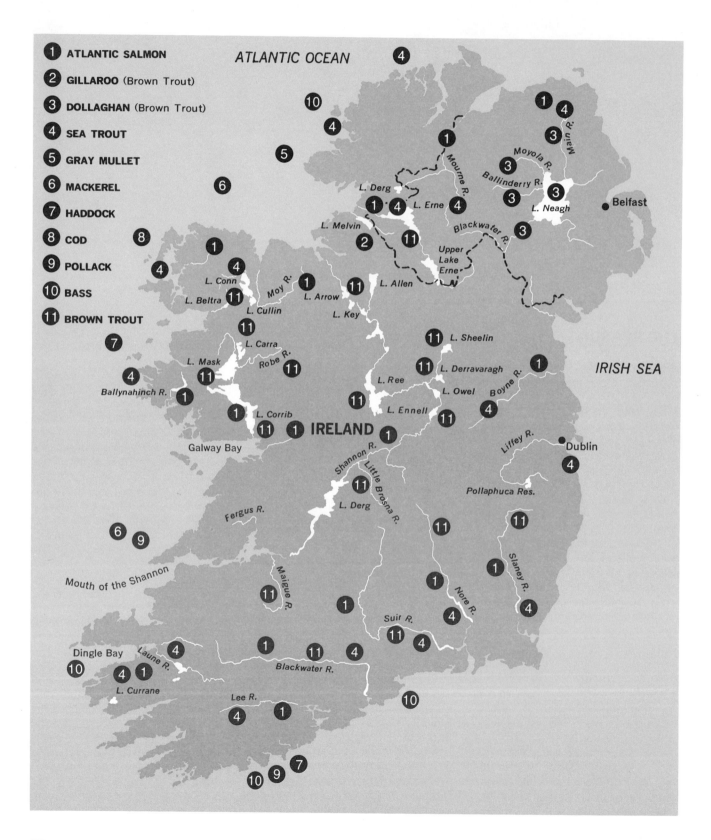

① ATLANTIC SALMON
② GILLAROO (Brown Trout)
③ DOLLAGHAN (Brown Trout)
④ SEA TROUT
⑤ GRAY MULLET
⑥ MACKEREL
⑦ HADDOCK
⑧ COD
⑨ POLLACK
⑩ BASS
⑪ BROWN TROUT

ATLANTIC OCEAN

IRELAND

IRISH SEA

Belfast

Dublin

Galway Bay

Dingle Bay

Mouth of the Shannon

L. Derg
L. Erne
L. Melvin
L. Allen
L. Conn
L. Beltra
L. Cullin
L. Carra
L. Mask
L. Corrib
Ballynahinch R.
Moy R.
L. Arrow
L. Key
Robe R.
L. Sheelin
L. Derravaragh
L. Ree
L. Owel
L. Ennell
Boyne R.
Liffey R.
Pollaphuca Res.
Shannon R.
Little Brosna R.
L. Derg
Fergus R.
Maigue R.
Slaney R.
Nore R.
Suir R.
Blackwater R.
Lee R.
Laune R.
L. Currane
Mourne R.
Main R.
Moyola R.
Ballinderry R.
L. Neagh
Blackwater R.
Upper Lake Erne

The waters of Ballynahinch Castle produce excellent salmon fishing with peak periods in June and September

The big lakes provide wet fly fishing in March, April, early May and September, and dry fly fishing during the Green Drake mayfly hatch (mid-May to early June) and during the summer evenings. The uniquely Irish sport of blow-line dapping with the natural insect is also practised on these lakes—with the mayfly during the mayfly hatch, and with the cranefly, known locally as the "daddy-long-legs" and grasshopper in August. The smaller lakes provide fishing with wet or dry fly throughout most of the season.

Some of the limestone streams provide excellent dry fly fishing for big trout, especially in late April, May and early June. Particularly good waters are the Robe (Co. Mayo), Black River (Galway-Mayo border), Fergus (Co. Clare), Maigue (Co. Limerick) and Little Brosna (Co. Tipperary). Many larger salmon streams provide wet and dry fly fishing for trout also.

A Gaelic distinction is made between two forms of brown trout in Ireland. The first of these is the *gillaroo*, a trout unique in that it has an unusual stomach similar to the gizzard of a bird. This horny stomach is used to aid the digestion of mollusks, which are the main items in the diet of this trout. The name gil-

laroo is derived from two words, *giolla* and *ruadh*, meaning "red fellow" (in reference to its reddish pink flesh). Gillaroo occur in several lakes but principally in Lough Melvin.

The other trout is the *dollaghan*. Found in Northern Ireland's Lough Neagh, this fish is a migratory lake-type brown trout which runs into tributary rivers. Dollaghan are the same form as Austria's *Lachforelle* or the lake-type fish found in many large North and South American waters.

The best dollaghan rivers are the Ballinderry, Moyola, Maine and Blackwater, all of which are within reasonable distance of Belfast. The Ballinderry and Moyola receive the earliest run of fish, the first flood in August usually bringing them up in large numbers, and from then till closing day, September 30th, splendid sport may be enjoyed if the water is right. They have been known to run these two rivers as early as the middle of July, but such an early run is exceptional. The Maine and Blackwater do not get a real run of fish till late August or early September, but these are heavier fish and the season has an extra month to run on these rivers, closing day being October 31st. Of the four rivers,

the Ballinderry is generally recognized as the best for fly fishing, and the Maine the best for those who prefer spinning.

SEA TROUT

Sea trout (locally white trout) are abundant in a number of rivers, estuaries and small lakes of the coastal regions particularly in west Cork, Kerry, Connemara, and Donegal. Runs start as early as May in some places but July and August are the peak months. The majority of Irish sea trout return to the rivers the year after they enter the sea, so that the average weight of the fish is low (1½ to 3 pounds) with anything over 7 pounds being rare.

The best sea trout waters are preserved either by private owners who let their fisheries by the month, week or day, or by hotels which reserve the fishing for their guests. There is, however, some good sea trout fishing controlled by angling associations, and there is good free sea trout fishing in several lakes (e.g. Lough Currane, Waterville; Lough Caragh, Kerry) and in some rivers. There are, too, many coastal streams which are free, and where there is some sea trout fishing after a flood. Sea trout can also be caught in salt water in a number of places, and this fishing is mostly free. In Irish lakes, sea trout will rise to the dry fly. In the rivers, they can be taken by spinning and fly fishing. The best time for fishing is in the evening or after a spate. They are often difficult to catch when the water is low. The most productive locations for sea trout are on the west coast, particularly the rivers of Counties Kerry, Mayo, and Donegal.

LICENSES

Ireland is divided politically into two areas: Northern Ireland, or Ulster, and the Republic of Ireland. Ulster is a part of Great Britain; the Republic is independent. Each has its own regulations and licenses, and the visitor who intends to tour around should bear in mind the boundary between the two countries.

Ireland is also divided into twenty-one districts—seventeen in the south and four in the north—for the purpose of issuing licenses for fishing for salmon and sea trout. Li-

censes fall into two categories—those only valid in the district of issue and those valid in either Ulster or the Republic of Ireland. The current prices in the Republic of Ireland are as follows:

All-districts, full season . . $9.60
Single district (specified)
full season $7.20
All districts, 21 days $7.20
All districts, 7 days $2.40

Most of the best salmon fishing is in the hands of private owners, and hoteliers and visitors are permitted to fish on payment of appropriate fees. As this type of fishing is often booked in advance, early application is advised.

A random sampling of some of the better known Irish salmon and trout waters would include the following:

BALLYNAHINCH RIVER

The Ballynahinch River is a short stream of less than 3 miles in length but it is one of the top salmon waters in Ireland. Located in County

Galway near Connemara the Ballynahinch (Sometimes called the Owenmore River) is wholly preserved but available to guests of **Ballynahinch Castle.**

The Hotel has the fishing rights on the total length of the river from the lake to the tidal waters on both banks. The river is divided into seven beats, and only two rods are permitted on each beat. There are two boats on Ballynahinch Lake with two rods per boat. Fishermen rotate on the river beats working downstream on a daily basis. Fishing beats are let for the whole day from 10 a.m. to 7 p.m. Salmon fishing extends from 1st February to the 12th October and sea trout from the end of June to the end of September. (All salmon caught by hotel guests from the river and lake are the property of the guests and may be sold to the hotel). Salmon average about 10 pounds but fish over 20 pounds are not uncommon. Occasional large brown trout are

The reward of Irish angling is not always the trout but the idyllic land through which its rivers flow

caught. The peak season for salmon is from the end of May through June, and again in September until closing day. During these periods the hotel is usually fully booked. Rod rates vary according to the months fished but average about $14.50 per day in the prime periods. Gillies wages run $2.50 per day which is the standard rate on most Irish waters.

Ballynahinch Castle, (Ballinafad, County Galway; telephone Ballinafad 2) was the ancestral home of the O'Flahertys, the 17th century chieftains of Connemara. The castle is not the traditional moat-and-battlement design expressed at Dromoland or Ashford but looks more like a great big country hotel despite having been the property of His Highness the Maharajah Jam Sahib of Nawanagar. This clubhouse atmosphere is perhaps the very trait that makes Ballynahinch so popular. Ask for a room with a tub if you have a choice. Rates run $15 single, and $21 double including meals plus a 10 percent service charge.

SUIR RIVER

The Suir (pronounced Sure) is 114 miles long. It rises in the Devil's Bit Mountain and flows south through Holycross, west of Cashel and through Newcastle before turning back on itself for some distance by the Knockmealdown and Comeragh Mountains. It then turns east and flows through Clonmel and Kilsheelan to Carrickon Suir where it meets the tide. The estuary extends for 30 miles to Waterford.

Above Thurles, the Suir is rather narrow and runs low in summer; it is best suited to dry fly and provides fair trout fishing. At Holycross, the river is bigger and there is more broken water. In its middle and lower reaches, the Suir is a big river, with deep pools and glides and there is excellent dry fly fishing. There is a Green Drake hatch, but it is erratic. Trout are plentiful and run big, as this is mainly limestone water. There is considerable free fishing, especially in the upper reaches,

and good club water, controlled by a number of angling associations. The Suir produced the Irish record Atlantic salmon of 57 pounds.

MAIGUE RIVER

This river rises on the Cork-Limerick border northwest of Charleville and flows east to join the Loobagh River. The upper Maigue, to the junction, is sand bottomed and slow moving but holds some good trout; it is excellent dry fly water. The gravelly Loobagh flows faster but its trout are smaller. From their junction, the lower Maigue flows more or less north through Bruree, Croom and Adare before entering the Shannon. The Maigue is a limestone stream and is a fair sized river in its lower section. Riffles alternate with pools and long glides which are sometimes divided into channels by beds of bulrushes. Aquatic insects are abundant including the Green Drake and Blue Winged Olive as well as the Caperer, Iron Blue Dun and Gray Flag Sedge. The Maigue tends to become low and weedy in summer and in parts is difficult to fish but it holds large trout (which have been caught up to 8¼ pounds on small dry flies). However, it is nearly always possible to find some trout rising, even on off days. It is preserved up to Cherrygrove Bridge above Croom; but the Maigue Anglers' Association has some water at Castleroberts (between Adare and Croom); and the **Dunraven Arms Hotel** at Adare has water for its guests in this area also. Rates run $5.40 per night—bed and breakfast.

ROBE RIVER

A good limestone river which produces nice trout. The Robe rises west of Ballyhaunis and flows southwesterly into Lake Mask at Cushlough Bay. Above the village of Claremorris, it is a medium-sized stream with a good deal of weed and bullrushes in some sections. Below Claremorris, it becomes a much larger stream. A favorite of dry fly anglers, the Robe produces an occasional 5- or 6-pounder, particularly during the mayfly hatches in May and June.

BLACK RIVER

A tributary to Lough Corrib rising near the village of Shrule and entering Corrib near Inchiquin Island. Much of its course forms the Galway-Mayo border. The Black is a fair-sized limestone stream which tends to become weedy in summer. Nevertheless it holds very good trout and is an excellent if somewhat difficult dry fly stream. Heavy browns (3 to 6 pounds) frequent the water in the vicinity of Ross Abbey. Around the village of Shrule the trout tend to run small but fair numbers of big fish occur in a short stretch near Headford. The Black River can be fished from **Ashford Castle.**

LOUGH CORRIB

This lake extends from near Galway city to the Mayo border, is a limestone lake of 44,000 acres in extent. There are many islands and numerous bays; and there is a great deal of shallow water, though there are also some deep gullies. Trout average about 1¼ pounds, but 3-pound fish are commonly taken on the fly. Very large brown trout are caught by trolling; one of 21 pounds 6 ounces was boated in 1959—the third largest authenticated Irish rod-caught brown trout. The Green Drake hatch occurs here about mid-May. There is fairly good wet fly fishing in spring and autumn, and the dapping with the daddy-long-legs in August and September is often very good. Salmon and sea trout are also caught in Corrib. Boats available at many points around the lake. Galway is a convenient location for fishing the southern portion of Corrib. The **Great Southern Hotel** located in the city of Galway and many smaller angling resorts around the lake shore provide accommodations. The **Oughterard House Hotel** (Connemara, County Galway) is a good location on the west shore. Unique and perhaps the most famous in Ireland is Noel Huggard's **Ashford Castle** (Ashford Castle, Cong, County Mayo; telephone Cong 3) located on the northeast shore which also gives access to

Irish anglers favor stout rods on open windswept lakes, such as Lough Doo, where trout and salmon occur

Lough Mask. Built about a century ago at a cost of over 2 million dollars the castle is a magnificent setting for the tourist angler. Rates at Ashford run about $7 to $9 per day per person for bed and breakfast. Mr. Huggard's cuisine is worth a detour. Boats with outboards and gillies are available.

LOUGH MASK

Lough Mask is about 10 miles long and averages about 4 miles width. Towards the southern end, some long, narrow bays thrust deep into the Mayo mountains to the west. It is a limestone lake. Trout average about a pound with good numbers of 3-pound fish. Some very big trout (several of over 10 pounds each year) are taken by trolling, especially in the vicinity of a deep gully that runs down the lake nearer to the western than to eastern shore. A very good wet fly lake; mayfly hatch in mid-May, and excellent dapping. Boats available at many points; shore fishing possible at several points, e.g., in the vicinity of Ferry Bridge, northwest of Clonbur.The nearest good accommodation to Loughs Mask and Carra is Una Lee's **Breaffy House Hotel** (Castlebar, County Mayo). The hotel can arrange for lunches, gillies, and boats. Rates here run from $8 to $12 per day single with meals.

LOUGH CARRA

About 6 miles long and of variable width, this lake is on the limestone plain. The water is crystal clear and the trout are very silvery in color. The browns here are a fast growing population and of large average size. A trout of 10¾ pounds was caught here in 1965 on a wet fly; the fish was only 5 years old. Carra gets a mayfly hatch somewhat earlier than Lough Mask; Carra is connected to Mask by a short river which also holds some good trout. Mask in turn is connected to Corrib by an underground river which surfaces as the Cong River, a broad limestone stream that flows past **Ashford Castle**. Occasionally a nice trout is taken in the Cong when the mayflies are on.

LOUGH CONN

This lake is about 9 miles long and varies from 2 to 4 miles in width. Conn is a limestone lake and the trout average about ¾ pound and run to 5 pounds or more. The wet fly fishing in March, April, May, and early September is often very good. There is a fair chance of hooking salmon here on wet flies, as well as by trolling. Conn's mayfly hatch is not as prolific as the emergence on other western lakes. Big trout (6 to 10 pounds) are caught each season on spinning lures but one of 11½ pounds was taken on the wet fly in 1968. Best accommodation is Brendon Geary's **Pontoon Bridge Hotel**, a typical Irish country hotel (Pontoon Bridge Hotel, Foxford, County Mayo; telephone Foxford 20). Rates run about $6 per day for bed and breakfast. Boats and gillies available. From Pontoon Bridge guests can fish the Moy River.

MOY RIVER

The Moy rises in the Ox Mountains and flows at first in a general southwest direction, passing 2 miles from Swinford. It then turns west, and then north again, through Foxford to Ballina, where it becomes tidal. The estuary is about 8 miles long and enters Killala Bay. The Moy is for the most part fairly swift and rocky; it is a fair-sized stream north of Swinford, and a big river from Foxford down. The Moy is noted salmon water, but is also quite a good brown trout river, though the fish, on the whole, are not very large. From Foxford down, the river is mostly preserved, and let by the period; in the upper reaches, there is a good deal of free and club water. The best salmon fishing on the Moy is from June through August with a peak in July; fish average about 12 pounds. The most suitable hotel here is the **Downhill Hotel** (Downhill Hotel, Ballina, County Mayo) at about $7 per day.

LITTLE BROSNA RIVER

This limestone stream is a tributary to the Shannon. It rises west of Shinrone and flows toward Roscrea, then turns north to the village of Brosna before heading toward Meelick. It is a rather small stream down to Brosna, with some deep sluggish portions near Shinrone, but with some nice dry fly water near Roscrea, Brosna and Sharavogue, and good wet fly water at Perry's Mills above Brosna. It becomes a fairly big stream below Birr; and at the New Bridge ("Anglers' Rest"), between Birr and Meelick, there is some nice wet fly as well as dry fly water, and some deep stretches holding heavy fish. The Little Brosna becomes weedy in summer, but is generally very good in late April and May. Has mayfly hatch in mid-May. Hatches of Grey Flag and B.W.O. bring on strong rises of trout. Trout average about ¼-pound with a good many fish of 2 pounds and over. Browns to 7¾ pounds have been taken on the dry fly. The stream banks are clear and there are many access points from numerous bridges. Fly fishing only is permitted on this stream.

BLACKWATER RIVER (CORK)
The Cork Blackwater is one of the most famous Irish salmon rivers. This 85-mile-long stream rises on the Cork-Kerry border and flows through Rathmore, Banteer, Mallow, Ballyhooley, Lismore, and Cappoquin to Youghal Harbour. The best salmon fishing is between Mallow and Lismore. There is some salmon fishing in the upper reaches of the Blackwater in the latter part of the season. A classic river with long glides, deep pools and pebble bottom it produces many fish of over 20 pounds each year. There is good trout fishing in parts of the Blackwater and sea trout in its lower reaches. The largest rod fishery on the river is The *Lower Blackwater Salmon Fishery* (Mr. S. H. Martin, Portmahon House, 77 Strand Road, Sandymount, Dublin). This encompasses 10 miles of excellent water near Ballyduff, Fermoy, and Ballyhooley. There are 10 beats averaging a mile in length (fished by two persons daily). There is also 2 miles of excellent sea trout and brown trout fishing as well as summer salmon and grilse on the main tributary—the River Bride.

Due to the salmon disease (UDN) the Cork Blackwater was seriously affected during the 1969 and 1970 seasons and the rod catch has been considerably below normal.

LAUNE RIVER
Although not as well publicized as other Irish salmon waters, the 14-mile-long Laune River draining the Lower Lake-of-Killarney and flowing into the head of Dingle Bay is well worth a detour. This beautiful stream fishes best in March and April but the fly rod angler may find good sport until the season ends on October 12th. Mr. Ernie Evans, who is variously a gourmet chef, angler, and your host at the **Towers Hotel** (Towers Hotel, Glenbeigh, County Kerry) can offer over 4½ miles of the Laune at $6 per day per rod, as well as beats on the Feale, Blackwater, Caragh, and Flask Rivers. He also has access to the Famous "Butler's Pool" which can be exceptional at times. His beat on the Blackwater is in the upper river which peaks late in the season. Days reserved on various rivers can be altered to suit water conditions so that you can be where the fishing is best.

The **Towers Hotel** is styled as a country-inn and is famous for its fine cuisine. Rates average about $6 per day single for bed and breakfast with weekly full board rates available.

LOUGH ENNELL
A limestone lake of 5 miles in length and about 2½ miles in width in County Westmeath near Mullingar. Ennell gets a great deal of rod pressure as the trout average nearly 2 pounds (14 inches is the minimum size). The record rod-caught trout for Ireland (26 pounds, 2 ounces caught in 1894) was taken from Ennell and is preserved in the Irish National Museum. Despite its popularity, the lake continues to produce exceptionally good fishing during duckfly and mayfly hatches. A substantial number of 4 to 7 pound trout was caught here in the 1969 and 1970 seasons despite the prolonged dry weather. The duckfly hatch commences about the beginning of April and occurs all over the lake but mainly in deep water. Olives emerge in early May followed by the Green Drake mayfly and various sedges. Boats and gillies are available. Best nearby hotel is the **Greville Arms** (Greville Arms, Mullingar, County Westmeath).

TACKLE
For trout fishing literally any fly rod is serviceable, as even the light-tackle fancier will find streams where fine lines and tippets can be put to effective use. On the big lakes, however, winds of almost gale force are not uncommon and a 9-foot rod calibered for No. 8 weight forward line is about right; this same outfit is quite adequate for Irish salmon fishing. Ideally you should bring along two outfits: a 7- or 7½-foot rod with No. 4 or No. 5 lines for small stream fishing, and a 9-foot general purpose rod. Spinning tackle with lines of 8- or 10-pound-test is suitable for casting and trolling spoons and spinners (¼ to ½ ounce class).

Local fly patterns are best. Ireland has many expert fly dressers and in dealing with highly selective trout it's worth while to stock imitations of the naturals particularly when they are emerging in quantities. The Green Drake (*Ephemera dancia*) is the best known aquatic which usually begins hatching about mid-May and lasts for a period of about five weeks on various lakes depending on the weather; the emergence occurs earliest on Lough Derg, a bit later on Lough Corrib, and the latest on Lough Erne so it's possible to follow the hatches. However, there are other naturals which bring on good rises; the Blue Winged Olive (*Ephemerella ignita*) which appears in June and emerges mainly in the evening during warm weather in July and August. Trout may become highly selective during a BWO hatch, taking only the nymph, dun, or spinner. The Iron Blue Dun (*Baetis pumilus*) is another mayfly that emerges on cold showery days early in the season, mainly in April and May. The Pale Evening Dun (*Procloen rufulum*) and the Yellow Evening Dun (*Ephemerella notata*) begin to occur in May, the former in slow flowing rivers, and the latter in fast shallow water. Various chironomids or midges also hatch in quantity creating some angling problems; the Duck Fly (*Chironomus anthracinus*) is a large, dark chironomid that comes on in the latter part of April and early May and again the trout will at times select the winged adult in preference to the pupa or vice-versa. The pupa is taken just below the surface and the activity of the fish may create the impression of a dry fly rise. Many caddisflies and some stoneflies are locally important such as the Caperer (*Sericostoma personatum*), Gray Flag Sedge (*Hydropsyche* spp.) Early Brown Stonefly (*Protonemura meyeri*) and the Large Stonefly (*Perla* spp.) Terrestrial insects such as grasshoppers, beetles, flying ants, and moths may bring on good rises and the imitations should be fairly obvious.

DAPPING THE MAYFLY

Although natural mayflies are the prototypes for literally hundreds of artificial flies, the live insect can be used as a bait. This method is almost unknown to United States waters, but the art of blow-line "dapping" is brought to perfection in the lakes of Ireland. It is most popular during the Green Drake hatch, but other insects such as grasshoppers are used when they are particularly abundant. The live mayflies are captured around the bushes or rocks near shore. They are placed in a small wooden box which has several large holes that are covered with perforated zinc; the box has two hinged lids for depositing and recapturing the insects.

The dapper uses a long (up to 17 feet), light rod and a plaited silk "blow-line" with a fine leader and small hook. One or usually two mayflies are impaled on the hook through the thorax. While drifting in the boat with the breeze, the angler lets the line blow out so that the mayfly just floats along on top of the water—well in advance of the boat. The mayfly drifts on the surface until seized by the trout.

SALTWATER FISHING

Saltwater angling in Irish waters does not have the same glamour as off the coast of Florida or Venezuela but it attracts some European tourists. Situated on the edge of the Continental Shelf and swept by the Gulf Stream, the west coast of Ireland is particularly productive of gray mullet, mackerel, haddock, cod, pollack (locally coalfish) and bass which appear inshore during the late summer and fall months. Shark and skate fishing provide the big-game thrills which may or may not be your bag. Actually, with quality freshwater angling available throughout the country you are not missing anything on the rolling Atlantic.

ACCOMMODATIONS

Pivotal stops when going east or west include: the **Limerick Inter-Continental** on the River Shannon overlooking the city of Limerick; the **Cork Inter-Continental,** 5 minutes from downtown Cork; and the **Dublin Inter-Continental** (near the American Embassy). Rates, including Continental breakfast, in the **Cork** and **Limerick Inter-Continental** are $8.50-$11.50 single, $14.50-$18.50 double; in the **Dublin Inter-Continental,** $11.50-$14.50 single, $18.50-$23 double; reduced rates mid-October through April. Among other fine hotels in Dublin are the **Royal Hibernian;** the smart **Gresham** and the **Russell;** the **Shelbourne** and **Jury's,** favorites for over a century; single rooms with bath about $12 during the peak seasons of June to September, and December. Good, but less expensive, are the **Central, Clarence** and **Wicklow.** Room rates in this type of hotel usually include a hearty Irish breakfast.

If you arrive at Shannon the best hotels are **Dromoland Castle** (Newmarket-on-Fergus, County Clare; telephone Shannon Airport 71144) which is just 8 miles from the airport and worth a detour no matter which way you are traveling, or the new

Clare Inn (Newmarket-on-Fergus, County Clare; telephone Shannon Airport 71161) a kind of elaborate motel just 9 miles from the airport. **Dromoland** rates vary widely from about $20 per day single with breakfast to about $50 per day double in a Presidential Room—breakfast included. The **Clare Inn** on European plan with twin-bedded rooms and private bath runs $12 to $18 single occupancy and $17 to $26 double occupancy; meals cost from $1.50 at breakfast to $4.00 for dinner.

Don't expect fancy food in Irish pubs. If they provide any food at all it runs from plain to inferior. Trenchermen will seek the known restaurants around cities and large towns, or at hotels. Some of the better dining spots are the *Gresham Hotel, Hotel Shelbourne,* the *Russell, Royal Hibernian,* and the *Old Dublin,* all in Dublin. *Ashford Castle* in Cong, the *Great Southern Hotel* in Galway, and for a bit of touristy shenanigans in 15th century finger-licking banquet style try *Bunratty Castle* not far from Shannon Airport on the road to Limerick; it's more fun than food but then you can always eat at the airport restaurant which is one of the best in Ireland—believe it or not. The most famous pub is *Paddy Burke's* in the village of Clarenbridge as you approach Galway from the south. Despite its uninspiring front (it's hidden behind two gas pumps) Paddy purveys the finest oysters on the Ol' Sod. Behind the bar you'll find Johnny Commins who is the present International Oyster Shucking Champion with a record 50 bivalves in 2 minutes 42 seconds. Mr. Commins uses a penknife and while he bleeds regularly in competition, nobody has come close to his mark. Best fare in Ireland is lamb stew, if you find a good one, pink hams and bacon, steak, chicken, Galway Bay oysters, smoked salmon, lobsters and above all the homemade brown bread with creamy rich butter. Dublin Bay prawns are less than spectacular although food writers tout them for some reason.

Jamaica

Long famous resort for the international set, Jamaica offers excellent saltwater fishing amid exotic surroundings.

This mountainous Caribbean island is approximately 90 miles south of the eastern end of Cuba. Jamaica is 144 miles long, and 70 miles wide between St. Ann's Bay on the north to Portland Point on the south coast. Anglers flying to Jamaica will either land at Montego Bay on the northwest coast or Kingston on the southeast coast. Both locations offer access to various kinds of fishing.

OFFSHORE FISHING

The undisputed king of the seas surrounding Jamaica is the blue marlin, and fish may be found there the year round. The average size is small, but they are plentiful. During one International Blue Marlin Tournament held during the first week in October off Port Antonio, 35 boats of all sizes raised 195 marlin in 5 days of fishing and brought to gaff 42. Nine of the boats hooked and caught doubleheaders, and two marlin were taken deep drifting. Most of the marlin are males, and will average 150 pounds per fish. One charter boat operating out of the *Blue Water Fishing Club* on the southwest coast hung 100 blue marlin in 3 months, the largest of which weighed 323 pounds and the smallest 90 pounds.

A few very large female marlin are taken each year by commercial fishermen when using wire lines for kingfish. In the autumn of 1962 one blue marlin over 600 pounds was taken by a local fisherman out of a large canoe. Although sharks are numerous, few marlin are ever mutilated. Some sailfish and white marlin are caught by fishermen, but these fish are not plentiful. Dolphin, wahoo, kingfish, blackfin tuna, common bonito, oceanic bonito, mackerel, as well as rainbow runners will be found to be abundant.

There are four main areas on the coast where at least one charter boat is usually available. Before any extended marlin fishing trip is scheduled, anglers should check on the availability of equipment and boats by writing the *Jamaica Tourist Board*. In the hands of an experienced angler, 50-pound-test monofilament, Dacron, or linen with matching tip and a 6/0 reel would be sufficient for 90 per cent of the marlin; however, most available equipment is either 24- or 39-thread and a 10/0 reel.

Fresh bait is usually available and generally consists of bonefish, mullet, mackerel, or bonito, and occasionally squid. The four major fishing ports from which marlin fishing is initiated are Port Royal near Kingston, Port Antonio, Montego Bay, and Whitehouse. Jamaica is fortunate in having several good currents and submerged mountaintops off its coast. Many of these banks are within an hour's cruising distance of the port with the exception of Montego Bay, which has a dropoff and currents but no bank within striking distance. Off Kingston and Port Royal, the most famous is California Bank. Two hours run farther south and slightly west is Bowditch Bank, larger than California, and the home of thousands of yellowfin tuna. The weather can get a bit testy off Bowditch, usually coming up rather severely in the early forenoon, and the run back to Kingston can be a miserable one quartering into a stiff sea breeze.

FISHING CENTERS

KINGSTON
Large schools of tarpon come into Kingston harbor in the late fall with the peak of the run showing best in November. Some tarpon are caught on fast-moving plugs and spoons, but the majority are taken on live minnows, finger mullet, or crabs while driftfishing. Kingston, the largest city in Jamaica, has several good restaurants and hotels. Guides and boats are available, and reliable fishing information may be obtained from personnel at the hotels. In addition to tarpon, jack crevalle, snook, mackerel, kingfish, and snappers may be taken in the harbor during most of the year. Spoons, wobblers, and white feathers are the best artificial lures for both trolling and casting.

WHITEHOUSE
Eighty miles west of Kingston is the small village of Whitehouse where the visiting angler may find some outstanding fishing. A charter boat with experienced skipper and crew is sometimes available at the *Blue Water Fishing Club* a few miles east of Whitehouse. There are two large banks within an hour's run of the club, Blossom and New Bank. A few small flats occur in this area, and some bonefish can be caught by wading and casting to the schools. Good accommodations are available if arranged for in advance.

MONTEGO BAY
One hour's drive north of Whitehouse is the plush resort city of Montego Bay. Many fine hotels and good food are available here, and there are charter boats for hire. This area is more developed than Whitehouse, and therefore it's easier for the average tourist to arrange his fishing in Montego Bay. Many fine marlin have been taken from this port as well as wahoo, dolphin, small tuna, and bonito. The trade winds prevail around Jamaica; so it is wise to fish east in the morning, and when the sea breeze comes up later in the day, a nice easy run with the sea may be made coming back to port.

PORT ANTONIO
Approximately one hundred miles to the east on the north coast we find the town of Port Antonio where an International Blue Marlin Tournament is held every fall. Each succeeding year has found more boats participating and more marlin being taken. This tournament is usually

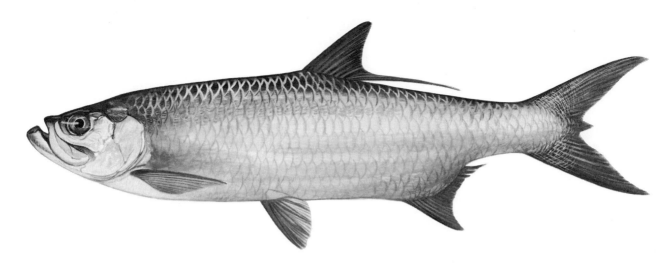

Tarpon concentrate at the river mouths and a "run" occurs in Kingston harbor

held in September or October; originated by sportsman Jim Paterson, President of the *Eastern Jamaica Anglers Association,* it is one of the outstanding events of its kind, attracting anglers from all over the world (for information contact: James B. Paterson, P.O. Box 140, Port Antonio, Jamaica, W.I.)

Port Antonio offers excellent accommodations and good food with charter boats stationed there the year round. There is one small bank called Henry Holmes and a larger one named Grappler Bank farther offshore. Despite its small size, Henry Holmes Bank attracts countless thousands of fish—yellowfin tuna, and rainbow runners gather there each year with the bulk of them congregating during the winter months. Unfortunately there are also swarms of sharks, but it is here that two opposite currents meet and a rip exists. Marlin abound in these waters, and several over 500 pounds have been taken by commercial fishermen.

There are two other outstanding fishing areas near Jamaica; one is the great Pedro Bank lying some forty miles due south of Portland Point and some sixty miles from Kingston, and Morant Cays lying some thirty miles south of Morant Point but sixty miles east southeast from Kingston. Both Morant Cays and Pedro Bank offer coral reefs above high tide and protection from high sea winds, but these expeditions should not be attempted unless a large, fast, well-equipped boat is available.

INSHORE FISHING

Tarpon and snook occur seasonally all around Jamaican shores; however, both species are numerous in brackish waters near river mouths and for varying distances upstream. The two largest rivers in Jamaica are the Black and the Rio Grande. The Black River originates in the Santa Cruz mountain range and terminates at the town of Black River on the southwest coast. The river is navigable from its mouth by outboard for some twenty miles upstream. It is perhaps the best river in Jamaica for tarpon up to 100 pounds, snook in the 20- to 30-pound class, snappers, and jack crevalle. Small boats and guides are locally available, but the angler must bring his own tackle. Accommodations can sometimes be arranged for in Black River or Mandeville, which is an hour's drive from Black River, has accommodations as well. The mouth of the Rio Grande, a few miles west of Port Antonio on the northeast coast, contains some very big snook, tarpon, snappers, and jacks. Good accommodations are available in Port Antonio. Medium to heavy bait-casting or spinning tackle is recommended for fishing the mouths of both the Rio Grande and the Black.

Bonefish, including an elsewhere rare second species, the longfin bonefish (*Dixenina nemeptera*), are common to Jamaican waters; however, there are comparatively few flats for the fly rod buff. There are several along the south coast at Whitehouse and near Montego Bay.

The longfins are usually caught near creek mouths but will sometimes school with the common bonefish (*Albula vulpes*). In general bonefishing here is a live bait, deep water proposition.

MULLET IN MOUNTAIN STREAMS

A zany, but popular diversion for the fly or spin-rod angler is fishing for the several species of mullet which inhabit Jamaican streams. The mountain mullet is usually caught on pieces of avocado pear by the local experts, but it will also strike artificial flies and small spinners. This little mullet lives in fast whitewater, and will run ½ to 2 pounds in weight.

In the quiet and slow reaches downstream lives another variety of mullet called the hognose. This fish is commonly taken on river shrimp as well as avocado, and will also hit a spinner. The hognose is a tough adversary and grows somewhat larger than the mountain mullet. Several hognose mullet have been taken in the 5-6-pound class.

Even farther down the river approaching its mouth lives still another mullet locally called the calopeva. This is the largest of the freshwater mullet and reaches a weight in excess of 10 pounds. Like the hognose it is an excellent fighter, but, once again, the lure needed to take it is most unusual. The calopeva feeds on river moss, and as far as is known will accept nothing else. This fish does not go to sea, but it does find brackish water in which it will spawn. Having done so, it will then return to the quiet pools of freshwater farther upstream.

Two popular spots for mullet fishing are located in the headwaters of the Rio Grande and just below the dam at Bog Walk on the Rio Cobre west of Kingston. There are hotels in Port Antonio where information is available on rafts and guides. The Rio Cobre can be reached only by car, via Spanish Town, the old capital of Jamaica. Since it is a forty-five-minute drive, the angler should make certain that he will have transportation back to Kingston, as there are no lodgings near Bog Walk.

LICENSES
None required.

TACKLE
Big-game tackle is supplied by the charter boats. For those who want to bring their own, a 50-pound class outfit should be a comfortable maximum on the marlin, and a 20-pound class outfit for all other trolling. If you want to pursue the mullet, any light spinning (ultra-light is ideal) or lightweight fly rod is adequate.

TRAVEL NOTES
No passports or visas are required for a stay of up to 6 months, provided the trip originates and terminates in the continental U.S. and the traveler has a return ticket and some proof of citizenship. Visitors fill in a Disembarkation Card prior to arrival, which must be returned to the Immigration authorities on departure. Vaccination certificates are required if the passenger comes from an infected area. No household pets are allowed. Allowed in duty free are: 1 carton of cigarettes; 50 cigars or ½ lb. tobacco; 1 pint of liquor or 1 quart of wine. No foreign rums are permitted. Also necessary for return entry is some sort of proof of U.S. Citizenship such as a birth certificate, naturalization papers or a passport.

ACCOMMODATIONS

MONTEGO BAY
The rates at Montego Bay hotels vary greatly in season and out; most are Modified American Plan, a few American Plan and fewer still European Plan. The winter prices range from about $25 to $70 per day per person in a double room. Among the popular hotels on the "Gold Coast" are the **Montego Beach** and **Sunset Lodge,** long-time favorites of the international set. Nearby is the luxurious and exclusive beach resort **Round Hill, Bay Roc, Casa Blanca** and **Tryall.** These are among Montego Bay's finest hotels. Most of them have private beaches. Directly behind Doctor's Cave Beach and overlooking the Caribbean is the **Casa Montego, The Beach View** and **Hacton House.** These are good hotels facing the sea. **Half Moon Hotel** and the **Royal Caribbean** are several miles out along the coast. **Miranda Lodge,** 2 miles from the airport and overlooking Montego Bay, is a self-contained resort with a fresh-water pool but it provides transportation to Doctor's Cave Beach, nightly entertainment. **Holiday House, Harmony House** and **Blairgowrie** are small but charming. The **Breezy Point Estate, Ltd.** is bright and new.

Doctor's Cave Beach Club is world famous for its coral sands and crystal-clear water. There is an excellent reef, and much of the area's social life centers around its Riviera-like setting. Membership is available to guests at all Montego Bay hotels, and water skiing, skin-diving and sailing are among the many aquatic activities it offers.

Ten miles inland from Falmouth, in neighboring Trelawny, is **Good Hope,** an 18th-century great-house in the center of a 6,000-acre cattle ranch. It offers horses and good trails for riding, and the easy, gracious life on a plantation home set in the midst of tall, waving cocoanut palms. It has its own private beach.

OCHO RIOS
About 65 miles east of Montego Bay is the Ocho Rios area, with numerous hotels and guest houses along a beautiful coastline. These include the luxurious **Plantation Inn, Carib Ocho Rios, Shaw Park Beach Hotel** and the **Island Inn.** Near St. Ann's Bay are the **Windsor,** the magnificent **Jamaica Hilton** and **Runaway Bay Hotel.** At the other end of the string, near Oracabessa, are the **Golden Head Beach** and the jaunty **Jamaica Playboy Club-Hotel.** In between lie peaceful **Jamaica Inn,** ever popular **Tower Isle,** which pioneered the gold rush of tourism to Ocho Rios, **Silver Seas** and the cottage colony of **Sans Souci.** Four miles from Ocho Rios village, Dunn's River tumbles down palm-shaded falls into the sparkling Caribbean. This is one of the island's best known beauty and bathing spots, where you can splash from the warm salt sea into the cool fresh foam of the falls.

PORT ANTONIO
Scene of the annual marlin tournament, Port Antonio has the island's heaviest rainfall and is consequently more lushly tropical. It boasts the fabulous resort of **Frenchman's Cove,** the **Jamaica Reef** of Errol Flynn fame, and charming **Bonnie View** from which—as the name implies—there is a superb view.

KINGSTON
The **Sheraton Kingston** is the largest hotel in the capital; $17.50 single, $11.75 per person double. The **Myrtle Bank** is conveniently close to the downtown shopping area; from $12 single, $20 double, the year round. In the Parish of St. Andrew, a suburb of Kingston, there is **Courtleigh Manor,** near Liguanea golf course. Also in this area are the **Mona, Blue Mountain Inn, Terra Nova, Liguanea Terrace, Flamingo** and **Green Gables.** These rates are per person in a double room. At **Morgan**'s **Harbour** in Port Royal is Kingston's only beach resort; yacht marina; from $8 per person double.

Kenya

This independent East African state bordering the Indian Ocean offers excellent saltwater fishing in season for black marlin, striped marlin, blue marlin, and sailfish and considerable freshwater fishing for Nile perch and tigerfish. Modest trout angling is also available in high altitude streams and largemouth bass provide some sport in Lake Naivasha. Kenya has a total area of 224,960 square miles but only about 3 percent of this is inland waters; its largest lake lying almost entirely within the country is Lake Rudolf in the northwest at the border of Ethiopia. The easterly shore of Lake Victoria indents Kenya at its western border with Uganda and Tanzania. Many sportsmen combine some angling with a hunting or camera safari. Kenya's numerous national parks are all easily reached by good roads where lions, elephants, hippos, and other free-roaming game can be viewed or photographed at close range. Sightseeing is an important part of any itinerary and complete 17- or 21-day tours covering all the major attractions in Tanzania and Uganda as well as Kenya are offered by *Kenya Flying Safaris* (Safari Outfitters Inc., 8 South Michigan Avenue, Chicago, Illinois 60603) which includes some fishing along the way. For itineraries with the emphasis on fishing with some sightseeing included *East African Fishing Safaris* (P.O. Box 4701, Nairobi, Kenya, East Africa) offers several trips by road and plane of 24 to 26 days duration which covers both freshwater and saltwater locations as well as game viewing.

THE SEASON

Extensive areas in Kenya have a mean annual rainfall of less than 30 inches. A large portion of northern Kenya has a mean of less than 10 inches. Low rainfall, high temperatures, and rapid evaporation create much aridity countrywide. Rains come as sudden heavy downpours usually from March to May while lesser rains occur from October through December. The best months weatherwise are from June through September with July and August the coolest months. Kenya is on the equator and the greater temperature differences come with altitude. The coastal region is hot and humid with temperatures from 75°F to 90°F. The inland plateaus to

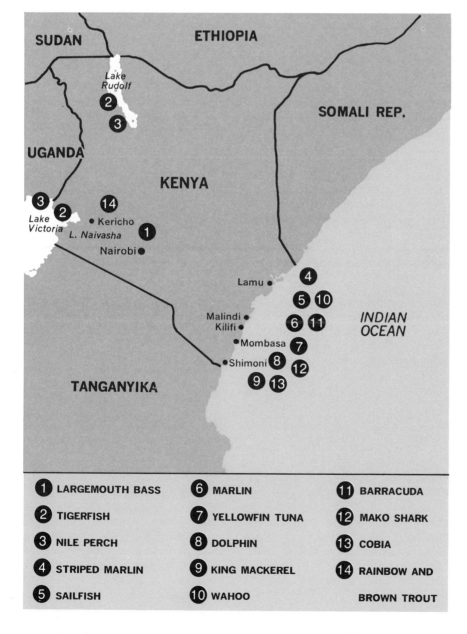

① LARGEMOUTH BASS ⑥ MARLIN ⑪ BARRACUDA

② TIGERFISH ⑦ YELLOWFIN TUNA ⑫ MAKO SHARK

③ NILE PERCH ⑧ DOLPHIN ⑬ COBIA

④ STRIPED MARLIN ⑨ KING MACKEREL ⑭ RAINBOW AND

⑤ SAILFISH ⑩ WAHOO BROWN TROUT

4,000 feet altitude are dry and hot with temperatures often exceeding 100°F. The highland region and Lake Victoria Basin (over 4,000 feet) usually have cool nights and warm days. The temperature range is from 45°F to 85°F.

FRESHWATER FISHING

Modest quality trout fishing exists in Kenya. In the lakes around Kericho rainbows will average about 1½ pounds with 5- and 6-pounders a possibility. In nearby streams such as the Kipsanoi and Itari the fish average about ¾ pound with the occasional large trout going 3 or 4 pounds. The **Tea Hotel** at Kericho is the comfortable headquarters for trout anglers in this area. Other popular trout rivers are the Chania, Gura, and the Sagana. Most of the fishing for rainbow and brown trout is in cold waters about 5,000 feet altitude in wild and beautiful surroundings. A number of hotels cater to anglers at distances from Nairobi varying between 56 and 230 miles.

There is no closed season but during the heavy rains from April through June the high run-off precludes these as fishing months. Full information can be obtained and trips organized by the *Brooke Bond Travel Ltd.* (P.O. Box 8726, Nairobi, Kenya, East Africa). This same outfit will arrange any type of freshwater or saltwater fishing.

Kenya may not have the biggest trout in the world but it boasts the largest fly-tying firm on the globe at *Kenya Fishing Flies Ltd.* (P.O. Box 20, Kericho, Kenya, East Africa). The plant has 223 men on staff, of which 190 are expert fly-tyers. The quality of their products is exceptional and prices extremely low.

Largemouth bass were introduced to Kenya some years ago and have thrived particularly well in Lake Naivasha, only 54 miles from Nairobi. In general the bass average about 1½ pounds although 5- and 6-pounders are not uncommon. The

same methods used in the U.S. are popular here.

Kenya's principal freshwater game-fish are the tigerfish and Nile perch in Lake Rudolf. The population of big perch is a sub-species (*Lates niloticus rudolfianus*) which is thought to exceed 250 pounds. The rod-and-reel record here for Nile perch is 238 pounds. Although Lake Rudolf is readily accessible by air from Nairobi, it lies in a desolate and otherwise waterless area, the home of the Turkana people, and it has hardly changed in a physical sense in a thousand years. The isolation coupled with the scenery and spectacular sunsets make for a rewarding visit. A popular fishing spot for both Nile perch and tigerfish is Ferguson's Gulf. Central Island, about an hour by boat from Ferguson's Gulf is one of the main breeding grounds of crocodiles on the lake and worth a side trip. The **Lake Rudolf Fishing Lodge** is headquarters on the gulf. On the west shore is *Lake Rudolf Fishing Safaris Ltd.* (P.O. Box 45, Nakuru, Kenya, East Africa) operated by Tony Partridge.

SALTWATER FISHING

Kenya offers excellent big-game angling from Lamu in the north, through Malindi, Kilifi, Momasa, and Shimoni to Mafia Island in the south. This section of the western Indian Ocean has more than 700 species of fish. Striped marlin is the principal gamefish along Kenya's Coral Coast. The fish usually arrive about mid-November and continue until mid-March with the peak in January. Sailfish may appear somewhat earlier in the northbound current but the best fishing occurs during the same period as the striped marlin run. Black and blue marlin are less abundant but some large fish are hooked, particularly in the waters off Shimoni. Other gamefish include the yellowfin tuna, dolphin, king mackerel, wahoo, barracuda, mako, cobia, and the occasional swordfish. Light tackle casters can find plenty of inshore

action with bonefish, jacks, ladyfish, barracuda, and the miniature Indo-Pacific tarpon (ox-eye).

Charter boats of varying quality are available in the major fishing centers. In general the rates run from $150 to $200 per day for a fully equipped, modern sportfisherman.

The most popular resorts on the Coral Coast are the **Dolphin Hotel,** the **Oceanic,** and the **Sea Breezes** in Mombasa; from $11 single and $19 double American plan. At Malindi try the **Eden Roc Hotel** or the **Sinbad** at about $11 per person American Plan. In Shimoni anglers headquarter at the **Pemba Channel Fishing Club** and on Mafia Island the **Mafia Island Fishing Club.** At Kilifi is the **Mnarani Club.**

TACKLE

All the necessary tackle for saltwater big-game fishing is available on Kenya's charter boats. Naturally specialists will bring their own. Resorts that cater to Nile perch anglers usually have suitable gear available. The standard tackle consists of a 9- to 10-foot-long surf spinning rod with a large capacity reel spooling 20- to 30-pound-test monofilament. The most popular lures are 6-inch-long plugs; jointed subsurface models are ideal. For tigerfish bring along a freshwater spinning rod or fly rod, lightweight but with a fairly stiff tip to facilitate hooking these toothy gamesters. The trout streams are not generally large and a 7- or 7½-foot fly rod calibered for a No. 5 line will prove adequate. *International Sports House Ltd.* (Northey Street, Nairobi) stocks a variety of tackle suitable for local angling.

TRAVEL NOTES

By Pan Am Jet Clipper from New York to Nairobi in 15¾ hours. Passport, visa ($2) and smallpox vaccination certificate required. Taxi fare from Embakasi Airport into Nairobi (8 miles) is 25 Kenya shillings or $3.30 plus 2 or 3 shillings tip. Bus fare is 5 shillings or 70 cents.

CLOTHING

Men wear shorts and open-neck shirts and women wear their coolest cottons the year around on the coast. Fairly warm woolens are needed in Nairobi and the highlands from June through August; lightweight suits and dresses the rest of the year, with something warmer for the cold nights.

ACCOMMODATIONS

NAIROBI

Advance hotel reservations are advisable at any time of year. In downtown Nairobi are the luxurious **Inter-Continental Nairobi,** single $14.30-$20, double $25.70-$31.45; and the **New Stanley** (Hilton), from $15.40 single, $25.20 double, rates are without breakfast (which other hotels include); the **Ambassadeur,** from $12.60 single, $22 double; **New Avenue,** from $11 single, $17.15, double. About half a mile from the center of town are the **Norfolk,** from $12.35 single, $23.10 double; and the **Panafric,** from $14 single, $26.20 double. Rates include service charges.

ELSEWHERE

No trip to Kenya is complete without a visit to **Treetops.** This world-famous hotel is built in an enormous fig tree in the Aberdare Forest west of Mt. Kenya in the Kikuyu tribe's realm. (Dress for cool weather at this elevation.) Guests must arrive early in the afternoon to avoid meeting the elephants, hippos and rhinoceros that come to drink at the water hole below the hotel. It is spotlighted at night, but the beasts think this is just another moon. A two-day tour from Nairobi for a night at Treetops costs less than $40 a person, all-inclusive. The elegant **Mt. Kenya Safari Club,** a 10 minute drive from Nanyuki Airport, is at 7,000 feet elevation; a fireplace in each guest room; heated pool; golf, fishing, riding; tribal entertainment; from $27 single, $45 double, with meals.

Mexico

From its 2,000-mile border with the United States, Mexico extends south and east 1,800 miles to its boundary with Guatemala. Although locations such as Acapulco, Mazatlan, and Cabo San Lucas are well known to fishermen, there are literally hundreds of remote villages along both coasts which are seldom visited by tourist anglers. Two areas that are becoming of increasing importance are the Yucatan Peninsula, which separates the Caribbean from the Gulf of Mexico, and the west-coast peninsula of Baja California. Saltwater fishing for striped marlin, black marlin, blue marlin, Pacific sailfish, tarpon, snook, dolphin, wahoo, roosterfish, yellowfin tuna, corvina, totuava, and many other game species is available. A limited amount of freshwater fishing exists also. Three-fourths of Mexico is mountainous, and many of the central plateau lakes and streams offer rainbow trout or largemouth bass.

Mexican charter craft are not usually as modern or well-equipped as stateside fleets. Small to medium sport-fishermen are the rule (24 to 32 feet) which are adequate for the normally flat to moderate seas encountered. There are comparatively few days when offshore fishing is scrubbed due to high winds. Although tackle is available on most charter boats, again it is only adequate and the visitor is strongly advised to bring his own. Twenty-pound-test class for small game trolling including sailfish and 50- or 80-pound-test class for marlin and swordfish is standard here.

Blacks of 500 to 1,000 pounds, while not abundant, are always possible, particularly in southern Baja waters.

Trolling large flyingfish baits (imported from California and currently $1.25 each) and sometimes mullet baits is the principal method used for marlin. Blind strikes are obtained but frequently the majority of the fish, including swordfish, will be sighted finning-out at the surface.

The Mexican method is to rush the baits to billfish at full throttle, then let them settle in front of a visible quarry or work the area in a trolling pattern.

THE SEASON

Climate in Mexico is determined more or less by altitude rather than distance from the Equator. The *tierra caliente* or hot land is from sea level to about 3,000 feet; the *tierra templada* or temperate land is from 3,000 to 6,000 feet; the cold land or *tierra fria* is limited to mountain tops and plateaus of 6,000 feet or higher. Though modified to some extent by the nearness of the sea, these differences hold throughout Mexico. The rainy season begins in June and extends to October; however, except for the rare "chubasco" (hurricanelike storm) the rains are not equatorially violent nor continuous. Northerly blows during the winter months sometimes confine ships to port on both coasts but these are normally of short duration. Temperatures run 85°F or more in the summer but average a pleasant 67° at other times of the year. November through June is the ideal period.

BAJA CALIFORNIA

The 1,015-mile-long peninsula contiguous to the state of California is part of Mexico and forms the western boundary of the Gulf of California, more commonly known as the Sea of Cortez. The Gulf supports an immense marine sport fishery. A rugged playground, Baja has everything from impregnable mountains to lonely deserts and thousands of isolated beaches down both coasts. The northern portion of Baja is separated from the south both geographically and politically; the upper half, Baja California Norte, is a state; the lower half, Baja California Sur, is a territory. From the tourist angler's standpoint Baja Sur has the most to offer. There are centuries-old missions to intrigue the sight-seer, legend to please romantics, and a languid subtropical climate for those who want to relax and get away from it all. Sunny skies prevail. The weather can be hot and humid during the summer months in Baja although ocean breezes and air-conditioning make life comfortable.

THE FISHING

Fishing is productive all year round in the Sea of Cortez. There is some debate about peak periods from one location to another but a distillation of opinions suggests the following: July to October is tops for blue and black marlin and swordfish. April to June is the peak for sailfish and striped marlin. California yellowtail and yellowfin tuna peak in the spring season, Wahoo are most abundant in the fall with November particularly good, while roosterfish peak during the summer in the northern half of the Cortez and during the winter toward the Cape. Billfish are most common from Buena Vista to Cabo San Lucas although sailfish and black marlin are occasionally caught in the Mulege area.

ACCOMMODATIONS

LA PAZ

This busy waterfront city of 40,000 founded in 1821 is the territorial capital of Baja. La Paz, the nearest commercial air terminal to the lower peninsula resorts, is not a major sport fishing area although boats are available for charter at $60 per day or $70 with tackle included. It's normally a long run (about 2 hours) to the nearest marlin grounds in the San Lorenzo Channel. La Paz has four tourist hotels. The best downtown facing the bay is **Hotel Los Arcos** where bungalow accommodations surround a swimming pool set among tropical plants. Rates run $15 per day single, and $27 double American plan; newer deluxe units are $20 single and $36 double. The main building across the street has a bar and open air patio for late dining.

Off the main thoroughfare and on the beach is **Hotel Los Cocos**. Originally a small home in a palm grove and now a spacious layout to which new buildings have been added, this hotel offers deluxe doubles in contemporary Mexican style at $30 per day and modern singles at $17.50 per day, both American plan. A large dining patio faces the pool and beach. Literally next door to **Los Cocos** and smaller in scope is **La Posada**, with cocktail lounge, pool, and an intimate club atmosphere. Singles at $17.50 per day and doubles at $30 per day American plan and also suites at $35 double and $20 single. Nearby but not on the beach is **Hotel Guaycura**, unpretentious but set amid lush gardens with pool. Units here are $15 single and $27 double American plan; newer and tastefully decorated wing goes for $20 single and $36 double.

LOS BARRILES

Popular and one of the oldest resorts in Baja is **Rancho Buena Vista** (P.O. Box 486, Newport Beach, California, or Rancho Buena Vista, Los Barriles, Baja California). The Ran-

Heavyweight marlin in Mexican waters

cho consists of a main lodge on the beach containing a cocktail lounge and dining room with separate motel type units at $15 per day American plan. Informality is the keynote here. Owner in residence Colonel Charles M. Walters is the troop leader at family-style meals while everybody swaps lies. Buena Vista has its own fleet of boats for offshore fishing at $65 per day. There is a 3,000-foot airstrip a short distance from the Rancho.

Nearby is **Bahia de Palmas** (Los Barriles, Baja California) small and relaxed with American plan rates at $10 per day per person.

SAN JOSE DEL CABO
At the tip of the peninsula lies San Jose del Cabo, a quaint town where one of the early missions is located. A tuna cannery attracts fleets of boats to "land's end" between the Pacific Ocean and the Gulf. The **Hacienda Cabo San Lucas** (P.O. Box 1775, La Jolla, California) directly on the beach is one of Baja's most distinguished angling resorts as the marlin grounds are only 15 minutes away and the layout is lavish; Spanish Colonial style, arched terraces, enclosed gardens and fountains make shorebound hours rewarding. Rates run $20 to $24 per person American plan with special summer prices from July to November. There is a 5,000-foot runway just four miles north of the hotel. To the west and also located on a beach is **Las Cruces Palmilla** (P.O. Box 40, La Paz, Baja California) another deluxe hotel with rates at $28 per person American plan. To the north, and not to be confused with the **Hacienda** is the **Hotel Cabo San Lucas** (P.O. Box 48747, Briggs Station, Los Angeles, California 90048) currently Baja's most deluxe resort. Situated on the hills overlooking Chilene Bay the hotel offers a dazzling view of the Gulf. A lavish dining room and lanai-type cocktail lounge compete with onyx-faced shower stalls and king-sized beds. A classic hotel by world standards, rates range from $22.50 to $30 sin-

Big roosterfish like this 71-pounder are rugged quarry taken on light tackle

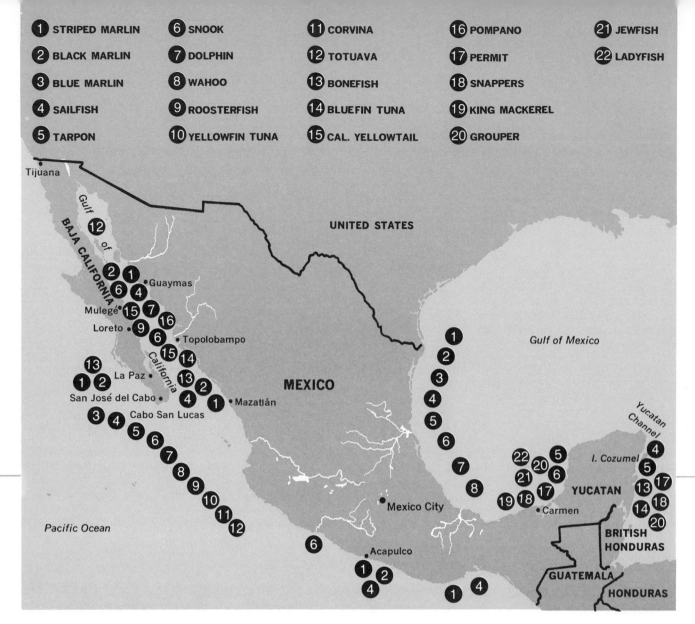

1 STRIPED MARLIN 6 SNOOK 11 CORVINA 16 POMPANO 21 JEWFISH
2 BLACK MARLIN 7 DOLPHIN 12 TOTUAVA 17 PERMIT 22 LADYFISH
3 BLUE MARLIN 8 WAHOO 13 BONEFISH 18 SNAPPERS
4 SAILFISH 9 ROOSTERFISH 14 BLUEFIN TUNA 19 KING MACKEREL
5 TARPON 10 YELLOWFIN TUNA 15 CAL. YELLOWTAIL 20 GROUPER

gle, or $20 to $30 per person double American plan according to the accommodation selected (room, studio, small suite, double suite, deluxe suite). From December to June reservations are tight despite the 160 guest capacity. Boats and tackle are better than average here; charter runs $65 per day. A 3,600 foot airstrip is adjacent to hotel.

MULEGE

Mulege is nearly 300 miles north of La Paz and 665 miles south of the U.S. border. Because of its location Mulege is extremely popular among California anglers who fly their own planes. Less arid than the Cape area, this section of Baja has mangrove shores and a freshwater river, the Estero. The fishing here is primarily for California yellowtail from November through February; roosterfish and dolphin from April through August, and pompano from June through August. The term

"pompano" in the Cortez includes permit, gafftopsail pompano, and the true pompano; the latter occurs on both the Atlantic and Pacific sides of Mexico and is similar to the Florida pompano. Groupers, snappers, cabrilla, sierra and black sea bass are caught the year round. Billfish are scarce this far north but a few sailfish and black marlin are taken in the late spring and summer months.

Popular and moderately priced is the **Serenidad** (Mulege, Baja California) which offers bungalows and rooms at $16 per day per person American plan with air conditioning or grass shack cabanas at $10 per day. There is a 3,000-foot airstrip facing the camp which is especially busy on weekends. Host Fernando del Moral keeps everybody oriented on the Unicom. Boats get $55 per day or $40 for a half day; outboards with guide are $35 per day.

On a hill outside of Mulege is the newer **Punta Chivato** (Mulege, Baja California) a deluxe layout with rates at $35 to $40 per day double American plan. Located on the left bank of the arroyo a short distance from a local landmark called El Sombretite (a small hill with a lighthouse) is the **Hotel Mulege**, formerly the Club Aero de Mulege. The hotel offers motel-type suites and a few bungalows. American plan rates are $20 per day single and $35 double.

Anyone who visits Mulege should spend at least one day on an excursion, preferably by water although you can get there by road, to Conception Bay, the inlet just to the south. Boats for the outing cost less than for big-game fishing. You can dive for scallops and lobster, scoop up butter clams and oysters by the bucketful, and, if you wish, sleep out overnight on a beach of your own discovery.

A marlin weighs in at Cabo San Lucas

Scenic luxury at Las Cruces Palmilla

Miles of uninhabited beach typifies Quintana Roo. Guides ready boat at Boca Paila

Aeronaves de Mexico flies in regularly from Tijuana to Santa Rosalia. Arrangements must be made in advance through your travel agent for automobile transportation from Santa Rosalia to Mulege.

LORETO
Loreto, which lies south of Mulege was the first permanent colony founded on the peninsula and served as Baja's capital from 1697 to 1829. Today it is enjoying a revival as a vacation spot. Aeronaves de Mexico has three flights a week into Loreto. The fishing here is the same as the Mulege area with emphasis on California yellowtail, roosterfish, dolphin, snappers, and other light-tackle gamesters. Roosterfish are especially abundant in Escondido Bay during the summer months.

The deluxe resort in Loreto is **La Mision de la Loreto** with rates at $35 double American plan. Rustic yet modern is the **Hotel Baja** with rates at $30 double American Plan. Small and almost lost in the acres of palms beside the Gulf is the **Hotel Oasis**, where the full tariff is $10 to $12.50 per person per day. Late-model fishing cruisers get $55 a day. **Flying Sportsman's Lodge**, something of a garden spot on the beach south of town, with flowering shrubs and lawn growing close to the sea is very popular. Air conditioning comes in all rooms at the Lodge. The food is good. American plan rates are $12.50 per person per day; fishing cruisers equipped for 4 persons are $55. Tackle rental is an extra $5 per day.

BAJA TRAVEL NOTES
Mexico is serviced by Pan American Jet Clipper non-stop from New Orleans and Houston to Mexico City, non-stop from Miami to Merida, and one-stop from Miami to Mexico City. Aeronaves de Mexico offers daily flights to La Paz from Mexico City; it also has a service called the "Sportsman's Route to Baja," which departs Tijuana on Monday, Wednesday and Saturday, flying to Santa Rosalia, Loreto, and La Paz. The return flight, with the same stops, departs on Tuesday, Friday and Sunday. Round-trip air fare on Aeronaves between Tijuana and Loreto is $80.

Relatively few anglers make the trip by road. From 160 miles south of the U.S. border to La Paz there's virtually nothing but desert. You have to be extremely well prepared to follow Mexico Highway 1 down the peninsula. This road is frequently no more than a desert trail and the going is difficult. The drive is not recommended for passenger cars. A jeep or a small truck is required, and even then there should be a caravan of at least two vehicles.

To reach La Paz, gateway to the southern resorts, you can drive down paved highway along the eastern coast of the Sea of Cortez (mainland Mexico) to Mazatlan and take the ferry across. Resembling a small cruise ship, this modern vessel transports 400 passengers and more than 100 autos, sailing twice a week on a 16-hour crossing. The quick way, of course, is by plane; La Paz is less than 2 hours from Los Angeles by jet.

Baggage handling around airports and hotels by non-professionals ranging in age from ten upwards is something of a national sport in Mexico. Veteran travelers carry plenty of one peso coins or notes. Except in metropolitan hotels change is always hard to get.

MAINLAND WEST COAST

GUAYMAS

An old seaport town, its main resort area is at San Carlos Bay which has developed into a yacht harbor with hotels, motels, and cafes. Miramar Beach is another popular spot and includes trailer camps as well as a large fleet of boats. There are motels in Guaymas proper; however, the vacation atmosphere is lacking. Sailfish occur off Guaymas from May through September; black and striped marlin are caught during the same period but are much less abundant. Fishing for dolphin, groupers, snappers, and corvina continues the year round. Two of the better hotels in this area are the **Hotel Playa de Cortez** with double rates at $29 per day American Plan and the **Miramar Hotel** at $14 per day double European Plan.

TOPOLOBAMPO

Below Guaymas there are several places where rough roads lead from the main highway to the sea but there are no shore accommodations except in the city of Los Mochis (**Hotel Santa Anita**) and at the modern **Yacht Hotel** in Topolobampo. Black sea bass, roosterfish, California yellowtail, snappers, snook, and several species of jack provide the major fishing. Sailfish and marlin appear in the spring with a peak in June but it's a long run out to the grounds. El Farallen, a 500-foot-high miniature of Gibraltar shared by sea birds and sea lions, rises from the Gulf about 20 miles from shore. A record 105-pound California yellowtail was caught in 1955.

MAZATLAN

This popular resort city has many fine hotels and charter craft available for offshore fishing. The angling here is principally for striped marlin from January through April. The sailfish and black marlin are most abundant from April through November with the best period for sails in June and July. April is a peak month for black sails and marlin. Blacks of over 600 pounds have been taken in Mazatlan waters. All other Sea of Cortez game species occur here, including some snook in the river estuaries and lagoons south of Mazatlan. Due to the fact that the best fishing grounds here are about twenty miles offshore it's important to charter a fast boat. The Star Fleet located near the lighthouse is recommended.

Beachside hotels include the **Hotel Cima, Hotel Playa, Hotel Belmar, Motel Playa del Rey** and **Hotel La Siesta.** European Plan rates are from $10 up double. The Balboa Club, a private club, will accept guests on a reciprocal basis with recognized fishing clubs, yacht clubs, or similar organizations. The club has excellent food and accommodations (Balboa Club de Mazatlan S. A., V. Carranza 103, Mazatlan, Sinaloa, Mexico). Mazatlan restaurants are famous for their seafoods especially oysters, shrimp, and lobster. Two popular spots are *El Shrimp Bucket* and the *Copa de Leche.*

ACAPULCO

Equally famous with jet-setters, Acapulco is also one of the major sail-fishing ports in Mexico during the winter and spring season (peak in April). Nearly all hotels can arrange for charter craft. Although not as numerous as they are on the Baja and Mazatlan grounds, both striped and black marlin occur here also and specimens of the latter exceeding 600 pounds have been taken. Acapulco is located on an oval bay surrounded by mountains and the scenery is fantastic. Hotels are numerous and range from super deluxe to modest. **Hotel Pierre Marques**, on Revolcadero Beach 12 miles from the city, is very swank with lavish entertainment; winter Modified American Plan (with 2 meals) rates from $22 per person. Also tops are the **Acapulco Hilton, El Presidente, Caleta, Ritz** and **Las Brisas** (has 100 swimming pools, one for nearly every room) with winter rates from $36 double, with breakfast. Excellent hotels with Modified American Plan rates include the **Playa Hornos, El Mirador** (dramatically perched on the Quebrada Cliffs), the **Costero, Las Hamacas, El Pozo del Rey** (American Plan), **Eleano** and **Majestic;** average Modified American Plan winter rate is $28 double. There are many good lower priced hotels: **Boca Chica, Club de Pesca, Maris, Papagayo, Del Monte; Motel Acapulco** and **Autohotel Ritz.** All rates are lower in summer. Swim at Caleta in the morning, at Los Hornos Beach in the afternoon; see the spectacular divers at La Perla Club. Shops are filled with handicrafts. Acapulco is one of the world's smartest winter resorts, but informality is the keynote.

YUCATAN PENINSULA

The Yucatan Peninsula on the east coast of Mexico facing the Caribbean has only recently begun to develop for the tourist sport fisherman. However, the number of established camps is still limited.

CARMEN

Located on Isla Aguada a short distance from the Carmen airport is **El Tarpon Tropical.** This camp has catered to anglers for many years. It consists of spacious cross-ventilated rooms in concrete buildings with palm thatched roofs, private showers and electricity. Rates here run $40 per day per person American Plan including boat and guide. Owner Andy Growich (Apartado 40, Cd. del Carmen, Campeche, Mexico) is the person to contact.

The season is from December until late August. Fishing here is done in the Laguna de Terminos, a 35-by 50-mile shallow lagoon, which is fed by three major rivers and innumerable streams flowing from southern Mexico and Guatemala. The many mangrove islands, grass flats, and deep channels make this a remarkable area for the light-tackle angler. The principal gamefish are tarpon, up to 100 pounds or more, snook, mangrove snapper, dog snapper, king mackerel, spotted seatrout, ladyfish, jewfish, grouper, red snapper, and jack crevalle. Beginning in early June, schools of permit frequent the flats also. Trolling and casting with plugs, spoons, flies, and jigs are generally productive.

The floating equipment of the Carmen camp consists of fifteen-foot skiffs with outboards which are designed for two anglers with guide. Fishing is customarily done from 6:00 a.m. to 6:00 p.m. with time out for a siesta from noon to 3:00 p.m. The lagoon is protected and the water is usually calm with one or two tidal changes per day. The climate is tropical (72°F. to 98°F.) with sunny weather the rule and showers of short duration.

ISLA MUJERES

The "island of women" is a comparatively recent tourist attraction which is now reached by the extension of a jungle highway from Valladolid, east of Merida, or by charter plane from Merida ($24 round trip). The last half of the bus trip to Puerto Juarez on the coast where you catch the ferry is rough. A low lying, 4½ miles long, Mujeres is a get-away-from-it all sanctuary (the village, population 1,000, consists of low stone and wooden houses behind unpainted plank fences and a Navy installation on top of the hill) which adventurous anglers might find interesting. There are two accommodations on the island at present—thatched huts at the **Zacil Ha** and motel units at **Posada del Mar** both at $18 single and $28 double American plan. Mujeres is currently the jump-off point for Isla Contey to the north, undeveloped and offering virgin fishing for tarpon, permit, bonefish, snook, large snappers, and groupers. Sailfish are abundant in the spring with a peak in April. The only way to make this trip is by charter boat from Mujeres to Contey stocking ample provisions and ice. Rates run about $35 per day provided you don't book through the hotels which nearly double the tab. For information contact: Pedro Gonzalez P., c/o Vienda Kodak, Isla Mujeres, Quintana Roo, Mexico.

COZUMEL

This 25-mile long island lying off the coast of the Yucatan Peninsula is fast developing as a major east coast resort. The island has a great deal to offer by way of fishing but the local building program can hardly keep abreast of the in-season tourist traffic. Despite the recent discovery (1968) of giant bluefin tuna in deep water between the mainland and the island during April and May, which adds a mighty plus to the marlin and sailfishing available, the number and quality of charter craft afloat is minimal. The best and popular hotels are the **Cozumel Presidente**, **Mayaluum, Cozumel de Caribe**, and the **Playa Azul** with rates between $22 and $40 per day double American Plan. Beautiful beaches and crystal clear water all around the island. The weather is hot and humid in the summer months so order air-conditioning in the off-season.

BOCA PAILA

One of the more unique permit grounds recently made available to angling is at Boca Paila in the Quintana Roo. This east coast Mexican location is drawing full house through the season at the **Boca Paila Lodge** (Calle 1 Sur, No. 11, P.O. Box 59, Cozumel, Quintana Roo, Mexico), operated by Antonio Gonzalez. Long known to a few pioneer anglers who used to make a rough seven hour boat trip down from Cozumel, then tent on the beach, young Tony put in a landing strip and hacked out an island paradise which offers all the amenities of civilization. Although small (2 to 3 pounds), bonefish are fantastically abundant on these shores, the permit schools are so numerous that you can cast to 40 or 50 fish per morning. Light tackle action for tarpon, snook, and numerous reef species including big dog snapper is top-drawer. The management restricts the permit and bonefish fishing to artificial lures only and allows the killing of only one permit per trip.

Boca Paila is best reached from Merida. Pan Am can make arrangements for a charter craft to meet clients at Merida for the one-hour flight to Tulum (rates vary according to the number of passengers but for two or more people it averages $70 round trip). The Tulum air strip is adjacent to Mayan ruins. A jeep meets guests for transport to camp; approximately a 40-minute ride through cocoanut groves and jungle. The rates at **Boca Paila Lodge** are $50 per day per person American Plan including local transportation, guide and boat. Lodge consists of cottages (each two rooms share bath). Food is excellently prepared, many native dishes, and drinking water is safe.

El Presidente hotel on Cozumel Island is air conditioned in hot, humid summer months, boasts beautiful beach, crystal clear waters

A prize gamefish, the ghostlike permit fins across a Yucatan flat

YUCATAN TRAVEL NOTES

The pivotal location in Yucatan air travel is the city of Merida. It is often necessary to overnight here for more remote trips. Pan American jets leave Miami for Merida Tuesdays, Wednesdays and Fridays.

From New Orleans, Pan Am jets fly Tuesdays, Thursdays and Saturdays. Compania Mexicana de Aviacion has daily jet service from Mexico City to Merida, where taxis from **El Tarpon Tropical** wait. Merida (pop. 17,000), the capital of Yucatan, has ten hotels that meet tourist standards. The **Hotel Merida,** with 110 rooms, has colonial Spanish charm and a swimming pool. It costs about $8 for a double room. The **Hotel Colon** has 20 rooms, each with bath and telephone and tiled steam baths adjoining a swimming pool, small in size but Roman in splendor. Double rooms are from $8 up.

MEXICO CITY

Tourists traveling to Baja, the Yucatan, and other angling regions frequently go by way of Mexico City or at least include it in their itinerary. Every type of hotel is available and

the following are quoted European plan.

The **Reforma Inter-Continental,** on the fashionable Paseo de la Reforma, with restaurants and night clubs. It is convenient to both shopping and entertainment spots; average rates $13 single and $22 double. Equally good and in a similar price range are the **Camino Real, Aristes, Continental Hilton, Alameda** (operated by Western Hotels), **Del Prado, Del Passo, Prado Alffer, Bamer, Plaza Vista Hermosa, Maria Isabel,** and the **El Presidente**. Good hotels in the moderate rate class (about $8 single, $10 double) are the **Ambassador, Cristobal, Colon, Monte Cassino, Premier, San Francisco.** Passable hotels in the $6 single, $8 double range are the **Francis, Geneve, Majestic, Metropol, Regis, Ritz,** and the **Romfel**. All the better hotels have good food, and some have beautiful rooftop dining rooms with music for dancing.

There are many outstanding restaurants in Mexico City and for a sampler you should include the *Hacienda del Morales, Del Lago,* and the *Rivoli*.

Nepal

Transportation on the Gogra River has not changed for centuries

The 54,363 square miles of Nepal lie almost entirely within the massive Himalaya Mountains. This independent kingdom was closed to all foreign visitors until twenty years ago. The country remains a mountainous enclave tucked between India and Tibet. It rises from the jungle lowlands of the Terai to the polar wastes of over-20,000-foot peaks approximately 100 miles away. Most villages have never been seen by tourists. The capital of Katmandu is still a medieval city with its roots over 2,000 years in the past, almost as old as Rome.

Katmandu alone is worth the trip. It lies unchanged in its high valley, almost a mile above sea level and sheltered in a giant amphitheatre of terraced mountains. There are temples and ancient *stupas* and monasteries. The streets are lined with shops like a continuous wall of mahogany-doored closets. Windows and eaves are an intricate lacework of rich carvings. The arcades are filled with water jars, silk from India, brightly striped bolts of cloth from Sikkim and Bhutan, spices and herbs, yeast roots for the ale-like *chang*.

The over-70-pound mahseer *(above)* is an unusually large catch in Nepalese rivers

A morning's bag on the Karnali. Heavy spinning tackle is standard equipment

For the tourist angler, Nepal offers excellent mahseer fishing. The mahseer (*Barbus tor*), an Asiatic member of the Cyprinidae, is a powerful gamefish and grows to weights of at least 120 pounds. Mahseer of 15 to 60 pounds are generally common both in Nepal and India. Although remotely related to the European carps, the mahseer is omnivorous and despite its rubbery lips, the jaws are extremely strong and its throat contains pharyngeal teeth. The mahseer has very large scales (to the size of a playing card on big fish) and exhibits a great variation in color from gold to almost black according to the habitat. Mahseer scales are often used for luggage labels and even menu cards by devoted anglers. When hooked the mahseer makes a typical long run of 100 yards or more. Subsequent runs may be shorter and punctuated with occasional jumps, especially from the smaller fish, but unquestionably the mahseer is difficult to subdue. Large mahseer (over 100 pounds) have required more than four hours to bring to gaff against heavy tackle.

The main western mahseer rivers in Nepal are the Karnali and Bheri (or Surju), and the Rapti, all of which join to form the Gogra which in turn flows into the Ganges. In central Nepal the principal streams are the Gandak and its tributaries, notably the Narayani, Seti, Marsyandi, Darondi, and Burhi Rivers. Elsewhere and to the east are the Indrawati, Sun Kosi, Dudh Kosi, Arun, and Tamur Rivers, all of which eventually merge and flow into India. Other important gamefish in these drainage systems include the Indian trout (*Barilius bola*), the silun, and the murrel.

THE SEASON
The best run of mahseer occurs in March and April and a fair run takes place in November, depending on how early or how late the monsoon clears. The climate varies with altitude. At low elevations it is subtropical with heavy rainfall, hot and humid in the summer but pleasantly cool during the winter. The uplands have comfortable temperatures dur-

ing the summer months and a cold winter with heavy snows above 8,000 feet. June, July, and August are the monsoon months.

PACKAGE TRIP
The only outfitter in Nepal is *Nepal Wildlife Adventure* (contact Mytravel Inc., 290 Madison Avenue, New York 10017) which is operated by Dr. Charles MacDougal, an American, and Colonel Adeyta Rana, a British Sandhurst graduate and now of the Nepalese Army. They have leased the very best river in Nepal—the Karnali—which flows from the Himalayan foothills in western Nepal. The basic trip provides 9 full days at the fishing camps at $1,890 per person. This includes all services from arrival at Katmandu to final departure therefrom including accommodations and breakfast in Katmandu at a deluxe hotel, accommodations in

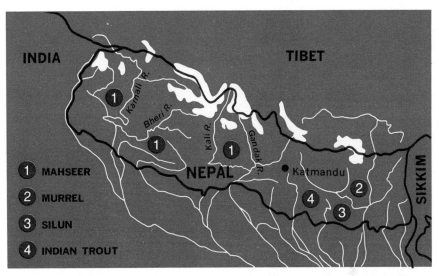

1 MAHSEER
2 MURREL
3 SILUN
4 INDIAN TROUT

tents or lodges, all meals elsewhere in Nepal, all transfers, sightseeing, local transportation including charter flights, English-speaking guides, fishing fees as utilized, service charges, and local taxes.

TACKLE
Standard salmon tackle is most suitable for mahseer fishing. Fly rods should preferably be 9 or 9½ feet long. The reel should be able to handle at least 250 yards of 30-pound backing. Leaders should be 20- to 30-pound-test since the mahseer is an extremely tough fighting fish and the currents are usually quite strong. Bright bucktails and streamers suitable for saltwater fly fishing are recommended. Hook sizes from 1/0 through 4/0. Standard spinning or bait casting equipment is also effective. Silver and copper spoons, and spinners with

1½-inch size blades are most commonly used. Be sure to bring a good supply of flies, leaders, and lures since none are available in Nepal. Mahseer over 100 pounds have been caught on spinning equipment.

TRAVEL NOTES
By daily 2¼-hour flights from New Delhi or Calcutta, which are on Pan Am's Round-the-World routes. Passport, visa (valid 7 days; extendable) from the Royal Nepalese Embassy, 2131 LeRoy Place, N.W., Washington, D.C. 20008, or the Consulate General in New York. Smallpox and cholera vaccination certificates. 100 cigarettes enter duty-free; no duty-free liquor allowance. Note: If you are arriving from and returning to India you will need a double entry visa for India.

ACCOMMODATIONS
The centrally located **Annapurna** has shopping arcade, central heating and air conditioning, excellent dining; $13.15 single, $22.80 double with meals. The **Soaltee**, 1½ miles from town, has pool, tennis, golf, shops, gambling casino, cabaret, discotheque, several restaurants, $9.85 single, $13.85 double without meals. Smaller and with more local

atmosphere: the **Panorama**, **Royal**, and **Shankar**, where rates with meals average about $9 single, $16 double. AP rates are about $8 single, $15 double at the **Coronation, Green,** and **Snow View**. A 5 percent tax and 10 percent service charge are added to bills. Tip 25 to 50 paisa for most small services.

Hotels often serve European-type food. Many European fruits and vegetables grow in Nepal. Try a local curry. Nepalese rice is very good, and the country produces a lot of cheese. Drink bottled water. Pasteurized milk is available. American cocktails are a rarity and drinks are sold by the bottle or by the "peg." Nepalese whiskey, gin, and rum, however, are only $2 a bottle and drinks are priced proportionately.

CONTACTS
Royal Nepalese Consulate General, 300 E. 46th Street, New York, N.Y. 10017. Tourist Information Center, Basantapur, Katmandu (Tel. 11293).

LANGUAGE
Nepali. Radio broadcasts in Katmandu are in Nepali, Hindi, Newari, and English. English is spoken in hotels and at the Karnali camp.

Netherlands Antilles [Leeward]

Fall and winter are the best periods for big-game fishing in the Antilles. Moderate seas are most common then

The Netherlands Antilles (formerly the Dutch Indies) consist of two widely separated groups of islands. To the Leeward Group belong Aruba, Curacao, Klein Curacao, Bonaire, and Klein Bonaire located in the southern Caribbean Sea. Aruba is less than 20 miles from Venezuela and 42 miles west-northwest of Curacao, the largest island, which lies about 38 miles from Venezuela. Bonaire is 30 miles east of Curacao. The Windward Group of islands is located 565 miles northeast of Curacao and consists of Saba, St. Eustatius, and the southern portion of St. Maarten. Both are part of the Lesser Antilles Chain but due to their wide geophysical separation, they present distinctly different angling possibilities.

The three major islands in Leeward Group are Aruba, Bonaire, and Curacao. Fishing here is for the rough-water sailor. Although these islands are south of the range of hurricanes, they are exposed to daily trade winds from the east-northeast and east at a steady 15 to 20 knots. Because of the wind direction and steep coral coasts, the best harbors are on the calmer west shores. The islands are volcanic in origin and have sharp dropoffs; the maximum depth between Curacao and Venezuela is over 500 fathoms. A deep trench, exceeding 800 fathoms, occurs between Curacao and Aruba; to the north of Aruba the bottom shelves down to 2,850 fathoms.

Due to the extreme drop-offs there are few reefs or extensive shallows around the Leeward Group and consequently only a very limited amount of inshore fishing for small-game species such as bonefish, barracuda, or snappers exists. The fishing is primarily for blue marlin, sailfish, dolphin, wahoo, occasional white marlin, king mackerel, and blackfin tuna.

Because of the semi-arid climate no freshwater fishing exists in the Leeward Islands. In the small basins where freshwater accumulates during the rainy season (November to March) so-called "tankies" consisting of several species of killifish, gambusia, and mollies occur as do one or two species of sleepers (Eleotridae).

THE FISHING

Ordinarily the big-game fishing period begins at the end of August and extends to April. The force of the Trades abates somewhat at the end of summer as the Leeward Group lies south of the hurricane zone and frequent low pressure areas to the north diminish the prevailing winds into the fall season. This may not provide the best fishing of the year, nor the kind of fishing you seek, but it's the best bet for calmer water. Blue marlin (locally balau blancu) fishing gets under way in the fall and extends through the winter tapering off toward April. Blues in the 300- to 400-pound class are fairly common. Sailfish (locally balau bandera) migrate through the Leewards during the same period. White marlin (locally balau cora) display no peak, are seldom numerous and may occur at any time. Wahoo (locally mula) occur in October and November and again in May. At other times of the year wahoo are scarce or totally absent. The waters around Klein Curacao are especially productive of wahoo averaging 30 to 40 pounds. Dolphin (locally dradu) are most abundant from April through the summer months and average a large size with 30-pounders not uncommon. King mackerel (locally konefes) occur from July to October.

Until recent years the boat situation in the Leeward group was poor, but with the upsurge in tourism, more and more charter craft are becoming available. Most hotels can arrange the details. Tour services such as *Coral Tours* (P.O. Box 2050, Curacao, Netherlands Antilles) or *Taber Tours* (c/o S.E.L. Maduro & Sons, Willemstad, Curacao, Netherlands Antilles) also handle charter bookings. Generally speaking, prices are slightly less than those in U.S. ports with the better offshore boats at $90 to $100 per day. Smaller craft for inshore trolling bring $60 per day.

TRAVEL NOTES

By Pan Am 747 Jet Clipper from New York to San Juan, with connecting flight to Curacao; Aruba is 6¾ hours direct from New York.

Birth certificate or naturalization papers and ticket to leave. Re-entry permit for resident aliens. No passport, no visa. Smallpox vaccination certificate required on entry. Visitors who stay 24 hours or less need no documents except proof of nationality to visit these islands.

Taxi fare from Plesman Airport into Willemstad (5 miles) is U.S. $3.50 Luggage porters get U.S. 25c (40c local) per bag. Departure tax U.S. $3 for Curacao only.

LEEWARD ISLANDS

1 BLUE MARLIN
2 SAILFISH
3 DOLPHIN
4 WAHOO
5 BLACKFIN TUNA
6 WHITE MARLIN

CARIBBEAN SEA

ARUBA
Sint Nicolaas
CURACAO
BONAIRE
Kralendijk
Willemstad
Peninsula de Raraguaná
Bonaire Trench

ACCOMMODATIONS

CURACAO

On Willemstad's waterfront and commanding a spectacular view is the Curacao **Inter-Continental** with terraces, gardens, a night club, a gambling casino, discotheque *La Cave de Neptune* built among the arches of the old fort, and a split-level swimming pool with portholes for spectators. Winter rates $26 to $28 single, $32 to $34 double European Plan. Most hotels are $7 to $9 less per person from May to December 15. The **Avila Beach Hotel**, a former governor's palace ¾ mile from town, offers old world charm with modern conveniences; beach, pool, outdoor dining and dancing pavilion; from $12.50 single, $20 double, Modified American Plan. The **Piscadera Bay Club**, 1½ miles out, has special facilities for children, swimming, tennis, boating; $20.75 single, $32.50 double, American Plan. The new **Curacao Hilton**, on Piscadera Bay, is a complete resort community; $35 to $37.50 single, $50 to $52 double Modified American Plan. **Coral Cliff Hotel**, 24 miles from Willemstad on St. Martha's Bay, offers fishing, water skiing, snorkeling, scuba diving, sailing; $25 single, $40 double, Modified American Plan. Convenient downtown hotels include the **Americano**, from $6 single, $10 double, European Plan; **Bellevue**, from $8 single, $15 double, American Plan; and the **Park**, from $9 single, $16 double, American Plan. **Hotel Bianca**, at the airport, is from $9.50 single, $14 double, including breakfast.

ARUBA

On a white sand beach, is the exciting **Aruba Caribbean Hotel** with a gambling casino, night club, fishing, sailing and all water sports; winter rates $29 to $35 single, $34 to $40 double, European Plan. The luxurious **Aruba-Sheraton Hotel & Casino** on Palm Beach also has every resort facility; $34 to $54 single, $50 to $70 double, American Plan. The new **Manchebo Beach Hotel**,

which also has a pool, is from $22 single, $25 double, European Plan. The **Coral Strand Hotel** only 5 minutes from Oranjestad's shopping center, overlooks the Caribbean and has a pool, beach and night club; from $27 single, $32 double, European Plan. The **Basi Ruti Hotel** on Palm Beach is also an atmospheric resort featuring water sports; $14 to $18 single, $20 to $24 double, European Plan.

BONAIRE

Hotel Bonaire with swimming pool, private beach with all water sports, gambling casino and nightly entertainment; from $28 single, $42 double, Modified American Plan. Accommodations also in bungalows at the informal **Flamingo Beach Club**; $22 single, $36 double, Modified American Plan. **Debonair Bungalows**, completely furnished with kitchenettes and TV, are $125 a week for 2; $170 for 4; maid service, daily rates also available.

In addition to the hotel dining rooms there are many good restaurants throughout these three major islands. Seafoods and the Dutch rijsttafel are local specialties. A popular native dish made of corn pudding called *funchi* is eaten with a peppery fish soup called *sopi de playa* or literally "beach soup."

CONTACTS

The Curacao Information Center, 604 Fifth Avenue, New York, N.Y. 10020. Aruba Tourist Board, 609 Fifth Avenue, New York, N.Y. 10017. Bonaire Tourist Information Office, 4 West 58th Street, New York, N.Y. 10019. Pan Am is at 21 Heerenstradt, Willemstad (Tel. 13853), and at Princess Beatrix Airport, Aruba (Tel. 2707).

LANGUAGE

The official language is Netherlands (Dutch). The native population in the Leeward Islands speaks a dialect known as Papiamentu, derived from Spanish, Portuguese, Dutch and English. In the Windward Islands English is also spoken.

New Zealand

The two most important freshwater fish in New Zealand are brown and rainbow trout (below). Abundant food creates full-bodied fish

New Zealand has some of the finest trout fishing in the world and excellent big-game fishing in its offshore waters. Consisting of two major islands and numerous smaller ones, the countryside varies from rolling farm lands to high mountain ranges, and except for the lower west coast region of the South Island, it is all accessible by road.

The South Island is the more mountainous with seventeen of its peaks exceeding 10,000 feet. The highest mountain in New Zealand is Mount Cook, 12,349 feet. In keeping with the dimensions of the mountain system, the South Island has some mighty glaciers. The largest is the Tasman which is 18 miles long and 1¼ miles wide. Some of the glaciers descend to unusually low levels. The Fox and the Franz Josef Glaciers terminate at less than 700 feet above sea level and reach into lowland vegetation. Lakes are numerous, many in the South Island being surrounded by forest-clad mountains. Lake Taupo in the North Island, 228 square miles in area, is the largest expanse of freshwater in the South Temperate Zone. The North Island has a thermal region occupying a belt about 20 miles wide and 150 miles long and extending from Mount Ruapehu in the south to the volcanic White Island in the Bay of Plenty.

The forests of New Zealand are highly interesting, and in many cases unique. In the northern part of the North Island are huge kauri pines, giants of the forest world. New Zealand has some beautiful flowers found in woodlands and mountain meadows. Outstanding among them are the scarlet rata and pohutukawa, the "mountain lily," feathery celmisias, and veronicas of numerous kinds. There are song birds, such as the tui and the bellbird, and the curious flightless birds like the kiwi, with its hairlike plumage, vestigial wings that cannot be seen and nostrils at the end of its long bill. In New Zealand is found the most extraordinary of reptiles, the harmless tuatara, with a third rudimentary eye—a survival from some prehistoric age. There are no predatory animals nor birds harmful to man, very few noxious insects, and no snakes or other venomous reptiles.

Trout are not native to New Zealand, but were introduced in the second half of the last century because the native freshwater fish were of little sporting or food value. Brown trout (*Salmo trutta*) were first introduced, but they were less successful in the northern half of the North Island than the rainbow trout (*S. gairdnerii*) which was introduced later.

THE SEASON

North Island to the north of Auckland is moist and semitropical. Situated below the equator, it is warmer in the north and colder in the south. South Island is slightly cooler and higher. Officially, summer runs from December to February, fall from March to May, winter from June to August, and spring from September to November.

NORTH ISLAND

The North Island is smaller than the South Island, and the general character of its fishing is different from the latter. Rainbow trout predominate here, and some of the lakes and rivers, such as Lake Taupo and the Tongariro River, situated in the center of the island are world famous. Generally speaking, the waters of the North Isand are at their best early and late in the season, from October 1st to November 15th, and again from April 1st to the end of May. Night fishing is very popular in New Zealand, and some large trout are caught during the height of summer (February) on flies after dark in North Island streams. A great deal of trolling is done in some of the larger lakes, primarily with spoons.

LAKE TAUPO AND TONGARIRO RIVER

In one recent season it was estimated that 50,000 anglers fishing 187,600 angler days caught over 300,000 trout averaging about 4 pounds in weight in Lake Taupo. This 228-square-mile lake is one of the most productive fisheries in the world. From the town of Taupo (population 8,000) where the Waikato River leaves the northern end of the lake, one may fish the quiet reaches of the outlet or proceed by launch to Western Bay or by the road to the streams entering from the east. A launch trip of three days or more is the most interesting and productive. There are numerous boats for charter at the Taupo docks. These are hired on a per head basis including meals and cost about $35 to $40 per day. The boats visit the rugged, poorly roaded western shore and fish at the mouths of tributaries such as Chow Creek, Boulder Stream, Waihora Stream, and Waihaha Stream. Fly fishermen can wade in crystal clear pebbly bottomed water. Best accommodations in Taupo are the **Wairakai Hotel** and the **Lake Taupo Hotel**.

The eastern shore of Taupo has many road access points to rivers such as the Waitahanui, Hinemaiaia, Tauranga-Taupo, and Waiotaka. These are all good fishing waters but the Tauranga-Taupo is above average. The upper reaches of the Waiotaka runs through a prison farm and permission to fish, easily obtainable, is necessary. The peak period on these streams is from March to May.

At the southern end of Taupo, anglers fish the famous Tongariro River. Accommodations can be found in Turangi and Tokaanu. The Tongariro, an outstanding rainbow stream, is turbulent, rising in inaccessible gorges, but creating an abundance of good pools, especially in its lower 12 miles. Near its delta (the river has five mouths) boat fishing is essential. The peak fishing on the Tongariro occurs in May, June, and July when the annual rainbow runs take place. Fish of 7, 8, and 9 pounds are not uncommon.

However, there are plenty of resident fish in the river, and a skilled angler might connect at any time. A fair number of large brown trout (5 to 15 pounds) are caught in Taupo, at the mouths of its tributary rivers and in the Tongariro.

Currently, the season at Lake Taupo is open 12 months of the year. Angling can be undertaken throughout the lake and over most of the streams, except for certain closed portions in the upper reaches, where the spawning areas are protected. The best months to fish the lake by trolling are October, November, December, June, and July. For fly fishing at the stream mouths, December, January and February. However, during the latter part of January and most of February, which is the height of the New Zealand summer, the fish become hard to catch during daylight, and are most successfully caught by fly fishing the stream mouths at night. The regulation governing angling on Lake Taupo is that there is no limit on the number of fish that may be caught, although anglers have to return all fish under 14 inches in length. Fishing is only permitted from 5 a.m. in the morning to 11 p.m. at night. While fishing at Lake Taupo during the months of March to October, it is desirable to have warm clothing, as the lake is situated 1200 feet above sea level and cool weather can be experienced.

LAKE ROTORUA AREA

Lakes Rotorua, Rotoiti, Tarawera, Okataina, Rotoehu, Rotoma, and Rotokakahi were formed by volcanic activity and lie in a fairly compact area. Actually, there are eleven lakes in this group ranging in size from 22-acre Lake Ngahewa to 26-square-mile Rotorua, but only the seven largest are of angling importance. These lakes are all easily accessible (within 15 miles) of the popular tourist center Rotorua with its geysers, thermal baths, and a model Maori village. All the Rotorua Lakes are rainbow trout waters; however, both Rotorua and Rotoiti also contain

brown trout. Fishing in general is best in spring and fall with trout running from 2 to 6 pounds and, of course, the occasional trophy of 12 or 15 pounds. Trolling is the most popular method in this region. The best dry fly fishing is found along the northeast shore of Rotorua for large brown trout. The legal season on Lake Rotorua is open 12 months of the year; however, rivers flowing into the lake are only open from December 1st to June 30th. The size limit is 14 inches in length for a legal bag of 8 trout.

Lake Tarawera, only ten miles from Rotorua, holds some of the largest rainbow trout in New Zealand with an average weight of about 9 pounds. Fish up to 12 pounds are not uncommon. However, it's quality rather than quantity here and the take can be sparse. The best fishing is had in October and again in the fall which peaks in May. This 17-square-mile lake fishes poorly in the summer months.

Lake Rotoiti is a 13-square-mile playground for New Zealand vacationists, and its beautiful shores are well developed for the holiday crowd. Nevertheless, it offers some fine fishing for rainbows averaging 4 pounds and browns in the 7 to 8 pound class. It is a good lake to wade. Fly fishing is best in November and after March, with trolling and spinning most successful in the warm months. The Kaituna River, the outlet stream of Rotoiti, offers a variety of big water for the fly fisherman and while the trout are not large by New Zealand standards, 2-to 3-pounders are not uncommon.

NORTH ISLAND RIVERS

In addition to the main lake fisheries, there is much good river fishing in all except the northerly parts of the North Island. The principal rainbow trout streams include the Waihou, Pokaiwhenua, and others near Okoroire and Putaruru in the Auckland Province, the Rangitaiki and Whirinaki at Murupara, the Tarawera, Waimana and Waioweka in the

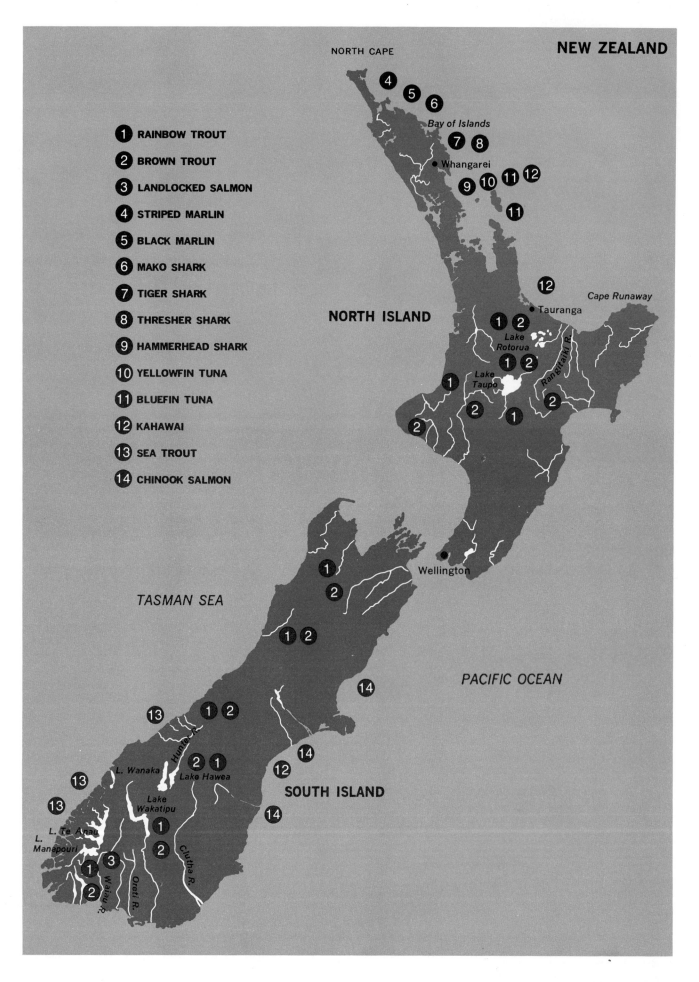

NEW ZEALAND

NORTH CAPE

1 RAINBOW TROUT

2 BROWN TROUT

3 LANDLOCKED SALMON

4 STRIPED MARLIN

5 BLACK MARLIN

6 MAKO SHARK

7 TIGER SHARK

8 THRESHER SHARK

9 HAMMERHEAD SHARK

10 YELLOWFIN TUNA

11 BLUEFIN TUNA

12 KAHAWAI

13 SEA TROUT

14 CHINOOK SALMON

Bay of Islands

Whangarei

NORTH ISLAND

Cape Runaway

Tauranga

Lake Rotorua

Lake Taupo

Rangitaiki R.

Wellington

TASMAN SEA

PACIFIC OCEAN

L. Wanaka

Hunter R.

Lake Hawea

Lake Wakatipu

SOUTH ISLAND

L. Te Anau

L. Manapouri

Waiau R.

Oreti R.

Clutha R.

Bay of Plenty, and the Ngaruroro in Hawkes Bay. The Wanganui and its tributaries above Taumarunui, the Tukituki and Waipawa in Hawkes Bay and Rangitikei River near Bulls offer good mixed fishing for brown and rainbow trout. Brown trout occur in practically all streams in the southern half of the Island. Some of the best brown trout rivers are the Mangawhero and tributaries near Raetihi, the Waiwakaiho near New Plymouth, the Kaupokonui and Kapuni near Hawera and a series of Manawatu tributaries at Pahiatua. Palmerston North is adjacent to productive portions of the Manawatu River and Masterton on the Ruamahanga River. Seasonal flooding in North Island streams makes fly fishing uncertain before December.

SOUTH ISLAND

The South Island is 550 miles long and has an average width of 120 miles. The magnificent alpine range, rising to 12,349 feet at Mt. Cook, runs west of the island's center. Many of the larger rivers rise in the peaks; during the early summer months these snow-fed streams are often highly discolored. However, there are other streams which do not get the melt and run clear. Perhaps the best period on the South Island is from November 15th to January in Canterbury and Nelson provinces, and to the end of March in Otago, Southland, and the Lakes District. Brown trout predominate on the South Island, and the average size varies according to the water fished. Fish of 1 to 2 pounds are common, and there are many locations, particularly at river mouths in lakes where a 3 pound average is possible. In addition to brown trout, the South Island offers some rainbow fishing in the high country and landlocked Atlantic salmon in the Waiau River system and its lakes. These landlocked salmon run from 2 to 6 pounds with the average closer to 2. Chinook salmon (locally Quinnant salmon) occur in the South Island's east coast rivers. There are so many productive brown

trout streams in Southland and South Otago that any selection is difficult. For spinning for sea-run trout in the early months of the season, the great lake-fed Waiau River in Southland is probably preferable to any other South Island river for abundance of fish in its lower reaches for natural beauty and for freedom from floods. Attractive fly

A reason to smile at Lake Rotorua

fishing rivers include the Aparima, Oreti and Mataura. Among the excellent small fly streams are included the Morley and other branches of the Orawia Stream through to its junction with the Waiau River above Tuatapere, the Otipiri, Lora and tributaries of the Makarewa from the Hokonui Hills across the plains to the Oreti River near Invercargill, the Wyndham and Mimihau entering the lower Mataura, the Waipahi and Pomahaka near Balclutha.

Farther inland, among high ranges, lie the great Southern Lakes: Te Anau, Wakatipu, Wanaka, and Hawea. These lakes contain moderate stocks of brown and rainbow trout of 2 to 6 pounds and also in Te

Anau, Atlantic salmon, and in Wakatipu, small landlocked Quinnat salmon. There is good hotel accommodation at Te Anau and Wakatipu. The upper portions of the two great river systems draining them, namely, the Waiau and Clutha, provide excellent spinning and fly water which is seldom influenced by flooding.

LAKE TE ANAU AREA

Of all the great southern lakes, Te Anau, the largest, has the greatest variety of scenic and sporting attractions. Te Anau is 98 miles from Invercargill and 89 miles from Gore over excellent sealed roads. The lake is 42 miles long and ranges from 2 to 8 miles wide, with a total area of 132 square miles. Much of its 330-mile shoreline is formed by fiords on the lake's western shore that run into the mountains for 12 to 20 miles. The eastern shore is low lying for the first 24 miles of its length and has little or no vegetation. Snow-capped peaks towering to 6,000 feet are clothed in dense bush from the snowline to the water's edge on the western and northern shores. The rivers of the western fiords are the best in the area and are seldom fished. It's worthwhile to hire a boat or charter an amphibian aircraft, as the waters are truly an angler's paradise. During westerly weather the first 7 miles of the eastern shore give many good fish to threadliners. Brown trout averaging 3½ pounds, rainbow averaging 3 pounds, and salmon averaging 2½ pounds are taken in these waters. Accommodations can be had at Te Anau in the **Te Anau Hotel** at $11 per person; the **Trans Holiday Motel** at $8 single and $13 double; or the **Fiord Land Motor Lodge** at $9 single and $16 double.

UPUKERORA RIVER

Rising in the high country east of Lake Te Anau, this river enters the lake about 3 miles from the **Te Anau Hotel.** The water courses at a fast pace over a rock bed. It is the only river in New Zealand in which Atlantic salmon has been successfully introduced. Brown and rainbow trout averaging 3 pounds and salmon averaging 2½ pounds may be taken. The river is restricted to fly fishing only.

EGLINTON RIVER

This river rises in the Livingstone Ranges, runs out of Lake Gunn down through the Eglinton Valley and into Lake Te Anau near the Te Anau Downs Station homestead. The Eglinton Road runs alongside the river for many miles making it easy of access, so the water is heavily fished. It contains rainbow trout averaging 2 pounds and brown trout averaging 3 pounds. The Eglinton is restricted to fly fishing only. Accommodation at Te Anau and Cascade Creek, 48 miles from Te Anau. Many camping grounds are to be found along the Eglinton Valley.

UPPER WAIAU RIVER

This outlet of Lake Te Anau runs through 12 miles of heavily wooded country into Lake Manapouri. The Waiau River has steep, rugged

banks and is inaccessible except at Horseshoe Bend and Rainbow Reach. It is very tough to wade. However there are boats available for hire at Manapouri from the Manapouri-Doubtful Sound Tourist Co. which also has a number of jet boats. Accommodation at Te Anau or Manapouri. Camping sites at Horseshoe Bend and Rainbow Reach. The average weights of rainbow and brown trout here are about 2 pounds with plenty of 4- to 6-pounders in the stream.

ETTRICK BURN

This water is situated at the entrance to Te Anau Middle Fiord. It offers fair fishing for rainbow and brown trout averaging 2½ pounds. There is good fly fishing at the mouth. Sandflies can be troublesome here.

UPPER AND LOWER HANKINSON RIVER

Good fishing for rainbow and brown trout averaging about 3 pounds. The fishing in Lake Hankinson is also good.

CLINTON RIVER

This excellent dry fly water is very clear and bouldery. Lower Clinton has steep, heavily forested banks and is difficult to wade. Trout up to 13 pounds have been taken here and 4 pound rainbows and browns are common. Rough accommodations at the **Glade House**.

WORSLEY RIVER

Another good stream for the fly fisherman. The average rainbow is about 2½ pounds and brown trout 3 pounds. Largest trout are caught here at night on big wet flies.

HAAST AREA

This is the sea trout (anadromous brown trout) area of New Zealand; fish enter most of the rivers between Milford Sound and Haast with the significant runs occurring in the McKerrow-Alabaster and Okuru-Turnbull watersheds. New Zealand sea trout follow the movements of whitebait and smelt into the coastal rivers and lakes between November and January, but because early runs sometimes take place, the angling season for these coastal waters begins on September 1st to coincide with the whitebait season. Presently, there are a few small motels in the Haast area but comfortable accommodations can be found at the **Franz-Josef Glacier Hotel** with rates beginning at $11 single and $15 double American Plan and the **Fox Glacier Hotel** at $9 per person American Plan. The following rivers and lakes are within easy driving distance:

MAHITAHI RIVER

This small river has a good population of sea-run brown trout, averaging 3 pounds, which may be caught by all methods at the mouth. A boat is necessary for fishing the upper reaches.

MAKAWHIE RIVER

Excellent sea-run brown trout average 3 pounds and are taken at the mouth by all methods.

PARINGA RIVER

Similar conditions to the Mahitahi River are to be found on this snow-fed river. There are a few big fish to

A young New Zealand visitor looks perplexed at the unusual road sign that points the way to good fishing spots in the lake region of North Island

be taken in the main river but the best fishing is at the mouth.

LAKE PARINGA

Slightly heavier brown trout are to be found in this lake, which offers good trolling, spinning, and fly fishing. Boats are available. There is a good camping site here, but sandflies and mosquitoes are very troublesome.

HALL RIVER

Heavy brown trout reside in this river, which also has a good run of sea trout when the whitebait season is on. There has been boat access only to this fishing water. However, a new road from Paringa has opened up this area. This also applies to the Blue River, which has similar fishing prospects.

LAKE MOERAKI

Sea-run brown trout and some excellent resident fish make this one of the best fishing waters on the coast. The road from Paringa gives access.

WAITA RIVER

This river contains excellent sea-run brown trout at the mouth, but access will be difficult until the new road from Paringa is completed.

HAAST, OKURU, TURNBULL, WAIATOTO, ARAWHATA, AND JACKSON RIVERS

All these waters are difficult of access but good sea-run brown may be found at the mouths of all except the Haast, which has poor fishing. When the Paringa-Haast road was opened, however, it made it fairly easy to get to all these rivers. Not much is known about the upper reaches, which run through difficult country.

LAKE ELLERY

An amphibian aircraft is necessary to gain access to this good brown trout water, but active anglers can hike to the lake over extremely difficult country.

WILKIN RIVER

This water is one of the largest tributaries of the Makarora River and spinning is most effective in the large clear pools of the Wilkin. Only fair fly fishing, wet and dry, is to be had. Brown and rainbow trout which average 3½ pounds can be taken almost anywhere on spoon. Fly fishing at the mouth.

HAWEA AREA

HAWEA RIVER

This water flows out of Lake Hawea and joins the Upper Clutha River at Albert Town, 10 miles away. It is fast, usually crystal clear, and its banks are scrubby with few open stretches. Brown and rainbow trout averaging 2½ pounds offer great sport to anglers visiting this river. From December onwards is the best time for fishing. All types of fishing are successful. Good camping sites are available at the outlet and at Albert Town. Anglers are warned against rises in the level of the river caused by water released from the hydro dam at Lake Hawea.

HUNTER RIVER

Flowing into the head of Lake Hawea, this river is generally clear and fast, but it is subject to sudden spates. The banks are open and fishing water accessible. Access is by road leaving the Makarora Highway at the neck. Road to Hunter by car in good weather only. The river carries rainbow and brown trout averaging 4 pounds and Quinnat salmon averaging 2 pounds. From December to March provides the best fishing. The salmon are taken on devons and spoons, and trolling is recommended at the mouth.

CLUTHA RIVER

The upper reaches of this river—Cromwell to Lake Wanaka—offer rainbow and brown trout averaging 2½ pounds. The banks are open and accessible, except towards Albert Town and Luggate. From the end of November onwards provides the best fishing. The fish are heavier and fight harder from the mouth of the Lindis River to the outlet of Lake Wanaka. There are many camping sites available at Luggate Bridge, Al-

bert Town, and the south side of the outlet of Lake Wanaka. Accommodation available at Cromwell, Lowburn, Luggate, and Wanaka. Care should be taken when fishing below the Hawea River confluence, as water levels fluctuate considerably with no warning because of the releases from the Hawea dam.

WAKATIPU DISTRICT

LAKE WAKATIPU

Queenstown, New Zealand's famous tourist resort on the shore of this lake, is the center of a district which provides all-year-round attractions for visitors. There are many popular fishing spots round the lake, but fishing is prohibited in Queenstown Bay, a sanctuary where 5- to 15-pound trout may be seen cruising around the jetty as they compete with ducks and gulls for the bread thrown by tourists. Good beaches between Queenstown and Kingston, at the head of the lake, offer excellent rainbow and brown trout and salmon. Fish average about 2½ pounds. The best fishing is in November and December and then again towards the end of the season. Fishing at stream mouths, except for the Dart and Rees Rivers, is restricted for fishermen in anchored boats for a radius of 200 yards. Trolling is good on the lake. Accommodations in Queenstown are the **Esplanade Hotel** at $16 per person American Plan, **Frankton Motor Hotel** at $12 per person with breakfast, **O'Connells Hotel** at $13 single and $24 double American Plan, and the **Wakatipu** at $11 per person.

LOCHY RIVER

Fly fishing only is permitted in this water, and dry-fly anglers do well when the river is normal or has a slight rise. The Collins River offers good fly fishing for brown trout, which predominate in this water. Fly fishing only is allowed in the Von River, where good fishing may be had at the mouth. Access is by boat to Mt. Nicholas and then a walk of one quarter of a mile around the north beach.

GREENSTONE AND CAPLES RIVERS

A boat is needed to reach the Greenstone River, which offers fine wet and dry-fly fishing at its junction with the Caples River. Above this fishing is spotty. Brown trout up to 14 pounds are taken from the Caples which is restricted to fly fishing only.

ROARING MEG

This fast-flowing stream enters the Kawarau Gorge and carries a few large brown trout averaging at least 6 pounds above the dam. It fishes best in warm weather and fly fishing is recommended.

NEVIS RIVER

The turnoff to this river can be found through Bannockburn. It is about 10 miles from the signpost to the Upper Nevis bridge. Then comes rough road access upstream for about 6 miles to the best fishing water. Dredge holes without outlets contain rainbow and brown trout which can be taken on fly and threadline tackle. The remainder of the area is reserved for fly fishing. Fish up to 15 pounds have been caught in the river. Access is limited to dry weather and in places the road climbs to almost 4,000 feet.

MANAPOURI DISTRICT

LAKE MANAPOURI

This is the deepest lake in New Zealand, (1,458 feet). It is well stocked with rainbow and brown trout and Atlantic salmon. The rainbows average 2½ pounds, the brown 3, and the salmon 2. Trolling is the most popular method of angling. A silver spoon or gold devon accounts for the most fish. However, fly fishing is good at the mouths of tributary rivers. The best fishing is towards the end of January. Sandflies are troublesome and a repellent should be carried. Accommodation is available at Te Anau.

GREBE RIVER

This water offers good fly and spoon

Trout like this 12-pound rainbow are not uncommon in New Zealand

fishing for about 6 miles. There are a fair number of brown trout in the large pools, but fly fishing is recommended at the mouth, where big boulders are seen. Outside these baitcasting and trolling are carried out with fair success. Brown trout averaging 3 pounds, rainbows averaging 2½ pounds, and salmon averaging 2 pounds may be caught here.

The many snow-fed rivers of the East Coast of the South Island such as the Waitaki, Rangitata, Rakaia, and Waimakariri are popular among New Zealand anglers for chinook salmon (locally Quinnat salmon). The fish begin arriving in February and the season peaks in March and April. These wide, silty, bouldery streams are not too attractive and the quality of the angling by American standards at least is poor. The average weight in New Zealand waters is about 12 pounds with fish over 30 pounds being exceptional. Casting with spoons and heavy tackle is the only method used. These rivers are frequently unfishable because of torrential rains and floods which makes a trip risky for the visitor with limited time and more rewarding choices available.

LICENSES

The general full-season license for

men costs approximately $5.00, but short-term licenses and women's and boys' licenses are available at lower fees. The general license covers all districts except Southern Lakes, Rotorua and Taupo where local licenses are issued. Fees are the same for residents and for non-residents, except at Taupo where, as part of the terms of settlement of Maori claims, non-residents pay more. There, tourists pay approximately $1.00 a day, $2.00 a week, or $10.00 for a full season.

TACKLE

Tackle can be purchased in any of the major cities or fishing centers such as Auckland, Rotorua, Wellington, Christchurch, or Dunedin. Generally speaking, the New Zealander favors somewhat heavy gear for freshwater fishing with powerful 9-foot to 12-foot (double handed salmon type) rods in the majority. To what extent this type of tackle is necessary depends on the experience of the angler. In lake fishing, a 9-foot rod calibered for a GBF (No.8) floating line, or sinking line is sufficient; the reel should have a capacity for 100 yards of 18-pound-test backing. The same rod would be suitable for fishing on large rivers. There is ample opportunity, however, to employ lighter gear on small waters provided the angler is a skilled caster.

Many rivers and portions of lakes (usually in the vicinity of river mouths) in New Zealand are closed to fly-fishing-only, but the fixed spool reel is used elsewhere both for casting and trolling.

The streamer fly is of more than passing interest in New Zealand trout fishing. The dry and wet fly and nymphs are effective on most

Western Bay region of Lake Taupo

rivers, but in the larger lakes where crayfish and forage species such as the native smelts (*Retropinna spp.*), bullies (*Gobiomorphus spp.*), galaxias (*Galaxias spp.*), and the juvenile galaxias or so-called "whitebait" are abundant, the streamer fly is more productive. Many imitative and fanciful local patterns have been devised but visiting American or Canadian anglers can rely on the White Marabou and Muddler Minnow; the former is an excellent representation of the smelt and whitebait, and the latter suggests the adult galaxias and bullies. Either of these patterns fished slow and deep with a sinking-type fly line are consistent trout catchers in New Zealand. At times when smelt or the transparent juvenile galaxias are shoaling near the surface of a calm lake, numerous rises may be seen that are easily mistaken for insect-feeding trout. Large rainbows and browns take the baitfish at

Florida visitor Richard Younger fly fishing the Waiau River

the top in what appears to be a leisurely rise to a mayfly. These "smelting" trout are highly selective and can only be attracted to suitable imitations.

Mayflies are the dominant aquatic insects in New Zealand and the more important species are somewhat large in size (*Ichthybotus hudsoni, I. bicolor*). Caddisflies, stoneflies, dobsonflies, and dragonflies (particularly the red dragonfly) appear in number regionally. Terrestrial insects are in many waters more important than the aquatics; the green manuka beetle, willow beetle, and brown fern beetle will bring on active rises, particularly in the early morning and evening.

INTER-ISLAND TRAVEL NOTES

As in any popular fishing country, the experienced angler will seek rivers and lakes away from the tourist centers and large cities. *Air New Zealand* services both islands, but it is advisable to use a rental car to cover a wide area. While there are some hotels or accommodations on the fishing waters, it's a logistical problem for the visitor to find meals or rooms in most places. There are only occasional widely spaced roadside restaurants (usually bus stops), and these are open at limited hours which seldom coincide with the an-

gler who fishes early or late. Hotel restaurants are similarly operated. Most New Zealand anglers camp out, which is not practical for the tourist without essential equipment.

Restaurant food in general tends to be hearty but uninspired. Quality meats, fruits, seafood, and vegetables are abundant but with exceptions few commercial kitchens know what to do with them. Reservations of all kinds, whether car rental, bus, air travel, or hotel, are vitally important, as facilities are always heavily booked. This is especially true in the summer season from December through January when everyone's on holiday.

SALTWATER FISHING

New Zealand has excellent saltwater fishing centered around 300 miles of its coast on the northern shores of the North Island. From Cape Runaway on the east to North Cape in the north, the major fishing ports are Whangaroa, Bay of Islands (Otehei Bay), Whangarei (Tutukaka), Mercury Bay (Whitianga), and Tauranga (Mayor Island). All fishing grounds are within a 4 hour drive from Auckland, or they may be reached by fast charter aircraft. The principal big-game species are black marlin, which have been caught here in weights up to 976 pounds, striped marlin, mako shark, thresher shark, hammerhead shark, tiger shark, yellowfin tuna, bluefin tuna, and Pacific yellowtail. The striped marlin are most numerous with 250-pound fish the average. Mako shark to 1,000 pounds are second in abundance. Swordfish occur, but only rarely.

New Zealand big-game ports have modern well-equipped charter boats ranging from 30 to 45 feet. The rates range from $50.00 to $60.00 per day.

THE SEASON
From January through April.

LOCAL REGULATIONS
Local marine department regulations provide that billfish can only be taken on rod-and-reel and the line cannot exceed 130-pound-test. Not more than four billfish can be killed from any one boat in any one day.

ACCOMMODATIONS
Resort hotels on the North Island marine fishing grounds are generally excellent and rates given are single. The **Hotel Whangaroa** at Whangaroa, $6.50 per day single; the **Fishing Lodge** at Whangaroa Heads, $7.50 to $12.50 per day; **Hotel Russel**, $8.00 to $9.50 per day and the **Otehei Lodge** in Bay of Islands, $8.00 to $12.50 per day; **Hotel Whangarei** at Whangarei, $9.50 to $11.00 per day; **Hotel Whitianga**, $9.00 per day, and **Hotel Tauranga** at Mercury Bay, $9.00 to $11.00 per day; the **Waitangi Hotel** at Waitangi, $9.00 to $11.00 per day.

FISHING FOR KAHAWAI
The number of small marine species in New Zealand which lend themselves to sport fishing methods by casting with artificial lures is limited. However, the kahawai (Arripis trutta) also known as Australian salmon, which has a superficial resemblance to a salmonid, as do some other members of the Sciaenidae, is a notable exception. Kahawai run from 3 to 10 pounds in weight, but individuals to 16 pounds have been reliably reported. Kaha-

wai can be caught by trolling and casting. They will accept almost any spinner or lure and a wide variety of natural baits. Often they are caught incidentally when an angler is fishing for tuna and yellowtail at sea, or fly fishing for sea trout in river mouths. They are the finest light-tackle game fish in New Zealand waters, and visiting American anglers have likened their fighting performance to that of tarpon. Saltwater spinning gear is becoming popular for kahawai fishing, with light lines down to 2-pound-test. Kahawai are strong, very fast swimmers, and frequently broach or "tail-walk" in an effort to throw the hook. They characteristically make a fast initial run, then zig-zag or swim towards the angler in wide circles (they are noted for line-tangling), and finally make short, rapid dashes in various directions when sighting the boat or nearing the shore.

Kahawai are most available in summer, when they form surface schools up to an acre in area. These appear to be mainly feeding concentrations, for they are usually associated with schools of herrings or anchovies, and planktonic crustaceans. The schools are followed by large flocks of sea birds, including terns (called "kahawai birds" by New Zealand fishermen because of their association with the fish), gulls, petrels, and shags. At times the schools are unaccompanied by birds; the kahawai swim with their mouths open, feeding not on small fish but zooplankton, particularly small shrimps or "krill." The spotted juveniles and the blue-green adults school separately. Each school normally contains fish of a similar size.

Other fishes may occur with kahawai schools, the main ones being trevally (Caranx lutescens), yellowtail (Seriola grandis), and southern mackerel (Scomber japonicus).

Schooling kahawai, often recognizable by their circular, swirling movements, may spend hours quietly moving with their prey organisms, herding them together at or near the

surface and rounding them up again if they disperse. Sometimes they sink quietly from sight, to reappear within a few minutes at a new locality, and sometimes they sound rapidly with much splashing, probably as a large predatory fish passes by.

Kahawai are preyed upon by larger pelagic fishes, including tuna and marlin, and because of their abundance, their suitability for trolling, and their acceptance by these fishes, they are a favorite bait used by New Zealand big-game anglers.

ACCOMMODATION IN TRANSIT
The best in Auckland is the **Inter-Continental Hotel**. Other Auckland hotels such as the **White Heron Lodge, Royal International** and the **De Brett** are the most modern hotels. Single from $10, double from $15, European Plan. Rates at the **Great Northern**, including breakfast, are from $11.00 per person. The **Star Hotel**, known for good food, charges $14.00 per person, American Plan. The long-established **Grand**, overlooking the harbor, is from $11.00 per person, American Plan. **El Cortez Motel** is from $9.30 per person, European Plan. There are also a number of less expensive hotels, motels and attractive guest houses (usually unlicensed for drinks). For an away-from-it-all treat, take the hydrofoil across Auckland's Waitenata Harbor (round trip $6.00) to the licensed **Motel Beach Haven** on Pakatoa Island; $6.00 per person.

TRAVEL NOTES
By Pan American Jet Clipper from San Francisco, Los Angeles, Seattle or Portland, to Auckland via Honolulu; or via Tahiti, from San Francisco and Los Angeles, about 15 hours elapsed time.

Passport and visa required. Also return ticket. Smallpox vaccination certificate. For one, customs declaration 200 cigarettes allowed duty free, or 50 cigars or ½ pound of tobacco. Also one bottle of liquor.

Fishing boats are shown docked at the Bay of Islands in New Zealand, an area well known for its striped marlin

Tongariro River in New Zealand, one of best known fly fishing streams in country, is located in North Island

Laje near Queensland, New Zealand, is a prime spot for the avid angler who enjoys fly fishing for brown trout

Nicaragua

SEE PAGE 85 FOR MAP

Tarpon leaps from the San Juan River at the Toro Rapids. Fish migrate upstream, with peak runs in February through March

Excellent fresh and saltwater angling can be found in this Central American country. Although organized facilities are limited, trips can be arranged in the capital city of Managua for tarpon and snook fishing in the larger inland rivers. The San Juan River at San Carlos, an outlet for huge Lake Nicaragua which flows about 120 miles into the Atlantic Ocean, is one of the more popular locations. Both tarpon and snook run to good size in the San Juan and can be taken by casting or trolling. Freshwater sharks inhabit Lake Nicaragua and occur also in many of the rivers. Snook and tarpon are numerous at the river mouths along the Atlantic side, and barracuda, king mackerel, various jacks, snappers, and groupers are abundant on the outlying reefs.

PACKAGE TRIPS

The easiest way to arrange your fishing in Nicaragua is through one of several travel agencies offering package trips. The only accommodation currently available is **Tarpon**

Camp Nicaragua located on the San Juan River. Situated upstream from the Toro Rapids and El Castille Rapids the camp provides exciting angling for tarpon in fast water. The fish are caught by trolling or by casting from an anchored dugout (cayuko). Plugs are the best bet here with darters and medium runners standard baits. Many fish are lost due to the current, rocks, and underwater snags, so bring plenty of lures for an extended trip. Fish run from 20 to 100 pounds with plenty in the 40- to 60-pound class.

In the package clients are met at Managua airport and transferred to a charter aircraft for a 65 minute flight to Los Chiles. Boats and guides meet parties at Los Chiles for the 1½ to 2 hour trip down river to **Tarpon Camp Nicaragua.** Unpretentious, the camp offers five comfortable bedrooms, good meals, and purified drinking water. The fishing is from January through June with a peak in February and March. Package rates vary from $420 per person for 4 days to $540 per person for 8 days. The following specialist tourist agencies book this package: *World Wide Sportsman, Inc.* P.O. Box 46, Islamorada, Florida 33036 or telephone: Area Code 305 664-4540 or 238-9252. *Safari Outfitters, Inc.*, 8 South Michigan Avenue, Chicago, Illinois 60603.

ACCOMMODATIONS

MANAGUA

Brand new and best in the city is the **Hotel Inter-Continental Managua** with 210 rooms and shaped like an Aztec temple. **Gran Hotel** and **Lido Palace Hotel** are old landmarks. Both have their own swimming pools. Rates about $10 single, $16 double, European Plan (without meals). Other hotels: **Hotel Nicaragua, Estrella, Santa Maria Ostuma,** a mountain hotel, 81 miles from Managua; the **Hotel Barlovento,** located in San Juan del Sur, a beach resort on the Pacific coast near the Costa Rican border, a 2½ hour drive from Managua.

Norway

In the geographically circumscribed world of the Atlantic salmon angler, the rivers of Norway represent an Olympian height. Each season fish of 50 to 60 pounds are caught in the fjord country, and the world record of 79 pounds captured in the Tana River has remained the standard bearer since 1928. Such angling is not something you just find; you may rent a beat which can vary in size from a small pool to a mile or so of river, or you may join a syndicate that controls the entire stream, or if money is no object you may rent the river for yourself. There are countless alternatives and none are cheap. On the better rivers in Norway today, such as the Driva, Maals, Flaam, Alta, and Laerdal, the prices vary from $450 to over $3,000 per week per angler. The torrent of shillings, francs, and dollars pouring down the fjords would stagger the imagination. Although fishing permits can be bought on a daily or weekly basis on mediocre rivers, this rarely results in a worth-while trip. Anglers contemplating a Norwegian vacation should rely on the services of an experienced outfitter such as *Mytravel* (Norway Travel House, 290 Madison Avenue, New York, N.Y. 10017; Area code 212 532-6055) to insure quality fishing and accommodations.

THE SEASON

Norwegian fishing gets underway in June and ends on the last day of August. The climate is nowhere near so forbidding as that might make you think. This is far north—and for three summer months it never gets dark in Norway, and at North Cape, for almost that long, the sun never goes below the horizon. But a strong modifying effect comes from the Atlantic drift, where the Gulf Stream ends its long flow northward; and the prevailing west wind carries warmth from the sea toward the land.

The Norwegian coast is the most complicated in the world, consisting almost entirely of fjords, peninsulas and islands. This interlacing of sea and land does much to moderate the climate. In the crumpled folds of the coastline are countless pockets in which warm maritime air accumulates. The price of warmth here is fog, and often rain. In the south of Norway precipitation reaches 85 inches a year, four times the amount that falls inland and farther north.

THE FISHING
Norway has stopped all drift-netting and long line fishing within the 12-mile limit except for the stationary nets belonging to farmers in the fjord areas. Very few fish with net marks were caught in the 1968 and 1969 seasons. However, the number of salmon caught in both years was very low due to an abnormally dry and hot summer creating low water levels. The fish did not run up in any quantity before the season ended. The Alta started slowly in 1969 but it finished with 800 salmon caught on eight rods in 5 week period; this is fairly close to its peak 1967 season when 900 salmon were caught by eight rods in the same period. The

low was in 1968 with less than 300 salmon registered. Prospects remain good throughout Norway for 1971.

AURLAND RIVER
The Aurland River is situated on the Sognefjord, a short drive from Flaam which is connected with Oslo and Bergen by rail. Aurland can also be reached by car from Oslo or Bergen on the new mountain road from Laerdal to Aurland. There are also excellent fjord steamer connections to the various villages on Sognefjord. The Aurland is probably one of Norway's most beautiful rivers and is famous for its fine run of sea trout. The river also holds a good number of salmon. Sea trout are usually caught on dry flies, and are considered even better sport than salmon by many anglers since light tackle can be used. Sea trout from 12 to 18 pounds are caught every year, and the average is around 6 pounds. Best salmon season is from mid-June to mid-July and top sea

trout season from mid-July to the end of August.

Accommodations can be arranged at Flaam, the **Fretheim Tourist Hotel,** which is situated 20 minutes' drive from the river. This is one of Norway's most charming fjord hotels.

LAERDAL RIVER
One of the best salmon rivers in Norway, the Laerdal, is approximately 50 miles long, of which there are about 16 miles of salmon and sea-trout water below an impassable falls. The river flows into Sognefjord, Norway's longest fjord, at the village of Laerdal. Nearly all fishing takes place from the banks or from specially constructed platforms built over the water. A few beats can be waded. No boats are used. The main road follows the river, and every pool is accessible by car. Visitors to the Laerdal travel by ferry steamer from Bergen to Laerdal in one day, or from Oslo by rail to Fagernes and then by bus to Laerdal (217 miles).

Laerdal salmon run 20 to 25 pounds. Fish of over 40 pounds are taken each season. The sea trout range from 8 to 15 pounds, but individual fish of over 20 pounds are caught.

The **Lindstrøm Hotel** dominates the village of Laerdal. As pine in functional design has become Early American, the well-built houses and the hotel, which reflect industry and thrift, might be called Early Norwegian. The main street is bisected here and there by forlorn little rivulets that come weeping down from the steep mountainside to seek their parent river. Lindstrøm's has been famous since before the turn of the century. This imperial playpen has been host to all of the crowned heads in Europe bent on catching salmon, the more successful anglers being celebrated by wood carvings and painted outlines of their prize catches which adorn the walls of the inn.

For some of its Laerdal fishing *Mytravel* offers the **Moldebo Lodge.**

Aurland in Norway is one of country's most beautiful rivers and famous for its sea trout. Specimen shown here was caught by happy fisherman

This consists of one main building and five log cabins as sleeping quarters. The cabins and main building are old farm houses from the 17th and 18th centuries, which have been collected from the valley and its surroundings. Completely modernized inside to give the finest comfort but without losing its traditional look. The main building has a dining room, sitting room with fire place, large terrace facing the river and rooms for servants. In front of the main building is a heated swimming pool. The camp has also its own sauna bath, smoke house and deep freezing room.

ALTA RIVER

The Alta River in Arctic Norway is rated as the finest salmon river in the world. Rising in the plateau barrens above Karasjok in Lapland the Alta flows through a forested valley toward the Altafjord, only a hundred miles south of the North Cape. Regular daily air service connects Oslo with Alta, and the fishing accommodations are along the river. *Mytravel* controls the arrangements for fishing the Alta, and occasional beats are available on a weekly basis. Prices are expensive and vary considerably with the specific beats and seasons, but fishing this almost legendary salmon river is an experience no dedicated salmon angler can afford to miss.

The people of the village of Alta celebrate Midsummer's Eve at midnight on June 23 each year. Everyone participates—men, women and children. Most of them preselect camp spots along the river, for public fishing is permitted and they are free to fish for salmon from the banks until midnight that day. They view this occasion, the day the sun never sets, as being second only to Christmas in importance. At midnight all public fishing ceases, for the 300 land owners along the river have formed "The River Company" which leases the river for the next five weeks, and only the lessee (*Mytravel*) and its clients can fish.

The Alta River produces exceptionally large salmon, but it is also one of the most expensive rivers in the world. Rates for the 1971 season will run about $3,000 per week

The fishing is exceptional. Skilled salmon anglers often kill as many as ten salmon averaging 27 pounds in a single night. Alta regulars sleep through the day and fish during the eight-hour twilight of the Midnight Sun. The flow in the Alta River is heavy even in July. To get a fly deep and to attract large salmon requires wet patterns such as the Dusty Miller, Red Abbey, Black Dose, Jock Scott, Silver Rat and Rusty Rat in sizes from 3/0 to 6/0; local preference is for double hooks in 5/0 and 6/0. A heavy sinking line (No. 11) with 220 yards of 30-pound-test backing is standard. Leaders testing 30 to 40 pounds are preferred. Traditional fly rods are two-handed 13-footers but single-handed 9- and 9½-footers are now in fashion. Fishing on the Alta is done from narrow 20- to 22-foot-long boats with substantial freeboard; they are quite stable in rough water and are maneuvered by a man operating a stern outboard motor and a "rower" who sits in the bow. The fishing is accomplished by slow drifting from the head of the pool to the tail. The angler, sitting amidship, casts quartering down on the fast water side allowing the fly to swing directly ahead of the boat. Thirty- to 40-pound salmon are not uncommon. The record Alta salmon weighed 61 pounds and was killed by the Earl of

Dudley in 1951. Such fly-fishing makes the Alta a unique salmon river.

MALANGSFOSSEN

This is considered the finest single salmon pool in the world. It is almost 250 miles north of the Arctic Circle in a valley of dense pines and spectacular mountains. Its excellence stems from the size of the river and its thundering waterfall, which churns through 500 yards of broken boulders and mossy ledges until it has dropped almost 75 feet into the pool. The falls block the entire spawning run of a major arctic watershed for almost two months. Sometimes thousands of salmon, darkening after weeks in the river and others still sea-bright and fresh, lie waiting in its tumbling currents until the right water level enables them to ascend the ladder in the falls; this usually occurs in early July.

The Malangfoss lies only thirty minutes southeast of the airfield at Bardufoss, with daily five-hour connecting flights to Oslo. *Mytravel's* lodge is located in a pleasant meadow surrounded with silver birches, sited on a quiet bend of the Bardufoss river, since the roar of the Malangsfoss waterfall itself makes sleep difficult. The pool itself measures almost 300 yards in diameter,

This over-60-pound salmon was taken on the Vossa River by Egil Larsen of Oslo

The Laerdal River produces salmon of over 40 pounds with an average of half that size. Sea trout fishing is excellent starting about July 15. Beats are in high demand

shaped like a gargantuan bottle with the waterfall in its narrow throat. The principal current-tongue churns deep into the maelstrom of whirlpools and white water at the head before sweeping almost 200 yards down the granite ledges across the pool. Strong reverse currents sweep back along the rocky fishing beaches toward the base of the falls, and the river is powerful enough that salmon are found facing reverse currents and eddies as well as the river itself. The spreading tail shallows divide at a downstream island, widening the river to almost 400 yards in places. Depending on the river level, there is ample fishing room for two to three boats on this tremendous pool.

The fishing at Malangsfossen is unique in terms of a single pool, since about forty salmon averaging 30 to 40 pounds are killed each summer, and the pool record is 57 pounds. Its depth and turbulence make fly fishing difficult until late July, and most of the fishing is done with an assortment of spoons and Devon minnows. Some bank-casting and wading is possible, but the best fishing is from boats. Some additional bank-casting and wading is available on the beats below the pool. Hip-length waders are recommended, since the fish are landed on the rocky beach after hooking them from the boats.

DRIVA RIVER

The Driva rises high in the barren Dovrefjell plateau, among the highest mountains in Norway, and flows north through one of the most beautiful valleys in Europe until it reaches the fjord at Sunndalsøra. Its pastoral farmsteads and emerald-green currents are enclosed in a high-walled valley, threaded with countless waterfalls tumbling more than a thousand feet from the snowfields and glaciers to the valley floor. The setting is spectacular.

The Driva lies about two hundred miles north of Oslo, with excellent train service to Oppdal and transfer by chauffeur-driven car the last 40 miles to the **Grand Hotel** in Sunndalsøra. The beats include several charming fishing huts along the river, and encompass the Hoven and Hol leases which are considered the best stretches. Some boat fishing is done on the larger pools, using small prams designed for such work, but other pools offer excellent wading and bank-casting.

Driva salmon average about 18 pounds and the sea trout about 3 pounds. Fly fishing becomes good after mid-July, and the sea trout begin arriving later. The record salmon for the river is 57 pounds, and its reputation places it among the ten best rivers in Norway.

SULDALSLAGEN RIVER

Also known as the Sand River, this beautiful stream is in Rogaland, about 200 miles southwest of Oslo, and its salmon run upriver about 15 miles between the Suldalsvatn lake and its mouth in the Saudafjord above Stavanger. Its valley varies between narrow gorges, where the river tumbles in white water chutes, to timbered basins where it flows past farms and small villages. Sand is located at its mouth on the fjord, and is a typical coastal settlement that once built sailing ships and now draws its livelihood from fishing and forestry.

British anglers have fished the river

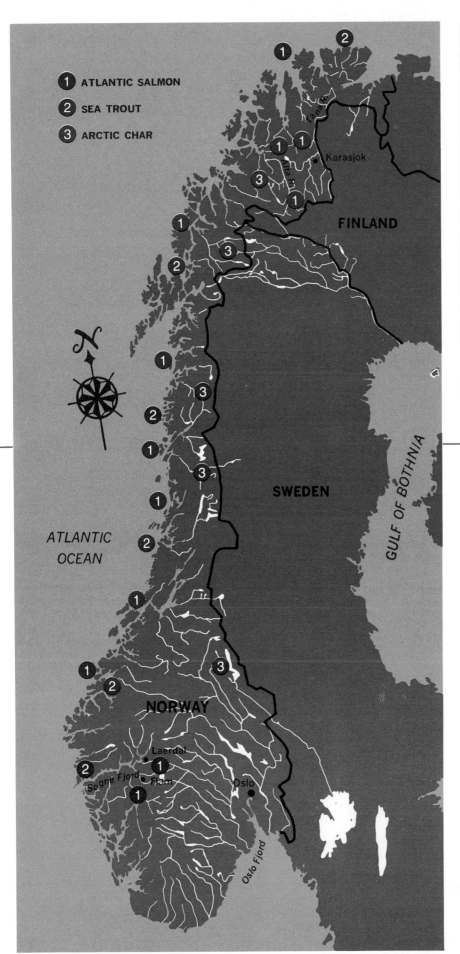

1 ATLANTIC SALMON

2 SEA TROUT

3 ARCTIC CHAR

ATLANTIC
OCEAN

FINLAND

Karasjok

SWEDEN

GULF OF BOTHNIA

NORWAY

Laerdal

Sogne Fjord • Flåm

Oslo

Oslo Fjord

The Driva River is one of Norway's best fly-fishing streams from mid-July on

since 1884, when its late summer run became known in the United Kingdom and dedicated anglers could travel to Sand when their own fishing slackened in midsummer. Suldalslagen was considered one of the best rivers in the world until about 1925, when its extensive spawning run and the high average weight of the salmon attracted commercial fishing interests and the fish were decimated.

Sport fishermen ended this period of exploitation, when all netting and trapping ended and the river was restored. These reforms have brought the river back considerably in the past ten years, until its salmon now average about 25 pounds and the river record of 64 pounds was made in recent years. The salmon run peaks in August and September, making it a late river for Norway. The Sand is reached via daily air service to Stavanger and hydrofoil-boat connections between Stavanger and the village of Sand. There is both boat fishing in the larger pools and bank-casting in other places. Your chances here are excellent for fish above 40 pounds.

Famed fly-caster Ernest Schwiebert of New Jersey
is an annual visitor to Norway's rivers

FLAAM RIVER

A relatively small Norwegian salmon stream, the Flaam has its source in the Storskavlen glaciers, about 200 miles northwest of Oslo in the mountains of the Sognefjord. This tranquil valley has picturesque villages, farms and waterfalls, and its crystalline pools hold salmon in about three miles of water between the fjord at Flaam and the Gilja waterfall upstream. The current is relatively smooth, since the river drops less than 200 feet between the waterfall and its mouth, but it is surprisingly swift.

Flaam is the terminal point of excellent rail service from Oslo, and much of its charm lies in its isolation from outside roads. Charming fjord steamers also serve Flaam from several villages on the Sognefjord. The Mytravel lease includes the entire three miles of river, with bankcasting and some wading throughout. There are nine pools in this reach of water, as well as a number of small holding-places at various levels of water.

The salmon run a little smaller than those of most Norwegian rivers, averaging about 14 pounds. There are also numbers of grilse and sea trout arriving after the middle of July.

Salmon of over 30 pounds are possible. A fish weighing 32 pounds was caught on the dry fly in 1968 by John R. Martin of New York using a single-handed 9-foot rod. The visitor cannot expect the same number of salmon on the Flaam as are killed on larger, more costly rivers elsewhere in Norway but it flows among some of the most spectacular mountains in Norway, and its charming **Fretheim** is one of the most pleasant country hotels in Europe. Fishing its pools is an angling experience of tranquility and comfort, in a high-walled valley almost unspoiled by civilization.

TACKLE

Norwegian salmon rivers are swift and their fish average close to 20 pounds, with fish between 30 and 40 pounds in good numbers. Strong tackle is advisable in Norway, although anglers experienced with big salmon on Canadian rivers can use single-handed rods of 8½ and 9½ feet. Longer two-handed rods between 10½ and 13½ feet are more commonly used in Norway, since there is considerable use for flies larger than 3/0. Sinking lines are required through most of the Norwegian season, although floating lines are useful in shallow holding-lies later in the summer. Fly-reels

should be sturdy, provide firm drag mechanisms, and have at least 200 yards of 20-pound backing line. Such flies as the Jock Scott, Silver Grey, Blue Charm, Black Doctor, Thunder and Lightning and Dusty Miller are in widespread use on Norwegian rivers, and an assortment between sizes 4/0 and 5/0 is advisable. Spoon fishermen will find light trolling rods valuable, fitted with heavy-duty casting reels and 30-pound line. Medium to heavy spinning gear is also useful. Spoons and Devon minnows and other lures are available throughout Norway, and the fisherman should perhaps purchase such equipment to meet local conditions. There are well-stocked tackle shops in Oslo, Bergen and Trondheim.

FISHING COSTS

The price of Atlantic salmon fishing continues to spiral upward. For 1970 the rates per rod per week on rivers serviced by *Mytravel* were as follows:

Malangfossen Pool	$750 from June 28 through July 19; $650 from July 20 through August 2.
Alta River	From $1,800 to $3,250
Aurland River	$550
Laerdal River	$1,100
Driva	$750
Suldalslagen (Sand) River	$750
Flaam	$750 from June 28 through July 26; $550 from July 27 to August 30.
Stjordal	$550 from June 28 through July 26; $450 from July 27 to August 30.

All above rates include fishing rights and fees, accommodations, meals, boats and ghillie services (except on Malangsfossen Pool where boat and ghillie cost an additional $2.50 per hour) as well as local transportation between fishing beats and the lodge or hotel.

Reservation: When making a reservation, a deposit of 25% of the total price is required. Balance is due three months prior to arrival in Norway (Alta, January 15).

Cancellation: If a cancellation is made later than three months prior to arrival, no refund unless the vacancy is resold.

Not included: Fishing tackle, liquor, beer and other items of personal nature.

Lease of beats: Each beat is leased to two to four rods at a time. If you wish to lease a beat for the exclusive use of one or two rods, apply for special rates. (Alta, eight rods in the whole river).

CLOTHING

Norway has a northern marine climate that is surprisingly mild considering its latitudes. Summer temperatures commonly vary between 50 and 80 degrees Farenheit. Visitors should bring a varied assortment of clothing. While the Gulf Stream along the coast of Norway prevents the extremely cold weather one often experiences on the North American continent at or near these latitudes, it is nevertheless cold and wet here too, most of the time. One should bring very warm clothing including thermal underwear, short insulated rubber boots, strong raingear with parka hood, rubber pants and plastic lined gloves for traveling on the river between pools. Bright weather makes it possible to fish in normal summer clothes of poplin or khaki, perhaps supplemented with a sweater or light windbreaker jacket. Sport coats and suits of medium weight are also useful, since Norwegian evenings tend toward coolness. Suitable clothing for such cities as Bergen and Trondheim and Oslo should also be in the luggage of anglers bound for Norway.

ACCOMMODATIONS

OSLO

Luxury hotels in **Oslo** are the **Bristol, Continental** and the **Grand.** Rates about $22 single, $40 double for room with bath. First-class hotels include the **Ambassadeur, Carlton,** the **KNA** (Royal Norwegian Automobile Club), the **Norum, Nobel,** the **Viking,** and the **Holmenkollen,** which is on the famous hill overlooking the city. Rates at these hotels average $17 single, $31 double. There is usually an extra charge of Kr. 2 if you stay only 1 night. There are also several "off-season" rate reductions during the year.

Advance reservations are recommended, especially in summer.

BERGEN

Best hotels in Bergen are the **Bristol,** the **Orion** and the **Norge.** Rates start at about $15 single, $30 double European Plan.

STAVANGER

Excellent hotels here are the **Atlantic Hotel, KNA, Esso Motor Hotel.** Rates start at about $15 single, $26 double European Plan.

TRONDHEIM

If you stop over here, try the **Britannia, Prinsen, Astoria,** or the **Bristol.** Rates start at about $15 single European Plan.

Breakfast and service charges are included in your bill, and no other tips are expected, except Kr. 1 per day to the head porter. Round off restaurant check (which has 12½ percent service charge) to the nearest krone; ditto for taxi drivers. Tip washroom attendants and hat-check girls 50 ore. Luggage porters get Kr. 3.50 per person. If you have more than the normal number of bags, Kr. 7 is customary.

There are many fine places to dine in the large cities which favor a continental cuisine; however, the cold buffet (*Koldtbordt*) is a notable feature of Norway and particularly in the fishing areas. Herring is featured in amazing variety. Fjord people are a vigorous race of farmers and fishermen, and thus the food is hearty— the pressed cod or *persetorsk* or for stronger stomachs the *lutefisk,* a cod prepared in potash lye. Another aged fish dish and one much appreciated in Norway is *rakørret* or raketrout, which is half fermented by storing the fish in a barrel with coarse salt and sugar and pressing them under a heavy weight for three months. Cattle are scarce and the staple meat is mutton in the form of *fenalor,* a cured smoked leg, or *pinnekjott,* the salted and dried ribs of mutton. Game birds come to the table often, and the favorite is *ryper* or ptarmigan, a delight to all people living along the south rim of the Arctic Circle. Venison or *dyrestek* is in Norway the reindeer. But salmon, particularly the *røkelaks* in smoked form, has the same prestige and market value in Norway as it does elsewhere in the world.

Don Carter of Dallas, Texas, fights salmon. Laerdal guide is famed Olaf Olson

Panama

Long a citadel for black marlin angling, this Central American country rates as one of the most productive saltwater fishing regions in the world. Bordered by the Caribbean Sea on the north and the Pacific Ocean on the south, Panama is tropical and has a dry season from December through April and a rainy season from May through November. The rainy season is typified by brief but heavy showers during some part of the day.

OFFSHORE FISHING

Until recently the prime fishing grounds in the Gulf of Panama at Piñas Bay were difficult of access. Adventurous anglers cruised from the Canal Zone with an overnight stop at Cocos Point to fish the Piñas Bay area for black and striped marlin, yellowfin tuna, Pacific sailfish, dolphin, amberjack, mako, and a great variety of reef species, including the corvina. Today, it can be conveniently reached by plane service from Tocumen Airport, and excellent accommodations as well as boats and guides exist on location. This is one of few areas where black marlin can be caught in quantity.

Pacific sailfish are boated the year round, but because the most effective Panamanian method of fishing for marlin is to use a whole bonito from the outriggers, many sailfish are not hooked on these 5- to 6-pound skip baits. A similarly large bonito is employed when live baiting on the flat lines. However, sailfish are readily caught on smaller whole baits as well as strip baits. Wahoo, dolphin, roosterfish, big-eye tuna, and amberjack also come to these smaller baits. Due to the great abundance of dolphin in these waters, many anglers use bait-casting and fly-fishing tackle.

THE SEASON

Black marlin have been caught in Piñas Bay during all months of the year. However, they are more abundant during January, February, and March. The boats at Tropic Star Lodge often average fifteen marlin strikes per day during this period. Some large black marlin (600-700 pounds) have been caught in the summer months, and it would appear that the heaviest fish occur here from July until early fall. Sailfish peak in the summer months.

Sailfish like this 140-pounder *(left)* are very abundant in the summer months. The Pacific form runs twice the size of its Atlantic counterpart. The cove at Tropic Star Lodge *(above)* is a well-protected anchorage for charter craft. Although normally calm the seas can build at times

ACCOMMODATIONS

PIÑAS BAY

The **Tropic Star Lodge** owned by Bud and Joan Williams. A deluxe resort hacked from the Darien jungle consisting of well-appointed, air-conditioned, individual bungalows and a main lodge. Food excellent. The Williams couple also own **Arctic Star Lodge** located on Great Bear Lake in Canada's Northwest Territories. The **Tropic Star** package price $1095 per person all-inclusive including round trip transportation from Panama City (150 miles from the lodge). A fleet of 31-foot twin diesel charter craft on premises. For reservations: Tropic Star Lodge, c/o International Inn, 1808 Wellington Avenue, Winnepeg, Manitoba, Canada.

CARIBBEAN SEA

COSTA RICA

Isthmus of Panama

CANAL ZONE (USA)

Golfo de los Mosquitos

Chiriquí Grande

Panama

PANAMA

Bay of Panama

Gulf of Chiriquí

Parita Gulf

PACIFIC OCEAN

PERLAS ISLANDS

Gulf of Panama

COIBA I.

CÉBACO I.

COLOMBIA

1	BLACK MARLIN	4	PACIFIC SAILFISH	7	MAKO	10	RAINBOW TROUT
2	STRIPED MARLIN	5	DOLPHIN	8	CORVINA	11	SNOOK
3	YELLOWFIN TUNA	6	AMBERJACK	9	WAHOO	12	TARPON

TROUT FISHING

There is some rainbow trout fishing in the Chiriquí Highlands of Panama. This is the coffee and sugar district bordering on Costa Rica. The streams around El Volcan, an 11,000-foot mountain peak, provide modest sizes and numbers of trout. There are guides and accommodations available locally. Best spots are the **Nacional Hotel** in David or the **Dos Rios** or **Hotel Panamonte** in Boquete. Guides are also available. There are regular flights from Panama City to David.

ACCOMMODATIONS

PANAMA CITY

All European Plan: **Hotel El Continental** is air-conditioned, has a swimming pool, gambling casino, night club, several fine dining rooms and a coffee shop open 24 hours a day. Double $14-$20 (December 16-March 31). The **Lux,** nearer the center of town, has year-round double rates from $13. The lavish **El Panamá Hilton** is situated in the residential section of the capital. Ultramodern studio-style bedrooms with private balconies are designed for beauty and comfort. Featured are an outdoor patio, swimming pool, cabaña and tennis club, dining and dancing, and gambling casino. Rates from $16 up, double (slightly higher January 6-March 31). The **Hotel Internacional** is in the heart of the theater and night-club section; year round from $10 double. **La Siesta Hotel,** at the airport, is a complete resort in itself with night club, pool and golf course. Year-round rates are $12 single, $16 double.

Marlin (above) are the mainstay of Piñas Bay angling. Anglers enjoy a very high ratio of success per trip. The red snapper (left) surfaces in such numbers at times that the ocean turns red for acres. Other prime table-fish such as corvina and dolphin are in constant supply at Tropic Star Lodge

Paraguay

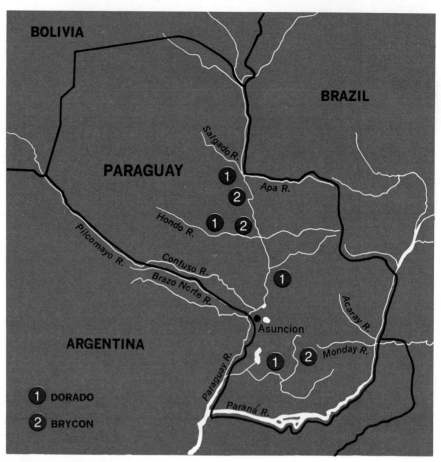

Legend on map:
- BOLIVIA
- BRAZIL
- PARAGUAY
- ARGENTINA
- Salgado R.
- Apa R.
- Hondo R.
- Pilcomayo R.
- Confuso R.
- Brazo Norte R.
- Asuncion
- Acaray R.
- Paraguay R.
- Monday R.
- Paraná R.
- ① DORADO
- ② BRYCON

Chicago angler James Bresley and dorado from Tiger Hill Safaris

This country in central South America has much to offer the sportsman, but the dorado fishing is clearly its best angling. Paraguay is the least populated country in South America (estimated less than 2 million) and many of its numerous rivers receive very little rod pressure. The land is not for the tourist who expects to find everything comparable to home; there is a great deal of primitive jungle and roads are non-existent in many areas. The river port capital, Asuncion, is the only concession to civilization, and here ox carts and donkeys plod among the taxis and imported cars. The best and easiest way to arrange a dorado trip here is through *Safari Outfitters, Inc.*, (8 South Michigan Avenue, Chicago, Illinois 60603, Area Code 312 346-9631). This specialized travel organization is the representative for **Tiger Hill Safaris** which maintains camps on a number of Paraguayan rivers. The accommodations may consist of hotels, ranch houses, or tents depending on the river being fished. All supporting equipment including small aircraft and car, service personnel, and a bi-lingual guide are included in these package trips.

THE SEASON
Dorado fishing in Paraguay starts and ends later than the same angling in Argentina. The best period here is from October through March. This is the summer season and temperatures ordinarily run from 80°F to 90°F, accompanied by moderate rainfall in the form of thundershowers.

THE FISHING
The techniques and tackle for dorado fishing are detailed under Argentina in this book. The same equipment and methods are used here.

COSTS
Safari Outfitters rates are $350 for one person on a six-day trip, $287 for two, and $234 for three persons; each extra day runs from $35 to $40.

LICENSE
None required.

ACCOMMODATIONS
ASUNCION
The best is the air conditioned **Guarani Hotel** which has swimming pool, theater, night club, and magnificent view of the city. Stop is included in *Safari Outfitters* tour, otherwise rates run from $13 single European Plan. Older is the **Gran Hotel del Paraguay** with single rates from $14 American Plan. Two best restaurants are *La Preferida* and *La Pergola del Bolsi*. For Paraguayan dishes and native music try *La Calandria* and *El Jardin de la Cerveza*. Tap water is safe in Asuncion but bottled *agua mineral* is a good policy.

TRAVEL NOTES
Passport, smallpox certificate both required. Duty-free allowances: 200 cigarettes, one bottle of liquor. Departure tax is G150 to G300, depending upon destination. The guarani (G), divided into 100 centimos, is currently valued at G100 to U.S. 70c. The First National City Bank of New York has a branch in Asuncion.

Puerto Rico

Puerto Rico is located 1063 miles southeast of Miami. From the air, the island looks like a dark green blanket that somebody folded carelessly and dropped on a bed of sand. Over the rain forest at El Yunque the clouds will hang like giant cotton balls and low to the southwest at La Parguera, where it never rains, the heat reflects pearl pink in the sky. Puerto Rico is bordered on the north by the Atlantic Ocean and on the south by the Caribbean Sea. It rises as a peak from the ocean floor. Nearby is the deepest spot in the Atlantic (30,246 feet) known as the Milwaukee Deep. The 100-fathom curve is within 3 miles of Arecibo and San Juan. It is also very close to shore west of Aguadilla and Rincón, and about 15 miles offshore from Mayagüez. This marine habitat is host to more than 500 species of fish, of which at least seventy are of angling interest. Big-game fishing, however, is the principal attraction in Puerto Rico. Both blue and white marlin are common. They frequent the waters off San Juan, Arecibo, Mayagüez, La Parguera, and probably surround the entire island, but few boats operate away from these four major ports. There are also yellowfin tuna, dolphin, wahoo, king mackerel, barracuda, tarpon, and snook in certain localities, and sailfish are present although they are not common.

THE SEASON

There are no real extremes in Puerto Rican climate. It's warm the year round with averages running between 75°F and 85°F. December through May offers the best weather. Because Puerto Rico is in the trade winds zone, fresh easterly or northeasterly winds are the rule. In the spring (March through May), there are strong winds averaging around 18 mph, with gusts to 30 mph. From August through October there is some fairly calm weather. Winds in June and July are stronger, and the waters tend to be rough on the north coast of Puerto Rico. In winter, especially January, there may be northers with a ground sea.

SALTWATER FISHING

NORTH COAST

The most convenient fishing for the vacationer is out of San Juan. The city has lush hotels, and charter boats operate from the docks at *Club Nautico.* Many visitors have hung at least one marlin on the gin-pole in a day's charter. Blue marlin, white marlin, sailfish, yellowfin tuna, and dolphin are likely quarry here. Blues are the most commonly caught billfish. They occur the year round but in comparatively small sizes between February and late May. In June, they begin to appear in numbers, and from July to October there is usually good fishing. The large blue marlin of over 400 pounds are caught from late June through August with a July peak. Usually, blue marlin vary between 225 and 450 pounds during the summer period. However, a world's all-tackle record was held twice in Puerto Rico. The heavier fish weighed 781 pounds. Several blue marlin have also been sighted or hooked which were estimated to be over 1,000 pounds. In September and October the weight averages drop and fish of 100 to 150 pounds are common. More than 100 blue marlin are caught in the San Juan area each year.

White marlin occur all season long but they seem to be more plentiful in April, May and June. The whites usually run 45 to 65 pounds with 80 to 90 pound specimens being exceptional. Sailfish appear on the north coast late in September and they are abundant from November to the middle of December. They disappear in the summer. Yellowfin tuna also occur here, and May through July seems to be the best period for this species. There are

days during the early summer months when very large schools may be seen feeding in the company of whale sharks. The usual size of the yellowfin tuna north of San Juan is large, running 60 to 150 pounds. The exceptional specimens caught in Puerto Rico approach 190 pounds. The north coast is also prolific in dolphin schools. Dolphin are abundant in the winter and the best month for fishing is February. The usual weight of these fish is 10 to 15 pounds; however, sizes of 30 to 50 pounds are not uncommon. In general, dolphin run quite large off Puerto Rico; two fish caught on the south coast in January 1964 weighed 66 and 68 pounds. This, of course, is a choice food fish and is eagerly sought during peak periods.

EAST COAST

The reefs on the east coast of Puerto Rico in the Fajardo, Culebra, and Vieques perimeter provide the best fishing of this kind on the island. This is principally for snappers and groupers. South of the island of Vieques there is an extremely sharp drop-off of over 1,000 fathoms. Very little sport fishing has been done in this area but marlin and sailfish have been taken. Off the mainland east coast a few miles from Guaynabe is the Grappler Bank; blue marlin have been caught here but the banks are better known for wahoo fishing in October and early November. There are few facilities on the east coast except at Guyama.

SOUTH COAST

In the south, reef-fishing is good between Ponce and Santa Isabel; few billfish have been caught in this area. Marlin, tuna, and dolphin are plentiful along the south coast from Guanica to Cabo Rojo, consistently more abundant south of Guanica

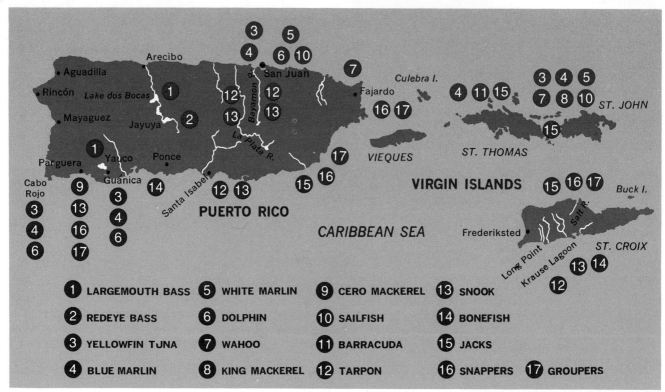

1 LARGEMOUTH BASS	**5** WHITE MARLIN	**9** CERO MACKEREL	**13** SNOOK
2 REDEYE BASS	**6** DOLPHIN	**10** SAILFISH	**14** BONEFISH
3 YELLOWFIN TUNA	**7** WAHOO	**11** BARRACUDA	**15** JACKS
4 BLUE MARLIN	**8** KING MACKEREL	**12** TARPON	**16** SNAPPERS **17** GROUPERS

and La Parguera. Billfishing and tuna fishing off the south coast begins in March, and it is good until May. Reef-fishing, including snappers, groupers, cero, king mackerel, and barracuda, is unusually good at La Parguera.

The road west from Salinas to Ponce, second city of Puerto Rico, passes through Santa Isabel. This sleepy port boasts a gourmet inn, *El Aquarium*, serving some of the best bouillabaisse this side of Marseilles.

The **Ponce Inter-Continental,** a modern oasis, perches high on a hillside. This handsome hostelry offers its guests swimming pool, night club, casino, tennis courts, side trips to the beach, a rum distillery and coffee plantation.

Flats are scattered both east and west with many good tarpon bays close to shore. Some of the flats like the one inside Media Luna Reef seasonally attract very large tarpon (100 pounds plus). Snook, known as *robalo* in Spanish speaking countries, trade in the mangroves east of La Parguera. Snappers, king mackerel, jack crevalle, and the usual populations of reef fish can be taken

by spin-casters in any of the bays. The **Villa Parguera** is a popular hotel here where host Carlos Quinones offers 32 double rooms, 19 of them air-conditioned, plus a swimming pool.

WEST COAST

On the west coast of Puerto Rico off Mayagüez, Rincón and Aguadilla, there is some blue marlin fishing. However, the Mona Passage can be disappointing. There is also some reef-fishing off Mayaguez, and occasional wahoo fishing around the Sponge Bank. Hotel here is the **Mayagüez Hilton** at $15 single and $19 double. The hotel offers facilities for offshore fishing.

TACKLE

Big-game fishing tackle can be supplied by the charter craft. However, serious anglers will want to bring their own. Generally speaking, Puerto Ricans favor the light side with 20-pound test on the flat lines and 50-pound test virtually standard for blue marlin.

Blind strikes are the rule here, and island skippers follow the booby

and frigate birds or look for concentrations of drifting Portuguese Man-of-War to locate fish. The most popular bait in Puerto Rican fishing waters is ballyhoo, which is used for small blue marlin, white marlin, sailfish, dolphin, and wahoo. However, small barracuda, white mullet and bonefish have been employed with success for large blues. The blue marlin in Puerto Rico display a varied diet with tunas, especially frigate mackerel, needlefish, pompano dolphin, snake mackerel, and round robins being important items of their food. The white marlin feed on squids as well as small fishes, such as the blue runner, surgeonfish, filefish, and little tuna. Sailfish utilize substantially the same forage and in addition occasionally flyingfish. Flyingfish are the chief item of food for dolphin in Puerto Rico. As in most big-game areas, the baits used do not necessarily reflect the actual diet of the fish sought.

Artificial lures, such as feathers, are used primarily for bonito fishing. There are very large schools of bonito present in the summer months.

FRESHWATER FISHING

Puerto Rico offers some good largemouth bass (locally *lobina*) fishing in twenty reservoirs which range in size from 15 to 970 acres. The local record is a 14-pounder from Lake Dos Bocas. At Yauco Lake skilled bass fishermen have averaged as high as 12 bass per angler per trip. Puerto Rican bass fishing peaks when the water is clear during the dry season, with January the best month. The poorest fishing is generally in summer and fall when the water becomes muddy after heavy rains. Redeye bass (*Micropterus coosae*) have also been stocked in a number of farm ponds as well as the Maricao, Jayuya, and Pitahaya Rivers. There are twenty large rivers on the island which hold populations of snook and tarpon. The best locations for this type of fishing are the Añasco, La Plata, Bayamon and Loiza Rivers. Other saltwater species come into the rivers, such as the jacks and ladyfish, and even permit have been caught in the lower Añasco River.

ACCOMMODATIONS

San Juan is a booming resort city offering a wide range of accommodations from beachfront hotels to guest houses. In-season rates (mid-December to May) are higher than the off-season prices and the following are in-season minimums on European plan. Two large Hilton Hotels dominate the Condado section of the city: the **Caribe Hilton** with a balcony and ocean view from every room at $33 single and $37 double, and the newer **San Jeronimo Hilton,** $26 single and $30 double. The **Da Vinci** is $20 single and $26 double. The colorful **Flamboyan** overlooks the sea and Condado Lagoon, single $29, double $34; the Spanish-style **Condado Beach,** $22 single, $26 double; the **Puerto Rico Sheraton** on the ocean, $21 single, $26 double, and the dramatic **La Concha** with its shell-shaped night club, $28 single, $33 double. In the Isla Verda section are the 400-room **Americana,** $29 single, $33 double; the **Racquet Club Hotel** with tennis courts and a racquet-shaped swimming pool, $24 single, $29 double; **El San Juan Hotel** on 15 ocean-front acres, $27 single, $32 double; and the attractive **Holiday Inn,** $21 single, $27 double. These hotels are air-conditioned, have bars, restaurants, their own beaches or pools, evening entertainment and sports facilities. In the heart of Old San Juan is the beautiful **El Convento,** a restored 17th century Carmeline convent furnished with antiques, $22 single, $27 double. **El Miramar** is equidistant from beaches and commercial centers in San Juan and offers spectacular views of the capital from its rooftop restaurant, $17 single, $24 double. The **Pierre Hotel,** Swiss operated, has rates from $22 single, $28 double; the **Excelsior,** new in the Santurce section, is from $10 single, $14 double. Smaller tourist hotels in San Juan include the **Condado Lagoon,** $19 single, $23 double. Twenty miles west of San Juan are two lavish hotels that are complete resorts in every way. The **Dorado Hilton** has an 18-hole golf course, among other facilities for sports and entertainment; MAP rates are from $50 single, $60 double. The **Dorado Beach** has two 18-hole golf courses, all kinds of entertainment including a Fiesta Jibara every Wednesday evening; modified American Plan rates are from $50 single, $60 double.

Flats on Puerto Rico's south shore offer some light-tackle casting to the wading angler or anglerette *(above).* **Best marlin fishing is from mid-July to early October**

Rhodesia

This landlocked southern African country boasts of one of the largest lakes on the continent, or at least its most extensive shoreline at its border with Zambia. Kariba Lake, a 190- to 200-mile-long impoundment formed by damming the Zambezi River, is celebrated for that African trophy, the tigerfish. Kariba Lake produces numerous tigerfish between Kariba Dam and Binga. Angling clubs meet here each September at Charara for an international competition. Tigerfish of 6 to 8 pounds are common, with 12- to 15-pound specimens a daily possibility. Fishing from boats and the banks is practiced—being careful to avoid crocodiles and hippos.

Many species of tilapia or "bream," which are considered valuable food fish, are locally popular. Tilapia are mainly omnivorous or vegetarian, but two species in Rhodesia are predatory and take artificial lures, the largemouth bream and olive bream of the Zambezi (*Sargochromis robustus*) with a record weight of 13 pounds taken on a bass plug. Large yellowfish also provide excellent sport in Lake Kyle near Fort Victoria.

Rhodesia offers a modest trout fishery in its eastern mountains near the Mozambique border around Mount Inyanyani (elevation 8,514 feet). The Inyanga Highlands, the vacation playground of Rhodesia, are the catchment area where tributaries of the Zambezi, Pungwe and Sabi rivers take their source. These streams are all from 5,000 to 7,000 feet above sea level. Much of the area falls within the Inyanga National Park, bequeathed to the people of Rhodesia by Cecil John Rhodes. Everything is well organized by the wardens of the Park, with good accommodations for anglers. Both

brown and rainbow trout thrive in the streams and in a number of artificial impoundments. The Mare Dam Hatchery maintains the trout population on a put-and-take basis, although there is some natural reproduction. Rhodesian trout average about ½ pound and fish of 4 pounds are uncommon. The Inyanga area is reached by good roads from Salisbury (160 miles) and Umtali (70 miles).

THE SEASON

Although fishing in Rhodesia is possible all year round for comfort, the cooler dry season of April to September is recommended.

FISHING SAFARIS

All-inclusive trips for tigerfish on Lake Kariba are arranged by *Rhodesian Safaris (1968) (PVT) LTD.* (P.O. Box 191, Salisbury, Rhodesia). This outfit provides 19- to 21-foot stern drive cruisers for fishing on the lake as well as spinning tackle, including ultra-light gear if you are so inclined; the present record is a 10-pound tigerfish taken on 2-pound-test line. Accommodations, meals, guide service, and transportation are included in the package.

TRAVEL NOTES

By Pan American flight to London, make connections with BOAC to the capital, Lusaka. Some connections with other air lines, New York to East Africa to Lusaka. Valid passport, current cholera, small pox vaccination required. Visitors should check with Rhodesian Tourist Board for last minute immigration regulation changes.

ACCOMMODATIONS

Situated in the heart of the Inyanga Mountains, and 6,600 feet above sea-level, the 54-room **Troutbeck Inn** offers good accommodations in a scenic setting. Private fishing in Troutbeck Lake is available to guests. On the eastern side of the Inyanga Mountains, with commanding views over the Manica Plateau in Mozambique, are the **Gleneagles Cottages.** The Gaeresi and Sumba rivers rise nearby, and the slopes of the surrounding hills are covered with scented pine woods and tangled escarpment forest. Fishing is for brook, tiger, brown, and rainbow

trout, at reasonable rates.

The rambling **Angler's Rest Hotel** offers good accommodations, cuisine and service. The hotel is situated close to Inyanga Village. It is an ideal base for the angler, as it is within a few miles of the Rhodes-Inyanga National Park, with its 50 miles of rivers and streams and Mare Dam.

At Kariba there are two hotels, both offering air-conditioned rooms with private bathrooms: The **Kariba Hotel,** 1,200 feet above the lake in the township, and the **Cutty Sark,** on the lake shore. Two motels, the **Lake View** on Camp Hill, and **Venture Cruises** on the lake shore, provide accommodation in an attractive setting, the **Lake View** particularly offering a range from air-conditioned self-contained lodges to inexpensive fishermen's huts. The hotels and motels are fully licensed. All hotels and motels have their own

swimming pools and other recreational facilities, and at one there is also a chip-and-putt golf course.

On the southern shore, is a **Bumi Hills Hotel,** which is situated on a promontory 400 feet above the lake. Game can often be seen on the shore below from the hotel verandah. The hotel can be reached by air or by boat.

At the western end of the lake reached from turnoffs from the Bulawayo-Victoria Falls road are resorts at Binga and Msuna Mouth, catering mainly to fishermen. There are at present no scheduled boat services traversing the length of the lake, but visitors can make the trip in their own craft. All visitors embarking on any journey on the lake, other than coastal cruises, should notify the Lake Navigation Control Office and acquaint themselves with regulations and safety procedures.

Tigerfish does not grow large in Rhodesian waters but what it lacks in poundage is not evident when razormouth like this one becomes airborne in survival fight

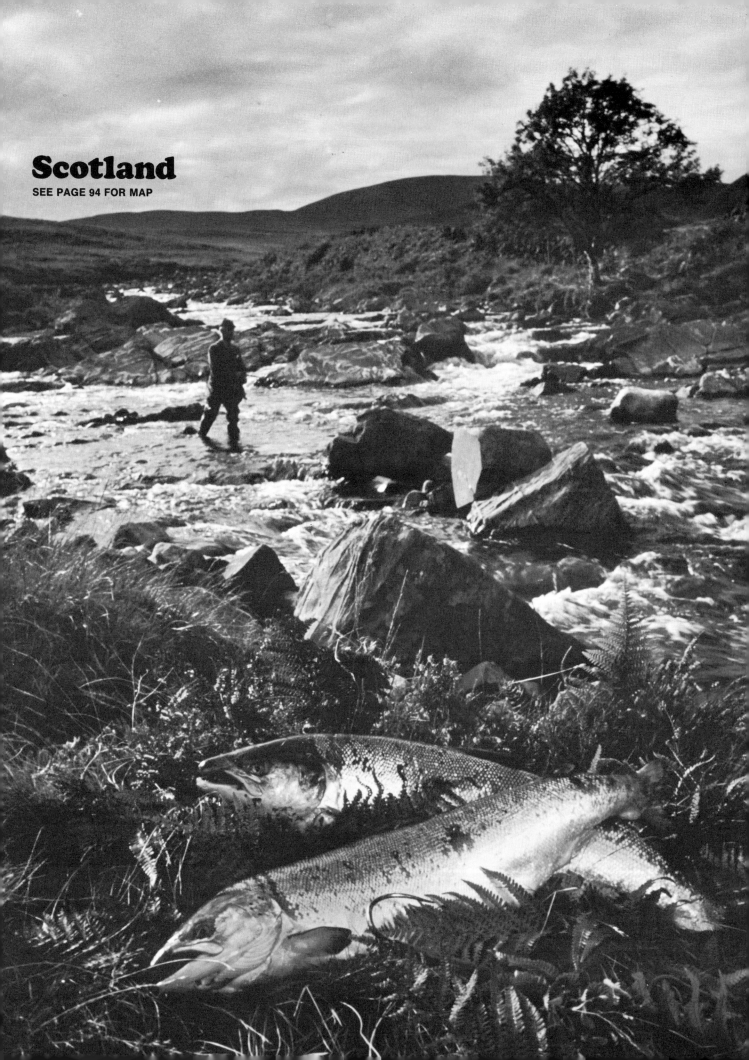

Scotland
SEE PAGE 94 FOR MAP

Some of the best salmon fishing in the British Isles is found in Scotland. This is Water of Fleet at Kirkcudbrightshire

Mountains mirrored by lochs, jagged headlands, coasts eroded by a pounding surf, and intensely green slopes make an idyllic background for salmon and trout fishing. Scotland is the perpetual fountain of whisky, a misty land with a tartan complex, home of the Loch Ness monster, bagpipes, haggis, and Bobby Burns. Roads wander whimsically through Lowlands and Highlands and driving is much the best way for an angler to see it. Though small as countries are measured (29,795 square miles including its 186 inhabited islands), Scotland is surprisingly "wild" outside of its major cities. Good salmon fishing in Scotland is not cheap but by world standards it is not expensive either; the only problem is the universal one of getting a beat on a top stream at the right time of the year and hoping the fish arrive. Although four Scottish rivers have become synonymous with the art of salmon fishing—the Tay, Dee, Spey, and the Tweed—there are fifty others such as the Nith, Awe, Oykel, Thurso, Glass, and the Beauly which give satisfactory sport and may at times outproduce the more celebrated waters. Quality sea trout fishing is common to Scotland, and brown trout are found in almost every loch, burn, and river.

THE SEASON

The salmon season in Scotland varies from river to river. The only month of the year when there is no fishing available is December; some rivers open as early as mid-January and all waters are open April 15th. Closing dates are also variable but the season is finished on December 1st. The closed season for trout runs from early October to mid-March. No fishing is permitted in Scotland on Sundays.

Scotland has a cool climate. The western coast of the mainland and the Hebrides have mild but wet and windy winters with temperatures in the 40°F to 45°F range during January while the east coast may be slightly colder and have less rainfall.

Spring and early summer are often relatively dry though remaining cool (April means at 43°F-45°F); midsummer to late summer conditions are often fairly cool with temperatures in the mid-50's in the extreme north, and the low 60's in the center and south. However, the weather can become briefly hot (in the high 80's) and drought conditions may occur particularly in the east coastal areas. Abnormally "good" weather in 1969 created extremely low water levels during the summer season. Because of the latitude, daylight lasts long in summer—until about 11:00 p.m.—and those additional hours are a bonus for anglers.

LICENSES

There is no national license required for fishing in Scotland. The waters are held by angling clubs, hotels, or the Crown and a fee is charged on a daily (day-ticket), weekly, or seasonal basis. The costs vary according to the quality of the fishing and range from less than $5.00 per day to $50.00 per day for a rod on a top salmon beat. To plan a trip to Scotland, write to the *Scottish Tourist Board* (2 Rutland Place, West End, Edinburgh 1) and enclose 70c for a copy of *Scotland for Fishing*. This comprehensive guide lists the fees for fishing as well as the rates for accommodations on every river and lake in Scotland. The following sampler is some of the better trout and salmon waters:

TWEED RIVER

Among Scotland's southeast rivers the Tweed is a classic. The river is approximately 100 miles long flowing into the North Sea at Berwick-on-Tweed and forms a considerable portion of the boundary between England and Scotland. It is an early river and yet it also has a very late run of fish in October and November. The Tweed is the only river in the British Isles which can be fished for ten months of the year—from February 1st to November 30th. February to May is considered the peak period, but November can be extremely good if the weather is normal. Salmon are plentiful in the Tweed but they average on the small side between 7 and 9 pounds; large salmon of 30 pounds or more are taken in the late, fall. Most of the fishing is done from boats although there are places where bank casting is possible. During the first two weeks of the season, only fly fishing is permitted to minimize rod pressure and allow a maximum stock of salmon to enter the stream. Beginning on February 15th spinning is allowed. Good fly fishing usually starts about the end of March. Advance bookings are essential for the lower beats below Kelso where the spring and fall fishing is in great demand.

The Tweed is also a first-class trout river and in April and May the fishing is particularly good. Any visitor staying in the district can find plenty of trout angling, as there are at least twenty tributaries to the Tweed which provide browns in good number, such as the Gala, Blackadder,

Teviot, Yarrow, and Rule Rivers.

Some hotels which offer Tweed fishing are the **Kingsknowes Hotel** in Galashiels, the **Castle Hotel** in Berwick, the **Newcastle Arms Hotel** at Coldstream, **Ednam House Hotel** in Kelso, the **Collingwood Arms Hotel** at Cornhill, and the **George** and the **Abbotsford Hotel** in Melrose. The general price range for accommodations varies from $36 to $70 per week.

LOCH LEVEN
North of Edinburgh across the Firth of Forth (via the new Road Bridge) is world-famous Loch Leven. Although Scotland has an abundance of brown trout waters, this lake is identified with a racial strain—the Loch Leven trout which is widely spread through the country. Brown trout from Loch Leven were introduced in the United States, and that name still persists in some Western states where heavily black-spotted trout are common. Loch Leven was acquired by the Kinross Estates in

1922, but visiting anglers can fish the loch for a nominal fee. Accommodations can be obtained at the **Green Hotel,** Kinross, Scotland. The trout population is entirely natural, as the mature fish spawn in tributary streams; the lake had a high level of production in years past with a rod catch as high as 86,000 fish in one season. Angling is restricted to fly-fishing in Loch Leven, and catches of 1½- to 3-pound trout have not been unusual. However, it did not fish well in the 1969 and 1970 seasons.

LOCH MAREE
Twelve mile long Loch Maree is one of the most productive waters in the Western Highlands. It flows into the sea through the 2-mile-long Ewe River. The average width of Loch Maree is about one mile but sea trout and Atlantic salmon are found along the shallow shores near rocky headlands and islands in water 8- to 12-feet deep. The salmon season starts in April and peaks in May. Salmon are caught by spinning and trolling as well as on the fly. However, after the sea trout appear in Loch Maree the rule is fly-fishing only. Sea trout begin running in July with the first summer flood tide; successive runs occur until mid-September but the fishing continues until the season ends on October 15th. The record sea trout for Great Britain (21 pounds) was caught on a fly in Loch Maree in 1948. Although the average weight for sea trout is slightly over 2 pounds, many 3- to 10-pound fish are taken each year. Brown trout up to 6 pounds produce good sport throughout the season. A popular technique in Maree fishing is dapping with the dry fly. The percentage of missed strikes is high but it does attract the fish. Dapping equipment (13- to 15-foot rods with blow-lines) is available for sale or rental locally.

Due to its popularity Loch Maree fishing must be booked well in advance; most reservations are made by January for the coming season. The hotels here are the **Kinlochewe**

Fighting salmon breaks free in the Thurso River, one of the largest in Scotland

Hotel (Kinlochewe Hotel, Kinlochewe by Achnasheen, Ross-shire, Scotland) offering adequate accommodations and food at about $7 per day and boat with ghillie at $14.25 per day. The **Loch Maree Hotel** (Loch Maree Hotel, Achnasheen, Ross-shire, Scotland) run by a brother of the film actor, the late Charles Laughton, is a quality operation at about $8.50 per day for room and meals and $14.40 per day per rod for boat and ghillie.

SPEY RIVER

The Spey is one of Scotland's great salmon rivers. It is big water, requiring deep wading but well suited to fly fishing. The Spey produces fish from the beginning of February in the lower reaches, right through to August in the upper reaches. Several waters can be rented by the fortnight or month. The best of the season would be from the beginning of April to about the middle of June. The fish average good size (about 12 pounds) and are strong fighters for their weight. There are hotels at Fochabers for the lower beats, Craigellachie, Archiestown, Aberlour for the middle river, and Grantown-on-Spey for the upper reaches. Nigel Grant's **Palace Hotel** at Grantown is popular. Spey fishing costs varied greatly in 1969 from as little as $2.40 per day on modest "ticket" water to $600 per beat per week (for 6 rods or $100 per person). The latter price included some of the best pools in the Spey and was the cost after May 5th.

In the offering for 1970 by *Scottish Tourist Promotion & Hotel Marketing* (19 Coates Crescent, Edinburgh, Scotland) were the following: one salmon beat on the Spey for three weeks in April (four rods are available on this beat); during the first two of these weeks the charge for each beat was $264 per week and on the third week the charge went to $392 per week. In May two beats were available (four rods each) at $660 per week each beat; in June two

Brown trout are found in almost every loch. Fishing Lochan na H'Achlaise in Argyll

beats were available (four rods each) at $396 per week each beat; and in July one beat was available for one week (four rods) at $264. These prices did not include hotel costs, which run about $65 per person per week including meals.

The Spey salmon stock was again hit by UDN in the 1970 season, and an active fry restocking program is underway. Sea trout have become very scarce.

TAY RIVER

For the fisherman who does not like wading, and for the one who likes to catch big fish, there are few Scottish rivers that can compare with the Tay. The season opens there on January 15th, and fish are caught on the opening day if the river is normal. The best fishing falls within a comparatively short season—February to the end of April—with a peak period in the last week of March and the first week in April. The seasons, however, vary, and the fish run earlier in some years than in others—but you would not go very far wrong in the periods mentioned.

Fishing in the Tay, which is a very wide and fast-running river, is practically all spinning or harling from a boat. The fish run large, averaging around 18 to 20 pounds, and big fish up to 40 or more pounds are killed there every year.

A popular location for many Tay beats is Perth. Beats are generally available and the cost is reasonable, which includes the hire of a boat and two boatmen or ghillies (the river is so strong that one man cannot handle the boat). Two people generally share a beat and boat, so the cost is not very extravagant. Hotels which offer Tay fishing are the **Birnam Hotel** and the **Dunkeld House Hotel,** both in Dunkeld. Accommodations here run from $50 to $55 per week. Beats are also available through P. D. Malloch (26 Scott Street, Perth, Scotland).

DEE RIVER

The Dee is the site of Balmoral Castle and is fished by Queen Elizabeth when in residence. The river rises in the Wells of Dee, a spring on the mountain slope of Ben Braeriach in the Cairngerms. It is little more than a brook as it runs through Mar Forest to Braemar; below Braemar it becomes a turbulent woodland stream gaining water from the rivers and burns that spill into it from the high hills along both banks. From Aboyne to Aberdeen the Dee becomes a large river meandering through broad fields rather than woods; the banks are carefully maintained with stone and concrete retaining walls at points where erosion would be a problem. Some stretches of the Dee through this area are so valuable that an 1,800 yard section sold for about $100,000 several years ago. However, there are numerous hotels with Dee fishing rights. The most prominent is the **Raemoir Hotel** at Banchory, which is owned by Lord Cowdray and has a most excellent cuisine. There is also the **Banchory Lodge Hotel,** which claims the advantage of having its fishing only sixty yards from the front door. For those who like to put up near big cities, there is the **Ardoe House Hotel** in Aberdeen which has its own reach of the Dee about two hundred yards away. Further upstream there are the **Invercauld Arms Hotel** and the **Loirston Hotel** at Ballater, and another **Invercauld Arms** at Braemar, all of which can supply Dee fishing. The open season for salmon on the Dee is February 1st to September 30th; the best months are March through May, although fresh salmon continue running in June, provided rainfall has been sufficient to keep the water level up.

Sample rates in the 1969 season on the Dee ran from $240 to $264 per week per rod (Upper Drum Beat through the **Netherley House Hotel**) in the peak period from February through May with a low of $24 in July and August. Drum is about ten miles upriver from the sea so it's primarily early water. An interesting elective in these prices: the charges are based on your keeping all salmon but as an alternate you can pay half price, then pay $2.40 per pound for all fish kept. So the optimist need have no worry about what to do with all those salmon he kills.

The hotel will always arrange the sale of them for him, and place a credit for the proceeds on his bill.

THURSO RIVER
Among the northernmost mainland waters beyond Inverness the Thurso rises in the moors near Knockfin Heights as two branch streams which form the river at Dalganachan. The Thurso is one of the largest rivers here, and while not in the same class as the Spey or Dee, it is an easy stream to fish from the bank. The Thurso is productive beginning in March and peaks from July through September. Since it is popular during the summer months, most anglers book their fishing a year in advance although it's sometimes possible to get a day on the river at short notice due to cancellations. The **Lochdhu Hotel** (Altnabreac, Scotland) controls ample water to accommodate its guests. Easiest way to book Thurso fishing in the U.S. is through *Winchester Adventures Inc.*, (100 Park Avenue, New Yor k, N.Y. 10017). The Winchester agency has package rates for fishing, accommodations, meals, and gillie ranging from $210 to $325 per rod per six-day week. Rates vary according to the period fished.

OYKEL RIVER
The Oykel north of Inverness and flowing into the Bornoch Firth is another good spot for both salmon and sea trout. The river is popular but a limited number of openings are available each season. Anglers stay at the recently modernized **Oykel Bridge Hotel** in Oykel Bridge. Rates run about $58 per week. The Oykel is a good wading stream and can be fished in part from the bank. Salmon average about 9½ pounds, with occasional large fish; beats are taken in daily rotation; fly-fishing-only is the rule. The lower 7 miles of river averages 730 salmon per year, but in the exceptionally dry summer of 1969 the total was 530 fish. The peak period is from the end of March to June 1st. Fishing charges in 1969 ran $150 to $250 per six-day

week per rod depending on the period fished.

SCOTLAND'S ISLANDS
Sea trout are common to Scotland but they provide the most fishing on the islands off the west and north coasts. Brown trout are abundant and some salmon fishing is available also. The Inner and Outer Hebrides encompassing islands such as Skye, Lewis, Harris, and North and South Uist attract good runs of sea trout beginning in June. There is a hotel on South Uist, which is well known for its excellent fishing and is worth a special visit from July to September, called the **Lochboisdale Hotel**. The **Horsacleit Lodge** at Tarbert on Harris Island and the **Lochmaddy Hotel** at Lochmaddy on North Uist are also popular. The Isle of Skye provides sea trout, brown trout, and salmon through the **Dunvegan Hotel** at Dunvegan; an old Highland inn, fully modernized and serving good food, this hotel has exclusive rights on a number of lochs and rivers. Another popular spot is the **Sligachan Hotel** at Sligachan.

To the northeast lie the wind-swept Orkney Islands which can be reached by air from Inverness or by car ferry from Thurso. Large sea trout and brown trout are caught here. There are about twenty-eight inhabited islands in the Orkney group but Kirkwall and Stromness are the two main centers. It is wild, hilly country with a definite fascination for visitors. Try the **Kirkwall Hotel** or the **Queen's Hotel** both in Kirkwall, or the **Stromness Hotel** in Stromness. Rates run from $45 to $55 per week. The principal lochs here are Loch Harray, Boardhouse, Hundland, Stenness, and Swannay.

Sea trout peak in the spring and fall and can be caught in bays and inlets around the island's shores.

The Shetlands are the most northerly group of islands and can be reached by air service from Inver-

The raw beauty of the Hebrides off Scotland's west coast is setting for the Sligachan Hotel on the Isle of Skye

ness or Aberdeen. Among the low hills and fjords there are a number of lochs and small rivers which hold brown and sea trout. There is a hotel at Lerwick, **The Grand** (Lerwick, Shetland, Scotland) which has fishing for its guests. July to the end of September is the best season.

TRAVEL NOTES
By Pan American directly to Glasgow through Prestwick Airport, four times weekly in winter and early spring with daily service during peak travel periods. Other connections include BOAC daily, SAS five flights per week. A valid passport and current small pox vaccination required.

ACCOMMODATIONS
PRESTWICK
Prestwick Airport is the major arrival point for overseas flights. This part of northern Scotland is convenient to many of the best fishing areas. If you have to overnight here, try the **Towans** near Prestwick which runs from $9 to $12 single, and $16 to $21 double or the **Turnberry Hotel** about 18 miles from the airport with rates at $11.40 per person.

EDINBURGH
The Scottish capital located on the Firth of Forth. A pivotal city in fishing the southeast coast. The better hotels include the **Caledonian** with rates starting at $14.40 single

and $23.60 double, the **Carlton Hotel** from $6.70 per person, **George Hotel** from $11.50 single and $23.60 double, the **North British** starting at $13.70 single, and $22.40 double, and the **Royal Hotel** from $7.20 per person.

There are few great restaurants in Scotland but "home cooking" can still be an accolade in many country inns, and the Scots eat bountifully. Roast beef and roast lamb, fresh trout and wild game vie with the rich soups, and Scotch kippers are a gourmet delight. Smoked salmon is the world's standard bearer here. The oatmeal bread and rich creamy butter is a meal in itself.

South Africa

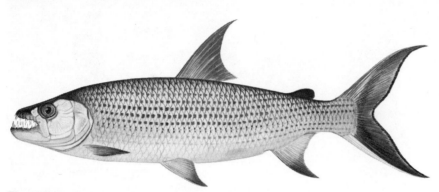

Tigerfish are found chiefly at Komatipoort and Pongola

A land of contrast from lush tropical beaches to rugged cold mountains and endless stretches of veld, South Africa offers considerable freshwater angling and excellent saltwater fishing to the tourist. Although the only trout endemic to the African continent is the Mediterranean subspecies of brown trout (*Salmo trutta macrostigma*) extensive plantings of both brown and rainbow trout from Europe since the turn of the century have become established in many watersheds, notably in the mountains of southwestern Cape Province, along the eastern escarpment of South Africa and in the Maluti and Drakensberg massif of Lesotho. In general, African trout attain only a moderate size, as their life span tends to be shorter in a warm climate outside of their native range. They thrive near sea level in streams of the wet-winter area within about 100 miles of Cape Town; but as one goes north into the summer rainfall areas, the heat increases in the low country and trout exist only by virtue of altitude in waters above 4,000 feet. There are no natural high-altitude lakes, but a number of artificial impoundments carry trout. In the majority of the trout areas rainbows predominate, but there are brown trout strongholds in the southwestern Cape and in Natal from the original plantings of the 1890's.

CAPE PROVINCE

The trout streams in the vicinity of Cape Town are all within a day's drive on good paved roads. The open season in Cape Province is from September 1 to June 1. The nearest stream is the Eerste River which holds a good population of rainbows; some "steelhead" or anadromous rainbows occur here also which range from 1½ to 5 pounds in size. Unlike the steelhead of western North America, which undertake extensive migrations and achieve heavy weights through sea feeding, these South African fish apparently do not wander far from the Eerste estuary. For topographical reasons most rivers in South Africa provide no trout habitat in their lower reaches but the Eerste is a notable exception.

Other trout streams within easy reach of Cape Town are the headwaters of the Berg River flowing to the Atlantic and of the Breede River flowing to the Indian Ocean. In addition to numerous rainbows these river systems have produced brown trout up to 8½ pounds. The Breede also produces good smallmouth bass fishing near Swellendam.

The Olifants River is one of the most interesting waters in the western Cape Province, both because of its size and its indigenous fish species.

It is the largest river system draining into the Atlantic Ocean south of the Orange River. One unusual gamefish found here is the Clanwilliam yellowfish (*Barbus capensis*). Native only to the Olifants, this species is distinct from the Orange River yellowfish (*Barbus holubi*). Members of the genus *Barbus* in Africa are related to the mahseers of Asia. Yellowfish are most commonly caught by bottom fishing with live baits but they are readily taken on artificial lures. In clear tributaries or the riffles of the main river the Clanwilliam yellowfish provides good sport on the fly rod and large specimens are frequently taken on spinning tackle in deep pools. This yellowfish is reported to weights of over 20 pounds although 7 to 15 pounds is the usual range in the Olifants River.

Another Olifants River species is the sawfin (*Barbus serra*), locally known as the "freshwater snoek" or "witvis," although its mouth is toothless and it is distinct from the witvis of the Berg and Breede river systems. It does not grow as large as the yellowfish and lacks the golden coloration. It has a long head and dark patches on the body, and the back fin has a serrated spine like a carp. The sawfin provides fair sport on light tackle.

The Olifants River is also one of the best smallmouth bass waters in South Africa and many fish up to about 4 pounds are caught. Fishing spots have to be selected, as long stretches of the river bed are covered with white sand where bass are scarce. Largemouth bass are also present, particularly around large irrigation dams on the river at Clanwilliam and Bulshoek, the record for the former standing at 7 pounds, 11 ounces. The most accessible fishing places for smallmouth bass and yellowfish are the runs below the Clanwilliam rapids and other rocky sections downstream, the running water at the top of the Bulshoek dam, and the large pools below the Bulshoek rapids. A rocky section known as the "Cascades" is a good

Heavy spinning tackle is standard equipment for fisherman after tigerfish

A number of streams from the Amatole Mountains, which were stocked in the early days from the Pirie Trout Hatchery, continue to yield trout up to 7 pounds. Across the divide on the headwaters of the western flowing Orange River, the Barkly East district at an altitude of 6,000 feet has more than twenty streams and is one of the richest districts for rainbows up to 7 pounds. It also has a number of stream-fed farm ponds which have produced rainbows from 7 to 10 pounds.

Tigerfish's interlocking canine teeth and strong jaws make it difficult to hook

Across the Kei River, the boundary between the Cape Province and the Transkei region, the High Drakensberg range begins, and upper tributaries of the Kei, Bashee, and Umtata rivers hold rainbows. The Umzimvubu River system, the largest on the eastern side of the Drakensberg escarpment, includes its large branches the Tsitsa, Tina, Kenegha and Umzimkulu, and reaches the sea at Port St. Johns. In the complete absence of all indigenous river fish, except eels and minnows, these streams were virgin waters for the exotic rainbow trout which were prodigiously successful in the early days, but later showed a tendency to overbreed, although good fishing is maintained in a number of well-known streams reached from various centers.

place. All kinds of spoons, plugs and spinners are effective.

There are good hotels at Citrusdal and Clanwilliam, and visitors will be able to obtain information about local fishing spots. As this district is usually very hot in the summer, the most popular times for this river are in spring, autumn, and winter.

Passing eastwards around the southern tip of Africa, there is a troutless gap for about 600 miles, as the streams are too heavily peat-stained and acid for trout. There-

after the real beginning of the eastern trout region of South Africa starts and extends along the eastern escarpments of the Cape, Natal, Transvaal and Rhodesia. In contrast to the rocky, bush-clad mountain streams of the southwestern Cape in the wet-winter area, the summer-rainfall trout streams of the eastern escarpment flow from high mountains through a very different type of country, where they meander through grass lands in the rolling uplands.

One of the most popular methods of fishing in South Africa is surf casting from rocks

There are 1,000 miles of streams in Natal

NATAL

The Province of Natal offers the most convenient trout fishing for visiting anglers, for its best streams, amidst wild and grand scenery, are in a compact and accessible area under the supervision of the Natal Parks, Game and Fish Preservation Board of Pietermaritzburg. All the most important streams are in the foothills of the Drakensberg at altitudes between 4,000 and 6,000 feet, and many contain brown trout from the original plantings. The Umzimkulu River system in the Himeville/Underberg district in the southwestern corner of Natal is famous for its rainbow trout. Facilities are well organized, as the Parks Board and the local angling association control long stretches of the rivers, with offices for the allocation of angling beats, and there are hotels and guest farms catering to anglers. The Parks Board has a hatchery at Underberg. The district has such famous rainbow waters as the Indowana, Ingangwana, Umzimouti, Umzimkulu, Umzimkulwana, and Polela rivers, open from September 1 to May 15. There are also some 25 ponds and small lakes, formed by dams across streams, stocked from the hatchery and producing trout up to 7 pounds from boat or bank.

Within easy reach of this center are the headwaters of the Umkomaas River system containing brown trout of good size. The Tugela River system, the largest in Natal, has a number of famous brown trout streams from the High Drakensberg range, flowing from several nature and game reserves which are a feature of this Province. The best known are the Mooi and Bushmans rivers. The Umgeni River system has a large catch area and tributaries nearer to the populated centers. Its population of brown trout is descended from those first available in Southern Africa in 1890.

The best months for trout fishing in Natal are September and October in spring, and April and May in fall, as the rivers are liable to be flooded with the summer rains.

BASUTOLAND

Some of the headwaters of the Orange River in the high Maluti and Drakensberg ranges in Basutoland (Lesotho) have proved very suitable for trout. In spite of its location in Southern Africa, Lesotho can be intensely cold on account of its high altitude, and frosts and snow can occur even in summer. It is also in a summer rainfall area, but serious droughts occur at times.

Repeated attempts were made without success from 1904 onwards to introduce trout from Cape eggs. It was not until 1935 that members of the Basutoland Mounted Police succeeded in transporting a few adult brown trout from the Bushmans River, Natal, over the Giant's Castle massif of the Drakensberg to the nearest river in Lesotho. Only seven brown trout survived the gruelling journey in five-gallon cans on mules, but they bred in the virgin water so successfully that in a few years it was overpopulated. In 1943 rainbow ova from the Pirie Hatchery were taken from the Cape Province by the rough Ramatseliso Pass to a trading post at Sehlabathebe in Lesotho, where the trader hatched them in a stream and stocked some high tributaries which were later to produce record fish.

These Durban anglers are launching shallow-draft 16-foot "ski-boats" which are used for dolphin, sailfish, and marlin

Trout fishing in the Eastern Transvaal

In 1952, local enthusiasts started a makeshift plant for hatching 20,000 Cape ova each year; and fry were transported by car, jeep, aircraft, horse, mule, and man to most of the suitable rivers, so that in time Lesotho became a recognized trout-fishing country. It is, however, a border-line country for trout, suffering from overpopulation by rainbows on the one hand, and kills from severe droughts, hailstorms, and floods on the other.

Apart from entry by difficult mountain tracks, Lesotho has a main road and short railway from the Orange Free State to its capital, Maseru; which is a good center for accommodation, the hiring of light aircraft to a number of landing fields and organized safaris on ponies. From Maseru, an all-weather mountain road runs for over seventy miles in the heart of the mountains to several trout rivers.

In addition to the rainbow trout, in some clear waters the indigenous yellowfish (*Barbus holubi*) up to about 6 pounds will take a fly and make strong runs before being landed. Semonkong in the Maseru district has a productive stretch of the Maletsunyane River above a sheer waterfall of 637 feet, and is reached by a short flight to a landing field, or by a longer approach on horseback. The first stocking of trout in this river in the 1950's produced some rapid growth of rainbows; 2-inch fingerlings grew to 13 inches during the four summer months, and two years after the introduction, a female heavy in roe was 28 inches long when caught and released. Both brown and rainbow trout up to 6 pounds were taken. A number of other productive streams in the district have to be reached on horseback.

Entering Lesotho further north from the Orange Free State, via Butha Buthe, the Oxbow area, now reached by four-wheel-drive vehicles up the very tortuous Moleng Pass, may well become one of the most famous trout areas when the proposed Oxbow Dam is constructed for power and water supply. Oxbow Dam rivers have already achieved fame, for many rainbows up to 6 pounds have been taken and hosts of smaller fish. There is a vehicle and visitors' camp service at Oxbow, running regular tours.

Entering from the Cape Province, the upper Orange River tributaries can be approached by road by the permanent Qacha's Nek Pass; but the famous rainbow trout streams at Sehlabathebe have to be reached by a very rough cutting up the Drakensberg. The Tsoelikana River in that area has yielded some of the best rainbows in Southern Africa, including the present record of 9 pounds 5 ounces, taken on a Jock Scott fly, and numbers from 5 to 7½ pounds.

A much more popular route into Lesotho for anglers is from Hime-ville, Natal, the base for the Sani Pass four-wheel-drive service, across the Drakensberg to Mokhot-long, where there is good hotel accommodation and the choice of several trout streams yielding brown and rainbow trout.

TRANSVAAL

Trout are established in streams and ponds in the foothills of the Trans-vaal Drakensberg range, which forms part of the Great Escarpment in the eastern side of the Province. These trout waters are in two main river systems flowing into Mozam-bique territory. The introduction of trout to the Transvaal occurred later than in the Cape and Natal. It was done by private effort, and the earli-est attempts in 1903 did not have much success.

In the same year a society was formed and a hatchery started on the Mooi River at Potchefstroom, with the services of an experienced operator. This again had only mod-erate success, and it was far away from the prospective trout waters, involving slow train journeys and slower hauls by ox-wagon over mountainous tracks. As was more appropriate, a private hatchery was started in 1910 at Lydenburg near the Eastern Escarpment, which later became the site of the Provincial Fisheries Institute. Local enthusiasts cooperated to hatch Cape ova in streams of mountain water, and fry were widely distributed in the dis-trict by primitive but successful methods of transport. Before the Transvaal Provincial Administration took over in 1947, some 600,000 ova had been bought from private funds, and hatched successfully, the fry be-ing spread to many streams of the Eastern Transvaal. As in the case of so many preliminary plantings of rainbows in virgin waters, there were many instances of rapid growth, before the fish bred too abundantly. However, in this region, like Natal and Lesotho, the trouble of overstocking and reduction of size is liable to be checked by cli-matic disasters—the ravages of drought and the destruction by sud-den hail storms which drop the wa-ter temperature too suddenly for the survival of fish. Thus the need for the continuation of hatchery work.

The Transvaal trout rivers, lakes, and farm ponds are 200 miles or more eastward of Pretoria; the best known are in the Belfast, Dull-stroom, Machadadorp and Waterval Boven districts; in the vicinity of the surface gold-mining camps of the early days at Sabie, Pilgrim's Rest, and Graskop, and further north at Haenertsburg and Magoebaskloof. There are considerable restrictions due to private ownership and the leasing of waters by syndicates.

SALTWATER FISHING

South African saltwater fishing runs the gamut from kite fishing for big sharks from shore to bay, party boat, and big-game trolling. Black marlin (local record 1,002 pounds), striped marlin, sailfish, dolphin, bluefin

Hybrid tiger trout—cross between brook and brown—has been introduced to some South American waters

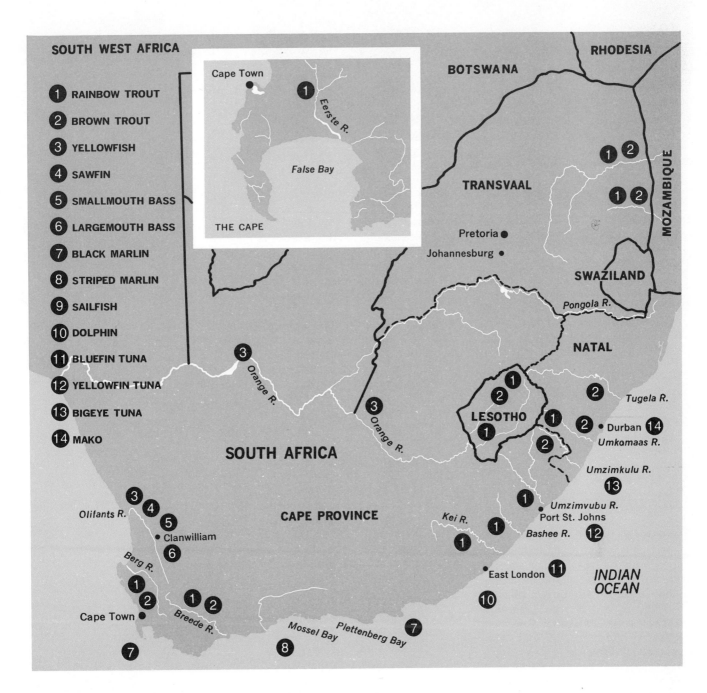

1 RAINBOW TROUT
2 BROWN TROUT
3 YELLOWFISH
4 SAWFIN
5 SMALLMOUTH BASS
6 LARGEMOUTH BASS
7 BLACK MARLIN
8 STRIPED MARLIN
9 SAILFISH
10 DOLPHIN
11 BLUEFIN TUNA
12 YELLOWFIN TUNA
13 BIGEYE TUNA
14 MAKO

tuna, yellowfin tuna, bigeye tuna, mako, and numerous indigenous game species occur along the 2,000 mile coast. Influenced by the Antarctic Drift whose cold waters circulate in the south and flow eastward and the warm Mozambique Current flowing south to become the Agulhas Current at the tip of the continent—South Africa has a diverse fish fauna of more than 1,300 species, most of which originate in the Indo-Pacific region. Seasonal migrations of large gamefish moving down with the Mozambique Current provide unusual angling out of Cape Town, Hout Bay, Simonstown, Kalk Bay, Gordon's Bay, Hermanus, Gansbaai, Mossel Bay, Plettenberg Bay, Port Elizabeth, East London, and Durban.

CONTACTS

Two big-game fishing clubs are established: the *South African Marlin and Tuna Club* (P.O. Box 1807, Cape Town) and the *Natal Deep Sea Rod and Reel Club* (Plaza Hotel, Broad Street, Durban). Organizations affiliated with the South African Anglers' Union are: *South African Anglers' Union,* (P.O. Box 36, Cape Town); *Eastern Province Angling Board of Control* (P.O. Box 624, Port Elizabeth); *Western Province Anglers' Union,* (9, Third Crescent, Vredelust, Belleville, Cape Province); *East London and Border Anglers' Union* (P.O. Box 412, East London); *Griqualand West Angling and Casting Union,* (7 Stanley Street, Beaconsfield, Kimberley);

An excellent fishing resort is located at Knysna Lagoon, Cape Province, on the Garden Route between Cape Town and Port Elizabeth

South African Underwater Union, (P.O. Box 41, Snell Parade, Durban); *Natal Angling Board of Control,* (29 Clement Avenue, Kingsview, Durban); *Game Fishing Association of South Africa* (P.O. Box 1236, Durban); *Southern Transvaal Angling and Casting Union,* (P.O. Box 2991, Johannesburg); *Eastern Transvaal Angling and Casting Union,* (c/o Mr. M. G. Human, Sallies Gold Mine, Brakpan); *Transvaal Angling and Casting Union,* (P.O. Box 360, Klerksdorp); *Orange Free State Anglers' Union,* (P.O. Box 302, Reitz, Orange Free State); *South West African Anglers' Union,* (P.O. Box 2818, Windhoek, South West Africa); *Northern Transvaal Angling and Casting Union,* (P.O. Box 1088, Pretoria).

ACCOMMODATIONS

JOHANNESBURG

The best hotels in Johannesburg are the **President,** (Eloff, Plein and De Villiers Streets); **Rand International,** 290 Bree Street; **Moulin Rouge,** Claim Street; **Criterion,** Jeppe Street; **Dawson's,** President Street; **Whitehall,** Abel Road; **Ambassador,** Pretoria Street; **Astor,** King George Street; **Skyline,** Twist Street; and the **Park Royal,** Plein Street. Rates average from $10 single, $18 double, with bath and breakfast.

CAPE TOWN

The most luxurious hotels are the **Mount Nelson,** Orange Street, slightly out of the city area and commanding a fine view of Table Mountain; and the **President Hotel,** Beach Road in Sea Point; from $14 single, $28 double, with bath and breakfast. Centrally located are the popular **Grand Hotel,** from $11.20 per person with bath, European Plan; the **Tulbagh,** from $9.80 per

person with bath and breakfast; **Tudor Hotel,** $3.85-$4.20 single, $8.40-$10 double, with breakfast. At nearby Sea Point, **Arthur's Seat** is on the Atlantic coast near a beautiful public swimming pool. Farther out is the **Clifton Hotel;** from $9.80 single, $19.60 double with bath and breakfast; good transportation facilities into the city. The **Alphen,** a skillfully restored Cape Dutch homestead, is 12 miles from Cape Town in Constantia Valley; from $8.40 per person with bath and breakfast. In lovely Stellenbosch Valley, 40 miles from Cape Town, is the excellent **Rawdon's Lanzerac** ranch-type hotel.

Drinking water is safe in South Africa. Locally made brandy and native wines are excellent. There is an enormous variety of fruit available and the oysters and lobster tails are great delicacies. Homemade sausage called *boerewors* (farm sausage) and steaks are South African favorites.

TRAVEL NOTES

Fishing tackle, cameras, and other personal goods are duty free but must be declared. Duty free allowances: 400 cigarettes, one opened bottle of liquor. Foreign currency can't be readily exchanged so take traveler's checks. Passport and visa necessary. Proof of sufficient funds and a return ticket, yellow fever and smallpox vaccination certificates.

THE SEASON

There are no extremes of climate, and a high average of daily sunshine. September is spring here, winter extends from May to August. The Cape has its rains during winter and the rest of the country during the summer. Except on the east coast in summer, there is little humidity.

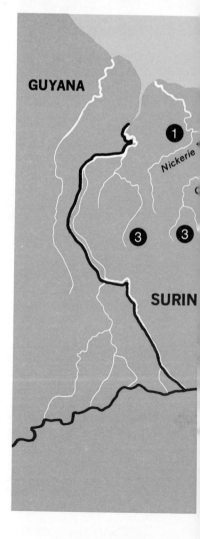

Bush Negroes of interior Surinam hunt the 6- to 8-foot-long pirarucu with bow-and-arrow

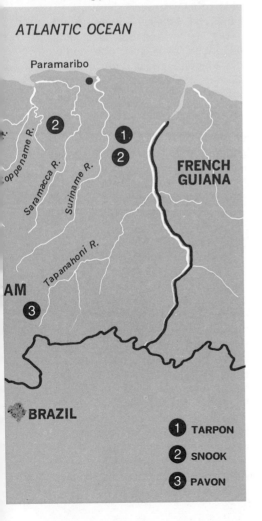

ATLANTIC OCEAN

Paramaribo

Oppename R.

Saramacca R.

Suriname R.

FRENCH GUIANA

Tapanahoni R.

AM

BRAZIL

1 TARPON

2 SNOOK

3 PAVON

Surinam

Surinam (formerly Dutch Guiana) is on the northeast coast of South America. Although a comparatively small country of 55,167 square miles, it has a vast network of freshwater rivers which provide an abundance of tarpon and snook fishing. The capital city of Paramaribo is the center of civilization in Surinam, but much of the surrounding jungle country is accessible. Surinam is equatorial in climate and while the temperature seldom exceeds 85°F, the humidity is often high and the rainfall sometimes heavy though sporadic, particularly from May to August. The temperature drops several degrees at night and the northeast Trade Winds modify the humidity considerably along the coastal areas. The high forests consist of greenheart, walaba, palms, giant mora, crabwood, and bulletwood trees. There is a diversity of plant life along the coast but the black mangrove is dominant.

The main watersheds in Surinam are the Nickerie River, Coppername River, Saramacca River, Suriname River, Marowijne River, and the Tapahony. Although facilities for fishing are not fully developed, the following agencies offer package trips into the interior jungle streams: *Andre's Tours* (P.O. Box 197, Paramaribo), *Tonee's Travel and Tour Bureau* (P.O. Box 1133, Paramaribo), *Surinam Safaris* (P.O. Box 1089, Paramaribo), and *Success Tourist Service* (P.O. Box 344).

ACCOMMODATIONS

PARAMARIBO
Set amid tropical gardens, with an olympic-size swimming pool, the luxurious **Surinam Torarica Hotel** is completely air conditioned, has a nightclub, and one of the most mod-

ern gambling casinos in South America. Winter rates: single $18-$22, double $23-$27, European plan. Less in summer. The **Surinam Palace Hotel,** also with casino and nightclub, is $11 single, $15.50 double, European plan. **Hotel Kersten,** convenient and immaculate, is $10-$13.50 single, $18-$22 double, American plan. Tip luggage porters SF .35 (18c) per bag. In the districts, you'll find government guest houses which are clean and spacious with good food at very reasonable rates.

Since Surinam is made up of peoples from many races, religions, cultures, and customs—Creoles, Hindustanis, Indonesians, Chinese, Bush Negroes, Amerindians, Dutch, and other European nationalities— the cuisine is highly varied. Among the best Paramaribo restaurants are: *Iwan's Deli, Hong Kong, Garuda, Padang, Bali-Lunapark.* A popular Dutch dish is *hutspot* which is a casserole of pork chops and potatoes. Indonesian *rijsttafel* consists of rice plus twenty or more separate dishes involving fish, fowls, fruits, sauces and condiments. *Satee boemboe* is barbecued meat with a curry tang. *Pisang goreng* is fried rib plantains. *Ajam-kening* is the highly seasoned local version of fried chicken. Peanuts (*katjang*) are widely used in soups and sauces. All sorts of drinks are available, but Holland gins, beers (Parbo is a local beer) and liqueurs predominate naturally. Tap water is pure and safe to drink.

LANGUAGE
Dutch is the official language, but English is widely spoken. Due to the many different races and nationalities which have preserved their own cultures, a number of other languages are also used.

CONTACTS
Surinam Tourist Bureau, 10 Rockefeller Plaza, New York, N.Y. 10020. *Surinam Tourist Development Board,* Kerkplein 10, Paramaribo, Surinam.

Turks and Caicos Islands

SEE PAGE 22 FOR MAP

Until recently known only to stamp collectors and geography buffs, the Turks and Caicos Islands formed an isolated British crown colony where a few thousand inhabitants raked salt and caught lobsters. Ignored by tourists because of the lack of facilities, the chief attraction was to small aircraft as a refueling stop and to yachtsmen for the best deep water harbor (Cockburn Harbour) north of the Windward Passage. Geologically, these islands are part of the Bahamas chain, but politically they are independent, a situation which European and American investors found attractive. The number of available rooms is still minimal although several new hotels and a real estate development are in progress. The islands remain unspoiled with miles of deserted beaches and literally virgin fishing.

The Turks Islands (Grand Turk and Salt Cay) lie east of the 22-mile-wide and 7,000-foot-deep Turks Island Passage. The Caicos Islands (South, East, North, West, and Middle Caicos, plus the island of Providenciales) lie to the west of the passage. Their total land area is about 166 square miles. Middle, sometimes called Grand Caicos, is the largest, being 25 miles long and 12 miles wide. The name Turks derives from a local cactus which resembles a fez, while Caicos is from Cayos, the Spanish word for cay.

THE SEASON

Warm, sunny skies prevail throughout the year with an average temperature of 77°F in the winter months and 83°F in summer. Rainfall averages only 26 inches annually. Low humidity and trade winds are fairly constant during winter and spring. The best fishing months are April, May, and June.

THE FISHING

The Caicos Islands are surrounded by extensive shallow bays and in many places by barrier reefs. Due to the size of the area involved and the lack of accommodations and therefore minimal angling pressure, it will be several years before the potential of the area is fully known. The bonefish is the principal flat species and small tarpon occur in tide holes at various points around the islands; tarpon are not abundant, however, and average 20 to 40 pounds. Bonefish are found along sandy shores and in the intricate network of marl-bottomed tidal creeks. There is no extreme rise and fall (2-1/2 feet average) of water except during spring tides. Snappers, notably the yellowtail and mutton snappers, crevalle, various groupers, barracuda, and cero mackerel constitute the bulk of inshore fishing along the reefs and in tide holes.

There has been no concentrated effort made at offshore sport fishing in the Turks and Caicos Islands. The potential is impressive, particularly around the more remote cays.

TRAVEL NOTES

By Pan American Jet Clipper to Nassau. It is possible to get through connections without overnighting in Nassau. Inter-island air taxi services from South Caicos are available. U.S. and British citizens are not required to have passports; passports are required of other nationalities.

The monetary unit of Turks and Caicos is the Jamaican dollar. Currency notes of the West Indies and Bahamas are also legal tender. American currency is negotiable but is not legal tender.

ACCOMMODATIONS

SOUTH CAICOS

Opened in 1963 and one of the pioneers of island resort development is the **The Admiral's Arms** (South Caicos, Turks and Caicos Islands, West Indies) owned and operated by Liam Maguire. Located in Cockburn Harbour, the Arms can accommodate 40 persons in 16 rooms (most with private bath). Dining family style and informality keynoted. Winter (December 1 to April 30) rates on Modified American Plan $20 single, and $35 double; meals from $2.00 to $5.50. Summer rates lower. Special rates for children under 14. Special rates for transient ferry pilots.

PROVIDENCIALES

The new **Third Turtle Inn** (inquiries to 2633 Lantana Road, Lantana, Florida; Area Code 305 967-2261) created by Fritz Ludington. Ludington also owns the **Two Turtles Inn** at George Town, on Exuma Island in the Bahamas. His Providenciales hotel is cliff-side facing a barrier reef on the north shore of the island. Winter rates (December 15 to April 30) on American plan are $40 double and $25 single. Summer rates at $30 double and $15 single. Special rates for transient ferry pilots. Several small boats (whalers) are available. No offshore charter craft are based here at present.

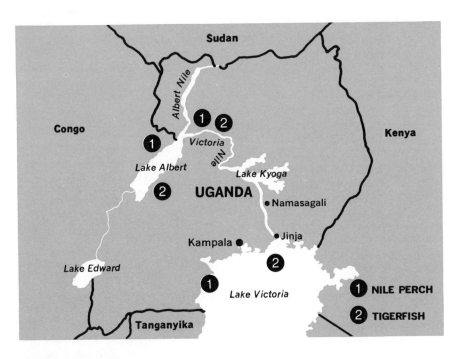

Uganda

This land-locked East African state lying west of Kenya and east of the Congo has a total area of 91,134 square miles of which about 16,400 square miles consist of lakes, rivers, and swamp. The northern half of Lake Victoria, the eastern portion of Lake Albert, and the northeastern corner of Lake Edward are Uganda territorial waters. The outlet of Lake Victoria is a powerful stream that passes through the Owen Falls Dam

at Jinja and forms the source of the Nile River. The Victoria Nile enters Lake Kyoga, then emerges from its west arm following a steep gradient before passing through a cleft less than 20 feet wide at Murchison Falls and entering Lake Albert. The Albert Nile continues across Uganda and becomes the White Nile at the Sudan border. Scenic attractions include vast Lake Victoria, mighty waterfalls, and the misty "Moun-

tains of the Moon" in the Ruwenzori Range that rises 16,794 feet, above the perpetual snow line despite lying on the equator. The national parks are unexcelled for their opportunities to see wild game at close range.

THE SEASON

Uganda has a higher mean annual rainfall than neighboring Kenya with few areas receiving less than 40 inches per year. Generally speaking the wettest months are March through May and to a less extent October through November. Typical of equatorial countries Uganda's temperatures vary with altitude, but over most of the country January and February are the hottest months and June through August the coolest. Most of the country lies at over 3,500 feet altitude so average temperatures range from 66°F to 80°F, providing comfortably warm days and cool nights.

THE FISHING

The principal freshwater gamefish in Uganda are the Nile perch and tigerfish. The former is most abundant in the Nile River below Murchison Falls and at Chobe (75 miles upstream). The fishing is done by casting from shore into very fast water using large plugs with heavy spinning or bait-casting tackle. At the Falls a 160-pound Nile perch was caught on 18-pound-test line

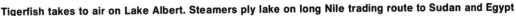

Tigerfish takes to air on Lake Albert. Steamers ply lake on long Nile trading route to Sudan and Egypt

which is the present rod record for the Nile. Casting from the rocks immediately below the Falls into strong currents adds some spice to the angling. At Parra several fish exceeding 200 pounds have been taken on handlines. Chobe also has some good fishing locations and the rod record here is 140 pounds. There is also excellent fishing for perch in Lake Albert where fish of over 200 pounds are possible. In the broad slow-moving reaches of the Nile at Namasagali, where it opens into Lake Kioga, about 50 miles from Lake Victoria, fish of up to 150 pounds have been taken. Bear in mind that these are maximum weights. For any number of Nile perch, say a dozen or more in a day's fishing, an *average* of about 35 pounds is considered good when both small and large catches are collectively totalled.

Despite its great size, the Nile perch is not a difficult or spectacular quarry in the sense of a tarpon, for example, with which it might be compared on the basis of weight and the tackle used. Small Nile perch (up to 50 pounds) are more active gamefish than the larger specimens which are inclined to sulk on the bottom. Occasionally the smaller fish will jump out of the water when hooked and big perch invariably shake their heads over the surface in an effort to break free, but it is mainly the size of the fish rather than its resistance that provides the angling thrills. Any kind of fish of over 100 pounds is awkward to handle especially when casting from the bank in a fast-flowing river.

By contrast the tigerfish doesn't compare to the Nile perch in size, but whatever it lacks in weight this remote relative of South America's dorado is a first-class gamester with acrobatics to spare. There are five species of tigerfish in Africa. The smallest of these is *Hydrocyon forskalii* which rarely weighs more than 2 pounds and the largest is *H. goliath,* found only in the Congo River watershed and Lake Tan-

ganyika, which grows to about 100 pounds. Between these extremes are *H. lineatus, H. brevis* and *H. vittatus.* Only *H. forskalii* (locally called "ngassa") and *H. lineatus* (locally called "wagassa") occur in Uganda. The latter has been recorded to weights of 35 pounds but the range of fish taken in Uganda ordinarily runs from 1 to 6 pounds. Tigerfish are found in the same waters as the Nile perch—in Lake Albert, and the Nile and its tributaries downstream from Murchison Falls. They are most common along rocky shores and in weedy bays but there is a seasonal variation in their distribution and numbers.

TACKLE
A medium-action bait-casting or spinning rod suitable for lures in the ½-ounce class is sporty equipment for tigerfish in Uganda. A 10-or 12-pound-test line is adequate for the average run of fish but still offers a margin of safety.

Tigerfish will take any form of live bait or lure that represents a fish. Often an angler trolling for Nile perch with a 6-inch-long plug will find tigerfish striking at the lure; some good fish are taken this way. They are not easy to catch. They hit voraciously but they are difficult to hook. Their mouths are extremely bony, and have few places where a hook will penetrate. Further, their jaws are immensely strong and can clamp down on a spoon so firmly as to resist even a heavy strike. For this reason some anglers use the heaviest tackle.

Live bait, dead bait, plugs, spoons, various spinners, and even flies can be used with success for tigerfish, but a lure with plenty of flash and movement such as a small bright wobbling spoon about 1¼ or 1½ inches long is ideal. Really big tigerfish are exceptional in Uganda and a spoon of this size is most effective.

TRAVEL NOTES
By Pan Am Jet Clipper to Entebbe in 19½ hours. Pan Am provides free

bus service from Entebbe into the capital city of Kampala. Internal air services connect Entebbe with small air fields at Jinja, Tororo, Soroti, Gulu, Arua, Murchison Falls, and Kasee. Passport, visa ($2.20), smallpox and yellow fever vaccination certificate required.

The Anopheles mosquito can be common anywhere below 5,000 feet altitude in Uganda and anti-malarial pills are strongly advised.

LANGUAGE AND PEOPLE
Uganda is ethnically and linguistically diversified. Bantu, Hima, Gisu, Gwere, Chiga, Nilotic Acholi, and other tribal groups are indigenous to certain regions. About two-thirds of the total population (over 8 million) is Bantu speaking. Europeans form a token percentage of the resident population. English is spoken in hotels and resorts.

ACCOMMODATIONS
Two first-class hotels are popular among anglers: the **Paraa Safari Lodge** and the **Chobe Safari Lodge.** Both are situated in Murchison Falls National Park where a profusion of wild game and bird life can be seen, together with magnificent scenery. Numbers of elephant, hippo, crocodile, buffalo, and waterbuck, occasionally the black and white varieties of rhino, and sometimes lion, can be seen. The bird-life includes many kinds of storks, ibis, herons, eagles, pelicans, skimmers, geese, and kingfishers.

Elsewhere in Uganda: Best and deluxe in Kampala, the **Apolo** is $12.35-$15.40 single, $18.50-$21.60 double. Rates at other Kampala hotels for rooms with bath: **Grand,** $10.80 single, $19.25 double; **Hacienda,** $9.10-$11.20 single, $16.80-$19.60 double. In Entebbe: **Lake Victoria Hotel,** $11.55 single, $20 double. Above rates include breakfast, but not the 10% service charge. There are modern, comfortable hotels at popular places around the country where rates average $10 per person, including meals.

United States

Bordered by the Atlantic and Pacific Oceans with a climate ranging from sub-arctic in Alaska to semi-tropical in Florida and Hawaii, the United States offers a tremendous variety of marine and freshwater angling. More than 60 million people go fishing each year in America and it's the nation's number one participation sport. Although sometimes viewed as a land of soaring skyscrapers and traffic jammed streets, the United States has vast forests, deserts, mountain ranges, an abundance of rivers and enormous lakes. Foreign visitors will have no difficulty in arranging a fishing trip as there are more camps and resorts catering to the sportsman here than anywhere else in the world. Wilderness float trips, mountain pack trips by horse or foot, big-game angling, stream trout fishing, surf casting, houseboat cruises and numerous other adventures are within easy reach of any port of entry.

Alaska

Viewed from afar Alaska is a land of giant brown bears, white whales, igloos, and bearded sourdoughs—straight out of Robert Service. While it is obvious that vast areas are barren and uninhabited (the population density is about ½ person to the square mile as compared to 50 people per square mile as the national average for the rest of the U.S.) most Alaskans live in towns and cities where all the amenities of modern civilization from TV to parking meters clutter the workaday world. Yet, the 49th State covers approximately 586,400 square miles making it one-fifth the size of the continental U.S. and inevitably quality fishing exists away from the main business hubs such as Anchorage, Juneau, and Fairbanks. Few of the great angling

Chum salmon on light tackle

areas can be reached by auto; the state has less than 5,500 miles of road and less than a thousand miles is paved. The bush pilot is the standard bearer for sportsmen who want wilderness, and Alaska boasts over 700 facilities for aircraft. Many waters have been overexploited, and others are devoid of fish at certain times of the year, so it requires expert local knowledge to enjoy what still remains the best fishing of its kind left in America. The principal species of gamefish sought are the chinook salmon (locally king salmon), coho salmon, sockeye salmon, rainbow trout, cutthroat trout, Dolly Varden, Arctic char, grayling, whitefish, northern pike, inconnu (locally sheefish), and white halibut.

THE SEASON

In the Arctic and in the area around Fairbanks, it is dry and cold with subzero temperatures in the winter, but quite warm and sunny during the summer months. Anchorage and the Kenai Peninsula area have weather comparable to the Midwestern states of the United States. The southern coastal areas are warmed by the Japanese current. Best months to visit are May through October. The most popular fishing months for tourists, July and August, are generally the warmest with average temperatures of 57°F and 56°F respectively. However, it can be cold at night and hot by day during the summer. A temperature drop has been recorded from 114°F to 30°F in a twelve-hour span on the Fortymile River. Thus the fisherman should select his wardrobe accordingly. One should be prepared for Alaska's most dangerous species, the mosquito, which is abundant through the early summer. A headnet is always a welcome haven, as are light gloves.

SOUTHEASTERN ALASKA

This section of Alaska is referred to as the Panhandle. It is the long strip of land that runs along the edge of British Columbia to the Kenai Penin-

sula. This coast is a complex of islands and bays, and is one of the least-known and most beautiful areas of North America. Huge forests of spruce, nurtured by a heavy rainfall and mild winters, follow the mountain sites right down to the saltwater. The streams are crystal clear (with the exception of the larger glacial runoffs) and cold. In the saltwater of the coastal inlets and channels, trolling for salmon and halibut provides sport for native and tourist alike, while the freshwater lakes and streams abound in cutthroat and rainbow trout, with salmon and steelhead as seasonal migrants.

Most of the Panhandle is true wilderness. There is no extensive road system, and villages are few and far between. Paradoxically, the area is very easily reached by commercial airlines or boat to Ketchikan or Juneau. Cabin or hotel accommodations are available close to the fishing grounds in these cities as well as Skagway, Wrangell, Sitka, and Petersburg. A major fishing layout here is **Bell Island Hot Springs Resort** leased by Alaska Airlines which flies its guests in from Ketchikan. Bell Island is on the Behm Canal, one of Alaska's top salmon spots from May through July for chinooks and July through September for coho salmon. **Clover Pass Resort,** a rustic cabin layout only fifteen miles from Ketchikan, is popular for overnight visits. Western Airlines offers package fishing trips to Panhandle resorts including **Yes Bay Lodge** for Dolly Varden, rainbow and cutthroat trout and an out-camp deluxe chalet on Humpback Lake for big cutthroat and brook trout. In Petersburg the **Tides Inn Motel** is base camp for Andy Mathisen (Box 316, Petersburg) who offers a variety of angling at $50 per person per day American Plan.

Boats for salmon fishing in the Panhandle are available in most cities and towns. A complete list of facilities can be obtained from local Chambers of Commerce or from the

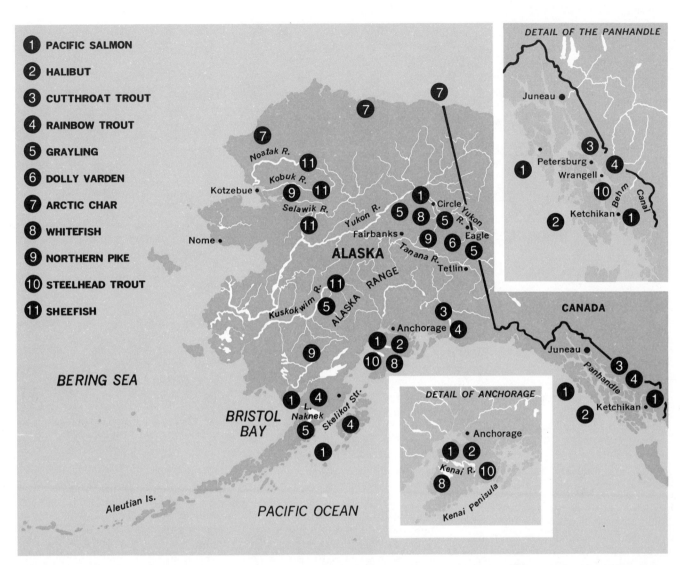

1 PACIFIC SALMON

2 HALIBUT

3 CUTTHROAT TROUT

4 RAINBOW TROUT

5 GRAYLING

6 DOLLY VARDEN

7 ARCTIC CHAR

8 WHITEFISH

9 NORTHERN PIKE

10 STEELHEAD TROUT

11 SHEEFISH

DETAIL OF THE PANHANDLE

DETAIL OF ANCHORAGE

Alaska Visitors' Association, Juneau. In Ketchikan, which claims title to the "Salmon Capital of the World," the Ketchikan Yacht Club will provide information on boat charters.

HIGHWAY FISHING

Although Alaska's highways are few and far between and heavily traveled, there is still good fishing to be had. However, to be successful, a knowledge of local areas is necessary. The Sport Fish Division of the Alaska Department of Fish and Game puts out an excellent guide to the roadside fishing of the state, and this guide (*Alaska Sport Fishing Guide*) may be obtained by writing to the Sport Fish Division, Alaska Department of Fish and Game in Ju-

neau. This manual leaves out one important road, the Taylor Highway, which joins Eagle, on the Yukon, to the Alaska Highway near the Canadian border at Tetlin Junction. This road crosses and parallels for some distance the brawling Fortymile River which offers wonderful grayling fishing over its length. At the last bridge there is a deep pool which yields an occasional sheefish and quite a few lingcod (locally, burbot). The latter species deserves recognition as one of the finest eating fish found in Alaskan waters. It is a member of the cod family and quite ugly in appearance. Its meat, however, is white and flaky, with a truly fine flavor. The natives prize the liver which they eat raw or fried.

Briefly looking at some of the fishing hot spots along the highways of the interior, we find excellent rainbow trout fishing in some of the lakes between the border and Delta Junction on the Alaska Highway. These are planted trout, and have done very well. The first is Deadman Lake at Mile 1251. The next and best known is Jan Lake at Mile 1324. The lake lies three-quarters of a mile off the road, but there is an excellent bulldozed trail to it. A third one is just south of Delta on the Richardson Highway. This is Bolio Lake and is also easily accessible from the road.

Further on the Richardson, on the other side of Black Rapids Pass, lie a series of lakes which offer year-

Bell Island Hot Springs Fishing Resort is located on Behm Canal near Ketchikan

An Eskimo ice-fisherman stacks a cord of 50-pound sheefish for winter food

round lake trout fishing. These lakes consist of Summit Lake, Paxon Lake, and then on the Denali Highway, Tangle Lakes. The best fishing here is right after ice-out in June or July, when the lake trout are feeding on the surface near the shores.

Driving north from Fairbanks the fisherman can travel on either the Steese Highway or the Livengood road, both good gravel roads. The Livengood fork crosses many good fly-fishing streams, such as the Chatanika River, Washington Creek, the Tatalina River, and the Tolovana. All these are heavily fished near the road, and the angler would be well advised to walk about a mile or so to get away from the traffic. Near the end of the highway the traveler crosses the Hutlinana River which features good grayling, salmon, and Dolly-Varden fishing in the spring and fall. The terminus of the highway is at Manley Hot Springs, where boats may be rented to try the excellent pike fishing in the sloughs.

The Steese Highway parallels the upper Chatanika for almost seventy miles. The whole stream is beautiful

grayling water and is the site of the University of Alaska's investigation on grayling biology. The Chatanika also has some feeder creeks on both sides of the river which harbor grayling. The highway passes the headwaters of Chatanika and then rises over Twelve-Mile Summit and drops into the Birch Creek drainage. This marks the site of another weeklong (or more) float trip, by canoe. Birch Creek is crossed by the Steese fifty miles further on, but in the meantime the stream travels 120 miles through the wilderness. Birch Creek offers near record-size grayling, whitefish, and pike, as well as sheefish in September. After leaving the headwaters of Birch Creek, the Steese Highway again climbs over another summit, passing through the caribou country. From this summit to Circle City the motorist passes over several small clear streams, which all offer fair-to-good fishing for small grayling.

KENAI PENINSULA

The Kenai Peninsula is one of the best known and most popular areas of Alaska. It can be reached by road from Anchorage. Chinook, coho,

and sockeye salmon, steelhead, and large halibut (fish of over 100 pounds have been taken on rod-and-reel) are the principal species in Kenai waters. The main stream on the peninsula is the Kenai River. The lower reaches are estuarine for some distance inland and provide accessible fishing through most of the season. Farther up the river, yet still within the reaches of the tidal effects, spring brings large runs of sockeye salmon and chinooks. The king-salmon run continues at a lower rate during the summer, and then is followed in the fall by a run of sporty coho salmon and Dolly Varden. During the early winter, the Kenai gets a run of steelhead trout, considered by some to be the greatest sport fish of all. Five-pound trout are not unusual, but fish of 10 pounds and better are often taken. The salmon vary in size with the

Hooked to a big rainbow on Upper Russian Lake. This is typical of Kenai's waters

Trout fishing out of Brooks River Lodge

pink or "humpback" running in the neighborhood of 5 pounds, the coho around 10 pounds. The kings, however, are behemoths. Commercial fishermen have taken chinooks up to 126 pounds in Alaska, but because of their tremendous strength and the powerful currents, fish over 40 pounds are very difficult to subdue in the river.

Farther upstream Beaver Creek joins the Kenai River, and there is a landing here where tourists can rent a boat. From here you can sample the Kenai itself or fish in Beaver Creek which yields good trout fishing for rainbows and some fair salmon fishing. Farther upstream is Eagle Rock, a well-known fishing site, which is usually very productive during the salmon runs. Two miles further up, the Kenai turns a right-angle corner, forming an eddy which is famous for the number of chinook salmon that congregate in the slack water.

Besides fantastic fishing, the Kenai offers many sights which are in themselves worth the visit. During the salmon runs the huge Alaskan brown bears congregate on the

sandbars, scooping up fish, while sea gulls hover around and dart after scraps. Bald eagles are a common sight along the river as they dive into the water and grab up a struggling salmon in their talons.

The Kenai is not the only good river on this peninsula. The Ninilchik, Anchor, and Mose rivers are all accessible from the road and offer fishing similar to the Kenai. The fisherman is better equipped on all of these rivers with a boat and a reliable motor. If the angler does not bring his own, there are numerous places where they can be rented. However, a word of caution; these rivers are all swift, rocky, and very cold. For the person not familiar with boating on such water, it is strongly recommended that the services of a guide be enlisted.

There are several large lakes on the Kenai Peninsula. They offer rainbow trout and Dolly Varden fishing. Accessible from the road is Siklak Lake, Kenai Lake, Russian Lake (a three-mile hike), Hidden Lake, Jean Lake, and many others. The Russian River is about a mile from the road on a good trail and was once the

outstanding rainbow trout stream in Alaska; it has been heavily fished in recent years although it still provides some sport.

SOUTHWESTERN ALASKA

This is bush pilot country. From Anchorage west, bounded to the north by the Alaska Range and Bristol Bay and to the south by the Shelikof Strait and the Pacific Ocean, it encompasses the Alaskan Peninsula which projects into the Aleutian Chain. It also contains the world famous Katmai National Monument. One of the oldest established camps in the Katmai area is **Brooks River Lodge** (Wien Consolidated Airlines, Anchorage, Alaska 99502). This camp is easily reached by daily flights from King Salmon. Rates run $40 per day per person American plan. Accommodations are mostly log cabins with modern facilities, as well as some tent houses. Huge brown bears, majestic moose, migrating salmon, and snow-splotched mountain peaks provide colorful subjects for the amateur photographer. Much of the wildlife footage in Walt Disney's now classic nature films was made in the Katmai region. Brooks camp is located on Naknek Lake, which is forty miles long and approximately fifteen miles wide, dotted with beautiful islands with many small streams and rivers that empty into the lake and the Naknek River, some twenty miles long, that empties into the Bering Sea.

The fishing is done in a rugged, mountainous landscape not far from the volcanic peaks of the Valley of Ten Thousand Smokes. Although there is some lake casting, the peninsula is drained by crystalline, gravel-bottomed rivers, which are easy to wade. Generally, you can get along with a pair of hip boots. Rainbow trout from 1½ to 5 pounds are numerous, and fish of 10 pounds or more are a daily possibility. The grayling usually run 1 to 2 pounds and provide excellent dry-fly fishing. More unique perhaps is the sockeye salmon, which in many parts of the Northwest rarely strikes artificial lures, but at Brooks River this species readily hits a streamer fly. The sockeyes vary from 5 to 10 pounds, while the acrobatic coho salmon are in the 6- to 12-pound class. Alaskan pike and lake trout are normally smaller than those found in the Canadian provinces, but they are numerous.

From Brooks River you can also visit **Kulik Camp** located at the mouth of Kulik River on the east end of Nonvianuk Lake. This is one of the better rainbow trout fishing streams to be found in Alaska. Kulik is situated just outside the boundaries of Katmai National Monument. Fly fishing, spin-fishing and trolling are all effective, but wading and fly fishing comprise 80 percent of the fishing here. The camp is limited to a maximum of twenty anglers at the peak of the season. Kulik boasts its own 4600-foot airstrip and is owned and operated by Wien Consolidated. Rates about $50 per person per day, American plan, including guide service.

Another Wien out-camp is **Grosvenor Camp** located between Co-

Migrating Pacific salmon are a common sight in Alaskan rivers. Sought chiefly in saltwater, seasonal runs of sockeye, coho, and chinook provide inland angling

ville Lake and Grosvenor Lake. The 50-mile-long American River feeds both lakes from the high country of the Katmai area. In turn Grosvenor and Coville drain into the Savanoski River—which empties into Naknek Lake. These lakes and their tributary rivers comprise some 163 miles of continuous waterway, most of which produces excellent fishing for rainbows, Dolly Varden, grayling, and sockeye salmon. Rates at about $40 per person per day, American plan including guide service.

Bristol Bay is another popular area. The saltwater yields excellent chinook and coho salmon by trolling. While inland, one finds rainbow trout, steelhead, Dolly Varden, sockeye, chinook, and coho salmon, as well as whitefish. Running into Bristol Bay are drainages which are very important to the Alaskan fishing scene. The Kuichak River drains Iliamna Lake, and the Wood River drains the Tikchik Lakes. The **Wood River Wilderness Camp** (P.O. Box 1631, Anchorage, Alaska 99501) covers over 800 miles of waterways in this area. Rates here run $375 per person American plan for five days.

Another popular operation based on Iliamna Lake is **Kokhonak Lodge** (Bud and Dennis Branham, P.O. Box 6128 Annex, Anchorage, Alaska 99502). In beautiful surroundings near Kokhonak Falls, the lodge is amid some of the best rainbow trout

fishing in Alaska. The minimum time you should plan for your fishing trip is 10 days, with longer being desirable. The Branhams take care of parties up to eight people, but they have to be separated into groups because of plane space. A party of one only would be handled in a Super-Cub, which is a two-place plane, while a party of two or three in a Courier. The costs are all-inclusive from the time you are picked up and returned to Anchorage or other prearranged commercial airport. The rates vary according to the size of the party; $200 per day for one person, $300 per day for two, $400 per day for three, and so on.

Just north of Bristol Bay lies the Kuskokwim watershed. Here again is a completely roadless wilderness, accessible only by air. However, there are several villages such as Bethel, Sleetmute, Stony River, and McGrath where guide service may be obtained. The Kuskokwim River is a silty stream like many of Alaska's big rivers, and the finest fishing occurs where the tributaries meet the main current, forming an interface of clear and muddy waters. Here two of Alaska's favorite sport fish are found in abundance. The Arctic grayling is a fly-fisherman's prize, with its huge sail-like dorsal fin and its dramatic way of engulfing a dry fly, then arching out of the water in a frantic jump before it dives for the safety of the bottom. The other trophy is the lantern-jawed pugnacious sheefish. The natives start catching these fish in March, through the ice, and fish for them until late into the fall. One of the many legends that has grown around the shee is that it never eats while in freshwater and therefore only strikes out of anger. Stomach examinations of this species show that this is false and that the inconnu is a voracious feeder on chubs, whitefish, salmon fry, grayling, sculpins, and other small fish. With this in mind, the prospective angler should arm himself with a spinning rod and a collection of wobbling spoons and spinners.

Eight pounders are common, but individuals of 50 pounds have been taken and the largest recorded is approximately 80 pounds. Sheefish justly earn their reputation of "Arctic tarpon" by putting on fantastic aerial shows and shoulder-jarring runs.

Some of the important waters of this drainage are the Holitna, the Hoholitna, the Stony, and the Aniak rivers. The latter contains the only native population of rainbow trout north of the Alaska range. All these waters also have superlative grayling fishing, and the slack waters of the sloughs of the lower reaches of all these rivers harbor northern pike.

YUKON-TANANA DRAINAGE

The Yukon-Tanana drainage stretches east and west from the Canadian border to the Bering Sea and from the Alaska Range to the south to the remote Brooks Range in the north. Much of the good water in the eastern section is accessible by road, but the area from Nenana west can only be reached by float plane or by river boat. The main species are grayling, sheefish, salmon, and pike.

The Tanana and Yukon Rivers, with their tributaries, form an extensive watershed, thousands of miles long. One of the best short trips by riverboat can be made from Circle to Ea-

Alaska's crystal clear streams yield such fish as grayling, char, trout, sockeye salmon among others

gle near the Canadian border. The Yukon River itself is not good fishing water, although it contains large chinook, coho, and sockeye salmon, as well as sheefish, grayling, and pike. Due to the eroding action of the river, the water is heavily silted. The tributaries are crystal clear and provide fast and exciting fishing for trophy-size fish. The first of these is the Charley River, which drains the hills south of the Yukon. It is navigable for many miles with a small riverboat, and its headwaters lie in some of Alaska's finest Dall sheep and caribou country. It is primarily a grayling stream, but salmon, sheefish, and pike may be encountered. The next stream upriver is the Kandik, draining the northern and eastern hills. At the mouth of this stream is a beautiful sandbar, which forms a perfect campground. The Kandik is fast and shallow but the mouth of the river is a deep bay, connected by a narrow channel to a series of beaver ponds. This channel and the bay provide some excellent fishing for pike. Due to the shallowness of the water the fish are forced to display all their aerial acrobatic ability, and they are worthy of the most enthusiastic user of light tackle. Further up the Kandik, grayling are abundant in ideal dry-fly water.

The Nation River is next on a journey up the Yukon. This is one of the most renowned grayling streams in Alaska. It might easily hold a fish of the world-record class. These grayling are at their best on light dry-fly tackle but are also sporty for the spin-fisherman. As with the Kandik, the Nation is also in the heart of bountiful big game and fur country. Wolves are common (though not often seen), and bears are abundant, as are the magnificent Alaskan moose.

The Tatonduk River is the next upstream and features grayling and sheefish, as well as pike in the sloughs and backwaters. For the late-summer fisherman, the sheefish is tops. These voracious whitefish migrate into the clear streams to

spawn and strike at spoons, plugs, and wet flies with a terrifying abandon. The shee is the most acrobatic of Alaska's gamefish, and although they do not seem to run large in size in the Yukon streams, 5 pounds of sheefish on light tackle will thrill the most jaded angler.

The whole trip from Circle to Eagle takes about a week, with time out to sample each tributary. It covers about 175 miles of true wilderness. However, the Yukon, like the Tanana, is a dangerous and tricky river. It is a mile wide at points but is very shallow in many places. The navigable channels are constantly shifting, and shoals present a continual hazard to the boatman. It is not a river for the novice in a runabout or power cruiser. The Alaskan riverboat is a piece of equipment designed especially for these waters, and it is advisable that guide services be secured for at least the first trip on the rivers of the interior.

The Circle-to-Eagle trip is only one of the many that may be undertaken. Another one can be started at Fairbanks, down the Chena River and into the Tanana, past the natives' fish wheels which scoop salmon from the river. Five miles down and across the river, Salchaket Slouth, a fast, deep cut-off from the mainstream enters. The fisherman follows up the slough for several miles and comes to a small clear stream entering from the right. This is Clear Creek and is one of the prettiest streams of the interior. Winding through vast stands of paper birches, it seems to be of another world. It features grayling and, after July, sheefish. It is a wonderful stream for the fly-fisherman and for the spin enthusiast, as well as the nonfishing bird watcher, for the area is populated with ducks, mergansers, and kingfishers, as well as all kinds of small songbirds. The Clear Creek trip is an all-day affair, and again a guide is needed, as threading one's way across the Tanana is a tricky business at best.

ARCTIC CIRCLE REGION

Moving north and west the next subdivision lies entirely within the Arctic Circle. There are three major rivers in this section, the Kobuk, the Selawik, and the Noatak, all with their mouths in the Kotzebue area. Sheefish are the prize, and it is here that they reach their maximum size. Again it is a totally roadless area, and the only practical means of transportation is by float plane. There are several towns that one can use for a base of operations, depending upon what kind of fishing is planned. The largest town is Kotzebue, on the coast, from which the angler can reach the lower sections of all three rivers, as well as Hotham Inlet and the huge inland lake which abound in sheefish up to 60 pounds and better. The Kobuk and Noatak fan into a delta, which holds pike of great size in all its sloughs.

Further inland, the town of Kiana lies on the Kobuk River. Bud and Dennis Branham have a camp here which specializes in sheefish. The layout consists of floored tent cabins with a central dining room. Their **Kobuk Camp** is in great demand and bookings should be made a year in advance. Rates run about $475 per day all-inclusive for a party of four. The fishing is prime from July 1st to about August 10th.

From the towns of Alatna, Allakaket, or Bettles (on the Koyukuk River) one can fly to the head water lakes of the Kobuk-Walker and Shelby Lakes, which hold good populations of lake trout.

The Noatak is prized for its Dolly Vardens and its beautiful and virgin scenery. The Selawik is a slow stream with large sheefish and pike. The native village of the same name is a good place to look for local guide service, or your pilot from Kotzebue will act as your guide in your quest for the inconnu.

North of here is the vast Arctic slope from the Bering Sea to the Arctic Wildlife Refuge and the Canadian border. Again the only practical

Fly-in camps are extremely popular and produce good fishing. **New York angler Warren Page** *(left)* with his catch on the Kobuk

transportation is by plane. In this area lie hundreds of lakes probably untouched by the white man. This is a last frontier for the adventurous fisherman. The principal known rivers are the Meade, the Colville, the Ikpikpuk, the Canning, and the Sagavanirktok.

TACKLE
A minimum of one fly rod and one spinning or bait casting rod is essential. Fly rods calibered for No. 8 or No. 9 line are suitable for salmon and steelhead and generally come in handy when winds are adverse. A lighter fly rod calibered for No. 4 or No. 5 line is also practical for the general run of trout and grayling fishing where fine leaders and small flies pay off. Popular dry-fly patterns are the Black Gnat, Mosquito, Royal Coachman, Yellow May, and the Parmachene Belle. Nymphs, large streamers, and wet flies of most of the common patterns are always good. For the spinning fisherman an ultralight outfit as well as a heavy-duty rig for salmon and sheefish are recommended. Most successful of the spinning lures are ¼- to ½-ounce spinners and red-and-white spoons, but almost any flashing

piece of metal will produce results with pike and sheefish.

It is always advisable to have enough extra tackle with you, as sporting goods stores are rare, although there are good ones located in the major towns. Guide service is available in all the main towns and in most of the smaller villages.

TRAVEL NOTES
By Pan Am Jet Clipper, non-stop service from New York to Fairbanks, 7½ hours flying time; from Seattle to Fairbanks, 3¼ hours flying time. Service also from Portland, Fairbanks to Juneau by Wien Consolidated Airlines, 2¼ hours; Fairbanks to Nome, 1¼ hours via Wien Consolidated. Anchorage is 40 minutes by jet from Juneau via Wien Consolidated or Alaska Airlines. The Alaska Highway, now partially paved, is reached through Alberta, Canada, or the Hart Highway through British Columbia.

Alaska encompasses four time zones: Pacific (the easternmost), Yukon, Alaska, and Bering (the zone in which lie most of the Aleutian Islands, which is a 1200-mile-long part of Alaska which is closer to Ja-

pan than to the rest of the United States). Nome, the state's most westerly city of consequence, is west of Honolulu.

ACCOMMODATIONS
The **Baranof-Western** in Juneau is one of the favorite hotels in Alaska and has music nightly in the *Latch-string;* $17 single, $22 to $45 double. In Anchorage the **Anchorage-Westward** is distinctive and features The *Top of the World* restaurant overlooking the city, harbor and mountains; from $15 single, $19 double. The new **Captain Cook** also has a panoramic view from its *Crow's Nest;* from $19 single, $25 double. Best in Fairbanks are the **Fairbanks Inn, Travelers Inn** and **Golden Nugget,** all $23 single, $29 double, and the **Nordate** with its typically "Alaskan atmosphere," $13 single, $20 double. In Ketchikan: the **Ingersoll,** from $13 single, $16 double; **Mary Francis,** from $14 single, $17 double. In Skagway: **Klondike Hotel,** from $18 single $22 double; **Golden North Hotel,** $13 single, from $18 double. Inns and motels charge about the same rates. City sales taxes are added to rates, which are often lower in winter.

Rare blueback trout from Wadleigh Pond

Down East Sampler

Sunapee trout isolated during Glacial Age

MAINE

Any visitor to the U.S. will enjoy a trip to Maine. The fishing is not always sensational, although it can be at times in the more remote waters. However, Maine has its own unique flavor with over 16 million acres of woodland and thousands of lakes, ponds, and streams in an idyllic setting of crying loons, soaring eagles, and tree-chomping beavers. There is still some relatively inaccessible brook trout fishing on such notable streams as the Allagash, Spencer, and Kennebago and for landlocked salmon as well as squaretail trout on the West Branch of the Penobscot, Moose River, upper Kennebec, and the outlets of Moosehead Lake. Much of the angling is done in lakes and connecting thoroughfares for brook trout, lake trout, landlocked salmon, and smallmouth bass. The rare blueback trout found only in Maine is limited to less than a dozen ponds today. Many lakes from central Maine to the coast also contain chain pickerel, white perch, and yellow perch. An Atlantic salmon restoration program has enjoyed a small success in establishing runs in five rivers; however, the quality of the fishing is not worth a detour at the present time. The total catch for all streams in 1969 was less than 400 fish.

Sea-run brook trout are also present in some coastal streams and the brown trout has been widely introduced to a number of lakes. Occasionally large browns are taken in Maine during the spring of the year. There is an established population of rainbow trout in Maine's Kennebec River in the Bingham area. Saltwater sport fishing in the state is dominated by the striped bass, pollock, and mackerel, but there is some offshore angling for bluefin tuna out of Ogunquit, Small Point, Boothbay, and Bailey Island.

The American sporting camp was created in Maine around 1840, when fishermen began visiting lumber camps to hire these professional woodsmen as guides. Soon the lumber bosses began putting up tents and taking in paying guests. There was hair in the chowder, plumbing was non-existent and anybody who survived one week was decorated for bravery. The reputable angling resorts in Maine today bear no resemblance to their prehistoric ancestors—in fact some are so lavish that they no longer qualify as sporting camps. The following is merely a sampler of the varied accommodations and angling:

WEST GRAND LAKE

Over in the southeast corner of the state is a major chain of lakes noted for smallmouth bass and landlocked salmon fishing. Near the village of Grand Lake Stream is **Leen's Lodge,** an angler's oasis on the shore of West Grand Lake. Situated among tall pines on a rocky promontory the lodge consists of ten cedar log cabins, paneled and handsomely furnished. The main lodge with its spacious dining room and game room overlooks the lake, as do many of the cabins. No place for calorie counters; Stanley and Barbara Leen specialize in Maine dishes which run the gamut from native blueberry pie to hulking red lobsters. Steak cookouts on the lodge's private coves and beaches accompanied by literal buckets of a Leen concocted daiquiri only compete with the guides' ambrosial handling of your morning's catch. Nothing is too good for a guest here, and the price is eminently fair at $22 single per day, and $19 per person double American plan. Leen's has family rates, also. Capable guides with boat and motor are available at $20 per day. The peak period here is the first three weeks of June for smallmouth bass through the whole lake chain including nearby Big Lake and well into summer for landlocked salmon. Nearby Grand Lake Stream has a few little salmon in it and while not a serious angler's river every once in a while some innocent catches a lunker.

SPEDNIC LAKE

One of the best smallmouth bass waters in the U.S., 27-mile-long Spednic Lake is located in northeast Maine at the New Brunswick border near Forest City. Studded with bouldery pine-covered islands Spednic is a beautiful angling arena which can be fished from **Wheaton's Camps,** (Box 48, Forest City, Maine), situated on nearby East Grand Lake. Ruth and Woodie Wheaton run a camp in the traditional sense and their guests come back year after year. The smallmouth fishing holds good here from late May through most of July and there's always a dividend of landlocked salmon which inhabit these same waters.

MOOSEHEAD LAKE

Moosehead is Maine's largest with an area of 74,890 acres. Its cold water drops down to 246 feet creating an ideal habitat for landlocked salmon, brook and lake trout. The west and east outlet of Moosehead merge and form Indian Pond, which flows into the Kennebec River. Moosehead has numerous fishing camps and the oldest of these is **Wilson's Camps** (Rockwood, Maine), located near the East Outlet Dam where the Kennebec River begins. In business for more than ninety years, Wilson's is an old favorite of fly fishermen. The brook trout and landlocked salmon fishing is especially good here in the spring and fall season. Wilson's is a cabin out in the woods set-up (no meals served) and the rates are modest.

To the west of Moosehead lie many noteworthy fishing lakes and streams. Up the Moose River from Rockwood is 8,979-acre Brassua Lake. Brassua is shallow (maximum depth 65 feet), but brook trout attain unusual size there. The 65-mile-long Moose River itself is an excellent salmon and trout stream for much of its length. It originates in Somerset and Franklin counties (in the Jackman area), and flows through several ponds and into Moosehead Lake. There are good salmon and trout ponds near the source of Moose River. East of Moosehead Lake are many fine trout waters such as Newsowadnahunk Lake (the correct Indian spelling for Sourdnahunk and recently changed on official maps) which has the reputation of being "the most natural trout factory" in Maine. A popular location here is **Camp Phoenix** (Millinocket, Maine) operated by George Emerson Jr. In this same general area, don't overlook Sebec Lake for its landlocked salmon.

Stable square-sterned canoe is ideal for working shoreline for smallmouths

Wooded hills surround Spednic Lake, one of the best springtime producers in Maine

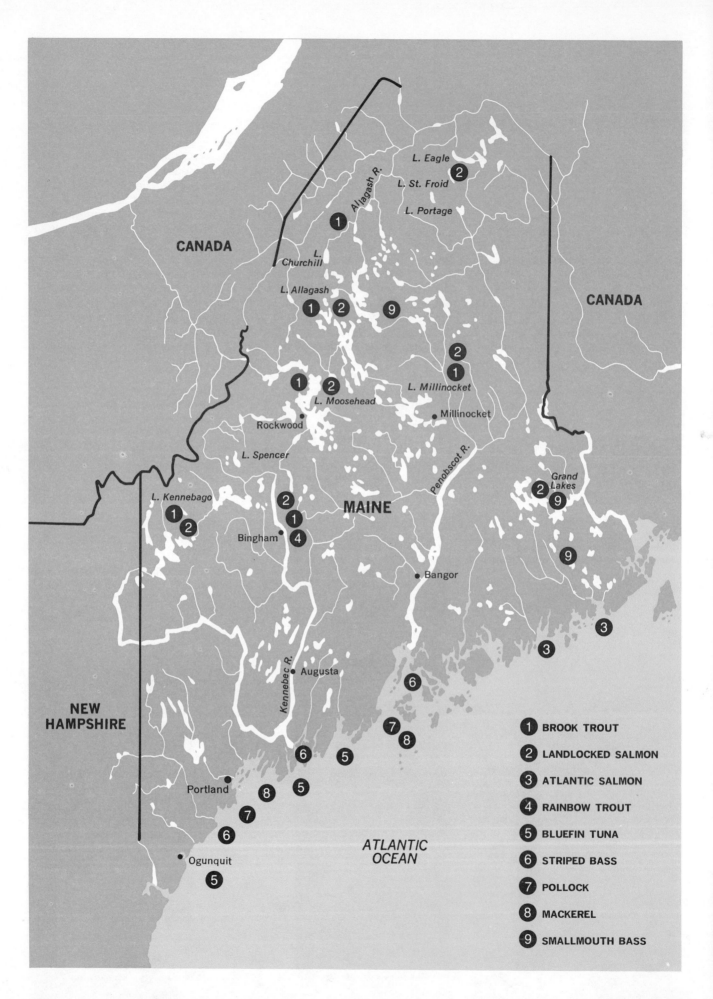

BROOK TROUT
LANDLOCKED SALMON
ATLANTIC SALMON
RAINBOW TROUT
BLUEFIN TUNA
STRIPED BASS
POLLOCK
MACKEREL
SMALLMOUTH BASS

WILDERNESS LUXURY

There are occasions when a family vacation takes precedence over a fishing trip in the sense that tennis, golf, water skiing, trap shooting, and other diversions must be available to keep everybody happy. **The Mount Kineo** (Kineo, Maine) is a luxurious resort located on a peninsula in Moosehead Lake. It can only be reached by water. Leave your car at the hotel's garage in Rockwood, not far from Greenville on Route 15. You will be met by the hotel's cabin cruisers for a one-mile voyage to the dock. The location is spectacular. Accommodations, cuisine, and wine list are excellent. Jacket and tie are required at cocktail time and the dinner hour, otherwise informality reigns. The usual fishing is available on Moosehead but the hotel also arranges for float plane trips into wilderness ponds and nearby Lobster Lake and Allagash River. Rates at the hotel and Oak Lodge run $40 to $45 single and $65 to $75 double. There are lower rates for extra persons sharing a room and for other quarters including housekeeping cottages.

KIDNEY POND

The full flavor of an oldtime Maine sporting camp (established 1902) exists 31 miles northwest of Millinocket at **Kidney Pond Lodge** (Millinocket, Maine). No outboard motors are allowed; you either paddle your own canoe or hire a guide. The only device permitted to break the blessed silence is the late Miss Ethel Barrymore's piano located in the lounge. Mrs. Ruth Morris's hostelry is located near Mt. Katahdin in a 200,000-acre sanctuary called Baxter State Park. The lodge can be reached via the park road about 30 miles from Millinocket. Fishing is with the fly *only* in most of eleven nearby ponds which are readily accessible over woods paths. Native brook trout averaging from 10 to 18 inches long are standard fodder for artful casters. An out-camp for guests on the West Branch of the

Penobscot River produces land-locked salmon as well as big brook trout. Wildlife including moose and black bears is abundant in this wilderness preserve. American plan rates at $18 per day per person or $115 per week. Guide fees run $16 per day when needed.

KENNEBAGO LAKES

The Kennebago Lakes are small by Maine standards but fish are plentiful. The Kennebago River runs through a series of ponds into 5-mile-long Big Kennebago Lake which contains brook trout and landlocked salmon. The stream has some excellent pools which are fishable from shore. Fly fishing remains good in this area right into summer with large fly hatches occurring in July and even into August. An 8-pound 15-ounce brook trout was caught at Kennebago in August of 1968. The famous resort here is the **Kennebago Lake Club,** (Rangely, Maine) established in 1872 and operated by Mr. and Mrs. Bud Russel.

The "club" now features a housekeeping plan composed of a community of modernized, fully equipped cabins with open log fires at $28 per day for up to four people. Guide rates run $20 per day.

FISH RIVER LAKES

This group of eight large connecting lakes is in the Fish River drainage located in Aroostook County. Long Lake in the eastern headwaters has an area of 6,000 acres and a maximum depth of 136 feet. Landlocked salmon were introduced into Long Lake at the turn of the century, and an excellent population has been maintained since. This lake is typical of others in the river system such as Mud, Cross, Square, and Eagle. Besides landlocked salmon the principal gamefish is the brook trout. Although the average salmon runs a bit less than 2 pounds, fish of 5 to 10 pounds are taken each year, particularly in Long and Eagle Lakes; the trout average about a pound but 3- to 5-pound squaretails

are occasional dividends here. Southwest of Eagle Lake lies St. Froid Lake, and farther south is Portage Lake. Fish River Lake is situated to the west of Portage Lake and until recently was inaccessible except by plane, but a woods road now leads into the area. The peak period in the Fish River chain is spring, right after ice-out which usually occurs about the third week in May. The entire region can be fished from **McNally's Camps** (Portage, Maine) which is located on Fish River Lake. Dana McNally, an established operator in this area, has a unique log cabin layout at about $18 per day per person American plan.

Charter aircraft can be arranged for visiting remote waters including the Allagash when guides are available.

ALLAGASH REGION

Maine is wonderful camping country for the angler. There are still some primitive trips to be made on several river systems and notable among these is the Allagash which lies west of the Fish River chain of lakes. This is cheerful water bubbling over beds of pebbles and boulders past pine and shaggy white birches. Until you've savoured a trout chowder and fresh blueberry fritters, or witnessed the marriage of a potato and onion in melted butter on the banks of a wilderness stream, you have left unclaimed the treasures inherent to angling. An ideal canoe trip on the Allagash is from Churchill Lake down to the river's junction with the St. John. There is only one short carry at Allagash Falls. There are good pools at the many tributary brook mouths and the trout will run from 10 to 15 inches with the occasional larger fish. Blackflies are something of a nuisance in late May and June. A beautiful time to be on the river without a bug problem is in early September. To arrange a visit to the Allagash, contact *The State Park & Recreation Commission* (State House, Augusta) and obtain a list of the guides available for the Allagash Wilderness Waterway.

FLORIDA KEYS

To an angler no other portion of the American coast is comparable to the Florida Keys—a 130-mile-long archipelago that stretches like a bared backbone between the Gulf of Mexico and the Atlantic Ocean. Over 300 species of fish roam the pale green and blue sea providing among other specialties the greatest tarpon fishing on the continent, and the *only* bonefishing in the Continental United States. The three main fishing centers in the Keys are Islamorada, Marathon, and Key West. In Islamorada **Cheeca Lodge** has become a platinum sanctuary for tourists looking for supreme comfort without formality. **Cheeca Lodge** offers a variety of quarters including a beach lodge room, $85 a day, a main lodge room, $70-$75 a day, and a poolside room at $50-$60 a day. But for luxurious living a double bedroom suite in a beach cottage with a sweeping view of sand and crystal clear sea is the ultimate. The plan is modified American which adds $10 per day per person for breakfast and dinner. The decor throughout, with a designer's taste for allegory, reflects the lazy beach life beginning with a fish-filled pool underfoot in the lobby entrance to the grass thatched huts facing the sea. The dining rooms are spacious and the bar offers music and dancing after dark. Between engagements with the tarpon you can wile away the hours in freshwater or saltwater swimming pools, on the tennis courts, or a putting green, a driving range, or a private 9 Hole, Par 3 golf course. (Contact: Cheeca Lodge, Islamorada, Florida; Area Code 305 644-4651).

Buccaneer Lodge located at Marathon is another popular resort for anglers who want the best in creature comforts. Sprawled along the shore of Vaca Key the lodge has sixty units including efficiency cottages for two, two-room villas and three-room villas (which includes two bedrooms, two tile baths, a living room, full kitchen and a screened patio facing the water). The prices are eminently fair and vary according to the season—a three room villa for example at $72 per day in the peak December into April period; from April to May it costs $60, and from May to December just $42. But a one bedroom efficiency runs from $18 to a peak season price of $32. **Buccaneer Lodge** operates on a European plan but meals are modestly priced. Dinner is by candlelight and you can dine and dance under the stars. Freshwater and saltwater pools, tennis courts, beach parties and other diversions are available during non-fishing hours. (Contact: Buccaneer Lodge, P.O. Box 428, Marathon, Florida: Area Code 305, 743-5511).

Sugar Loaf Lodge is the best accommodation in the Key West area (17 miles north of town) and it has every facility for the vacationing angler. The lodge has a 3,000-foot landing strip and will also pick up guests at the Key West commercial airport. Rates run from $20 single and $22 double, European Plan. (Contact: Sugar Loaf Lodge, Sugar Loaf Key, Florida: Area Code 305-745-3211)

THE FISHING

Offshore trolling from a 40-foot cruiser for sailfish, king mackerel, dolphin, and the occasional blue marlin is abundantly successful even for the uninitiated. A day's charter costs $90, and as many as four anglers can fish in comfort. You can also explore the "back country" or Gulf side flats. This is done from a large skiff. The basic rig is an 18-foot fiberglass hull with a 6-foot beam. Powered with a 90 hp engine, or a twin equivalent, the boat can barrel along at 25 to 30 knots while drawing a minimum depth of water. Bonefish, barracuda, red drum, ladyfish, mackerel, spotted seatrout, and a variety of other gamefish are abundant in this area at all seasons, but from April through June the lordly tarpon is supreme.

Tarpon can be pursued in various ways but clearly the most challenging form of angling is with the fly rod. The intricate pattern of chan-

Florida

nels and flats that form the Keys are uniquely suited to light tackle fishing because tarpon cannot be sighted easily or played readily in deep water. Here the giant silver acrobats come into the vast shallow banks beginning in April, and until June it is not unusual to see a thousand fish in a day. The actual fishing is accomplished by stalking. The guide either sights a moving school and poles his boat within range or, relying on his knowledge of the banks that tarpon frequent, he will stake out and wait to intercept them. On a glassy morning as hundreds of

WILDERNESS LUXURY

There are occasions when a family vacation takes precedence over a fishing trip in the sense that tennis, golf, water skiing, trap shooting, and other diversions must be available to keep everybody happy. **The Mount Kineo** (Kineo, Maine) is a luxurious resort located on a peninsula in Moosehead Lake. It can only be reached by water. Leave your car at the hotel's garage in Rockwood, not far from Greenville on Route 15. You will be met by the hotel's cabin cruisers for a one-mile voyage to the dock. The location is spectacular. Accommodations, cuisine, and wine list are excellent. Jacket and tie are required at cocktail time and the dinner hour, otherwise informality reigns. The usual fishing is available on Moosehead but the hotel also arranges for float plane trips into wilderness ponds and nearby Lobster Lake and Allagash River. Rates at the hotel and Oak Lodge run $40 to $45 single and $65 to $75 double. There are lower rates for extra persons sharing a room and for other quarters including housekeeping cottages.

KIDNEY POND

The full flavor of an oldtime Maine sporting camp (established 1902) exists 31 miles northwest of Millinocket at **Kidney Pond Lodge** (Millinocket, Maine). No outboard motors are allowed; you either paddle your own canoe or hire a guide. The only device permitted to break the blessed silence is the late Miss Ethel Barrymore's piano located in the lounge. Mrs. Ruth Morris's hostelry is located near Mt. Katahdin in a 200,000-acre sanctuary called Baxter State Park. The lodge can be reached via the park road about 30 miles from Millinocket. Fishing is with the fly *only* in most of eleven nearby ponds which are readily accessible over woods paths. Native brook trout averaging from 10 to 18 inches long are standard fodder for artful casters. An out-camp for guests on the West Branch of the

Penobscot River produces landlocked salmon as well as big brook trout. Wildlife including moose and black bears is abundant in this wilderness preserve. American plan rates at $18 per day per person or $115 per week. Guide fees run $16 per day when needed.

KENNEBAGO LAKES

The Kennebago Lakes are small by Maine standards but fish are plentiful. The Kennebago River runs through a series of ponds into 5-mile-long Big Kennebago Lake which contains brook trout and landlocked salmon. The stream has some excellent pools which are fishable from shore. Fly fishing remains good in this area right into summer with large fly hatches occurring in July and even into August. An 8-pound 15-ounce brook trout was caught at Kennebago in August of 1968. The famous resort here is the **Kennebago Lake Club,** (Rangely, Maine) established in 1872 and operated by Mr. and Mrs. Bud Russel.

The "club" now features a housekeeping plan composed of a community of modernized, fully equipped cabins with open log fires at $28 per day for up to four people. Guide rates run $20 per day.

FISH RIVER LAKES

This group of eight large connecting lakes is in the Fish River drainage located in Aroostook County. Long Lake in the eastern headwaters has an area of 6,000 acres and a maximum depth of 136 feet. Landlocked salmon were introduced into Long Lake at the turn of the century, and an excellent population has been maintained since. This lake is typical of others in the river system such as Mud, Cross, Square, and Eagle. Besides landlocked salmon the principal gamefish is the brook trout. Although the average salmon runs a bit less than 2 pounds, fish of 5 to 10 pounds are taken each year, particularly in Long and Eagle Lakes; the trout average about a pound but 3- to 5-pound squaretails

are occasional dividends here. Southwest of Eagle Lake lies St. Froid Lake, and farther south is Portage Lake. Fish River Lake is situated to the west of Portage Lake and until recently was inaccessible except by plane, but a woods road now leads into the area. The peak period in the Fish River chain is spring, right after ice-out which usually occurs about the third week in May. The entire region can be fished from **McNally's Camps** (Portage, Maine) which is located on Fish River Lake. Dana McNally, an established operator in this area, has a unique log cabin layout at about $18 per day per person American plan.

Charter aircraft can be arranged for visiting remote waters including the Allagash when guides are available.

ALLAGASH REGION

Maine is wonderful camping country for the angler. There are still some primitive trips to be made on several river systems and notable among these is the Allagash which lies west of the Fish River chain of lakes. This is cheerful water bubbling over beds of pebbles and boulders past pine and shaggy white birches. Until you've savoured a trout chowder and fresh blueberry fritters, or witnessed the marriage of a potato and onion in melted butter on the banks of a wilderness stream, you have left unclaimed the treasures inherent to angling. An ideal canoe trip on the Allagash is from Churchill Lake down to the river's junction with the St. John. There is only one short carry at Allagash Falls. There are good pools at the many tributary brook mouths and the trout will run from 10 to 15 inches with the occasional larger fish. Blackflies are something of a nuisance in late May and June. A beautiful time to be on the river without a bug problem is in early September. To arrange a visit to the Allagash, contact *The State Park & Recreation Commission* (State House, Augusta) and obtain a list of the guides available for the Allagash Wilderness Waterway.

FLORIDA KEYS

To an angler no other portion of the American coast is comparable to the Florida Keys—a 130-mile-long archipelago that stretches like a bared backbone between the Gulf of Mexico and the Atlantic Ocean. Over 300 species of fish roam the pale green and blue sea providing among other specialties the greatest tarpon fishing on the continent, and the *only* bonefishing in the Continental United States. The three main fishing centers in the Keys are Islamorada, Marathon, and Key West. In Islamorada **Cheeca Lodge** has become a platinum sanctuary for tourists looking for supreme comfort without formality. **Cheeca Lodge** offers a variety of quarters including a beach lodge room, $85 a day, a main lodge room, $70-$75 a day, and a poolside room at $50-$60 a day. But for luxurious living a double bedroom suite in a beach cottage with a sweeping view of sand and crystal clear sea is the ultimate. The plan is modified American which adds $10 per day per person for breakfast and dinner. The decor throughout, with a designer's taste for allegory, reflects the lazy beach life beginning with a fish-filled pool underfoot in the lobby entrance to the grass thatched huts facing the sea. The dining rooms are spacious and the bar offers music and dancing after dark. Between engagements with the tarpon you can wile away the hours in freshwater or saltwater swimming pools, on the tennis courts, or a putting green, a driving range, or a private 9 Hole, Par 3 golf course. (Contact: Cheeca Lodge, Islamorada, Florida; Area Code 305 644-4651).

Buccaneer Lodge located at Marathon is another popular resort for anglers who want the best in creature comforts. Sprawled along the shore of Vaca Key the lodge has sixty units including efficiency cottages for two, two-room villas and three-room villas (which includes two bedrooms, two tile baths, a living room, full kitchen and a screened patio facing the water). The prices are eminently fair and vary according to the season—a three room villa for example at $72 per day in the peak December into April period; from April to May it costs $60, and from May to December just $42. But a one bedroom efficiency runs from $18 to a peak season price of $32. **Buccaneer Lodge** operates on a European plan but meals are modestly priced. Dinner is by candlelight and you can dine and dance under the stars. Freshwater and saltwater pools, tennis courts, beach parties and other diversions are available during non-fishing hours. (Contact: Buccaneer Lodge, P.O. Box 428, Marathon, Florida: Area Code 305, 743-5511).

Sugar Loaf Lodge is the best accommodation in the Key West area (17 miles north of town) and it has every facility for the vacationing angler. The lodge has a 3,000-foot landing strip and will also pick up guests at the Key West commercial airport. Rates run from $20 single and $22 double, European Plan. (Contact: Sugar Loaf Lodge, Sugar Loaf Key, Florida: Area Code 305-745-3211)

THE FISHING

Offshore trolling from a 40-foot cruiser for sailfish, king mackerel, dolphin, and the occasional blue marlin is abundantly successful even for the uninitiated. A day's charter costs $90, and as many as four anglers can fish in comfort. You can also explore the "back country" or Gulf side flats. This is done from a large skiff. The basic rig is an 18-foot fiberglass hull with a 6-foot beam. Powered with a 90 hp engine, or a twin equivalent, the boat can barrel along at 25 to 30 knots while drawing a minimum depth of water. Bonefish, barracuda, red drum, ladyfish, mackerel, spotted seatrout, and a variety of other gamefish are abundant in this area at all seasons, but from April through June the lordly tarpon is supreme.

Tarpon can be pursued in various ways but clearly the most challenging form of angling is with the fly rod. The intricate pattern of chan-

Florida

nels and flats that form the Keys are uniquely suited to light tackle fishing because tarpon cannot be sighted easily or played readily in deep water. Here the giant silver acrobats come into the vast shallow banks beginning in April, and until June it is not unusual to see a thousand fish in a day. The actual fishing is accomplished by stalking. The guide either sights a moving school and poles his boat within range or, relying on his knowledge of the banks that tarpon frequent, he will stake out and wait to intercept them. On a glassy morning as hundreds of

On the hook, tarpon may leap 10 feet in air. This one is performing in Florida's Shark River

silvery specters appear over the sand bottom, they can appear so awesome that neophytes have been known to "freeze" and let the schools pass without making a cast. A fly rod, even a heavy 9-footer suitable for beating Persian rugs, somehow feels puny at the moment of truth. When hooked, a tarpon may jump ten feet into the air and clear almost twenty feet horizontally; this animated fighting machine with bulldog jaws can be whipped by a skilled angler in less than an hour (40 minutes for a 100-pounder is considered very good time), but each season tarpon in the 150-pound class blast over the sunlit water for six to eight hours before breaking free.

PERMIT IN A PACKAGE
The Atlantic permit, which as a trophy ranks along with bagging Afghanistan's Marco Polo sheep, is also common to the Gulf flats. To be reasonably certain of a successful trip for both tarpon and permit requires an experienced guide, and there are many capable men in the Keys. One of the top guides in years past, George Hommel, is now operating a travel service (*World Wide Sportsman, Inc.*, P.O. Box 46, Islamorada, Florida: Area Code 305, 664-4615) which among countless other angling tours offers an all-inclusive "back country" package covering four days and nights at a top hotel, rental car, guide, boat, and other needs at $326 per person. This is an eminently fair price under expert supervision. The Hommel headquarters contains one of the best stocked tackle shops in Florida where custom crafted gear is a speciality.

Angler Ed Reddy displays spotted seatrout

Air boat fishing, a Florida invention, is ideal way to travel in remote Everglades

Posh Remuda Ranch Grants near Naples on Florida's Tamiami Trail

First permit or last, you never forget any of them because nobody catches enough to become blasé on the subject. Permit fishing differs from the tarpon in that the fish are seen "tailing" as they feed head down on the sand flats. The gleaming caudal lobe of the tail flickers over the surface as the permit grubs for crabs and mollusks in the bottom. Here again, it's a game of stalking your quarry with a guide at the pushpole. A flighty, snubnosed fish ranging from 20 to 40 pounds in weight, the permit is not an aerialist; when hooked it charges over an aquatic obstacle course of sea fans, sponges, and coral heads with the determination of a French cab driver entering the Place de la Concorde. As a rule, the fish has to be followed a half mile or more at breakneck speed before it even slows down. With any luck you will boat a 20-pound permit in thirty or forty minutes.

During the two best months of the year, in February and March, it is possible to sight a hundred permit in a single day. To hook two or three per outing requires some luck and to whip one demands considerable skill. Most guides supply 8-pound-test spinning tackle rigged the way it will do the most service. If fly fishing is your forte—bring a 9-foot saltwater rod with a No. 9 or No. 10 floating line. Trolling tackle and spinning tackle can be supplied by guides throughout the Keys but with a few exceptions the more customized fly tackle is a personal elective. The acrobatic tarpon, bonefish, red drum, barracuda, and the complete list of shallow water gamesters add spice to angling in the Keys back country.

BOCA GRANDE

Boca Grande Pass lying at the entrance of Charlotte Harbor on Gasparilla Island is one of the most famous fishing grounds in the world. Long before Florida became a booming tourist state the *ancien riche* from distant lands made their annual pilgrimage to this aquatic playground in the season known as the "big tides." A June moon may symbolize the transcendent ecstasies depicted in romantic novels but to an angler its gravitational force is

Traditional run of the Palm Beach sailfish fleet at the opening of Master's Tournament

Acrobatic tarpon on the Florida Keys flats
A 41-pound jack crevalle taken on the fly

as compelling as the suicidal march of the lemmings. At its first full phase in our six month the moon reaches a position with relation to sun and earth which causes the water to run swiftly out of Charlotte Harbor through Boca Grande Pass — sweeping with it countless millions of shrimp, crabs, and helpless baitfish into the mouths of waiting tarpon who are massed in silvery legions for their summer invasion of the Gulf Coast.

In the eyes of many experts the tarpon is the most dynamic gamefish in the sea. Those ordinarily caught at Boca Grande range from 40 to 125 pounds. But when 4 to 6 feet of chrome plated violence erupts from the water, the tarpon appears twice its size and the angler is as easily unnerved as the *matador de toros* facing his first bull. But where the *torero* has a pop bottle throwing audience as his alternative, the Boca Grande tarpon angler is surrounded by thirty or forty boats engaged in the same madness. Tourists even watch the fishing with binoculars from the beach. The typical craft, all inboards from 24 to 32 feet in length, work so close together at

times that big tarpon have been known to jump over an innocent boat, and the skill of their captains in maneuvering away from the fleet with a running fish is legendary. Accommodations here are the **Boca Grande Hotel;** the **Gasparilla Inn,** and the **Waterfront Motel.** Rates according to season. Guides get $95 per tide.

THE FISHING

Fishing in the Pass is done by drifting. The Big Hole is some 90 feet deep and the object is to drop a bait, either a sand bream or squirrel-fish, among the tarpon. This makes casting impractical. Although there are plenty of shallow river mouths and lagoons up and down the coast where an artfully worked plug or fly will get results, the Boca Grande regular is essentially a bait fisherman. Of course, the fishing isn't limited solely to the period of the June tides; the season may begin as early as March and last until September or October, but it has its peak from mid-May into early summer. There is a large fleet of charter boats available at Boca Grande and most guides fish two lines which means that a pair of anglers can share the cost.

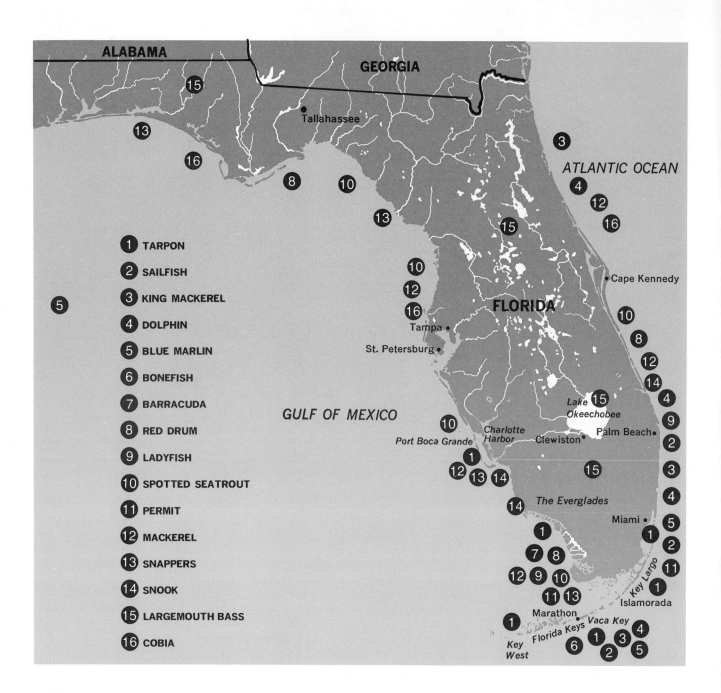

ALABAMA

GEORGIA

• Tallahassee

ATLANTIC OCEAN

FLORIDA

• Cape Kennedy

GULF OF MEXICO

Port Boca Grande

Charlotte Harbor

Lake Okeechobee

Clewiston

Palm Beach •

Tampa •

St. Petersburg •

The Everglades

Miami •

Key Largo

Islamorada

Marathon

Vaca Key

Key West

Florida Keys

1 TARPON

2 SAILFISH

3 KING MACKEREL

4 DOLPHIN

5 BLUE MARLIN

6 BONEFISH

7 BARRACUDA

8 RED DRUM

9 LADYFISH

10 SPOTTED SEATROUT

11 PERMIT

12 MACKEREL

13 SNAPPERS

14 SNOOK

15 LARGEMOUTH BASS

16 COBIA

Even when the tarpon fishing is not "red hot" (and that can happen the world over) there is plenty of sport to be had with spotted seatrout, snappers, snook, redfish, mackerel and many other varieties in nearby bays and channels.

The tarpon is one of the few fishes with the ability to survive in freshwater or saltwater. Unlike salmon, for example, which must become acclimated to a changing environment, tarpon can be abruptly transplanted from seawater to freshwater and back again with no ill effects. Despite the fact that stray tarpon have been caught as far north as Nova Scotia, they prefer warm temperatures and in fact will

die during those rare severe cold spells that hit the Gulf area. Peculiar also to the tarpon is that the fish has a lung-like gas bladder and is frequently seen "rolling" on the surface to take in atmospheric air. Schools of thirty or forty rolling fish commonly surface at Boca Grande —a sight which causes that squirrels-in-the-stomach feeling peculiar to tarpon fishermen.

FOR WOMEN ONLY

One of the things that creates the mystique of tarpon fishing is the fact that the fish is conserved not by law, but human consideration. Tarpon have no real food value and except

for the occasional trophy, few anglers ever kill one. The peculiar fascination of the sport may be explained as the nobility the tarpon inspires in man—or for that matter woman. The International Women's Fishing Association has held nine tournaments in the Pass and to prove that the hand that rocks the cradle has a calloused thumb—thirty competing members of the IWFA released 168 fish in one three-day vendetta. The winner boated a 150-pounder. This annual IWFA tournament attracts women anglers from all over the country. So the tarpon seems to have been created especially for fun-and-game. At the very least it's a sure cure for insomnia.

NIGHT FISHING

The tarpon possesses an unusually large eye which reflects its predilection for feeding at night. Anglers, of course, have never been known to miss an opportunity and thus a coterie of nocturnal specialists drift the Pass after dark. The ghostly leap and resounding crash of a moonlit tarpon is compelling, even frightening, and newcomers have been known to go around the clock in what neutral observers must view as the craziest art form since turtle painting. In an attempt to set some kind of record, a man once drifted the Pass for forty-eight hours and while his score was unimpressive (due to frequently falling asleep on the second day) he became what one critic said of the patron saint of angling, Izaac Walton, "not so much unrivaled as absolutely alone."

PALM BEACH

Palm Beach is the hub of Florida's sailfish sector, which extends roughly from Stuart to the Keys, and while allegiances vary, it is here that the annual Invitational Masters Angling Tournament takes place each January 5 to 10 with fifty of the world's most talented anglers afloat. There are more fishing boats, both private and charter craft in these waters than in any comparable area of the United States.

Some idea of the quality of the fishing off Palm Beach is relected in the fact that around 185 to 195 sailfish are caught and released during the contest period. However, more than a thousand sails are boated by visitors and these vie for honors in the Silver Sailfish Derby, which is open to the public and runs through the winter season. Palm Beach is also headquarters for the International Women's Fishing Association, which sponsors several tournaments for lady anglers. In effect, the tide marks of Palm Beach's society are the windrows of sargassum weed drifting with the Great Blue Stream.

Tourists can charter boats at the *West Palm Beach City Docks* (just across the Royal Poinciana Bridge) or at the *Sailfish Center* on Palm Beach Shores. All the major hotels (the **Colony,** the **Breakers, Palm Beach Towers,** and the **Biltmore**) are within minutes of the fleet. Palm

Beach offers more diverse facilities than Stuart, but the latter is uniquely an angling town with excellent family-style accommodations at the **Port St. Lucie Country Club** and **Villas.**

Due to the proximity of the Gulf Stream to Florida's coast in the Sailfish Sector, the fishing hours begin almost immediately after you leave the inlet at eight a.m. and continue to a reasonable period after four p.m., allowing sufficient time for your skipper to make port before dark.

The club's two 18-hole golf courses, the PGA-famous Saints and Sinners —plus skeet shooting, tennis, sailboating, horseback riding, and guided hunting tours are among its many assets. Port St. Lucie's one- to three-bedroom villas are modestly priced and few resorts can match the cuisine and wine list found in its $600,000 clubhouse, which is a short drive from the Stuart docks.

The standard rate for a day is from $100 to $125 depending on the crew and type of equipment offered. Many tourists fish on "make-up" charters in which the cost is prorated with other anglers who want to share a boat. All craft can comfortably fish two people at a time, and as many as four if, for example, two couples want to split costs. Make-up parties are arranged with the skipper, and for information on charters you can call the West Palm Beach Fishing Club after you arrive.

Trolling and drift-fishing are the principal techniques for catching sailfish. Instruction and the correct tackle are supplied by the charter boat. Your chances of raising at least one sailfish per trip are good, and ordinarily you will get several strikes on an average day. During peak periods, notably in January when the fish are schooling, and later in February, catches of five to ten sailfish per boat are not unusual, and a few experts have billed as many as thirty in one day. The fish run 6 to 8½ feet long and weigh 35 to 90 pounds. Sailfish are strong light-tackle fish (12-pound-test) but are no less acrobatic or powerful against the 20-pound and 30-pound lines spooled by most charter skippers. On occasion both white and blue marlin come to sailfish baits in this area.

Beautiful largemouth bass was fished from waters in Florida

The Ten Thousand Islands are a complex of creeks and bays bordering the Everglades. Light-tackle fishing is exceptional

Everglades National Park (1,400,533 acres) encompasses most of Florida's Ten Thousand Island region plus a vast area of creeks and hammocks which is one of the most unique attractions in North America. Bordering the Gulf of Mexico, this mangrove-dominated estuarine habitat holds vast populations of tarpon, snook, red drum, mangrove snapper, spotted seatrout, and numerous other light-tackle gamefish. Spring and fall are the best fishing seasons; winter can be good if there are no northerly blows, while summer angling is limited by normally heavy rains. Navigational charts are necessary if you travel without a guide in this complex of meandering waterways.

At the north end of the Park and situated in the Ten Thousand Islands is **Remuda Ranch** (Box 188, Goodland, Florida: Area Code 813 394-3101). This above-average sportsman's resort is reached from Miami on U.S. 41 (78 miles) or from other east coast cities via Alligator Alley. A 200-room "spread," the ranch offers everything from sauna baths to skeet-and-trap shooting in a Spanish decor. Boats and guides are available as are launching ramps if you trailer your own craft. Guides get $65 per day for a roomy 19-foot skiff suitable for two casters. Rooms run $12 to $16 per day single, and $14 to $18 per day double, European Plan according to season. Meals at nominal prices. A 2,500-foot strip for light aircraft on property.

In Everglades City proper is the newly refurbished **Rod and Gun Lodge** (Everglades City, Florida: Area Code 813 695-2101). Built about fifty years ago, the lodge is something of a local landmark. Rates here run $26 per day single, and $32 per day double, European Plan. It offers a screened pool and 42 air-conditioned rooms. Guides with skiffs available.

At the south end of the Park on Florida Bay and 39 miles in from the main gate is **Flamingo Lodge** (Everglades Park Company Inc., 3660 Coral Way, Miami, Florida: or call direct, Area Code 813 (695-3101). The lodge offers 120 motel-type air-conditioned units. Rates are $20 per day single, and $22 per day double, European Plan. Large dining room offers meals at nominal prices. Outboard skiffs rent for $15 per day with 10 hp. motors. Guides available at $48 per day. Slips and launching ramps for transient boats.

Hawaii

When the average mainlander thinks of Hawaii, his impressions of the 50th State are geographically confined to the Island of Oahu. It brings to mind Honolulu, super-markets, Waikiki Beach, Diamond Head, and hula-girls in a kind of Miami *cum* pineapples. But the Hawaiian archipelago is composed of eight islands with a total area of 6,435 square miles, and once you leave Oahu, the picture is quite different. Almost half of the island's population lives within ukulele range of Honolulu and just across the water along the Kona coast cruise some of the biggest Pacific blue marlin in the world. The clouds which curdle and thicken behind Kailua at noon are like a giant umbrella—so pre-

dictable that the only coffee plantations in Hawaii exist on those slopes. Yet, against the gloomy backdrop, schools of flyingfish zip across the sea like silver bullets in the sun. There is an even greater sense of perspective when Mauna Loa suddenly pokes out of the clouds, sleeping for the moment, but still one of the world's most active volcanoes. The ocean is not silent for long, however. Sometimes the sapphire water is shattered by acres of bonito and screaming birds, then it erupts behind the boat as a pair of *mahi-mahi* slam the dancing baits.

THE SEASON

There is no distinctly wet or dry season, but rather a climatic division between the windward and the leeward sides of the islands. Prevailing northeast trades spill their moisture against the peaks, and the annual rainfall in different locations varies in the extreme. Some leeward areas get no more than 2 to 3 inches of rain annually, while windward slopes such as Waialeale on Kauai are bucketed under 400 inches. Occasionally, a "Kona" or southerly wind brings muggy weather and heavy rains to the lowlands, but in general the climate is civilized and you can wear an Aloha shirt with

comfort. Although the wind is called Kona because of its direction in relation to the other islands, the Kona coast can be a millpond.

OFFSHORE FISHING

Saltwater fishing is of prime interest in the 50th State. In general, most of the common species of gamefish can be found almost anywhere in the Hawaiian chain, depending on the individual topography of the bay, channel, or bank. Fishing off the north and northeast sides of all islands tends to be good most of the time. However, the seas, driven by the prevailing trade winds, are often rough. The best plan is to make arrangements locally with charter-boat skippers who are familiar with the immediate fishing and weather conditions.

The most popular big-game fishing grounds are out of Honolulu on Oahu Island and at Kailua-Kona on the big island of Hawaii. The boats out of Honolulu range over the Molokai Channel to just offshore of Molokai and Lanai islands, or along leeward Oahu to Kaena Point. Marlin have been caught within one mile of the harbor. The Waianae grounds, off the lee coast of Oahu, can also be reached out of Honolulu's Kewalo Basin. A 30-fathom shoal (Penguin Bank), southwest of Molokai, is also reached by boat from Honolulu. The lee shore of Kauai in the Kaukahi Channel is another productive spot for trolling. The Kona coast of the island of Hawaii is the state's prime marlin ground.

Smooth seas and the possibility of record marlin make it a favorite. Too far away for a one-day boat trip from Honolulu and back, it is reached by plane either directly from Honolulu or by way of Hilo. The *Hawaiian International Billfish Tournament* is held in Kona waters early each summer (the 13th Annual will be held in 1971). There's no long run to reach the productive locations, as marlin are jumped within two miles of shore and instead of an endless

A greyhounding striped marlin comes back to the boat. Billfish are big attraction

Lare Point on Oahu is a favorite among "ulua" anglers who take these jacks in the surf

ocean you can survey at leisure the ever-changing panorama of the mountains.

The principal big-game species in Hawaiian waters are the Pacific blue marlin, striped marlin, yellowfin tuna, wahoo, and dolphin. Marlin are present all year round although the fishing peaks from late June through to November. You may be lucky and go out for one afternoon and boat a 700-pounder, or you may troll for several days and never see a bill. But the area offers an opportunity to get hooked up with some immense blues. Fish over 1,000 pounds have been caught off the Kona coast. Artificial lures known as knuckleheads which consist of a large-diameter plastic tubing with a squid-simulating skirt attached are the most popular baits for marlin as well as other gamefish. Dolphin also average a large size and the local record is close to 70 pounds. Yellowfin tuna are caught here in record sizes and are most common in the summer season.

CHARTER BOATS
Hawaiian charter boats are in general well equipped. Tackle and bait are included in a full charter. Food and drink are supplied by the fisherman, but ice and galley services are available. Some boats run on a per-person basis (split charter) if a full boatload is not available. However, prevacation correspondence is recommended to insure space at the exact time preferred. Hawaiian islanders are avid fishermen, and an unexpected run of any of the big gamefish quickly draws enthusiasts away from their offices and down to the docks for impromptu trips.

CONTACTS
For offshore fishing from the island of Oahu the fleet is located at Honolulu's Kewalo Basin which is five to ten minutes from downtown hotels. Rates here run from $95 to $125 for a full day charter depending on the size of the boat and equipment; half-day charters are $65 to $75. For bookings or information contact: *Island Charters, Sport Fishing Hawaii,* or *Deep Sea Fishing of Hawaii* all at Kewalo Basin.

For Kona coast fishing on the big island of Hawaii rates run a bit higher at $125 to $150 for a full day charter

Cast-net fishing for "uouoa," or mullet

and $75 to $90 for the half day. To make bookings contact the *Kona Charter Skippers Association* (P.O. Box 806, Kailua-Kona, Hawaii 96740), or the *Kona Inn* (Kona Inn, Kailua-Kona, Hawaii 96740). The demand here is considerable so inquire well in advance.

On Maui charter boats base at the old whaling port of Lahaina. Rates here run from $100 to $125 for a full day charter and $75 for a half day. There is no skippers association on Maui but charters can be arranged through your hotel.

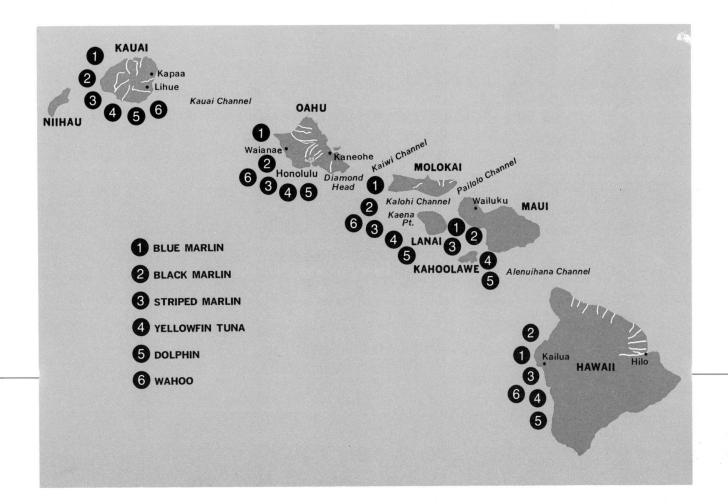

KAUAI
Kapaa
Lihue
Kauai Channel
NIIHAU

OAHU
Waianae
Kaneohe
Kaiwi Channel
Honolulu
Diamond Head
MOLOKAI
Kalohi Channel
Wailuku
Kaena Pt.
MAUI
LANAI
KAHOOLAWE
Alenuihana Channel
Pailolo Channel

1 BLUE MARLIN

2 BLACK MARLIN

3 STRIPED MARLIN

4 YELLOWFIN TUNA

5 DOLPHIN

6 WAHOO

Kailua
HAWAII
Hilo

On the island of Kaui there are several charter boat bases. Generally speaking, the rates run from $90 to $125 for a full day and $65 to $75 for a half day. At Hanalei contact *Hanalei Plantation Hotel* or write to Capt. Henry Gomez (P.O. Box 7, Hanalei, Kauai, Hawaii 96714). For Port Allen contact *Sport Fishing Kaui* (P.O. Box 302, Waimeax, Kaui, Hawaii 96796). At Nawiliwili Harbor contact the *Kaui Surf Hotel* or *Aloha Kai Sportfishing* (Box 322-P, Kapaa, Kaui, Hawaii 96746).

INSHORE FISHING
The light-tackle spinning and fly-rod caster will not find the same potential sport as the big-game man. The most common species of tropical Pacific reef fish are almost entirely absent from local waters. Why there is a gap between small and large carnivorous fishes is not known.

The inshore fauna of islands from Tahiti to Japan contains approximately forty different species of groupers and snappers; yet these reef dwellers do not frequent Hawaii. Bonefish (locally o'io) are not absent, however; the islands have produced several world's records, including a former 18-pound 2-ounce all-tackle record taken in Kauai. But here again mainland bonefish anglers may be disappointed, as there are few flats in the Florida sense of the game and no fly-fishing. Most of the coastline drops from volcanic rock cliffs to coral shelves and into deep water. Where beaches exist, they are subjected to running surfs. Bonefish are caught chiefly by bottom-fishing with live bait in the sand holes between reefs at 20- to 25-foot depths. They often come as a dividend to anglers seeking the ulua (jacks).

FRESHWATER FISHING
Freshwater species have been introduced into Hawaii in recent years, and have become fairly well established although the fishing is not significant. Regulations and information are available from the State of Hawaii, Division of Fish and Game, Department of Land and Natural Resources in Honolulu.

Rainbow trout have been planted in the mountain streams of Kokee, on the island of Kauai. The season generally opens the first Saturday of August, and for 16 days continuous fishing is permitted; thereafter, fishing is permitted only on week ends and state holidays in the remainder of August and in September. The limit is 10 fish per day, and the minimum size is 6 inches.

The season on largemouth and smallmouth bass is open all year.

Netherlands visitor Glenn Reece took his marlin at Kona after hour battle

Despite the chrome *cum* pineapple atmosphere of Honolulu, native Hawaiians in the out-islands still pursue an ancient method in spear fishing by torchlight

These can be found in streams, estuaries, and reservoirs on Oahu, Kauai, Hawaii, and Maui.

TRAVEL NOTES

Hawaii is reached non-stop via Pan Am's new 747 Clipper from Los Angeles or San Francisco, or via 707 from Seattle or Portland. All islands have daily service from and to Honolulu via Hawaiian and Aloha Airlines.

LANGUAGE

English with many Hawaiian words or phrases which are easy to learn. Newcomers are called Malihinis; old timers, Kamaainas; and warm friends, Aikanes. Aloha, of course, is the traditional expression of greeting or farewell.

ACCOMMODATIONS

OAHU

The **Royal Hawaiian** (Sheraton) on Waikiki Beach, the best-known hotel in the Islands, has everything; rates about $25 to $37 double European plan. The **Halekulani,** also on the beach, is quiet and pleasant; $18 to $24 double. Other good hotels on Waikiki, all European Plan, (with

Best marlin season is from July to November, with peak in August

double rates quoted), include the **Moana,** $15 to $21; the huge **Hilton Hawaiian Village** with cottages and hotel rooms from $19 to $37; the **Reef,** $14 to $24 and the **Surfrider,** $18 to $29. There are a number of newer hotels: the **Kahala Hilton,** overlooking Waialae Golf Club, $28 to $45; the **Colony Surf,** $25 to $30; the **Princess Kaiulani,** $15 to $22; the stunning new **Ilikai,** $22 to $30; and the lovely **Waikikian,** with its authentic Polynesian atmosphere, $16 to $28. There are also many small hotels and apartment hotels which are available by the day, week or month. Rates given apply the year around; make reservations in advance.

HAWAII

The "Big Island" and major game-fishing area located on the Kona coast. Popular hotels include the **Kona Inn, Waiaka Lodge, Hotel King Kamehameha, Kona Hukilau, Kona Palms** are here, and the elegant **Mauna Kea Beach Hotel** is not far away. This island, three times larger than all others combined, offers greater scenic variety and more striking contrasts than any others of the group. Here you can see lava flows, the chain of craters, and fern tree forests in Hawaii Volcanoes National Park. And from the palm-treed shores of Hilo Bay, you can see far-reaching fields of sugar cane topped by lofty, snow-capped peaks of Mauna Kea and Mauna Loa.

MAUI

Among the island's luxury hotels, are the **Hana-Maui, Sheraton-Maui, Kaanapali Maui Hilton,** and **Royal Lahaina Beach Hotel,** $48 to $66 double American plan. More moderately priced is the very good **Maui Palms Hotel** in Wailuku. **Napili Kai Beach Club** has very nice studios with kitchens for $21.50 double. The **Hale Napili** is also popular. The eastern half of this exquisite island is a massive volcanic peak with a huge crater 20 miles wide. West Maui's attractions include Iao Valley and its much-photographed Needle, the historic whaling town of Lahaina, and the new Kaanapali resort area with superb beaches and championship golf course. While on Maui, try to see a Hukilau, or community fishing party, at Hana.

KAUAI

Called the Garden Island because of its foliage. The **Coco Palms Hotel** and **Kauai Surf Hotel** at Lihue are modern and excellent. They have everything from swimming pools to Saturday-night hula shows. The **Waiohai** is more restful. Less expensive are the **Seven Seas** and **Prince Kuhio.** This is an island where you will do well to hire a U-Drive car or a private car, for you will have more fun and see more that way. Hanalei on Kauai is one of the finest beaches on the islands; the luxurious **Hanalei Plantation Hotel** overlooks this idyllic South Pacific seascape. Capt. Henry Gomez operates from the hotel's dock both for offshore trolling and bonefish. Near the mouth of the Wailua River is the **Coco Palms Hotel.**

MOLOKAI

This island is still not over-developed. There are ranches, pineapple plantations and ancient temples. Wild deer roam part of the island. Hotels here are the **Puu-o-Hoku Lodge** and the **Molokai Hotel.** Boats from Honolulu and Lahaina fish the Penguin Bank located off Molokai's southwest shore.

Pacific Salmon

European anglers visiting western North America are usually puzzled by the Pacific salmon which presently only occur in the Barents Sea of Russia where they have been stocked since 1956. The two species used in the Soviet experiments (the chum and the pink salmon) are commercially important but of minor sport interest. There is some similarity between angling for Pacific salmon and angling for Atlantic salmon insofar as two other species are concerned, the coho and the chinook; however, geography and season play an important role in the methods used.

The six species of Pacific salmon are in a separate genus (*Onchorhynchus*) from the Atlantic salmon and are thought to be the least primitive of the salmonine fishes. Five species occur in North American waters—the chinook (*O. tshawytscha*), coho (*O. kisutch*), sockeye (*O. nerka*), pink (*O. gorbuscha*), and the chum salmon (*O. keta*). The sixth species is the cherry salmon (*O. masou*), which occurs only in Asia. The genus has a range from Formosa to San Diego, California. All six species spawn in freshwater in gravel from June (chinooks in Siberia) to February (coho in Oregon) and die shortly thereafter. The young (alevins) remain in the gravel until the large yolk-sac is wholly or almost absorbed and then emerge to go to the ocean immediately as with the chum and pink or remain in freshwater for 3-4 months, as does the fall chinook, or for a year or more, as with coho, spring chinook,

and sockeye. The kokanee or resident sockeye spends its entire life in freshwater. The ocean life is varied, from 2 years with pinks and cohos to 7 or 8 years with some sockeyes. Most of the species and races probably feed in the north Pacific and the Gulf of Alaska. As the fish mature and reach spawning time, their silvery appearance with blue backs and some spotting changes to shades of red, yellow or black, dependent on the species and sex and the males develop a hook (kype) on the tip of the lower or both jaws.

MIGRATIONS

The chinook, sockeye, and chum salmon from North America travel great distances to reach their ocean feeding areas. Chinooks from the Columbia River have been known to travel 2,500 miles to the Aleutians. Sockeyes swim over halfway to Asia from British Columbia. Chums from southeastern Alaska journey to the Aleutians. Pink salmon from southeastern Alaska cross the Gulf of Alaska. The coho from Oregon and Washington is not given to extensive migration. They are caught in the ocean by commercial fishing fleets from Northern California into British Columbia. Some of the northern stocks of the species travel into the Gulf of Alaska.

There is considerable intermingling between populations of widely different origins while at sea. Chum salmon, for example, tagged within a relatively small area of the Gulf of Alaska, provided returns from Japan, the USSR and as far south as

the state of Washington, which is practically the entire geographical range of the species.

Comparatively little is known of the vertical distribution of Pacific salmon while in the ocean. On the basis of echo sounding experiments by Japanese researchers in the Aleutian region, it was observed that salmon were closest to the surface after sunset and descended after daylight. The concentrations of fish shifted in relation to the depth of the thermocline. Canadian researchers found that sockeye and chum salmon exhibit differences in behavior toward the thermocline; this cold layer of water appears to act as a barrier through which the sockeye will not pass either during the night or day, whereas the chum salmon found the thermocline a barrier only during hours of darkness in the late season.

Salmon which survive to maturity in the open ocean return with a high degree of constancy to the freshwater rivers of their origin. This phenomenon has been the subject of extensive research to isolate the homing mechanism. The well-ordered direction and timing of the shoreward migrations from the high seas are relatively rapid journeys which do not appear to be oriented by currents, temperatures, or salinities. It has been suggested that the detection of odors of certain rivers near coastal localities is the homing mechanism but this does not explain orientation in migration and would require strict adherence to a shoreline after making a blind landfall. It is known that salmon can maintain widely divergent courses while hundreds of miles at sea and arrive at a coastal locality, converging with a high degree of precision at their place of origin. Salmon also show a keen awareness of changes in light intensity and length of day which suggests that ocean life is an integrated whole involving the seaward migration of young, seasonal movements and exploitation of the environment during the ocean years before returning to the river.

CHINOOK SALMON

The chinook salmon, also called king salmon and tyee, is the largest of the Pacific salmon. Although the average catch is close to 18 pounds, it has been recorded to a weight of 126 pounds (Alaska). There are several races, distinguishable by the time of river entrance which varies from January to late fall. The fish are thus termed spring, summer, or fall chinook. The chinook salmon often travels great distances from the sea, as much as 2,000 miles in the Yukon, and seems to prefer large rivers. It spawns in June to November of each year. In the Columbia River the spring race has little tendency to spawn in the main river, entering side streams from near the mouth to the headwaters. The fall fish spawned almost entirely in the main-river system, but the advent of multiple dams has created slackwater, eliminating most of the available spawning area. The race is rapidly declining in the river system.

The species matures at 1 (males only) to 8 years of age. The 1-year-old mature males become ripe before going to saltwater, and some, at least, recover to reach saltwater and return. The young chinook emerge from the gravel and may go to the sea immediately; others may not migrate for a considerable period. As a rule, the fall chinook goes to sea at 3 to 4 months of age while the spring chinook usually remains in freshwater for approximately eighteen months. At spawning time the fish is less emaciated than other species of Pacific salmon, and especially is this so of the female which may be plump and clean five hundred miles from the sea. The male gets progressively blacker with the passage of time spent in the spawning area while the female may take on a rich brassy color.

Chinook salmon can be caught by many methods, but they are most commonly taken by trolling. The standard tackle consists of a conventional trolling rod or boat rod, with a star-drag reel and 20- to 45-pound-test line; a saltwater spinning rod 6½ to 7½ feet in length may also be used with a sturdy reel. The line capacity in either case should not be less than 150 yards. Dacron, nylon, and monofilament are popular line materials, but many anglers prefer wire (.016- to .024-inch diameter); wire lines should be spooled on oversize-frame reels made for that purpose.

Salmon trolling is practiced in the ocean near shore, in large protected straits or sounds, or in river estuaries. Ordinarily, more fish over a longer period will be taken in the ocean, but there are local exceptions. Ocean trolling can be done with large plugs or spoons, but these are not as popular as bait. Nearly all Pacific salmon are taken on herring, anchovy, candlefish, or, when available, the Pacific sardine. The herring or other baitfish must be presented to the salmon in a particular way, dependent upon the method of bait attachment or use. In trolling, two hooks are ordinarily used. They are small, about No. 2/0, the upper one being free to slide on the line but not so free as to lose the position at which it may be set. Usually both hooks pass through the snout and down through the "chin," the upper hook remaining in that position and the other passed through and inserted near the tail in such a manner as to bend the body of the herring slightly. The bend will cause the fish to gyrate slowly as the lure is trolled if the hooks are properly positioned.

Locating the fish can sometimes be difficult. Often the success of other anglers can be noted. Birds may work on small fish at the surface to give an indication of the possible presence of salmon nearby. The surfacing, feeding fish may be obvious. There may be a traditional trolling "slot" that seems to have fish in it consistently. The mouths of rivers are usually most productive. Tiderips are also favored fishing spots. They are easily located by the floating eelgrass or other debris which strings out in a narrow line over the surface. Sometimes a rip is marked by foam on the surface. Under the worst conditions the angler may have to prospect for fish with no signs to offer help, and this may be particularly true of chinook which are deep-running. The time of day can be significant. The early angler who is on the water at daybreak will usually be the most successful in taking salmon.

A typical salmon troller on Lake Michigan. Heavy seas are not unusual in Great Lakes

Michigan angler Bing McClellan displays a nice coho taken near Traverse City. Both coho and chinook are abundant in Lake Michigan. Deep trolling is the rule here although the fish school near surface in spring migrations and in autumn

COHO SALMON

The coho salmon is found from California to Japan. It has also been widely introduced to large inland freshwater lakes such as the Great Lakes, and in New England rivers tributary to the Atlantic coast of the U.S. Unlike the chinook salmon which undertakes long migrations, the coho salmon ranges in a more confined area with populations from one state overlapping into adjacent states. The coho originating in northern California contribute primarily to the fisheries of that state, but also range as far north as Washington. Populations in Oregon streams range from northern Van-

couver Island to northern California. Cohos from British Columbia streams mainly concentrate offshore north of Vancouver Island, but these are mixed with salmon from the rivers of Washington. Cohos from Washington rivers travel as far north as the Queen Charlotte Islands and south to northern California. Populations originating in Alaska are predominantly local in movement and contribute principally to the Alaskan fishery.

Coho spawn in gravel in the headwaters or near the sea in streams, usually entering coastal rivers beginning in July and spawning from October to February. The spawning

is completed by the end of December. Most young fish migrate to the sea when a year old, but some may go earlier or wait until the third year. Maturity is usually reached at 3 years of age, but some of the males and a few females mature at 2 years and a few come into the river in the fourth year. Their food consists of fishes, squid, and crustaceans.

Coho fishing is an exciting game. These salmon are strong, fast running, and acrobatic when caught in saltwater. The coho fights on the surface, sometimes making six or eight jumps one after the other; it will run directly at the boat, then turn away with electric speed. A bright coho has all the steam of a summer steelhead or an Atlantic salmon. Coho feed heavily in their short life span. In British Columbia waters the average fish weighs from 10 to 15 pounds at the end of its three years. There have been some 4-year olds recorded, and one 5-year old, which is the world's record (31 pounds), taken at Cowichan Bay. But it doesn't matter whether the fish are just average or big—when coho are raiding the kelp beds gulping herring and candlefish, the sight of a rolling school is a heart stopper. Three- to four-inch-long polar bear hair streamers in patterns such as the Coronation, Howell's Coho Fly, and the Candlefish on hook sizes from 2/0 to 4/0 with either 3X or 4X long shanks are typical attractors. The reason for the long shank hook is to keep the wing length at a point just slightly beyond the barb. This prevents it from twisting under the shank when casting and eliminates short strikes. For trolling flies, straight eyed hooks are preferred and some tyers add a trailer hook secured with a piece of nylon. Big coho have sharp teeth and it's important to dress the fly with durability in mind—tying a tight wing and lacquering the head and body thoroughly. Coho flies are mainly three-color wing streamers; in the blue, white, and red Coronation, for example, the blue or overwing represents the back of a herring

Chum salmon is sporadic lure taker but valuable for red "caviar"

while the center or median line is suggested by a strip of red hair and the white portion or underwing over the silver tinsel body suggests a herring's belly. The addition of a small spinner at the head of the streamer greatly enhances its fish appeal. No weights are used; the lure is tied directly to the leader or line.

Anglers who specialize in trolling, and there's no denying that it's the most productive technique even with flies, use a variety of equipment such as a spinning outfit with 300 yards of 8- to 10-pound-test monofilament line, a standard 9-foot fly rod and reel (spooled with mono instead of a tapered line) and even conventional bait-casting gear. For surface trolling, monofilament has a lot less drag in the water than a fly line and at times some coho experts troll so fast in the wake of a motor that the streamer fly skims over the top. Always circling ahead of the

salmon school the troller jinks around in a zig-zag course presenting the fly in the manner of a panic-stricken candlefish. It's also possible to cast to them when coho are visible. It is no different from casting to a rising trout with the exception that the fly has to be retrieved at a quick pace. Often you'll see a coho following the streamer and usually a couple of hard pulls on the line will induce a strike. So for the most fun bring along two outfits; you can rig one fly rod or spinning rod for monofilament trolling and the other fly rod with a GBF for casting.

After the coho move into a river, the bear hair streamer loses its effectiveness. Here the smaller Atlantic salmon and steelhead wet patterns can be used with some success as can a variety of casting lures, particularly wobblers and spinners. As spawning time nears, coho become very fussy and the rule then, for whatever generalizations are worth,

is to use slow, deep retrieves when stream casting. Some of the best coastal anglers let their lures "hang" for two or three minutes in the same spot. There's no doubt that coho display a decided interest in being caught after getting a long, teasing look at the feathers or hardware. This is generally achieved by maneuvering yourself in such a position that you have the current to work with—by standing upstream from the holding water and drifting your lure into it—rather than casting from a position in which the lure passes over the fish quickly. Of course, highly water-resisting baits such as the Flatfish plug are ideal for this kind of angling.

SOCKEYE SALMON
The sockeye salmon is found from Japan to California, but appears south of the Columbia River only as a stray. It enters rivers, usually those that are fed by lakes, in March to July with some variation in time. A few spawn in streams without lakes. Spawning takes place in lakes or immediately adjacent in inlet or outlet streams from August to December. Most of the adults are 4 to 6 years old, but some reach 8 years of age. The young spend 1 to 3 years in lakes, migrating to the ocean in

Pink salmon *(right)*, readily caught in some rivers but not at all in others

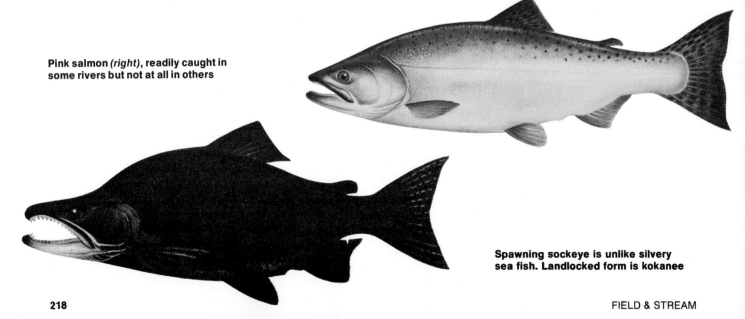

Spawning sockeye is unlike silvery sea fish. Landlocked form is kokanee

March to May. Some fish enter the sea as fry. Non-migratory races are known as kokanee and are widely popular among sportsmen because they are often abundant, easy to catch, and delicious to eat. Some sockeyes of sea-run stock have been known to live their whole lives in freshwater. Vast numbers of fish utilize a relatively small area in spawning. For example, the optimal number of fish utilizing the outlet of Chilko Lake in British Columbia is 500,000 over a 3¾-mile reach of the stream, covering 269 acres or roughly 2 square yards per fish.

Food of the sockeye in the ocean consists of Euphausiids and other small crustaceans. As kokanee the species subsists largely on water fleas and copepods. Its weight at maturity is 5 to 7 pounds and the maximal weight recorded is 15½ pounds. The kokanee has a wide range in length at maturity, dependent upon freshwater food supplies, varying from 4 to 24 inches.

PINK SALMON

The pink, or humpback salmon is the smallest member of the family found along North American shores. It usually weighs 3 to 5 pounds at maturity, reaching 10 at maximum. The size varies with the abundance of year and classes. It is recognized by the large, oval, black blotches on the caudal fin, and its small scales. The young pinks have no parr marks.

The fish reaches maturity in two years. At that time males develop a large hump on the back in addition to a hooked snout. Spawning takes place in September and November in freshwater, usually near the sea, but a few races migrate several hundred miles. They enter the river as early as July. The timing of runs varies widely from odd to even years to disproportionate numbers between years or to more or less even numbers between years. Its food con-

Dog salmon is one of the many different kinds of fish to be found in Alaska. This one was caught in wild country to north of the lower 48

sists largely of crustaceans but sometimes includes fish and squid.

CHUM SALMON

The chum salmon is distinguished by having no large black spots on fins or body, a slender caudal peduncle, black-tinged fins (except dorsal), dark bars or streaks on body at or near spawning time.

Runs of chums are marked by wide yearly fluctuation in numbers. It matures at 4 to 5 years of age. In part of its range it is represented by two forms, a summer and a fall fish. The summer fish enters the river earlier, reaches maturity earlier, is smaller, and does not travel up the river as

far. Entrance to the river takes place from July to December.

Though the species is usually given to spawning in the lower reaches of rivers, it is to be found near the head of the Yukon River in Teslin Lake, which is approximately two thousand miles from the sea. It spawns in November and December. The egg of the chum is large, approaching 5/16 inch. Its range is from northern California to Korea and Japan. Its food consists largely of fish and crustaceans. Only rarely is it ever taken by the sport fisherman. It is third in value of Pacific salmons, exceeded by the sockeye and pink. The chum reaches a weight of 33 pounds but is usually taken in sizes from 8 to 18 pounds.

Rocky Mountain Trout Fishing

Perhaps the best inland trout fishing found in the United States today exists in the Rocky Mountain region. Whether you stay on a dude ranch or in a hotel or motel, no visit is complete without making a wilderness pack and at least one float trip on a major trout stream. In the old days when Wyoming was still part of Oregon Country (adjoining the Mexican Territory), professional *tourists* like Jim Bridger and Kit Carson would rendezvous with the Utes, Nez Perces, and Shoshones along the banks of the Green River to swap trade goods and whiskey for beaver pelts. The next travel stimulus was to the northwest corner of the state with the creation of Yellowstone Park in 1872—which remains one of the garden spots of the world. Today hundreds of thousands of people visit the Park each summer just to gawk at the tilted landscape and its wilderness attractions such as smelly geysers, roadside bears, nearsighted moose, and tumbling

waterfalls. The traffic jam at summer's peak can be staggering. However, there are miles of unsullied country in all directions just off the highway. If you have to see Old Faithful, Mt. Moran, the Gertrude Vanderbilt Whitney Gallery of Western Art, and the Buffalo Bill Museum, charter a small plane and fly over Jackson Lake for a closeup look at the whole Teton range, then over Yellowstone where you can see all the geysers puffing before heading for Cody to visit the very worthwhile museums. Staying in two or three places in your allotted holiday time is infinitely more rewarding. One does not casually catch a trophy golden trout in a quick visit. So whether you allow three weeks or three months for a Western Roundup, it should be staged to include an exotic ranch, such as the **A-Bar-A,** a family table ranch with the extraneous furbelows but with a comfortable as an old shoe atmosphere such as the **Circle S,** then, depending on

The dude ranch has become an American institution. Many vacationists combine western outdoor living with their fishing

221

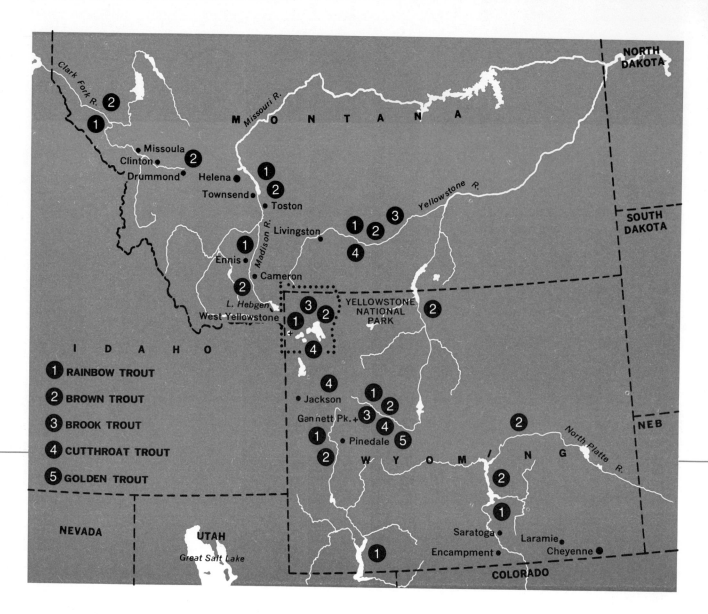

1 RAINBOW TROUT

2 BROWN TROUT

3 BROOK TROUT

4 CUTTHROAT TROUT

5 GOLDEN TROUT

your inclination, a pack horse trip into the Bridger Wilderness or the Bob Marshall Wilderness for trout fishing.

WYOMING

The **A-Bar-A** is located 85 miles southwest of Laramie or 200 miles northwest of Denver at Encampment, Wyoming. A 6,000-foot hard-surfaced runway is available for guests who fly or charter their own aircraft. It's not unusual for antelope, deer, cattle, or all three to be walking on the strip; however, the management clears it quickly when alerted on the Unicom. The ranch itself covers more than 75,000 acres and offers rooms or cottages in a western decor. The tariff for an A-Bar-A holiday is an eminent bargain at $34 per day for each of two persons in a twin-bedded room when you consider that in addition

to the accommodations and excellent meals, you have 24 miles of private water on the North Platte River with superlative fishing, a saddle horse and wrangler service, a large heated swimming pool (rare in the Rockies), golf on a 9 hole 3 par course, the use of an electric skeet and target range, the services of a children's counselor who organizes their program, and a variety of ranch activities from moonlight horseback riding to barbecue cookouts.

As a rule the A-Bar-A closes on September 15, simply because it's too big to operate after the regular tourist season, but even a brief stay will be memorable. Here, 2- to 4-pound rainbow and brown trout are commonplace, and few guests fail to catch 20 to 30 fish a day—and that, as anyone knows, is fishing! This section of the river is restricted to fly fishing.

In Saratoga you can stay at the newly refurbished **Saratoga Inn.** Rooms are from $15 to $20 per day, and meals are extra. The local guide is Len Benson (Area Code 307, 326-5426) who specializes in float trips on the North Platte. He covers a 10-mile or more leg downstream from Saratoga and while the average catch is from 1 to 3 pounds, skilled casters can often expect 5- to 7-pound browns.

The **Circle S Ranch** is located in the upper Green River valley, adjoining the Bridger National Forest and Wilderness, 30 miles north of Pinedale, or 60 miles south of Jackson Hole. For the flying sportsman there is a good hard-surfaced runway in Pinedale, and the ranch provides local transportation. The owners in residence of the Circle S are Mari and Elmer George. Mr. George, an auto racing champion who retired from

A nice rainbow from Montana's upper Madison River

Floating is an ideal way to fish on big western rivers

Pack train heads into Jim Bridger Wilderness

the track to have more time for hunting and fishing, and his wife Mari, daughter of Indianapolis Speedway's Tony Hulman, saw the ranch as a fine place to stable her appaloosas. This casual approach to a

successful business has obviously influenced their guest list which contains some of the giants of American industry. The rates here, and again fair, differ in accordance with the more complex services afforded; a cabin with bath on the American plan for one person is $18.50 per day; deluxe cabins with larger rooms for a party of two, four, or six persons run $20 per day or $135 a week per person. Incidentally, children under 10 are charged one-half the adult rate. A pack trip into the Bridger Wilderness which spirals up to 13,785 feet at Gannett Peak encompassing 1,200 lakes (all out of the bikini littoral) costs $33 a day per person in groups of eight or more, $39 a saddle in parties of five to eight, or $200 a day in groups of four or less. The cost rises simply because it requires the same amount of gear and guides to lead four people into the high country as it does to bring eight dudes above timberline. Pack trips are very popular, however, and with a little advance notice to the management you can be enlisted in a "makeup" group. While the pack trip for high-country fishing is an experience of a lifetime—so much so that people re-

peat it year after year—it is limited to July and August before early snows block the mountain passes.

By now the dude ranch is an established institution. The Wyoming Travel Commission in Cheyenne publishes a descriptive directory of one hundred or more (*Motels, Hotels, Dude Ranches, Outfitters, Resorts*) which is a reliable Baedeker for the neophyte. All ranches are members of a self-inspecting association with rigid standards and at the very least you can expect comfortable accommodations and excellent meals. Western style cuisine reckons with the inner man. The fare is hearty and well prepared. Regional specialties such as sourdough pancakes, smoked sausages, buffalo steaks (which vie with the finest sirloin), charcoaled butterfly lamb, stream sweet trout, and of course, the native cheese are without peer. There are two local cheeses, one a cheddar and the other an Emmenthal or so-called Swiss cheese, which are of exceptional quality and worthy of shipping home. These are churned on the rich Mormon farmlands of the Salt River valley between Sayre and Afton.

Angler casting on big cutthroat water of the Grand Canyon of the Snake at Thayne, Wyoming

MONTANA

Although a jacket and tie is customary at the A-Bar-A during dinner hour, female guests do not compete with Rudi Gernreich but tend toward tailored informals; at the Circle S dress is also casual and after the first blush of arrival, dudes often come to the table in their blue jeans and buckskins. In the outcamps, of course, everybody looks and feels like Kit Carson.

MONTANA

If you draw a circle with a 200 mile radius from West Yellowstone, it would encompass most of the classic stream trout fishing in the U.S.

today. Within this area flow all size waters from infant brooks to great torrents that roar through remote canyons. Naturally, some streams are better than others, and if you want to explore the park with the benefit of an experienced guide, one of the better professionals is Bud Lilly, who can be contacted at *Bud Lilly's Trout Shop* in West Yellowstone, Montana (Area Code 406, 646-7293), just a short drive from the West Entrance. Mr. Lilly is a big-fish specialist who caters to serious fly fishermen.

The rivers of Yellowstone Park proper may be unapproachable in

the fall period (roughly September 20 through October) if early snows at altitude close the roads. Nevertheless, there's an abundance of fishing at lower elevations outside the park. It would be hard to beat the run of spawning browns which move into the upper Madison River from Hebgen Lake (and if the park is open a similar run coming into the Moose River from Lewis Lake).

Nearby Wade Lake also produces phenomenal fishing in October for browns in the 9- to 12-pound class.

A record 29½-pounder was caught there in 1966. A popular accommodation in this area is the **Parade Rest Ranch** (Area Code 406, 646-7217) operated by Wells Morris, or you can stay in any of the motels in West Yellowstone. From here you can pick up U.S. 287 at Hebgen Lake if you plan on continuing north to sample the lower Madison River. Headquarters for the lower Madison River is at Ennis, Montana. There are several guides and motels, such as the **El Western** and **Sportsman's Lodge** in the village. Although the entire river is open to the wading angler, you should take at least one float trip with a local expert. The standard rate here is $35 to $40 per day for two people in a modified double-ender. The usual float on the Madison (the upper river cannot be floated) is from the Varney Bridge near Cameron to Ennis Lake; however, don't overlook the run from the Gray Cliffs Access into the headwaters of the Missouri River, or from Toston to Townsend on the Missouri itself. The latter is a two-day trip, but brown trout of 3 pounds are fairly common.

At the North Entrance to Yellowstone Park in Gardiner, Montana, you'll find the *Parks' Fly Shop* (Area Code 406, 848-7314), which is operated by Merton Parks. Both Merton and his son Richard make a specialty of float trips on the Yellowstone River on a 30-mile leg between Gardiner and Livingston. As a rule they float five to ten miles, beginning at 9 a.m. and fishing until dark. Their rates are $25 per day for one angler, and $30 for two. Yellowstone anglers headquarter in Gardiner or Livingston; the latter has several motels and visitors can obtain all information on the area at *Dan Bailey's Fly Shop* (Area Code 406, 222-1673). Most devotees stay at the **Island Resort Motel** in Livingston. New and also recommended is the **Yellowstone Valley Ranch** located about fifteen miles south of Livingston. More in the dude ranch style is the **Lazy K Bar** and the **Sixty-three Ranch** near Big Timber.

Another popular location is Bruce Elliot's **Rock Creek Lodge** just east of Clinton, Montana, on U.S. 10 (Area Code 406, 825-9191), which is headquarters for both Rock Creek and the Clark Fork of the Colombia River. The Clark Fork has an abundance of big brownies as does Rock Creek in its lower reaches. The fall season is a prime time for browns, and you might find excellent angling anywhere between Drummond and Superior on the Clark Fork. Here 3- and 4-pound fish are not out of the ordinary. Like most big streams it provides quality rather than quantity, although remarkable catches have been scored on both counts by some of Elliot's clients. There are plenty of motels, restaurants, and trailer parks in the vicinity of Missoula, and Bob Ward of *Ward's Tackle Shop* can post you on immediate conditions.

On the way to the Clark Fork you might consider a float trip either with your own raft or with a local pro. However, allow plenty of time if you are going to do the whole leg. It starts on the Big Hole, which fishes well through the entire season. You can put in at Melrose and float all the way to Three Forks, a distance of about 100 miles. At Twin Bridges, where the Big Hole joins the Beaverhead to form the Jefferson, is the most interesting part of the trip from the standpoint of scenery, and here hefty brownies are numerous. The Big Hole has a steep gradient, plenty of snags, and side channels. However, the Jefferson portion is an easy float and at times it fishes better than the Big Hole. If you want to cut the trip in half, start at Twin Bridges and allow three or four days for leisurely angling on those broad sparkling riffles. The local contact in Twin Bridges is Frank Rose of *Frank's Tackle Shop* (Area Code 406, 684-5651). Frank knows all the hotspots for miles around.

MONTANA DUDE RANCHES AND OUTFITTERS

For wilderness fishing in Montana

contact one of the following: **Diamond L Bar Ranch,** Box W, Seeley Lake, Montana 59868, Mission Mountain Wild Area. **KNL Spotted Bear Resort,** Walter and Rhoda G. Cook, Hungry Horse, Montana 59919, Bob Marshall Wilderness and South Fork of the Flathead. **Elk Creek Ranch,** Babe and Addie Sayre, Box 323A, Augusta, Montana 59410, North Fork of the Blackfoot and Upper Dearborn River drainage —Scapegoat. **JJJ Guest Ranch,** Herb and Leona Stevens, Box 383, Augusta, Montana 59410, Bob Marshall Wilderness Area. **Cheff Guest Ranch,** Adelle and Bud Cheff, Box W124, Charlo, Montana 59824, Bob Marshall Wilderness Area. **V-A Ranch,** Gene and Martha Youderian, Box 162B, Lincoln, Montana 59639, Bob Marshall Wilderness and Lincoln Back-country Wilderness. **4C Ranch,** Ted Thompson, Big Timber, Montana 59011, North of Yellowstone Park and Thompson Falls Area. **White Tail Ranch,** Tom and Helen Edwards, Ovando, Montana 59854, Danaher Valley Bob Marshall Wilderness and North Fork of the Blackfoot—Scapegoat. **Circle Eight Ranch,** C. H. Gleason, Choteau, Montana 59422, Bob Marshall Wilderness Area. **Sixty Three Ranch,** Box W676, Paul E. Christensen, Livingston, Montana 59047, Absaroka Primitive Area. **J-L Outfitters,** Gene and Don Johnson, Sand Coulee, Montana 59472, North Fork of the Sun River. **33-Ranch,** Buff Hultman, Box 113, Seeley Lake, Montana 59868, Bob Marshall Wilderness Area. **Ford Creek Ranch,** Roy and Rena Coghill, Augusta, Montana 59410, Bob Marshall Wilderness Area and Sun River Drainage. **Sun Canyon Lodge,** Glen Roberts, Box 327W, Augusta, Montana 59410, North Fork of the Sun and White Rivers. **Seven Lazy P Guest Ranch,** Chuck and Sharon Blixrud, Choteau, Montana 59422, South and Middle Forks of the Flathead River and the Sun River Area. **Diamond T. Ranch,** Gene Fox, Swan Lake, Montana, Bob Marshall Wilderness.

Random Casts

All the fishing in the United States is by no means limited to Florida, the Rocky Mountains, and New England. In fact there is so much of it in the states of Hawaii and Alaska that these are treated as separate entries in this guide. Much of the fishing we do in the southern section of our country and the Midwest and in the Pacific region is vastly different from the kind of angling described so far. So the random sampler that follows are some of the high spots in these regions which we feel would interest foreign visitors.

STEELHEAD

Although rainbow trout have a world wide distribution, it is only in North America that sea-run fish of this species occur in large sizes and numbers. The southern boundary of the anadromous rainbow on this continent is the Russian River north of San Francisco in California. However, the most productive streams today are in the Pacific Northwest (Washington and Oregon), British Columbia, and Alaska. In common with Atlantic salmon fishing the game is wholly dependent on an-nual runs of steelhead returning to the rivers. These migrations may take place only in the fall and winter seasons, or on some rivers summer runs occur also; this presents a variety of angling conditions. In summer when the water is low and clear, it may require fine terminal tackle to earn strikes and exceptional skill in handling large trout. Fall will bring occasional storms which may raise and discolor the river for a short time, but one can usually depend on weeks of excellent water and good fishing. Winter presents a real problem to the dedicated fly man, as rivers are high and roily with only short periods of clearing or lowering water. Close contact by telephone with local tackle firms or anglers is essential. When the word is favorable, get there immediately, as the river can change in just a few hours.

Steelhead move into the rivers in groups, and a stretch of stream that was productive last week may be empty until a new group arrives. Often, a riffle that produced a steelhead in the morning may have another fish in the same spot by late afternoon. The angler's ability to lo-cate or anticipate good holding water is no small part of the charm of this kind of fishing. As the fish travel upriver, they will follow identical routes through each riffle and pool, as they have for countless generations before. They will rest in the same spots, bunch up in certain pools, or stay in a favored 5- to 10-foot area in a riffle that may be 100 yards long. This will be repeated year after year unless a flood scours and alters the stream bed. Oldtimers learn these spots through constant fishing, and by trial and error. Many experts can look at a strange river and instantly pick out the best riffles. Submerged ledges, changes in the bottom revealed by a slight variation in the surface flow, and the location of rocks—all of these have their special meaning. You can save a lot of time by avoiding the kinds of water that steelhead will not hold in and the places that cannot be fished properly even if the trout are present. For example, water that is extremely fast is not likely to contain steelhead. They prefer moving water, of course, but as a rule of thumb, if it is flowing too fast to wade comfortably it is too fast to fish. Dead water is a poor producer on most rivers, although there are a few exceptions. The reliable places are the slicks above a rapid, which are usually created below big pools where the stream spreads out. Another kind of water that is consistently good is a long, uniform flow of moderate speed. Steelhead habitually lie in the channel of a run of the latter type, and it pays to study the deeper sections carefully.

TECHNIQUE

The basic technique of steelhead fly-fishing is to wade in the head of a run and cover the water with cross-stream casts until every por-

Lone fisherman practices his art on bubbling stream in quest of trout

tion of the riffle is reached. The fly will swing around in arcs, and you are most likely to get a strike between the time the line tightens as it quarters downstream and when it completes the swing directly below you. Keep your rod low and pointed toward the fly. You can let the fly drift dead or jiggle it a bit either by twitching the rod or pulling the line. Try both methods. Make three short casts in all; then, having covered the close water, extend the line 10 or 15 feet. Make three more casts, and then extend the line again to reach the maximum distance so the entire run has been covered from one side to the other. Now wade eight or ten steps downstream and repeat the procedure until the length of the riffle has been fished. This is the standard method. You can vary it, of course, by changing the direction of your casts, working the fly deeper by casting upstream, and running it near the surface by casting more directly downstream.

Catching steelhead is not difficult. The technique is quite simple compared to some other types of trout fishing. The ability to "read" the water and to cast a long line is most important. Wading ability also goes a long way in successful steelhead fishing because of the volume of flow typical of most coastal rivers.

STEELHEAD TACKLE
Steelhead fly tackle is heavier than ordinary trout gear. Rods of 8½ to 9½ feet in length are standard. In bamboo, some of the favorites are made in fluted hollow construction; these are extremely powerful for their weight and were responsible for many tournament distance records when they first appeared on the market. Fiberglass rods have, of course, captured a large audience, and one development in that construction is a method of joining the sections by using hollow glass as a ferrule to keep the total rod weight down and to produce an action very similar to one-piece blanks. Regardless of the construction, the empha-

sis is on power; the tip must not be soft, and the action must extend well down into the butt. The guides should be correctly spaced, and of large size to permit smooth shooting of the line. A screw-locking-type reel seat is essential.

The reel must be large enough to accommodate at least 100 yards at 15- to 18-pound-test backing as well as the fly line. If the angler plans to fish some of the Canadian waters where steelhead in excess of 25 pounds may be encountered, it is advisable to use a reel that will hold at least 150 yards of backing. A single action reel with an adjustable brake is most popular, although some casters use automatic fly reels. In most models the 3-⅝-inch and 3-⅞-inch sizes (spool diameter) are suitable for steelhead fishing. Although brakes are usually of the friction type, at least one reel has a floating disc brake which eliminates brake failure and heat distortion.

The majority of fly lines used for steelhead are of the sinking type, either shooting heads or weight forward tapers. An occasional river will offer dry-fly fishing but such conditions are rare. The rod, of course, will determine the correct line weight to use.

The following are some of the most popular Washington and Oregon rivers. Despite being very heavily fished, they are highly productive:

KALAMA RIVER
The Kalama River, from its source near snow-capped Mt. St. Helens, runs through rugged canyons and timbered slopes for approximately 40 miles before it joins the Columbia River near the town of Kelso. It is one of very few streams in the Northwest drawing three distinct runs of steelhead. A substantial run enters the Kalama in March and continues until early May. The fish are large and 12-pounders are not uncommon. The "springers," as the local anglers call them, are strong,

and good equipment is needed to slow them down in the high run-off. Fly fishing is only fair during the spring season, however, as the water is usually milky from the melting snow. At times, depending upon the severity of the preceding winter, the water may be clear enough to allow the use of flies with success.

In June a second run of fish starts up the Kalama River, and this summer run attracts many fly fishermen until August. Above the Puget Sound Power and Light Company flume the Kalama is restricted to fly-fishing-only during the summer season. The water is usually crystal clear at this time and early morning fishing (at dawn) is most productive. These steelies average about 7 pounds and the Kalama produces about 4,000 such fish each summer.

From late November until the following March winter steelhead are in the river. This cold weather fishing is done chiefly from boats in the lower stream in the section from the power plant down to the mouth by bottom bouncing with bait (salmon eggs). Winter steelhead average good size with fish of over 18 pounds not uncommon.

The Kalama River may be reached by going north on Highway 99 from Vancouver, Washington. Accommodations may be had at the town of Kalama and also at the resort near the mouth of the river where the highway crosses it. The resort also offers boating and guide service through the winter and spring fishing in the lower river below the power flume. A good road parallels the river along most of the fishable water, and access to the stream may be gained at various points along the road.

STILLIGUAMISH RIVER
Rising in the Cascade mountains in Washington's Mt. Baker National Forest, the North Fork of the Stilliguamish offers little in the way of steelhead fishing until it reaches the confluence of Deer Creek at the village of Oso. Deer Creek provides

Steelhead rivers of the western U.S. are big streams requiring powerful fly-rod tackle

the major spawning area for the Stilliguamish and is closed to angling, but from that point downstream to its junction with the South Fork the river offers some of the finest fly fishing water in the West. The North Fork of the Stilliguamish is open only to angling with an artificial fly. The first of the summer-run fish are usually taken around July 4th, and from that date on the summer fishing improves. By the middle of August, the fish are sometimes caught on a dry fly as well as the usual wet patterns. The Stilliguamish is a slow moving stream in the section immediately below Oso and the method of fishing is similar to that used on quiet pools and runs in other streams. The fly is cast upstream with plenty of slack line and allowed to drift deep with the current. The character of the stream affords little cover other than depth itself, and the fish usually hold near the bottom. In early morning and late evening, however, the steelies may be on the move and very often are taken in rather shallow riffles.

The fly fishing continues to be good during most of the winter when the water is clear. At times the water is discolored due to a clay slide on the upper stretches of the river, and fishing drops off considerably.

The South Fork of the Stilliguamish has a winter run of steelhead, and they may be angled for with bait or other lures.

The Stilliguamish may be reached by going north on U.S. Highway 99. A paved secondary highway follows the river from Arlington to Oso. Accommodations may be had at either Oso or Arlington.

SKYKOMISH RIVER
The Skykomish River is one of the favorites of Washington steelhead anglers. Starting high in the Cascade Mountains, as does the Stilliguamish, the Skykomish drops swiftly from two forks, the South and the North, which join near the town of Index. From this point downstream, there are approximately 30 miles of excellent fishing water.

The summer fly fishing extends from July through September. The Skykomish is unusually clear during the summer, and therefore extremely light terminal tackle is necessary. This clear water also requires more delicate casting than is usual when fishing for steelhead.

Winter fishing begins in December and runs through February. Large fish are occasionally taken during the winter run with flies, although the water conditions are subject to quick changes, making fly fishing unreliable.

The Skykomish may be reached either from U.S. Highway 97 by turning off on Alternate Route 10 at the town of Peshastin, not far from Leavenworth, or by going to Everett and taking Alternate Route 10 up the river from that point.

Accommodations may be had at the towns of Monroe, Sulton, and Goldbar, and at various camps along the river.

ROGUE RIVER
The Rogue is about 200 miles long and enters the Pacific at Gold Beach. Over 30,000 anglers work the river mouth in Rogue River Bay each season, mainly in boats, although there is some casting from shore. The run of spring fish in 1969 exceeded any previous record for the last 25 years according to the counting station at Gold Ray Dam. The peak of its migration is in April and May, while the fall run is at its height

in September. Coho salmon are also taken in September and October, but the fishery is in the lower river. In the vicinity of Grants Pass, the spring chinook salmon fishing is best in May, while in the upper river, near Gold Ray Dam, June is the best month for the spring fish.

Steelhead trout are taken by fly fishing from shore in the lower Rogue during September while in the middle course of the river the best fishing is to be had in October. In both regions, the fish are in the river through December. Accommodations are plentiful throughout the Rogue River Valley. **Morrison's Lodge** (Merlin, Oregon) is a popular spot here.

UMPQUA RIVER

The Umpqua River in Douglas County is approximately 192 miles in length, nearly all of which can be reached by paved or improved roads. Chinook and coho salmon, cutthroat and steelhead trout, striped bass, and shad are all available in season.

A generally successful summer sport fishery for salmon is practiced during July and August at the mouth of the Umpqua for feeding fish. These chinook salmon are thought to be destined for migration into other streams, but they enter the mouth of the river to feed on pilchard and herring. In addition to the summer fishery, a substantial salmon run occurs during September and October, from the mouth of Winchester Bay to the Forks.

Winter steelhead fishing is practiced in January and February. Summer steelheads may be taken from July to September in the upper reaches of the river, except where it is closed by angling regulations of the Oregon State Game Commission.

The main Umpqua is formed by the North and South Umpqua near Roseburg. The North Umpqua is considered to be superior to the South in both quantity and quality of its game fish population. The nature of the South Umpqua watershed is such as to contribute to heavy flooding in the winter, and to warm and low water in the summer, whereas the North Umpqua is generally clear and its summer temperatures are not excessive. Frank Moore's **Steamboat Inn** is headquarters for visiting fly fishermen on the North Branch.

In common with most large Oregon rivers of similar nature, the North Umpqua was populated in former years by resident trout in considerable numbers to the extent of supporting a quasi-commercial fishery which supplied the eating houses of the area. Presently, success in trout fishing in the Umpqua is largely dependent upon fish of legal size stocked from hatcheries, and on a run of cutthroat which appears in the river toward the latter part of April, and which is caught generally from August to October. Resident cutthroat are most often taken in June and July. Brown trout occur in the upper North Umpqua and they seem to be most easily taken during July.

Accommodations are not plentiful in the Umpqua watershed. The larger towns offer the best opportunity to obtain meals and lodging, except on the North Umpqua where three resorts are to be found.

Winter steelhead are readily caught on bait-casting or spinning tackle

NORTH CAROLINA MARLIN

The Outer Banks, composed of Hatteras and Ocracoke islands, form the eastern perimeter of Pamlico Sound. These two thin strips of sand and scrub trees protect the eastern shore of North Carolina from the cruel buffeting of the Atlantic Ocean. As the mainland falls sharply off toward the southwest, Hatteras Island, separated from Bodie Island by Oregon Inlet, runs almost due south for 45 miles before turning abruptly westsouthwest to meet Ocracoke Island and eventually join up with the mainland again. Hatteras Island, from the Oregon Inlet at the north end to the town of Buxton 40 miles south, at no point exceeds 1,000 yards in width. The largest part of the island is dominated by the famous Cape Hatteras Lighthouse guarding the west end of the Diamond Shoals. This shoal extends 12 miles into the Atlantic, and it constitutes one of the most dangerous sailing areas in the world. The brave little Diamond Lightship rides at anchor 15 miles out in the Atlantic night and day to warn the unwary ship of this treacherous hazard to navigation.

The Gulf Stream most closely approaches the United States coast after it leaves Florida before turning northeasterly into the Atlantic. The other current, which hugs the inner side of the Stream, is an extension of the Labrador Current coming down from Greenland and Nova Scotia. This junction of two major currents creates a condition favorable to fish, but it also creates a rough sea, so the angler must also be a good sailor to test these waters properly.

The waters in the Gulf Stream near the Diamond Lightship consistently produce big fish. A large blue marlin weighing 810 pounds was taken near the lightship during the summer of 1962 on an artificial bait. The run from Hatteras to the fishing grounds takes a minimum of one hour to perhaps two hours depending on whether the Gulf Stream is running inshore or offshore. It can be as close as 12 miles or as far as 30 depending in large measure on the wind and the strength of the current that is pushing down from the north. The best wind for fishing seems to be a northeaster, but this wind also produces fairly lumpy water since it is going against the Stream. The local boats and crews available at Hatteras are excellent for this particular type of fishing and under the rough conditions which are likely to be encountered. The men are expert seamen, and the boats are safe.

In addition to blue marlin, there are also white marlin, sailfish, king mackerel, wahoo, dolphin, bonito, oceanic bonito, blackfin tuna, and yellowfin tuna. The big bluefin also passes close to Hatteras on the annual migration to the north. A 400-pounder was washed up on the Hatteras beach which seems to bear out this theory; however, they probably go by too deep for fishermen. The numerous wrecks which dot the area around Diamond Shoals provide excellent fishing for amberjack, barracuda, bluefish, sailfish, kingfish, and mackerel. If an angler tires of skipping baits for big fish, he can enjoy a change of pace by using lighter tackle and fishing the drop-offs near the sloughs and shoals. One of the greatest concentration of dolphin exists off Hatteras during the summer and extending into the fall. They range up to 40 pounds, and an angler can enjoy great sport with spinning tackle along the weed lines or logs which float with the stream. However, the angler must be prepared to sit it out on shore if the weather gets nasty. Any boat captain taking a private fishing boat to Hatteras should consult the local guides for inlet conditions and the latest information on the position of the sandbars at the mouth.

ACCOMMODATIONS

For Hatteras fishing from Buxton try the **Cape Hatteras Court** at $9 single and $12 double for a room, or $100 to $150 per week for one of 15 cottages. The Court has a swimming pool and marina. Also in Buxton is the **Cape Pines Motel** at $10 per day single and $12 double. In the village of Hatteras try the **Hatteras Marlin Motel** at $10 per day single or $12 double. Cottages are available. The **Sea Gull Motel** is another popular spot at $10 to $18 single, and $12 to $18 double. Apartments are available. All rates quoted are lower in the off season (spring and fall).

CHARTER BOATS

Fully equipped modern sportfishermen are available for marlin fishing off Hatteras. Rates range from $100 for a 12-hour trip to $150 for a 24-hour trip for a party of six or less. Tackle is provided but lunch and beverages are extra. The variance in offshore charter rates results in part from a difference in the service offered. At Morehead City, for example, parties often sleep aboard ship the night before a trip offshore. Time and distance also are factors. The usual blue water trip begins at 4:30 to 5:00 in the morning and ends approximately 12 hours later. But a trip out of Southport or Morehead City for Gulf Stream species like the blue marlin will begin as early as 2:00 a.m. and continue until sundown. Parties after marlin often make a 24-hour trip of it.

The fleet at Hatteras Marlin Club

FOR PURISTS ONLY

When in California you can hardly afford to miss a day on Hot Creek. Once a campsite of Paiute Indians, **Hot Creek Ranch** (Hot Creek Ranch, Route 3, Box 206, Bishop, California 93514; Area Code 714 935-4214) provides over two miles of beautiful winding meadow stream restricted to the *dry* fly only. You can't even dunk a nymph which is the ultimate test where 2- to 4-pound brown trout are not uncommon and a 14¾-pounder is the record to date. These are stream spawned fish, not hatchery fodder. Delicate tackle is a *must.* Situated on the eastern slope of the Sierras at a bit over 7,000 feet elevation, the ranch consists of nine completely furnished cabins, each with private bath, double beds, refrigerator and all appurtenances necessary to housekeeping. Grocery stores are three miles away but there are several restaurants nearby if you have an aversion to dirty dishes. Ranch is 283 miles from San Francisco, and 290 miles from Los Angeles over good highway. There is also a small airstrip nearby for light aircraft. Host Lee Willardson can expert you on how to match-the-hatch. Rates are $17.50 per day for double occupancy in a cabin with special rates for children and weekly rates. Minimum week-end is three days at $67.50 for two persons. An eminent bargain for purist anglers. Fishing season same as the State of California legal period for trout.

LUXURY PARTY BOAT FISHING

Only in California would the tourist find an incongruous combination of the last word in resorts with sinker-bouncing, but every game has its Taj Mahal and the **San Luis Bay Inn** (Marre Ranch, Avila Beach, California 93424; Area Code 805 595-2333) looms large on the horizon. Managed by Fritz Hartung, the inn offers exquisite rooms and gourmet cuisine. There is an 18 hole golf course, tennis courts and surf or pool bathing to keep the family happy. All rooms have private balco-nies affording views of the ocean or the encircling wooded hills. Modified American Plan rates (including dinner and breakfast) are $40 up for double rooms or $28 up for single occupancy.

Port San Luis was the outstanding harbor in California for the salmon catch in 1969 with over 5,000 brought in by sport boats (not including the commercial haul). Prospects for 1971 look as good, with size ranging from 30 to 35 pounds. They have a very good albacore season running August through November, and a good bonito run about the same period. Excellent bottom fishing the year around for ling cod, red rock cod and caba-zone. Good halibut fishing inside the Bay for small-boat fishermen. Party boats accommodating about 20 people sail daily. For salmon, boats leave the dock at 7:00 a.m. and return at 2:00 p.m. Charge per person is $8 without tackle or $10 with tackle furnished. For albacore, boats leave about 4:00 a.m. and return about 4:00 p.m., and the charge is slightly higher.

ACCOMMODATIONS

Visitors from abroad can now tour the United States far less expensively than before with the Visit the U.S.A. Hospitality Card, which permits hotel room rate discounts of 10 percent to 40 percent in many of the best hotels and motels in the country. The discount card, with a booklet listing all the hotels and other facilities participating in this great travel bargain, is available at Pan Am ticket offices, travel agencies and American Express offices outside the United States.

As in all other countries, hotel rates in the States are noticeably lower in small towns than in large cities. In non-resort communities which are busy the year 'round, hotel rates are fairly stable all year. Some hotels charge extra for the television set in your room. It is free in the better hotels. All the better hotels are air-conditioned. There is no extra charge for steam heat, of which America seems to have an overa-bundance. While it is sometimes dif-ficult to get room with a private bath in many countries, the room-with-bath combination is standard in all modern American hotels and motels throughout the country. "American Plan," in which the room rate includes all meals, is seldom found nowadays except in an occasional resort. Only a few hotels include continental breakfasts in their room rates. In southern resorts such as Miami Beach, rates are lowered drastically during the summer months. Northern resorts either close entirely or cut rates in winter, unless they are in snow-sports areas.

TRAVEL NOTES

Pan American Airways has a wide choice of money-saving travel plans. The Extra Cities Bonus Plan takes you to any gateway city of your choice: Seattle, Portland, San Francisco or Los Angeles on the West Coast; Houston, Dallas, Atlanta, New Orleans or Miami in the South; Boston, New York, Philadelphia, Baltimore or Washington, D.C. in the East; Chicago or Detroit in the Midwest. You can then tour the country by domestic airlines and see any number of U.S. cities for just the price of a single round-trip ticket to the most distant destinations. Group Fares, Family Fares and Excursion Fares also offer an appreciable savings on flights. Your travel agent can help you plan a trip which best fits your time, taste and budget.

Bus fare from John F. Kennedy Airport into Manhattan (16 miles) is $2.50; taxi fare is at least $7, plus 20 percent tip. Customs inspects most luggage. Tip air terminal porters a minimum of 25c per bag. No departure taxes.

To visit the United States, for business or pleasure, you need a passport, visa and international small-pox vaccination certificate. In most countries, it is no longer necessary to appear in person at a U.S. Consulate to obtain a visa. You can do this by mail merely by sending in your passport and one photograph. Pan American Airways sales offices can furnish application forms printed in your own language.

232

A peacock pavón takes to the air. Fly fishing in the Orinoco's upper tributaries is among world's best. Fish average 8 pounds or more

Venezuela

In that half-dark hour when the blast furnace sun slides around the equator, you can ride the funicular to the top of the mountain which isolates Caracas from the rest of the world and see the night lights come on—a billion blinking eyes opening from their drugged sleep. Beyond that electric glare on the Llanos where tourists rarely go, and black gold bubbles out of the oldest graves in the earth, there is only wakening sound—a mournful A-minor chord held on a guitar, an organ chorus of howler monkeys, and the piercing night hunger scream of the jaguar. Much of the 260,000 square miles of Llanos is unknown even to the people living there. The vast grassy flatland fingered by green *quebradas* is as primitive as our Wagon Wheel West.

The Llanos, or plains, is veined by rivers flowing generally southward from the coastal mountains and uplands to the Orinoco. These streams are clear, never muddy in the dry season, but they become raging torrents in the rainy season. Where there is water the jungle growth is lush. Between rivers the land is less verdant, and becomes grassy and flat like the African veldt with occasional umbrella-shaped trees. Larger than the combined states of Texas and Minnesota, the 352,143 square miles of Venezuela are only sparsely populated. The tropical interior, which is dominated by the

1 WHITE MARLIN	**6** DOLPHIN	**11** CAHAMA
2 BLUE MARLIN	**7** TARPON	**12** DORADO
3 SAILFISH	**8** SNOOK	**13** BRYCON
4 SWORDFISH	**9** PAVON	**14** PIRANHA
5 BLUEFIN TUNA	**10** PAYARA	**15** CATFISH

The pavón is most common native game fish

Orinoco watershed, has over 1,000 rivers which support such endemic species as the pavón, payara, pacu, dorado, piranha and numerous catfishes. These constitute an immense and largely unexploited fishery. Few anglers visit the Venezuelan jungle country.

The coastal saltwater fishing, which is centered on blue marlin, white marlin, sailfish, and tarpon, is of unusual quality yet facilities are limited. There are excellent accommodations but charter craft are not numerous. An annual marlin tournament held at La Guaira each September has resulted in some remarkable catches, but this is an invitational match for private boats. So the overall picture is great fishing — but not easily arranged.

THE SEASON

The southern border of Venezuela runs to within one degree of the Equator but the country's climate is tropical, modified by elevation and prevailing winds. The hot zone, from sea level to about 3,000 feet, averages 85°F except where cooled by winds from the sea. The leeward or southern slopes of mountains, together with the Llanos, cut off from prevailing trade winds by the peaks of the coastal mountain range, are generally the hottest. The coast itself, though fanned by on-shore breezes, is often oppressive because of high relative humidity.

Much of inland Venezuela, however, is above the hot zone, in a moderate range from 3,000 to about 6,000 feet, where the annual mean temperature runs about 65°F. Here the warmest months are April and May, the coolest December and January. The wettest months are July and August, the driest is February. Because of the cooling effect of altitude, probably the most pleasant climate in Venezuela is found fairly near the Equator — in the high jungle country south of the Orinoco.

FRESHWATER FISHING

Except for a few remote American oil camps which are not available to the public, there are no facilities or resorts on the interior Venezuelan rivers catering to anglers. There is only limited road access across the Llanos, although some streams can be reached by a four-wheel-drive vehicle. Essentially, however, this is for the more adventurous sportsman. During the rainy season, the Llanos becomes a flood plain, and the rivers are not approachable. During the dry season (from January through May) auto travel is rough, but feasible. The angler must be prepared to camp out. Outfitters who have the equipment for such a trip are seldom available in Caracas.

Easy to attract but difficult to hold, a payara will strike at the lure repeatedly

Some of world's best white marlin fishing takes place each September off La Guaira

Canine teeth of payara can puncture lures

The outstanding and most widely distributed native gamefish is the pavón (*Cichla spp.*). Pavón occur in most rivers tributary to the Orinoco.

There are at least four species found in Venezuela; among the largest is the peacock pavón (locally pavón cinchado) which has a probable maximum weight of 30 pounds with an average of 6 pounds. Equal in size is the spotted pavón (locally pavón truchas) the strongest and most spectacular cichlid in South America. The third species is the butterfly pavón (locally pavón mariposa) which averages 2½ pounds with a maximum weight of about 11 pounds. The butterfly inhabits slower water than the peacock and spotted pavón and is somewhat easier to catch. Comparable in size and found in fast-flowing sections of stream is the royal pavón (locally pavón real) which is common to the upper Orinoco tributaries in the vicinity of Puerto Páez.

Of comparable distribution and usually found in the same waters with the pavón is the payara. A payara has the vicious nature of a bluefish,

Continued on page 241

For Adventurers Only: A Journey In Tropical South America

It is difficult if not impossible to visualize the immensity of South America's watersheds. The Orinoco rises in the Parima Mountains of southern Venezuela, almost on the Brazilian border, and flows 1,281 miles draining countless tributaries in an area of roughly 360,000 square miles including one-fifth of Colombia. Near its headwaters the river divides as it leaves the Great Plain where a branch stream, the Casiquiare, turns into the Rio Negro, which joins the Amazon. The Amazon alone is almost 3,300 miles in length and the brown weight of it is so great that if the flow of the Mississippi were added there would scarcely be a change in water level. It stains the ocean a hundred miles offshore. About 2,000 different species of fish occur in this tropical ecosystem, ranging from the little four-eyed *Anableps* to giant pirarucu which grow to 12 feet in length.

No footprints will be seen over millions of acres of rain forest. Isolated nomadic Indian tribes live in Amazonia but much of the back country is uninhabited, especially in the upper reaches of the Orinoco. There are only two accommodations for sportsmen in all of this vast wilderness: one in Colombia near Miraflores, and the other on Bananal Island in the Matto Grosso of Brazil. No camp exists as such in Venezuela. A 75-foot houseboat operates from Bananal (which has a hotel with the unlikely name **Hotel John Kennedy**) along the Araguaia River. Otherwise a trip to the interior is strictly for adventurers. This is done by river boat, flying in small aircraft, and in some areas by four-wheel-drive vehicle.

There are two seasons in the tropics —wet or *invierno* and dry or *verano*. The dry season in the Orinoco is generally from January into April and on the Amazon to the south from late June to November. During the wet season these rivers rise 20 to 50 feet over their banks and flood the surrounding lands for twenty miles or more. Fishing is possible only in the dry season. High temperatures prevail in the lowland jungles and plains with daily maximums in the 90's and occasionally over 100°F., particularly toward the end of the dry season.

Although the main rivers are muddy for the most part, the upper tributaries flow clear over sand and rock bottoms. In the brief months between rains their luminous beauty has no equal. The fishing, on a river such as the Ventuari (Territorio Amazonas, Venezuela) is without parallel. Catching fifty or even a hundred pavón in one day, averaging 8 pounds or more, is the norm. Whether you use fly, plug, or spoon, many other gamefish such as the powerful and leaping payara, various brycons, pacu, trachira, pike-characins, and the acrobatic striped catfish will take the lure just as readily.

The jungle and its wildlife is no small part of the enjoyment in a South American trip. Jaguar, puma, tapir, capybara, wild boar, and deer are sometimes seen along the river banks, and the green canopy of trees is often teeming with howler monkeys. It is a bird watcher's paradise, where dusky skimmers do their surface-cleaving quadrille over the water while herons silently watch the performance. Native wild turkeys, bellbirds, and colorful warblers (which vie with the butterflies in brilliance) flush at the passing of a boat. There are piranha, cayman, crocodiles, electric eels, giant anaconda, and stingrays in all of the upper streams, and of these potentially dangerous creatures, the stingray is most feared by the Indian. The freshwater ray is more potent than its marine counterpart, as it has two or more toxic barbs—one extending out to the tip of its tail. But caution is the keynote in an alien environment and few adventurers have returned with anything more harrowing than a mosquito bite.

At present there are several travel agencies at work organizing trips for anglers to the Orinoco and Amazon wildernesses. These will be reported on in subsequent issues.

Florida angler Vernon Ogilvie hooks a royal pavon on the Ventuari River. Frequent sandbars provide easy wading and casting to deep shores. The Parguaza River in the largely uninhabited State of Bolivar, Venezuela, *(lower left)* joins the Orinoco just behind the hills; this crystal clear stream has a vast gamefish population. A mountainous divide *(lower right)* separates the Parguaza from another great stream, the Chivapuri. The jutting rock peak was recently split in half vertically by an earth tremor. Only a few nomadic Indians hunting cayman and turtles ever appear in these jungles. The way to fish the area is by flying in and camping out. This heartland of South America is the last great wilderness in the world.

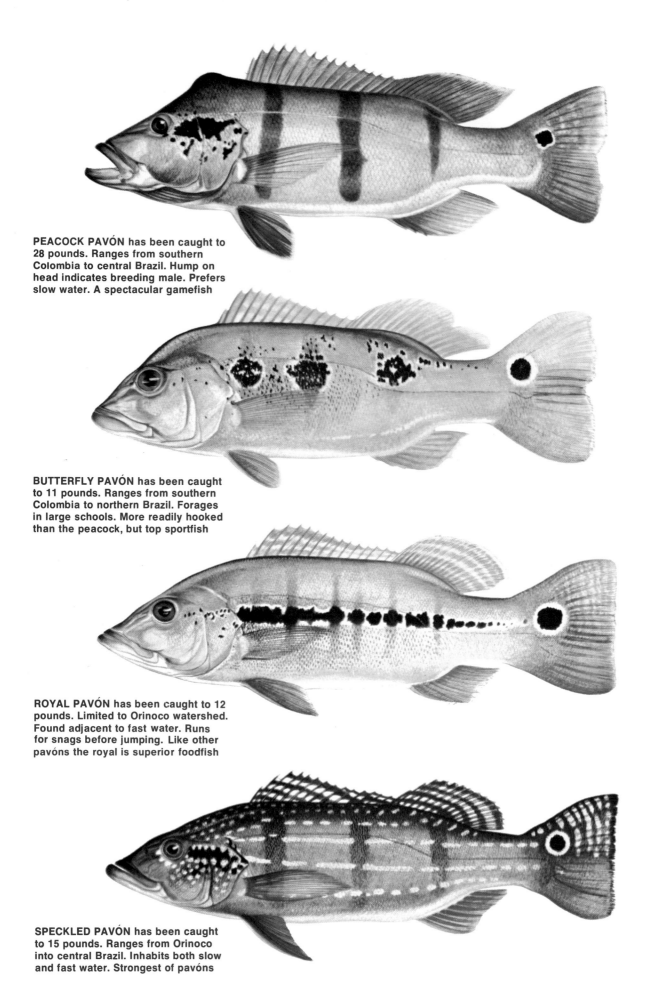

PEACOCK PAVÓN has been caught to 28 pounds. Ranges from southern Colombia to central Brazil. Hump on head indicates breeding male. Prefers slow water. A spectacular gamefish

BUTTERFLY PAVÓN has been caught to 11 pounds. Ranges from southern Colombia to northern Brazil. Forages in large schools. More readily hooked than the peacock, but top sportfish

ROYAL PAVÓN has been caught to 12 pounds. Limited to Orinoco watershed. Found adjacent to fast water. Runs for snags before jumping. Like other pavóns the royal is superior foodfish

SPECKLED PAVÓN has been caught to 15 pounds. Ranges from Orinoco into central Brazil. Inhabits both slow and fast water. Strongest of pavóns

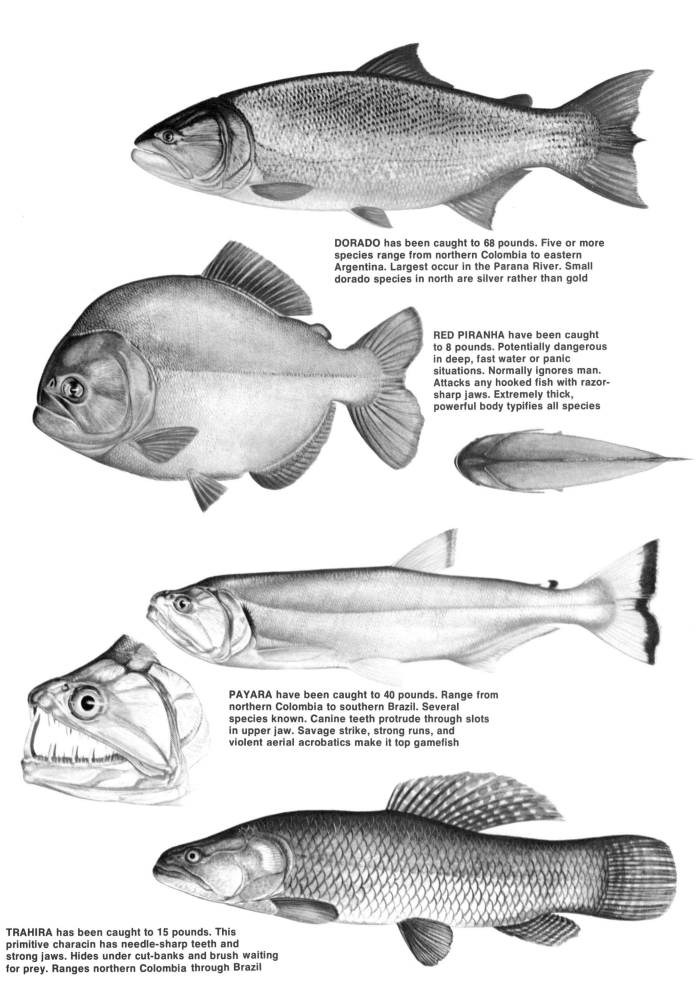

DORADO has been caught to 68 pounds. Five or more species range from northern Colombia to eastern Argentina. Largest occur in the Parana River. Small dorado species in north are silver rather than gold

RED PIRANHA have been caught to 8 pounds. Potentially dangerous in deep, fast water or panic situations. Normally ignores man. Attacks any hooked fish with razor-sharp jaws. Extremely thick, powerful body typifies all species

PAYARA have been caught to 40 pounds. Range from northern Colombia to southern Brazil. Several species known. Canine teeth protrude through slots in upper jaw. Savage strike, strong runs, and violent aerial acrobatics make it top gamefish

TRAHIRA has been caught to 15 pounds. This primitive characin has needle-sharp teeth and strong jaws. Hides under cut-banks and brush waiting for prey. Ranges northern Colombia through Brazil

Variety Is Endless In Tropical Rivers

During the dry season tropical rivers such as the Cinaruco *(top left)* drop to fishable levels

Peacock pavón of 12 and 13 pounds and butterfly pavón of 5 pounds *(lower left)*, make camp fare on the Ventuari River. Pavón flesh is firm, finely textured and has few bones

Shadlike fish *(top right)* is one of numerous brycons in South America. Brycons take flies, jigs, and small spinners, and are excellent gamefish on light tackle. Brycons range from Central America through northern Argentina. Though bony, they are esteemed foodfish

A pikecichlid *(second down)* is one of the smaller species. These slender fish live under rocks, ledges, and sunken logs. Needle-sharp dorsal spines and sharp teeth make it tricky to unhook

A piranhalike characin *(third down)* genus and species unknown is common to the upper Orinoco. This fish has grinding teeth and is probably related to the pacu. It mangles lures and bends hooks

The long, slender gar-shaped fish *(fourth down)* is called a picuda which simply means beaked or pointed. It is a characin of the genus *Hydrocinus*. The upper and lower jaws are of equal length but the upper one has a fleshy extension which is bright red in color. This obvious appendage may be a "lure" to its prey There are many species and some grow quite large. This fish "sleeps" at night and can be dipped up with a net in very shallow water. Large picuda are acrobatic gamefish and make long arcing leaps. The freshwater stingray *(Paratrygon laticeps)* ranges up to 40 pounds in weight. The short multibarbed tail is lethal. Indians have lost feet and legs due to toxic infection, and death is not uncommon. Careful foot shuffling is essential when wading. If "stung," tetanus vaccine and hospitalization is a must

continued from page 235

the poise of a rainbow trout, and when hooked, the jumping ability of a tarpon. Its mouth is nearly hook-proof. Equipped with sharp canines including two front teeth which fit in sockets on top of its head, the payara can chop through plastic lures and wire leaders quite easily.

There are three species found in Venezuela. The most abundant is *Hydrolicus scomberoides* which attains weights over 30 pounds. They will take literally any lure or bait and display a particular enthusiasm for topwater plugs. On light casting tackle payara put up a terrific scrap, making powerful runs and frequent jumps.

In contrast the pacu (*Colossoma spp.*) looks more like an overgrown bluegill in shape. The pacu is one of the strongest fish in South American rivers—not a jumper but a determined body-shaking bottom plunger. Pacu weigh from a 5 or 6 pound average to 40 pounds or more. There appears to be two common species, the blue pacu (locally cachama azul) and the red pacu (locally cachama roja). Although this fish is primarily herbivorous, it can be taken on artificial lures, particularly small spoons and spinners.

Pacu inhabit swift-water streams as well as standing waters and are often associated with dorado throughout their mutual range from Colombia south to northern Argentina.

Dorado have a more spotty distribution in Venezuela than the pavón.

They do occur, however, in gravel-bottomed streams in the Barinas watershed, such as the Paguey and Canagua Rivers. They are also found in rivers to the west as far as Barcelona and south to the Meta River on the Colombian border. This species of dorado (*Salminus hilarii*) is not as heavy as the dorado of Argentina, Paraguay, and Brazil. An 8- or 9-pound dorado is considered quite large in Venezuela.

JUNGLE HAZARDS

The chief danger in remote country is not understanding it—or being careless. There are ticks, chiggers, mosquitoes, and a type of black fly locally known as jejen (pronounced hayhen) on the Llanos. The fly quietly settles on you and punctures your hide, leaving holes which begin to itch, then fester. A long-sleeved shirt, high socks, and plenty of insect repellent are adequate precautions. Two other pests are the army ant and the rove beetle. The army ant is an animated blowtorch—and one reason for sleeping in a hammock. Rove beetles are not common, but occasionally people get smeared by them in the jungle. A rove beetle exudes an oil irritant that leaves red welts and swelling.

Snakes are not numerous in Venezuela. There are certain areas where they are abundant, but ordinarily only the harmless tree boas and water boas are found along the rivers. The tree boa, or constrictor, grows to ten feet in length; the water boa, or anaconda, is twenty-five feet long at full growth. Because of their size, people fear them, but actually they are too big to stumble over and too sluggish to be aggressive. There are, however, bushmasters, coral snakes, rattlers, and fer-de-lance. The two poisonous snakes you may not be familiar with are the fer-de-lance and the bushmaster. The fer-de-lance is generally from five to six feet long and has a lance-shaped head. The snake is deadly. The bushmaster, or "silent rattler," is the largest of all vipers, growing to nine feet in length. But if you're cautious about jumping over logs, climbing ledges, and scrambling around jungle potholes, you have about as little chance of being struck as of winning a $200,000 parlay in the Caracas races.

Of all things to be careful about, none is more deadly than microscopic one-celled amoeba. Water is the greatest killer in the tropics. If you are staying in the back country for a long time, you must accept the fact that you are subject to dysentery. There are two standard items you should have in your first-aid kit, however: Entero-Vioform, which you can take daily to kill stray amoebae; and Lomotil, which you take if the former fails. A good broad-spectrum anti-biotic is also essential; consult your physician.

With respect to the caribe, or piranha, these fish are not ordinarily dangerous. Naturally, if there is blood in the water, the caribe will not hesitate to attack. Also depth seems to be a factor in their aggressiveness. If you don't wade deeper than your knees, you are likely to be safe. Freshwater stingrays are very common and much more feared by the Indians than the caribe. If you must wade—wade cautiously.

TACKLE
There are no soft-mouthed gamefish in the Orinoco country so the emphasis should be on fairly stiff, if not heavy, rods. A stout 5½-foot bait casting rod equipped with 15-pound-test line, or a 6½-foot spinning rod and a minimum 10-pound-test mono is about right. Your fly-fishing equipment should be steelhead caliber. For lures, you need heavy-hook streamer flies in a good range of sizes. Mostly you will use No. 2 to No. 2/0, with yellow or white wings predominating.

The best all-round lures for spinning and bait casting are wooden plugs with heavy-gauge hooks. Big pavón have powerful jaws and toss their heads like fighting bulls, twisting out hardware and straightening ordinary hooks. They also bite through plastic lures. Payara are natural plug busters with their long canine teeth. Dorado have relatively short but nevertheless sharp teeth. The pacu has molars like a horse— oversize grinding teeth with jaws like a vise. A 20-pound pacu can crush a plug to splinters if he grips it right. You will lose many plugs; so it's advisable to bring along a few dozen. Spoons designed for salt-water casting are usually effective and not easily damaged. Bring plenty of wire leaders: 18-inch long stainless steel coated with vinyl in 30-pound test provides ample protection.

SALTWATER FISHING
Venezuela has over 1,700 miles of coast which is bathed on its north shore by the North Equatorial Current and along the east coast by the Guiana Current which receives freshwater, especially in the rainy season, from the Amazon, Orinoco, and many lesser rivers. These river waters are rich in nutrients which favor the growth of aquatic life on Venezuela's continental shelf and inshore areas. Generally speaking, the season for white marlin is from July through September, but blue marlin are present all year. The whites, which peak in September, are of large average size, with the majority of fish weighing over 60 pounds; the blue marlin average about 225 pounds, with 400- to 450-pound fish being the exception. Most of the marlin fishing is done 15 miles west northwest of the port of La Guaira. Some sailfish are taken in this same area, but larger concentrations appear to exist near Isla de Margarita. Swordfish and bluefin tuna also occur off the Venezuelan coast notably around the island of La Blanquilla. Dolphin are common to all marlin grounds and run to a large size with 25- to 40-pound fish being fairly common. Charter boats are scarce in Venezuela but bookings can be made through the larger Caracas hotels. The *Go-Marina* next to the **Hotel Macuto Sheraton** has a variety of craft available. Rates for a full day run $150 to $200.

Schools of tarpon appear along the coast during the summer months (July through September) and are often caught from small boats and in the surf. However, there is some tarpon fishing in bays, lagoons, and rivers at all times. Snook are very abundant in the surf as well as all brackish-water coastal lagoons such as Sinamaica, Tacarigua, Unaré, Piritu, and Arestinga.

ACCOMMODATIONS
In Caracas, the **Hotel Tamanaco**, with its superb view of the city, luxurious studio bedrooms, attractive *El Toledo* night club, extra-large swimming pool, many shops, good bars and lounges, is a resort in itself, and makes a convenient headquarters. Rates about $15-$20 single and $19.50-$24 double. The **Hotel Avila** is another luxury hotel; single from $13, double from $19.50 Others are **Comercio, El Conde, Mara, Potomac, Tiuna,** and **Waldorf.** The luxurious **Macuto-Sheraton** is on the beach, 20 miles from Caracas, with rates from $11.50 single, $16 double. The Venezuelan government has built a chain of hotels across the nation including the elaborate **Hotel Maracay** with golf course, swimming pool, and movie theater at Maracay. Other hotels in this chain (CONAHOTU) are the **Bella Vista** at Porlamar on the Island of Margarita, and in the Venezuelan Andes the **Aguas Calientes,** the **Moruco,** the **Prado Rio,** the **Tama,** and the **Trujillo.** Good hotels, many of them with air conditioning, can be found throughout the country.

Although the Caracas water system supplies abundant potable water, it is recommended that bottled water be used, particularly during a stay of short duration. Mineral waters are available in most restaurants and hotels. In the interior, drink sealed bottled waters.

Best restaurants would include *Hector's, Chicote, Monseigneur, Rossini's, Anatole, Tarzilandia, Tyrol, Dragon Verde, El Palmar* (Chinese), *Vert Galant, Casa Italia, Lee Hamilton's Steak House, Rincon Bavario.* For Argentine-style steaks: *La Estancia, Shorthorn Grill, Zig-Zag, El Caney.* For seafood: *El Mar, Porlamar, Cubaqua, Rio Chico.* Typical Venezuelan dishes at *El Campo* and *La Carreta.* For French cuisine: *Henry IV, Biarritz Abadie, Ambassador, La Cascada.* One of the most expensive is the exclusive *La Belle Epoque* in Colinas de Bello Monte.

Daily service by Pan Am Jet Clipper, only 4½ hours non-stop from New York to Caracas. Flights from Miami, 2¾ hours. Direct service also from Los Angeles and San Francisco.

Caracas is 2 hours from Panama, where connections are made with Pan Am flights from other points.

Regular taxi rates are not much higher than in any large U.S. city, but establish the fare before a long ride or tour. The ride from the airport up to Caracas costs $7.50. Inter-city bus service is fairly frequent. Rental cars are available and Venezuela has over 5,000 miles of paved road.

Smiling fisherman holds magnificent pavón he landed. Fish is native to South America

Wading In Semi-Tropical And Tropical Waters

Due to the warm climate in many popular fishing areas from Florida through Central and South America, as well as in the Indo-Pacific region, boots or waders are not always desirable. In bonefishing, for example, the angler usually wades "wet" by wearing bathing trunks or old trousers and a pair of rubber-soled canvas shoes. Trousers offer the most protection from the sun (reflected light underwater can cause severe sunburning on sensitive skin) and from organisms such as sea nettles, jellyfish, stinging coral, and fire sponge. The footgear provides additional protection from sea urchins, crabs, bristleworms, sharp coral, and to some extent possible contact with stingrays. Ordinarily, by wading carefully and shuffling one's feet along soft sand or muck bottoms, there is little risk of coming in contact with harmful aquatic life. It should be noted, however, that dangerous fish are present in freshwater *and* saltwater, such as freshwater sharks in parts of Central America; piranha, electric rays and stingrays in tropical South American streams; and various venom-producing species such as scorpionfish, toadfish, and stargazers common to all tropical seas. In areas where schistosomiasis is known to exist (parts of Asia, the Philippines, the Middle East, Africa, the West Indies, and tropical South America) do *not* enter the water at all.

Virgin Islands SEE PAGE 168 FOR MAP

Although the Virgin Islands may rightfully claim some of the finest blue marlin fishing in the Atlantic, the area offers an amazing variety of marine species for the offshore troller. These beautiful islands are really the peaks of submerged mountains that form the eastward extension of a submarine plateau which is the base of the Greater Antilles. Deep water, sharp drop-offs and vast concentrations of baitfish create prime fishing grounds and the existence of over 1,000-pound blue marlin is not to be doubted here. Being in the Trade Winds zone where fresh easterlies are the rule, the sea gets rough at times. However, some fairly calm weather occurs in the spring and from late August through October. Island skippers not only rely on the Fathometers to locate fish but they are also passionate bird watchers. Wheeling and diving booby and frigate birds will usually reveal action on the surface below. Huge schools of blackfin tuna and oceanic bonito foraging on small anchovies attract the marlin, sailfish, big yellowfin tuna and various other large gamefish. Strikes of some kind are invariably obtained under the birds and at times it's actually difficult to keep a bait in the water.

THE SEASON

Blue marlin (record 845 pounds) are caught the year round on the drop-off around the islands from St. Thomas to Anegada, but the peak period is from July through September. This is where the ocean floor drops to 100 fathoms and deeper. It is approximately 15 miles from St. Thomas. The drop-off also produces white marlin and wahoo. Whites, although not as plentiful as blue marlin, have been caught up to 100 pounds, and wahoo to 124 pounds. Both generally are year-round fish. St. Croix features deep water right off the coast on the north and west, and blue marlin can be caught within one-half mile of shore. Two reef areas are especially good for wahoo fishing from fall to spring.

These are Barracuda Sea Mount, southeast of Virgin Gorda, and Lang Bank, just east of St. Croix. Dolphin run the deep water in winter and spring, and have been caught up to 53 pounds. King mackerel can be found year-round both inshore and offshore. They run big on the drop-off and off St. Croix where they have been boated up to 70 pounds. Yellowfin and blackfin tuna appear year-round both offshore and inshore. Sailfish are most numerous in winter and spring. Scattered sails show up on the north drop-off in late September, and the fish start moving to concentrate on the inshore shelf just north of St. Thomas and Tortola in mid-November. The sails remain through March. The fish average 40 to 45 pounds and most are released.

Species taken along the edge of the shelf or close inshore include, besides the king mackerel, the little tuna, cero mackerel, blue runner, bar jack, horse-eye jack, various snappers, groupers and barracuda. The shore fisherman may find tarpon throughout the islands on occasion but chiefly along the north coast of St. Thomas and around St. Croix at Pelican Cove and Salt River Bay. Due to the mountainous nature of the islands, bonefish flats are both scarce and small except along the south side of St. Croix. The most popular spots are at Long Point and Krause Lagoon between Frederiksted and Christiansted. Snook and ladyfish are also caught around St. Croix. Large permit appear throughout the Virgins, often coming up on small coral flats. While inshore fishing is satisfactory it is not of the offshore caliber which has made the Virgins famous.

TACKLE

Big-game fishing tackle is supplied by the charter craft. However, 80- and 130-pound-test class tackle is mostly used here due to the depth of the water (2 miles down in places) and the size of the marlin encountered. Lighter tackle is used on the flat-lines, either 30- or 50-pound-test class, for smaller baits and smaller fish. Except around St. Croix the inshore fishing possibilities are limited, so optionally you may want to bring along a saltwater bait-casting, spinning, or fly rod.

ACCOMMODATIONS

Although the U.S. Virgin Islands consist of St. Thomas, St. Croix, St. John, and about fifty smaller islets, in the contest of fishing, Virgin Gorda, a British possession, is often included in the angler's itinerary. Virgin Gorda is serviced by charter craft either from Tortola or the Red Hook Marina out of St. Thomas.

ST. THOMAS

Many and varied accommodations are available on St. Thomas which has the largest population and includes the busy capital city of Charlotte Amalie. Some of the more popular hotels are the **Caravan Hotel** with 150 rooms facing the waterfront; $25 and $30 European Plan. The **Bluebeard's Castle,** $46 and $56, overlooks town and sea. The luxurious **Virgin Isle Hilton,** $44 and $54, has a beautiful pool, two cork tennis courts, dancing nightly, each room with private balcony; **Dorothea Beach Club,** secluded cottages in formal beach resort; $47.50 double, European Plan. The **Water Isle Colony Club,** on an island in the harbor, has fine facilities for snorkeling, sailing, spearfishing; $48 double. **Pineapple Beach Club,** on the east coast, offers both sea and pool swimming; $56 double. **Island Beachcomber,** beach resort and efficiency units. **Morning Star Beach Resort** has luxuriously appointed beach facilities; $25 and $30, European Plan. The elegant **Pelican Beach Club** is quietly se-

cluded; $44 double, European Plan. **Sapphire Bay Resort,** with all kinds of water sports, is five miles from town: $30 and $35, European Plan. The new **Pavilions** offers complete apartments, each with its own swimming pool and maid service; $44 double, European Plan. **Shibui Hotel** is a colony of attractive Japanese-style cottages with pool and a view; $30 double, European Plan. **Yacht Haven Hotel** with pool and yachting center, $24 and $32, European Plan.

ST. CROIX

Christiansted area: The **Buccaneer Hotel,** with accommodations on beautiful beach, $30 and $55. **Grapetree Bay Hotel & Villas** on a 750-acre estate, $38 and $52. **St. Croix By The Sea,** with beach and pool, $32 and $48. **Queen's Quarter,** pool and cottages, $15 and $30, and **Pelican Cove Beach Club,** efficiency units with pool and beach, $19 and $38, European Plan. **Beach Hotel of St. Croix** has air-conditioned beachfront lanai suites, $18 and $47. **Tamarind Reef Hotel,** $28 and $42. **Cruzana Hotel,** $28 and $38.

Christiansted Town: **Old Quarter Hotel,** $22 and $28, European Plan. **King's Alley Hotel,** $25 and $28, European Plan. **Comanche Hotel,** $15 and $24 with breakfast, **Mahogany Inn,** $12 and $24, European Plan. **Pink Fancy Apartments,** $15 and $20. Cane Bay, on the north shore midway between the two towns, has several small quiet cottage colonies with kitchenettes, such as **The Waves,** $125 weekly; **Village at Cane Bay,** $210 weekly; and **Diamond Fancy,** $150 weekly, all double. **Cane Bay Plantation** has cottages, $20 double, European Plan, and rooms with balconies at $32 and $50, Modified American Plan.

Frederiksted area: **Cottages By the Sea,** $145-$185 weekly. **Royal Dane Hotel,** $26 and $38, Modified American Plan. **Sunset Beach Cottages,**

$20, European Plan. **Estate Good Hope,** with beach, about $50, Modified American Plan. **Clover Crest Hotel,** with pool, $28 and $40, Modified American Plan. **La Grange House,** about $35 and $42, Modified American Plan. **Sprat Hall,** with beach, $22 and $40, Modified American Plan.

ST. JOHN

Not a resort in the usual sense of the word, exotic **Caneel Bay Plantation, Inc.,** is a wholly owned corporation of Jackson Hole Preserve, Inc., a non-profit foundation, and all income is devoted to the operation, maintenance, and improvement of the facilities as well as conservation projects. The Plantation is located on the northwest tip of St. John, smallest of the three main United States Virgin Islands and the site of the Virgin Islands National Park. Caneel Bay is just four miles and only twenty minutes by motor launch from Red Hook Landing on St. Thomas. **Caneel Bay Plantation** has a total of 130 double rooms in beachfront units with a maximum capacity of some 298 persons. Some of the beachfront rooms connect in pairs, if desired, and each has bedroom and lounge areas, tiled bath, dressing alcove, private entrance, and an open-to-the-sky patio. The resort is open all year with off-season rates (during best fishing period) effective from April 15 to December 14. In-season rates American Plan are $48 to $73 per person per day, $60 to $85 double.

VIRGIN GORDA

The **Little Dix Bay Resort,** developed by Mr. Laurance S. Rockefeller, occupies a 500-acre tract on the northwest corner of Virgin Gorda, third largest of the British Virgin Islands. This archipelago is linked geographically and economically with the U.S. Virgin Islands. Virgin Gorda is 10 miles long and two miles wide, and is 12 miles east of Tortola, capital of the British Virgin

Angler Elliot Fishman of St. Thomas captured this record 845-pound blue marlin on 80-pound-test line over the 100 fathom curve

Islands, and some 26 miles northeast of St. Thomas, capital of the U.S. Virgin Islands.

The **Little Dix Bay Resort** has a total of 50 rooms located along the wide crescent of Little Dix Bay beach. The reefs and offshore islands afford a variety of protected sailing areas and anchorages. Trade winds in Sir Francis Drake Channel by Virgin Gorda provide some of the Caribbean's most challenging and exciting sailing. In-season rates are $75 to $80 single per person per day and $85 to $90 double.

Executive twin-engine air service direct to Virgin Gorda connects with daily jets arriving at San Juan, Puerto Rico, and St. Thomas, V.I., from New York, Miami, Chicago and other principal U.S. cities as well as South America and Europe. There are no visas, passports, or vaccination records required for U.S. or British visitors. United States cur-

rency is the medium of exchange in the British Virgin Islands.

Reservations for **Caneel Bay Plantation** and **Little Dix Bay Resort** may be made through travel agents; through Resort Representation in the East—New York, 30 Rockefeller Plaza West (telephone CIrcle 5-8055); Chicago, 20 Michigan Avenue (telephone 922-4139); Washington, D.C., 1627 K Street, N.W. (telephone 347-4951); through Glen W. Fawcett, Inc., in the West—Los Angeles, 510 West Sixth Street (telephone MA 6-7581); San Francisco, 629 Russ Building (telephone 434-0660); Seattle, 726 Joseph Vance Building (MU 2-1981); Dallas, 211 North Ervay (telephone RI 1-6814); or directly with the resorts: **Caneel Bay Plantation,** St. John, U.S. Virgin Islands, Box 1091, St. Thomas, Virgin Islands, USA. (Cable: Caneelbay, St. Thomas; telephone 744-1090). **Little Dix Bay,** c/o International Airport Post Office, San Juan, Puerto Rico, (Cable: Dixbay, Virgin Gorda, B.V.I.)

VIRGIN ISLANDS NATIONAL PARK

Information, maps, literature on fish, plants, and island history are available at the park visitor center. Several exhibits and orientation talks at 10:30 a.m. and 11:00 a.m. give you a general introduction to the natural and human history of St. John.

Hiking trails on St. John are numerous, from easy walks to difficult climbs; well maintained to brushy; and short to long—¼ mile to 6 miles. Bring good hiking shoes and cool clothing. Small knapsacks and belt canteens are handy. Water is not available along hiking trails.

For you-drive-it jeeps at $12 to $15 per day—also by the week—make reservations well in advance. A temporary Virgin Islands driver's license ($1) and a valid state license (U.S. or foreign) are required.

Guided snorkel trips are conducted

weekly as well as history and nature walks. One is an all-day guided hike into the Reef Bay Valley to see the famed petroglyphs (ancient stone picture writings). For illustrated evening campfire programs and other activities, check the weekly schedules posted at the visitor center in Cruz Bay, Cinnamon Bay Camp Store, and Caneel Bay Plantation.

Swimming and snorkeling are excellent at St. John's many fine beaches when weather and sea conditions are good. You may rent snorkel equipment at Trunk and Cinnamon bays. Ask a lifeguard about the safety features of the equipment you are using. Scuba also can be rented and serviced on both St. John and St. Thomas. Spearfishing and water skiing are strictly prohibited in park areas.

Virgin Islands National Park is administered by the National Park Service, United States Department of the Interior. Address all inquiries to the Superintendent, Box 1707, St. Thomas, U.S. V.I. 00801.

CAMPING ON ST. JOHN
Cinnamon Bay Campground, with the beach nearby, is located five miles from Cruz Bay on a paved road. It has tables, charcoal grills, and water (should be boiled). While there is no definite rainy season, tents are advised because of unexpected rain showers. Camping limit is 30 days in any 12-month period. Insect repellents are needed. No electricity and no bath or laundry facilities are in the park, but a laundry is located in Cruz Bay. Pets are not permitted in the campground.

At **Cinnamon Bay** you may rent complete camping equipment for $35 per week for two, plus $8.75 per week for each additional person. Also available are screened and furnished beach cottages with patio and outdoor cooking facilities; a modern comfort station is nearby.

Cottage rates are $10 per day per couple; $2 each additional person.

The concessioner provides cots, bedding, linen, and cooking utensils, and the camp store has essential groceries, ice, charcoal, and some other supplies. A variety of foods are available at Cruz Bay, and supermarkets are on St. Thomas, but purchases must be carried to camp personally by taxi and ferry. Cottage and campground reservations must be made well in advance because both equipment and cottages are limited. Write to: The Concessioner, Cinnamon Bay Camp, St. John, U.S. Virgin Islands 00830.

CONTACTS
Captain John Harms of the Lagoon Marina at Red Hook on St. Thomas has the largest charter fleet in the Virgins. Captain Harms pioneered and did much to develop the big-game fishing here, and can help tourist anglers get oriented.

There are a number of fishing tournaments throughout the year in the islands. Included are a year-round sailfish release tourney, a Memorial Day event, and the Annual July 4th Open Tournament. Visiting anglers are invited to come and talk fishing with members of the island's two clubs, the Virgin Islands Game Fishing Club, which meets the first Thursday night of each month at Lagoon Marina, St. Thomas, and the St. Croix Sports Fishing Club, which

meets the second Tuesday night of each month at Club Comanche, Christiansted, St. Croix.

TRAVEL NOTES
By non-stop Pan American Clipper to St. Thomas 3½ hours from New York; 3½ hours from Miami. Pan Am's non-stop service is daily. If you are planning a three-week or less vacation, check the 21-day excursion fare. To reach the Virgin Islands National Park on St. John from Charlotte Amalie on St. Thomas, go to the public dock at Red Hook by taxi ($3 one person, 50c each additional). Also a public bus (40c per person) operates between Charlotte Amalie and Red Hook. The Ferry across Pillsbury Sound from Red Hook to Cruz Bay ($1 per person) operates daily from 7:30 a.m. to 5:30 p.m. After hours charter service only is available at $10 to $12 per boat. A special boat for Caneel Bay Plantation guests runs between the Red Hook Ranger Station and Caneel Bay.

DOCUMENTATION
All regulations applicable to the USA apply. Canadians and British subjects coming from or passing through adjacent islands should carry Int. Certificate of Vaccination and passport. All others require passport.

Sport Fisherman boat designed for fishing plies waters of the Virgin Islands

Wales

A Welsh angler spins for salmon on the Towy. Pastoral countryside is typical of this mountainous section of Great Britain

The Principality of Wales is the mountainous area of Great Britain bounded on the south by the Bristol Channel, on the west by St. George's Channel and the Irish Sea, on the north by the estuary of the Dee, and on the east roughly by the line of the river Severn. As different from England as is Scotland, with its own language and its own traditions, Wales possesses some worthwhile fishing for the tourist. Atlantic salmon, brown trout, and sea trout (locally called sewin) are the principal gamefish sought. Here as elsewhere in the British Isles most of the angling is made available through hotels and local angling associations.

THE FISHING

The Severn, once a great salmon river, is, through wise management, rapidly regaining its stature. Its tributaries, both in Wales and along the border, also provide excellent trout fishing. The Wye, accepted as

the best salmon river south of Scotland, likewise affords excellent trouting in its upper waters and feeder streams such as the Lugg, Irfon, Ithon, Monnow, and Honddu.

Pre-eminent among Welsh rivers is the Usk. Once the finest salmon river of its size in Europe, it still has a good run of fish averaging 10 to 12 pounds. The Usk also holds many brown trout usually from ½- to ¾-pound, and draws minor runs of sea trout in early spring and summer.

The charge for fishing varies according to the beat but there are a number available. Except when the water is high and badly discolored after heavy rains, sport can generally be relied on with the fly. Chest-high waders are desirable for the Usk is a big river, by British standards. The Usk can be fished from the **Gliffaes Country House Hotel** which controls about 2½ miles of water. Most of the stream adjoins the hotel grounds but there is an ad-

ditional beat some miles downstream near Abergavenny. Visitors can also go to Usk Town where the local Fishery Association holds about two miles of water and issues a limited number of day tickets for trout fishing only. This is some of the finest water in Wales.

The Teifi (pronounced Tie-Vee) and the Towy are both good salmon and trout streams and particularly good sea-trout rivers. The Cothi, a tributary of the Towy, is an outstanding stream for the latter fish. A popular accommodation here is the **Talbot Hotel, (Talbot Hotel,** Tregaron, Cardiganshire, West Wales). A small, inexpensive country inn, it does not control water but is convenient for visitors who can get fishing rights through the local Tregaron Angling Association. A weekly visitor's ticket for salmon and for trout or a season ticket is available from Barclays Bank in the village square near the hotel. A River Board license can be bought from the local drug store. A helpful map issued by the association explains the main Teifi water and designates the salmon pools in which spinning is permitted. Elsewhere, below Glanbrenig Bridge, Tregaron, the rule is fly only. Night fishing is not allowed, nor is Sunday fishing. This remote part of Wales is Welsh-speaking, and at night the talk in the hotel bar is in the ancient tongue.

Salmon are not plentiful; their presence is dependent on water conditions, which also govern the sea-trout run in the summer. Brown trout fishing opens about mid-March and is particularly good in April and May. Trout average over ½-pound as a rule, but there are plenty over 1 pound with an occasional 2-pounder or better. Above Tregaron the water flows through a Nature Reserve, the desolate, curlew-haunted Tregaron Bog. Below the village there is some most attractive dry-fly water on such reaches as Abercoed, Nantdderwen, and Pont Llanio.

The Dovey and the Conway are excellent sea-trout rivers. Each season, large numbers of fish over 8 pounds are taken from both of them. Both hold salmon, and the Conway (and its tributary the Lledr) is a popular river in Britain for these fish. The **Gwydyr Hotel,** one of the best in Wales, controls about 30 miles of the fishing in the Conway, Llugwy, and Lledr. It also offers trout fishing on Lakes Elsi and Siabod (**Gwydyr Hotel,** Betws-Y-Coed, Caernarven, Wales, telephone: Betws-y-Coed 217).

Besides these well-known rivers there are many other smaller streams which have a run of salmon, often a big run of sea trout, and which hold, of course, resident brown trout. There are also many lakes, natural and man-made, which provide good trout fishing.

The following are typical hotels and inns with facilities for angling in Wales:

Royal Goat, Beddgelert Tel. 224	Salmon, sea trout and trout fishing on river and lake.
Pen-y-Gwryd, Nant Gwynant Tel. Llanberis 211	Salmon, sea trout, and trout fishing on river and lake. Tickets available at hotel.
Snowdonia Park Motel Tyn-y-Maes Tel. Bethesda 548	Salmon, sea trout and trout fishing on river and lake. Tickets available at hotel.
Saracen's Head Hotel Beddgelert. Tel. 223	Salmon, sea trout and trout fishing on river and lake. Hotel private water.
Tan Lan Hotel, Betws-y-Coed Tel. 232.	Salmon, sea trout and trout fishing on river Conway. Association waters but weekly tickets available at hotel.
Dolmelynnllyn Hall Ganllwyd Tel. 211	Hotel private water. Salmon sea trout and trout fishing on River Mawddach and lake. Welsh Manor House, dates from 12th century. Owned by National Trust.
Tyn-y-Groes Ganllwyd Tel. 205	Hotel private water. Salmon, sea trout and trout fishing on River Mawddach available to guests. Tickets obtainable from hotel.
Blaendyffryn Hall Llandyssul Tel. 2377	Hotel private water. Salmon, sea trout and trout fishing on River Teify.
Castle Malgwyn Llechryd Tel. 382	Hotel private water. Salmon, sea trout and trout fishing in grounds. License locally.
Hand Hotel Llanarmon Dyffryn Ceiriog Tel. 296	Trout fishing adjoining hotel. Old inn now modernized. Licenses available at hotel.
West Arms Llanarmon Dyffryn Ceiriog Tel. 205	Hotel private water. Trout fishing on adjoining river. Example of 17th century Welsh Inn. Licenses at hotel.
Tyn-y-Wern Llangollen Tel. 2252	Salmon and trout fishing on River Dee available to guests. Tackle obtainable locally.
Golden Pheasant Llwynmawr Tel. Clynceiriog 281	Hotel private water. Trout fishing; three miles on River Ceiriog. Salmon fishing also available.
Ruthin Castle Ruthin Tel. 2664	Hotel private water. Trout fishing in grounds for twelve miles. Tickets obtainable from hotel. Fly fishing only.

Yugoslavia

Best known for huchen and brown trout, the Neretva River *(left)* flows through Mostar. Deluxe accommodations such as the Golf Hotel *(top)* are available in many angling centers. Excellent fly fishing is found on the Sava Bohinjka River *(top right)*. The Una River *(center)* has more than fifty waterfalls in its 133-mile course. New York visitor Peter Barrett found a pram helpful in maneuvering through this Gacka River tributary *(below)*. The Gacka is considered a classic European chalk stream. The Buna River *(far right)* is a tributary to the Neretva; in addition to brown and rainbow trout it holds the rare softmouth trout, which has plicate mobile lips similar to those of a sucker

The most Western and independent of the Eastern-bloc nations, Yugoslavia is free of Red tape and is enjoying an unparalleled tourist boom. Embracing the western half of the Balkan Peninsula and bordered by Austria, Italy, Hungary, Rumania, Bulgaria, Greece, and Albania, this small (98,766 square miles) European country has such a variety of landscapes, from Alpine peaks to rolling hills and a spectacularly precipitous coast spilling into the sea, that it refers to itself as a traveler's "compact." There are more than 1,000 islands off its Dalmatian Coast of which about a hundred are permanently inhabited. The annual array of cultural and sporting events with the jazz festival at Bled, the International Motorcycle Rally at Crikvenica, the Adriatic Grand Prix at Opatija, the Film Festival at Pula and even a jousting on horseback tournament at Sinj attract aficionados in such numbers that from mid-June to September Yugoslavia is literally overrun with tourists. Aside from its physical and intellectual assets, Yugoslavia offers bargain prices in accommodations and food which has not escaped sharp-eyed West

Europeans. The fact that fishing exists at all is almost anti-climactic and while the overall picture is modest, no angling education is complete until you've sampled a beautiful river like the Sava Bohinjka or puzzled over Yugoslavia's exotic salmonids. Almost the entire country is based on limestone (every street and every building in the fabulous old city of Dubrovnik is made of limestone) a geological endowment that is the hallmark of fertile trout streams. By the same token its seawater is so clear that plankton and marine plant life is relatively poor along the Adriatic shore and saltwater fishing is limited to a small number of reef species — although it is a paradise for the skin or scuba diver.

One way to cover Yugoslavia's rivers is to rent a car in one of the major cities and follow the road map. For a guide book get a copy of *Fishing In Yugoslavia* from the Tourist Association of Yugoslavia (Beograd, Nusiceva 9/V, POB 595). This 26-page booklet is more accurately compiled than most government publications although the scientific names of fishes are in some cases

incorrect or outdated. The translation of species into English may sound a bit strange such as "largetooth trout, softmouth trout, or badmouth trout," but they are literal. In general all north to south highways are excellent and all east to west roads are terrible.

The other way, and certainly the easiest for non-Slavonic speakers, is to have a travel specialist arrange the trip for you which solves all problems including the driving. *Safari Outfitters, Inc.* (8 South Michigan Avenue, Chicago, Illinois 60603) offers a Yugoslavian package tour at $220 per person (excluding air fare) for seven days.

THE SEASON

May and June are the best months for Yugoslavian trout fishing. Average daily temperatures will range from 63°F to 68°F and rainfall during this period averages about 15 days out of each month. The summer season can be very hot with a mean in July of 75°F but daily maximums running to 85°F or more. Good fishing can be obtained in high altitude streams during summer months.

THE FISHING

Yugoslavian freshwater fishing is primarily for brown and rainbow trout. The brown is native to Yugoslavia and the rainbow was introduced from California. Grayling are also native to the country. However, rivers draining into the Adriatic contain post-glacial species which, with a possible exception in the Ohrid trout (*Salmo letnica*) do not occur elsewhere. A similar relict species, the Lake Garda trout (*Salmo carpio*) exists on the Italian side of the Adriatic. A brood stock of Ohrid trout is presently maintained at the Manchester, Iowa, Federal hatchery in the U.S.A. The species is being considered as a possible alternate for the brown trout in lake environments. In addition to the Ohrid trout, Yugoslavian angling may produce marble trout (*Salmo mormoratus*) which grows to very large sizes exceeding 40 pounds, and the softmouth trout (*Salmo obtusirostris*) which weighs up to 10 pounds. Another primitive genus of salmonine fishes is *Hucho*, a strictly Eurasian freshwater group composed of four species and commonly known to most Europeans as huchen. A large, landlocked salmonid (one species *Hucho taimen* which occurs in Russian Arctic rivers from the Pechora River east attains a recorded weight of 176 pounds although the Yugoslavian species *Hucho hucho* is known to exceed 80 pounds) the huchen is highly regarded by anglers. Huchen are caught primarily by casting spoons, spinners, and plugs. The fight consists of long, hard runs at great speed. It is a strong fish and fairly heavy spinning tackle is favored. Huchen are essentially a river species usually found at the bottom of deep pools near fast water. Numerous attempts have been made to introduce huchen to European rivers which are not suited to Atlantic salmon, but none of these introductions has been successful.

The body shape of the huchen is very similar to the Atlantic salmon, *Salmo salar*. It is, however, rather more cylindrical than the salmon, with a proportionately larger head and adipose fin. The back is colored dark brown to violet, or even gray-green. The sides often have a reddish hue, deepening with age. The belly is white or silver, and the entire

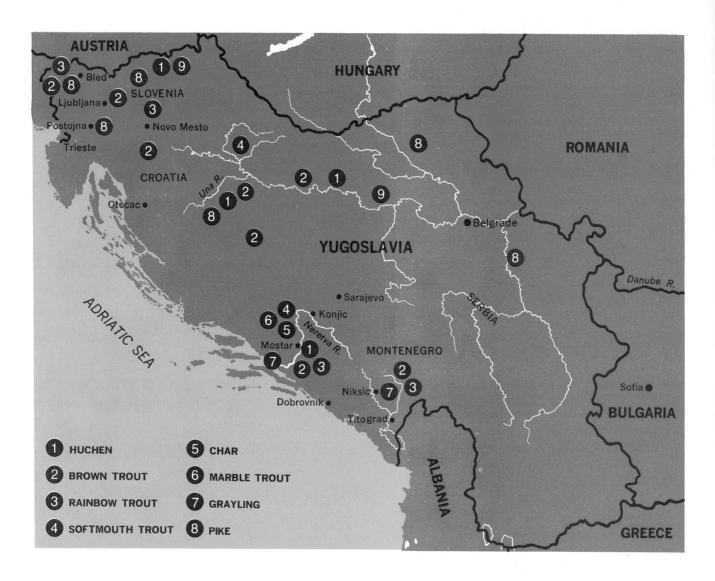

1 HUCHEN 5 CHAR

2 BROWN TROUT 6 MARBLE TROUT

3 RAINBOW TROUT 7 GRAYLING

4 SOFTMOUTH TROUT 8 PIKE

body surface is covered with many minute black spots. In contrast with the brown trout, which it generally resembles when small, only black spots are present. The latter species may have orange or red spots as well—the huchen does not.

There are few quantitative differences between the huchen and the salmon or trout. Huchen have by far the smallest scales of these three species, 180 to 200 in the lateral line. Brown trout in comparison have only 110 to 120 lateral line scales and Atlantic salmon 120 to 130.

Huchen caught by angling are usually from 24 to 48 inches in length. While their growth rate is initially slow, after maturity 2 pounds per annum is considered the norm and a 4-pound increment has been recorded. In general, Yugoslavian rivers have a rich supply of small forage fishes and are therefore capable of supporting large predators

such as the huchen and marble trout. To what extent these species will be affected by the growing number of hydroelectric impoundments is not known.

The following are some of the major fishing streams in Yugoslavia:

SAVA BOHINJKA RIVER
Located in Slovenia, the Sava Bohinjka is a crystal-clear gravel-bottomed stream that rises in Lake Bohinjka which nestles among the Julian Alps. Although the highest peak, Triglav (9,393 feet), is of modest stature when compared to other mountain ranges, the heavily glaciated limestone and granite walls are remarkably beautiful. The river offers many miles of first-class fly fishing for rainbows, browns, and grayling. The fish in this stream are plump and colorful with an average of about ¾-pound and the occasional 2- or 3-pounder. Dry flies and nymphs are most effective. The river

is easy to wade. Look for the larger trout along undercut banks and willows.

Literally situated in a corner opposite Austria and Italy, the resort city of Bled offers every amenity to the traveler from casinos to sauna baths and a variety of lakefront hotels. Recommended here is the **Golf Hotel** (Golf Hotel, Bled, Slovenija, Yugoslavia) a modern, first-class operation with excellent food. Situated on a hillside overlooking Lake Bled, the rooms offer a spectacular view. Rates run $7 to $9 single, and $6 to $8 per person double including meals (the plan is called Full Board in Yugoslavia). July and August prices run about two dollars higher. It's only a ten-minute drive from the hotel to the river. The hotel doorman is an ardent angler and taxidermist; check him for best spots. A fishing license is about $4 per day and can be obtained from Zavod za ribistvo (the Fishing Institute) in Ljubljana, Zupanciceva 9, telephone 20-702, which manages these waters; the Tourist Society of Bled, telephone 77-409; the travel agency Kompas at Bled, telephone 77-235 and 77-245; Ribogojstvo (the Fish-Hatchery) Bohinj at Bohinjska Bistrica, telephone 76-116, and from the Tourist Society Bohinj in the Tourist Office at Lake Bohinj, telephone 76-105.

KRKA RIVER

The Krka River (pronounced Kur-ka with a rolled *r*) is not far from the city of Ljubljana. Except for the farm houses with their red tile roofs the countryside is very similar to the Catskill Mountain region around the Beaverkill River. However, the rivers are distinctly different. The Krka is mainly a slow-flowing stream with long, deep stretches that flow be-tween steep hills; comparatively lit-tle of the trout water between its source and the village of Zuzemberk is wadable. About every quarter mile or so the Krka flows over shallow limestone ledges of several hundred yards in length which offer access to the river. Despite this limited wading area numbers of fine trout can be caught especially during the fre-quent mayfly hatches. The average size is about 1 pound although the river holds very large browns and rainbows and 5- and 6-pounders are not uncommon. The lower river, from Zuzemberk to Novo Mesto is primarily grayling and huchen wa-ter. The Krka is noted for its large huchen which average about 15 pounds. From Novo Mesto down-stream the river becomes broader and slow moving; northern pike and walleye are common here.

For the Krka you can find accommo-dations at the **Hotel Otocec,** an old castle situated on an island in the river at the village of Otocec. Actu-ally, it doesn't put you any closer to the fishing because you'll still have to drive almost half way back to Ljubljana to reach the better trout water so it's just as easy to stay in the city at the **Hotel Lev** where the food and amenities are first class.

GACKA RIVER

The Gacka River (pronounced Gots-ga) in Croatia is one of the most fer-tile chalk streams in central Europe. At one time it produced very large brown and rainbow trout (to 20 pounds) and although occasional big fish are still caught, their num-bers have declined and the stream average is about 1½ pounds. The

The resort city of Bled in the Julian Alps. Nearby Sava Bohinjka, tributary to Bled Lake, is one of Yugoslavia's better trout rivers

One of the best grayling streams (and not listed in the guide books) is the beautiful Unica River in the meadows of Postojna

Gacka is intensively fished particularly in the prime season from May through June after which the angling tapers off with some fair catches being made on evening rises. However, due to a great abundance of aquatic foods, the fish are highly selective and the angling is not easy. Long a favorite of German and Italian tourists, the Gacka gets plenty of rod pressure even in summer months. There are no good accommodations near the river. The choice is to stay at the **Park Hotel** in Otocac (pronounced Aw-toe-shots) which is a lower than B Category hotel but within 5 miles of the river, or at the A Category **Plitvice Hotel** located in the National Park 25 miles from the Gacka at Plitvice. The drive from Plitvice to the Gacka is about 25 miles in a large part over switchback road that takes one hour. The **Plitvice Hotel** is a mecca for park visitors—heavily trafficked but well run.

NERETVA RIVER
The Neretva River is one of the largest in Yugoslavia and is usually fished from the town of Konjic or Mostar. This broad, slightly turbid river has a daily fluctuating water

level due to a hydroelectric impoundment near its headwaters. The level may increase from 2 to 4 feet depending on demand with the stream at its low stage in the morning hours and rising by mid-day. Any wading must be done very cautiously. However, the Neretva contains a variety of salmonids including brown, rainbow, softmouth, and marble trout. It also produces some exceptional huchen in the 60-pound plus class. Chiefly, this is a stream for the spinning rod as it is almost all bank casting and over much of its length the Neretva is about a quarter mile wide. Ideally, you should fish the Neretva early in the morning while the water is low, then drive to the Buna River for an afternoon of trout fishing. Stay at the **Bristol Hotel** in Mostar. There are several others in town but it's the best choice.

BUNA RIVER
The Buna River, a tributary of the Neretva, is located near the city of Mostar. This charming stream has many good riffles and pools and produces rainbow, brown, and softmouth trout. The popular fishing area is from the riverside restaurant

at its source (the Buna emerges from a great spring in a cave at the foot of a mountain) to about 5 miles downstream. Although this upstream section is productive, with an average of about ¾-pound, any of the lower beats are preferable.

UNA RIVER
One of the most scenic rivers in Yugoslavia, the Una has a great number of waterfalls (at the rate of about one at every 1½ miles in its 133-mile course) which creates the impression of a chain of narrow lakes rather than a river. The Una and its tributaries—the Unac, Klokot, Krusnica, Bastra, and Sana Rivers, are principally grayling and brown trout streams although large huchen occur in the Una from the waterfall at Kosteli downstream; a popular 12½ mile stretch is at Bosanska Krupa. The main fishing center for the Una is at Martin Brod.

UNICA RIVER
Overlooked in the official guide books but about an hour's drive south of Ljubljana near the town of Postojna, the Unica is one of the best, if not *the* best grayling stream in Yugoslavia. A narrow, meander-

ing river, it is quite easy to fish with a fly. You can headquarter either in Ljubljana and drive, or stay at the **Hotel Kras** in Postojna. The road from Ljubljana is terrible. It's the main artery into Trieste and points south on the Adriatic. Many switch-backs in the highway with heavy commercial traffic. To reach the best fishing on the Unica, take the road from Planina towards Rakek. After a half mile turn left at the bridge. After a quarter mile you will see an unlikely track sloping down into the field on the left. Follow this until you arrive at a big loop in the river. Good fly water here and 60 to 80 grayling in a day would not be unusual. Fish average about ¾-pound with the occasional 2-pounder.

MORACA RIVER

Flows through Titograd in Montene-gro and is one of the better marble trout streams in Yugoslavia. A 46½-pound marble trout was caught here in 1968 (this species is known locally as *glavatica*). The Moraca also contains large brown and rain-bow trout. A road parallels the river for almost fifty miles so the water is accessible. Like the huchen, marble trout tend to stay in deep places (the Moraca has many steep gorges) and make strong runs when hooked but rarely jump. Spinners, spoons, and plugs are favored for these large trout. Two other streams worth ex-ploring in this area are the Cijevna and Zeta Rivers. Accommodations can be found in Titograd at the **Podgorica Hotel** or in the village of Niksic at the **Onogost Hotel.**

TACKLE

Any standard trout fly rod according to preference. Most Yugoslavian waters can be fished with fairly light tackle, however, as a second rod, bring along a 9-footer with a No. 8 line if you plan to fish a weedy river like the Gacka. It takes a stout rod to hold big trout out of the cress beds. Too, the Gacka flows through open country where winds are a problem. All the usual trout patterns in dry

Scenic Lake Bohinj in Yugoslavia offers angler a choice of brown or rainbow trout

and wet flies will take fish, but nymphs are often most effective and make sure to stock a supply in cream, grays, and browns. Much of this fishing is in crystal-clear water, so long, fine leaders (9 to 12 feet and from 3X to 6X) are a must. Spin-ning or bait-casting tackle for the huchen should be calibered at 12-pound-test minimum; wobbling spoons, spinners and small plugs are effective.

LICENSES

Yugoslavia consists of six separate socialist republics: Slovenia, Bosnia and Hercegovina, Croatia, Mace-donia, Serbia, and Montenegro. Each has its own system of licensing which is really not as complicated as it reads. When in doubt your hotel or the local tourist office can direct you to the correct address. Basically, you will need a separate permit for *each* river and a fishing card aver-ages about $4 per day. Yugoslavia has a very active staff of game pro-tectors so don't get a lapse of mem-ory about which stream you are on, or whether the permit covers that particular day. Size and bag limits are strictly enforced and also vary according to the waters fished; this information will appear on your per-mit. The following may serve as a general guide:

SLOVENIA

For all detailed information foreign

visitors can approach these organi-zations: Ribiskazveza Slovenije, Zupanciceva 9/11, Ljubljana, or Uprava gojitvenih lovisc, Zupan-ciceva 9, Ljubljana.

CROATIA

Permits are issued by district peo-ple's committees (-Opstinski narodni odbor-) or by fishing as-sociations or by tourist organiza-tions. If writing from abroad, the address is: Sportsko ribolovno drustvo in care of the particular republic.

Information for fishing in rivers and lakes can be obtained from -Savez, sportskih ribolovnih drustava Hrvatske-, Palmoticeva 7/I, Zagreb, (Union of fishing societies of Croatia).

BOSNIA AND HERCEGOVINA

Permits for the whole Republic (for all its waters) are issued by -Savez udruzenja ribolovaca-, Stros-majerova 1/II, Sarajevo, (Union fishermen's associations) and by lo-cal associations of anglers and by district people's committees for all the waters on their own territory.

MONTENEGRO

Permits are issued by district peo-ple's committees. Information is given by -Udruzenje sportskih ribolovaca Crne Gore-, Titograd, (Association of sports fishermen).

SERBIA

Fishing permits are issued by district people's committees or Udruzenje sportskih ribolovaca Srbije, Strahinica bana 66 A, (Association of sports fishermen of Serbia). For the region Pancevacki Rit permits are issued by the same Association or by the travel agency -Turist Expres-, Beograd. For the fishing region of Lake Vlasina permits are issued by Lovno gazdinstvo, Marsala Tita 14, Beograd, or by Uprava rezervata at Vlasinsko Jezero, by -Turist- at Leskovac and by -Turist Expres-, Beograd.

MACEDONIA

Permits are issued by fishing societies and by district people's committees (Opstinski narodni odbor). Information can be obtained from Savez sportskih ribolovaca NR Makedonije, -Partizanka- VI adm. zgrada, Skopje, (Union of sports fishermen of PR Macedonia).

ACCOMMODATIONS

BELGRADE

The best hotel in Belgrade is the **Hotel Jugoslavia;** expensive by local standards, rates run about $20 per day single and $24 per day double American plan. Modern with spacious public rooms and excellent restaurants the **Jugoslavia** is a good jumpoff point to the fishing regions. Other hotels are the **Metropol, Majestic, Slavija, Moskva, Palace,** and **Excelsior** with rates ranging from $12 to $15 per day single including meals.

DUBROVNIK

Called the "Pearl of the Adriatic" with its ancient walls and winding narrow streets. Fort Lovrjenac, built in the 14th century, is often the setting for festival performances of Shakespeare. The Rector's Palace, completed in 1441, is now a palatial museum and inside the West Gate is a pharmacy that has been in business since 1318. Dubrovnik is

easily reached by sea, highway or air. Best hotels: **Excelsior, Argentina, Adriatic, Neptun, Dubrovnik, Petka.** Don't miss *Restaurant Prijeko,* a small bistro in the old city. Try the stuffed squid.

SPLIT

Located in the center of the Dalmatian coast, Split treasures the immense 4th-century palace of the Emperor Diocletian and makes it the setting for its annual summer festival. The town is a gem of Venetian-Gothic architecture, and folk dance performances, opera, ballet and concerts offer music the year around. Advance hotel reservations are advisable at the **Marjan, Park** and **Bellevue.**

OPATIJA

Former resort of Austro-Hungarian nobility. Opatija revels in a balmy climate with lidos, lovely walks through luxuriant woods, and many excellent restaurants. The old casino is active. Best hotels are **Kvarner, Slavija, Belvedere, Krystal** (with a good night club), **Jadran, Atlantic** and **Ambassador.** The town is a convenient headquarters for excursions to Pula with its amphitheater; the spectacular Plitvica Lakes lying on 16 levels connected by waterfalls; Rovinj; and the beautiful Postoina Caves. Other popular seaside resorts are Budva, Crikvenica, Hercegovina, Portoroz and the islands of Rab, Hvar and Sveti Stefan (a whole medieval village turned into a hotel).

LJUBLJANA

A good jumpoff point for many streams. You can even stay in Ljubljana and fish rivers such as the Krka, Sava Bohinjka, and the Unica which are all within an hour's drive of the city. Best hotel here is the **Hotel Lev,** modern, unpretentious, with an excellent cuisine. Other hotels include the **Turist** and **Slon.**

ZAGREB

A pivotal point for streams to the south. Zagreb has the **Palace** and **International** hotels but the best

and deluxe is the **Inter-Continental Esplanade;** run by one of the top hotel men in the business (Branko Jakopovic) this establishment has a *fin-de-siecle* elegance and an exceptional cuisine. If desserts are your bag, try the pancakes with nuts and chocolate sauce.

In general, food is good throughout Yugoslavia and gourmet caliber in the deluxe or Category A hotels. Encompassing so many cultures you'll find appetizing dishes from Turkey, Italy, Hungary, Austria, Russia, and France as well as the native delights. Seafood is served everywhere and fresh trout appear at every inland restaurant. Smoked Dalmatian ham is a *must* at breakfast, lunch or dinner. Accompany these with one of the dark, almost black red wines from the Carso mountains; there are *merlot, blatina* and *Zilavka,* which are grown in the vineyards near Mostar. Slovenia's best red wines are *teran* and *pinot,* and wine is produced on the great majority of Dalmatian islands; white vintages that will interest you are *vugava* and *grk.* Meat menus list regional specialties such as Turkish-inspired ragouts of veal and chicken, and *raznjici,* which is shish kabob. Top one of these off with some of the world's sweetest, most inspired desserts and a cup of rich Turkish coffee (to be followed, perhaps, by a glass of *sljivovica,* which is plum brandy, Yugoslavia's well-known—and highly potent—national drink.

LANGUAGE

It can be a real problem for the English speaking tourist. A knowledge of German or Italian is a great help. Slavonic languages are spoken by 90 percent of the population which includes Serb-Croat; Slovene and Albanian among the non-Slavonic speakers in western Macedonia. All major hotels employ somebody who speaks English so don't worry about fundamentals. Do learn the correct pronunciation of river names or you'll wind up on the wrong stream; there are confusing similarities such as Una, Unac and Unica.